Identity in Organizations

FOUNDATIONS FOR ORGANIZATIONAL SCIENCE

A Sage Publications Series

Series Editor

David Whetten, *Brigham Young University*

Editors

Peter J. Frost, *University of British Columbia*
Anne S. Huff, *University of Colorado* and *Cranfield University* (UK)
Benjamin Schneider, *University of Maryland*
M. Susan Taylor, *University of Maryland*
Andrew Van de Ven, *University of Minnesota*

The FOUNDATIONS FOR ORGANIZATIONAL SCIENCE series supports the development of students, faculty, and prospective organizational science professionals through the publication of texts authored by leading organizational scientists. Each volume provides a highly personal, hands-on introduction to a core topic or theory and challenges the reader to explore promising avenues for future theory development and empirical application.

Books in This Series

PUBLISHING IN THE ORGANIZATIONAL SCIENCES, 2nd Edition
Edited by L. L. Cummings and Peter J. Frost

SENSEMAKING IN ORGANIZATIONS
Karl E. Weick

INSTITUTIONS AND ORGANIZATIONS
W. Richard Scott

RHYTHMS OF ACADEMIC LIFE
Peter J. Frost and M. Susan Taylor

RESEARCHERS HOOKED ON TEACHING:
Noted Scholars Discuss the Synergies of Teaching and Research
Rae André and Peter J. Frost

THE PSYCHOLOGY OF DECISION MAKING: People in Organizations
Lee Roy Beach

ORGANIZATIONAL JUSTICE AND HUMAN RESOURCE MANAGEMENT
Robert Folger and Russell Cropanzano

RECRUITING EMPLOYEES: Individual and Organizational Perspectives
Alison E. Barber

ATTITUDES IN AND AROUND ORGANIZATIONS
Arthur P. Brief

IDENTITY IN ORGANIZATIONS: Building Theory Through Conversations
Edited by David Whetten and Paul Godfrey

PERSONNEL SELECTION: A Theoretical Approach
Neal Schmitt and David Chan

David A. Whetten
Paul C. Godfrey

Identity in Organizations

Building Theory
Through Conversations

Foundations for
Organizational
Science
A Sage Publications Series

SAGE Publications
International Educational and Professional Publisher
Thousand Oaks   London   New Delhi

For information:

SAGE Publications, Inc.
2455 Teller Road
Thousand Oaks, California 91320
E-mail: order@sagepub.com

SAGE Publications Ltd.
6 Bonhill Street
London EC2A 4PU
United Kingdom

SAGE Publications India Pvt. Ltd.
M-32 Market
Greater Kailash I
New Delhi 110048 India

Printed in the United States of America

Library of Congress Cataloging-in-Publication Data

Main entry under title:

Identity in organizations: Building theory through conversations/
   edited by David A. Whetten and Paul C. Godfrey
      p. cm.—(Foundations for organizational science)
   Includes bibliographical references and index.
   ISBN 0-7619-0947-8 (acid-free paper)
   ISBN 0-7619-0948-6 (pbk.: acid-free paper)
   1. Organizational behavior. 2. Psychology, Industrial. 3.
Corporate culture. I. Whetten, David A. (David Allfred), 1946- II.
Godfrey, Paul C. III. Series.
   HD58.7 .I34 1998
   302.3'5—ddc21   98-19757

98 99 00 01 02 03 04 8 7 6 5 4 3 2 1

Acquiring Editor:	Marquita Flemming
Production Editor:	Astrid Virding
Editorial Assistant:	Denise Santoyo
Typesetter/Designer:	Danielle Dillahunt
Cover Designer:	Ravi Balasuriya

Contents

PART III: How Do People Identify With Organizations?

Preface:
Why Organizational Identity,
and Why Conversations?

DAVID A. WHETTEN

WHY ORGANIZATIONAL IDENTITY?

Stuart Albert and I began using the concept "organizational identity" out of necessity— we needed an interpretive framework to make sense out of our experience as faculty members at the University of Illinois during a period of financial turbulence. In 1979, the state legislature cut the university's budget by 2%. In the contemporary higher education financial scene this is hardly reason for alarm. However, prior to 1979 the University of Illinois had "always" received budget increases. So, in response to what one University of Illinois administrator referred to as a pending financial disaster, the president organized a series of focus group discussions with faculty members to explore the organization's options.

Stuart and I were intimately involved in this process, and we were perplexed by the intensity of the debates. The incongruity between the relatively benign environmental stimulus and the incredibly animated organizational response seemed especially puzzling to a couple of business school professors who were at that time discussing in their classes the "real" financial crisis at Chrysler Corporation and the merits of the government's $100 million commitment to save that company. Our university administration was not considering shutting down any departments, firing any faculty, or even significantly downsizing any of the core academic programs. However, although the impending budget adjustment posed no real threat to those attending our discussion groups, they framed this legislative mandate as a profound threat to the organization and their membership in it. As we listened to faculty and administrators debate questions like "Has the legislature lost confidence in the university?", "Is a geography department a necessary component of an

American research university?", and "Would important constituents still think of us as the University of Illinois if we cut out the aviation program, or cut back on agricultural extension services?", we began to realize that concerns about identity are just as profound as concerns about survival.

The requirement to make, for the first time in the modern history of the organization, even a modest reduction in programmatic budget allocations required a justification so convincing that it quickly escalated into a full-blown identity crisis. The need to reduce the organization's commitment to something introduced the possibility that the organization might be willing to give up everything. By extension, some faculty worried that if the administration was willing to eliminate anything in order to balance the budget, it undoubtedly didn't care about those elements of the University of Illinois that were essential to their personal identity as academics. In brief: Although the existence of the organization was not in question, its identity was, and although the employment relationship between individual faculty and the university was not at risk, their identification with the university was.

What we observed was the anguishing personal and collective examination of members' taken-for-granted assumptions about what was core, enduring, and distinctive about an American research university in general, and the University of Illinois in particular, exacerbated by the terrifying prospect that the slightest reduction in the current organizational configuration could precipitate an uncontrollable erosion of organizational, and by inference personal, identity. Because the current faculty had never observed the university undertake a budget cut, they had no concrete experience to check the contagious fear that once they started down the slippery slope of budget cuts there would be no way to stop short of cutting out what for each individual member constituted the core of a university.

Writing the 1985 ROB article on organizational identity was both a highly frustrating and rewarding experience. It was difficult to construct a new logic and language, but it was immensely gratifying to make sense out of our anomalous observations. Drawing upon the literature on identity in related disciplines, we crafted a theoretical lens that afforded us a better understanding of the incongruous response-to-stimuli behavior on campus. Soon after the completion of this project, Stuart joined the faculty at the University of Minnesota and our scholarly interests followed divergent paths. After a circadian-like period of dormancy, the concept of organizational identity started sprouting up all over the place. We began getting papers to review from colleagues who reported similar experiences—they were observing emotionally intense debates between key organizational stakeholders about profoundly significant issues and they found the concepts of "identity of" and "identification with" extremely useful interpretive fimneworks.

In 1994, I moved from the University of Illinois to Brigham Young University to direct the Center for the Study of Values in Organizations. My felt need to publicize our new Center and my revitalized interest in organizational identity gave rise to the "Sundance Conference on Organizational Identity" in September 1994. 1 invited 30 colleagues to meet for a two-day conference at Robert Redford's resort at the base of majestic Mount Timpanogos in Utah. This meeting resembled a brainstorming session in which small groups spent several hours discussing questions like "What is organizational identity?", "How should it be measured?", and "How is it similar to and different from related topics like organizational culture?" At the conclusion of our final plenary session, the only thing that I could get the participants to agree on was that they wanted to return for "Identity II." So, the next fall we met at Deer Valley, a ski resort near Park City, Utah. This time we narrowed the invitation list to scholars who were actively involved in theory development and research on this topic. Whereas Identity I had been organized as an extended brainstorming session, this time we invited participants to share their work-in-progress. Our discussions about "what is" being done proved to be a nice counterbalance to the Identity I focus on "what if." At the conclusion of Identity II the participants felt we were ready to meet a year hence and work on a book.

WHY CONVERSATIONS ABOUT ORGANIZATIONAL IDENTITY?

The design of Identity III was tricky, because the organization of the conference needed to be consistent with the organization of the book. We intuitively felt that the traditional conference-to-book format, in which participants present formal papers at the conference and then revise them for the book based on feedback they receive during the conference, was inappropriate because it was out of character with both the culture of our previous conferences and the nascent stage of our collective understanding of the topic. After months of contemplation and debate we selected the modality of "conversation" as the core design feature of both the conference and the book. Publishing a set of structured conversations about organizational identity satisfied our criteria of being congruent with the informal nature of our previous meetings and the emergent nature of the subject matter. As a bonus, we realized that it also mirrored the cocreative, discursive process whereby organizational identities are created, sustained, and modified. And, besides, we thought it would be lots more fun.

However, as the meeting date drew closer and some our collaborators began asking us if we really thought this idea was going to work, we became concerned about the lack of structure and clarity inherent in the conversation format. In response, we sent out a list of questions and topics for participants to begin contemplating, as well as a basic set of readings to review before the meeting. We also asked Blake Ashforth, Denny Gioia, and Rhonda Reger to serve as conversation leaders for three general topics. Our apprehension as organizers was further reflected in my opening remarks at the conference, which focused on what we meant by a "structured conversation" and why we felt this was the appropriate medium for the conference and the book. Following my part frame setting, part pep talk, part legitimacy-seeking opening presentation and a vigorous question-and-answer period, one of the participants grumbled, "Let's stop talking about doing it, and get started. We won't know if this is going to work until we see what we have to say." With that bit of encouragement, we split up into three groups and started conversing.

A NOTE TO THE READER

As you look over the organization of the book you will observe that each of the discussion leaders has provided a brief description of how their group proceeded to fashion their version of a conversation about organizational identity. In addition, Paul Godfrey has written a very thoughtful conclusion about using conversation to generate theory. We also commissioned a background paper for each of the three conversation topics, which appears at the beginning of each section, to help you understand the scholarly grist each group brought to their conversation mill. In addition to these conversation-specific introductions, we asked Stuart Albert to provide a brief introduction to the basic logic and language of organizational identity.

Our overall objective in framing a series of conversations about organizational identity was to invite you, the reader, to join in. We have attempted to provide sufficient background information so that, regardless of your previous exposure to this literature, you will understand the issues that framed our discussions. We have also worked hard to provoke your interest in extending and expanding these initial, tentative conversations. Speaking for *all* the contributors, we would love to reconvene at Sundance someday and continue our conversations—better informed by your contribution and participation.

A PERSONAL NOTE

I want to acknowledge a key role played by my colleague Hal Gregersen in organizing Identity I and II. I'm sorry that his schedule did not allow him to reprise his role at Identity III. It was fortuitous that Paul Godfrey's interest in identity was on the upswing at that time. His contribution to planning and managing Identity III was indispensable. But more important, Paul did most of the editorial legwork involved in assembling the materials contained in this book.

When my oldest son was considering various career options, he asked me why I had chosen to be an academic. I don't remember the details of my answer, but I know it included references to the joys of learning and creativity and especially to the pleasure of insight. I remember wishing that I had a more concrete way of sharing the best of my professional experiences with him. If he asked me that question today, I'd simply say Identity I, II, and III. Thank you to 45 wonderful colleagues and friends who contributed to our great conversations and fun (even funny) encounters with nature. Let's do it again.

ACKNOWLEDGMENTS

We would like to express appreciation to the many individuals who helped make this 4-year process, encompassing three conferences and this book, both possible and enjoyable. In particular, there were several secretaries and students who played critical roles, including, Marlow Christensen, Tim Simmons, Jean Hawkins, Rose Marie Morrell, and Amy Lilly. We also appreciate the support of our families during the hectic period of meeting editorial deadlines.

A number of colleagues participated in the first two identity conferences but were unable to join us for Identity III and the ensuing book project. We would like to recognize Jane Dutton, Charles Fombrun, and John Kimberly who made important contributions to our discussions at both Identity I and II but regretfully are not among the contributors to this book.

Finally, we are especially grateful that Denny Gioia, Rhonda Reger, and Blake Ashforth willingly expanded their roles as group discussion leaders by helping us edit the conference transcripts and coordinate the writing projects within their respective groups. Each clearly warrants the designation of Section Editor in this book.

1

The Definition and Metadefinition of Identity

STUART ALBERT

To introduce is to mediate an encounter between strangers, to diminish threat, render intelligible, suggest common purpose, and promise rewards. All new work bears what Harold Bloom has called the anxiety of influence: It must distance itself from the past so as not to be engulfed or demoralized by the insights of work that has gone before it. There is also a deep fear of revisiting or repeating a topic, particularly if, in the eyes of some, it has been exhausted. (Is identity culture? Is identification commitment?) On one hand, a topic must be new, or else it is not news—but it cannot be so new as to be unintelligible or irrelevant, and certainly, it must not be threatening unless the intent is to provoke a fight. Thus, on encountering the new or unknown, one immediately asks for a definition. What is it? Is it new or old, threatening or useful? The new must be categorized (if not pigeonholed), given boundaries and fixed nature, so that it is safe to use or discard.

In the pages that follow, the reader will find a provocative set of metaphors for understanding and investigating organizational identity and for thinking about the process and objects of identification. Identity must be viewed as a theory, an asset, or a resource (Chapter 5), a stellar constellation (Chapter 7), and so on. In line with the focus on metaphor prevalent in this volume, let me offer a brief reflection on the origin of the religious and business metaphors in Albert and Whetten (1985).

Dave and I were both at the University of Illinois at a time when Illinois was struggling with retrenchment. At one point in the informal seminar that ran every Friday morning for several years at the Center for Advanced Study, someone related the reaction of the Dean of Engineering on hearing that one of his faculty was leaving the university for a higher-paying job in the private sector. The dean's reaction, it was reported, was filled with moral indignation: How *could* the faculty member be leaving *just* for higher pay? To capture that sense of *moral* indignation, Dave or I (I do not remember who) remarked that it was as if the Dean of Engineering viewed engineering as almost a religious calling rather than simply a job or profession. A day later, we had a brief working note to ourselves on the university as a religion. Because the context was retrenchment, and because Dave and I were affiliated with the business school (Dave as faculty, I as visitor), elaboration of the metaphor, the university as a business, seemed natural. The rest of the paper simply developed the implications of those two lenses. We remain indebted to Barry Staw, our editor at *Research in Organizational Behavior,* who welcomed the paper. Our paper offered, even if tentatively and metaphorically, a religious account of a secular world. That one needed a religious language to describe the world of the university and the dean's reaction constituted a refusal to accept the unchallenged sovereignty of psychological categories and language. We could not reduce what we had observed to stress or distress, anger or incredulity. It required a descriptive language of a different kind.

The present volume records the thinking and conversation of a group of researchers that met for several years at Robert Redford's resort, Sundance, in the Rocky Mountains in the summers of 1994, 1995, and 1996 under the auspices and support of Brigham Young University. The purpose was to investigate the topics of organizational identity and individual identification with an organization.

THE PROBLEM OF METADEFINITION

Organizational Identity as
Construct, Question, or Metaphor

Individuals inevitably bring to any subject matter pre-existing habits of thought and standards or judgment. Sometimes, it is useful to challenge them, and so, in the spirit of this volume, with its unconventional format and ideas, I would like to make some brief comments on the nature and functions of definition.

When we ask what identification and organizational identity are and how these concepts can be treated scientifically, we are tempted to think in terms of constructs. But the appeal of the term *construct,* a fabrication that rests on a spatial metaphor, may not only be illusory, but also damaging. If one considers identity or identification as constructs, the next questions that are inevitably asked are: How can each be measured? What is its relationship to other constructs? When there are no clear answers, the construct is dismissed as vague, ambiguous, or ill-defined; for scientific purposes, it is useless. But an idea that is vague, hard to pin down, elusive, or multifaceted may not be useless at all. An idea may have value not because it can be weighed and measured, not because it conforms to the hidden criteria of an optical metaphor—that of the visible, distinguishable object, which achieves its status as a scientific criterion in part by preying on our fear of the dark—but because it is a question.

If one considers identity to be a question, then the next step is not measurement—one does not measure a question—but rather a discussion of why identity is relevant or important within a particular context, what kinds of answers to the question of identity might be provided, and how adequate they are, and so on. Identity may be precisely that kind of question that eludes standard conceptions of measurement—that may be one of its defining properties. Just as Maslow concluded that people dislike being categorized, it may be essential that one's identity not be measurable, with all of the connotations of measurement—that of being pinned down, confined, revealed, invaded, and ultimately subject to control. A person's (or an organization's) identity may be the last refuge of the qualitative in a world of invading armies wielding rulers and compasses. Identity may define the boundary between utilitarian and deontological logics; it may express a need for uniqueness and privacy. It honors the ineffable. To measure identity may require that one measure its reluctance to being measured, that one study the genius of its disguises and the way it eludes capture while still claiming presence as a core defining feature.

From this perspective, the relationship between identity and culture is clear: A particular culture (or image or reputation) may, or may not, be part of the answer to the identity question: Who am I? What kind of firm is this? Relations with others, the kinds of interorganizational alliances into which a firm enters, for example, may be its most defining element. That one may not have agreement on how to define culture or how to measure it may not matter. Regardless of which way one chooses to define or measure culture, the question is only the extent to which some definition of culture (or element of culture) enters into the answer one gives to the identity question. And of course, different people or organizations may give different answers under different conditions. Niels Bohr is reported to have said that the opposite of something that is true is not something that is false; rather, the opposite of a profound truth is another profound truth. From that perspective, rather than hold that the first task of science after construct definition is measurement, one might argue that consensus on measurement should be among the final tasks to be attempted, and then only after an "industry standard" has evolved with respect to what should and should not be part of the concept. That is not to say that one should not do empirical work, merely that one should not expect to define the construct and agree on its measurement except after a long process of empirical inquiry and questioning. From this perspective, the definitional clarity of a construct and the adequacy with which it is measured should be a retrospective achievement, not a precondition for serious work. This is not to say that those seeking to measure identity or identification will not find in the papers of this volume many useful ideas, only that the absence of agreement about definition and measurement is what makes the topic so fertile. Furthermore, if identity is a metaphor rather than a construct, the question for measurement is what metaphors different individuals choose to apply to the organization, on what occasions, and for what purposes. One does not measure a metaphor but rather assesses its insightfulness, unexpectedness, aptness, and so on. As readers of this volume will discover, identity provokes a rich store of metaphors.

From one perspective, it is not difficult to define what *identification with* an organization is. For an individual to identify with an organization is to treat the organization *as if* it were, in some sense, an extension of the self. (See Chapter 6 for a review of definitions.) The problem with this definition is not merely the phrase "in some sense," or the metaphoric "as if," or the meaning of the term "self," but the deeper issue of how one would know whether any definition is a good one. What is it that definitions are supposed to do, and how do we know when they have done it? I address this question by enumerating a number of purposes or functions that definitions may serve. Not all of them are necessarily compatible, although they may be. How a particular definition addresses or satisfies these functions is its metadefinition.

Definitions Serve Five Functions,
Including the Search for Identity

Definitions serve five functions: They function as statements of *identity*; as a way to define *competitive* and *cooperative* relationships with other terms; as a way to end conceptual disputes and thus prepare the way for measurement—its *preoperational* or *premeasurement function*; as a way to locate a term within a particular context—its *orienting* or *contextual* function; and as a way to generate new ideas— its *generative* or *revelatory* function. I take up each in turn.

A good definition defines the *identity* of a term or concept; that is, a good definition tries to capture the core meaning or essential nature of a term, concept, or construct as it is distinguished from related terms or concepts (while being similar to others) in a way that is enduring (that fixes the meaning) so that a cumulative tradition of research and scholarship is possible without having to retrace one's steps endlessly. *To define a term is to give it an identity, to indicate with which scientific and intellectual traditions it is to be identified.* (In the chapters that follow, for example, the relationship of identity to culture and the relationship of identification to affiliation and commitment are considered.)

Some, by temperament, like what is sharply defined and clearly bounded; others find beauty and precision in fine gradations of gray. Some like their set boundaries fuzzy, others like them knife-edge sharp. Those who ask whether identity is different from culture—or any other concept—whether identification is different from commitment, sometimes demand what I call Level 1 distinctiveness, that is, that a concept be pure and unique, and that it not overlap with others that compete for the same or similar terrain. The alternative, of course, is distinctiveness (Level 2), not absolute difference. For Level 2 distinctiveness, what is required is that a concept be distinguished from others by a unique pattern of overlap and nonoverlap with other concepts from the same family. (See Pratt, Chapter 6, for a more complete discussion.) There is no reason to believe that a Level 1 concept is more powerful than a Level 2 concept. A nonoverlapping concept may be less useful than a unique hybrid or blend. Independence and individualism are, after all, not universal values, and it may be that the value-neutral methods of science are more culture bound in this instance than we might have thought or desired. Perhaps for some theoretical purposes it may not matter that identification and commitment overlap; in fact, it may be their intrinsic overlap that best accounts for why one leads to the other, or why an individual may not know which is which, and finds that his behavior is motivated by that enduring confusion. Concepts that have a distinctive overlap with their neighbors rather than concepts that are completely walled off from them may turn out to be the most useful. I suspect that identity and identification are in this category.

To define a term or concept is also to *specify* and *clarify* its core, to distinguish what is essential from what is accidental, peripheral, or superficial. One must decide where to place the boundaries around the concept: Is an antecedent process an antecedent, or, in fact, a part of the concept itself? Definitions settle, if only provisionally, boundary disputes. The clarifying function of any definition is to demystify, to draw lines, to pin down, and to make precise.

Although computational linguistics is in its infancy compared to computational mathematics, I suspect that construct validation in the future will compile a set of sentences of all kinds and all levels of complexity that exhibit or express what is core, distinctive, and enduring about a concept. Some sentences in the test bank may come with a paragraph-long description, and each sentence could be given a weight to express its centrality to the concept. This set of sentences will constitute a qualitative test bank that will form an industry standard for that concept. Rival concepts claiming the same conceptual-empirical territory will try their hand as substitutes for the nouns or phrases representing the old concept in all of the sentences in the test bank that define its identity and comprise its definition. One may be able to substitute the word *commitment* for identification in some sentences in the test bank but not in others without altering the truth, logic, reasonableness, or intelligibility of the sentence (as determined by judges). One can then compute a similarity score between two concepts without sacrificing any of the qualitative detail and complexity associated with the concepts. In the "new construct valida-tion," the qualitative is placed on an equal footing with the quantitative rather than being seen as a first step. Its purpose is to supply a degree of precision unavailable to the purely quantitative. The new construct validation will have the identity of a genuine hybrid: It will both qualitative and quantitative.

Defining a term or concept distinguishes it from others with which it may be confused. If a term cannot be distinguished from others that already exist, it will be denied entry into the literature. By carefully distinguishing one concept from another, a definition limits, restricts, or confines a concept's monopolistic and imperialistic impulses, which might otherwise allow it to claim more territory and importance for itself than is legitimate. I call this the *competitive* or *distinguishing function* of definition. Definitions that serve a competitive function are worded not merely to describe accurately a physical or conceptual reality, but to win battles.

Not all distinctions are involved in competitive struggles, however. For example, what is distinctive about the concept of identifying with an organization is the direction of the arrow from the self to the organization. To *identify with* an organization implies a movement *outward* from the self as well as a suspension of immunological defense, so that what is reached outside can be held and felt as part of what is inside. A term that is defined by an outward movement raises questions about whether there is a reverse process, not merely one of deidentification from the object of identification, which is often a painful process, but a movement inward without prior outward attachment, a progressive drawing in of the boundaries of the self.

In contrast to the competitive and distinguishing function, a definition also needs to identify terms or concepts that are similar or identical to the term being defined. This is the *cooperative* or *familial* function of definition. Defining a term means locating which other terms or concepts are members of the same family and which may therefore do the same conceptual or analytic work. Whereas the academic may wish to distinguish among processes of identification, attraction, commitment, and internalization, the practicing manager seeking to bond a new employee to the organization may wish to know that all of these processes are members of the same family, and that, under certain circumstances, one may substitute for another, or that several may be added together for special impact. A definition serves a cooperative function when it identifies which concepts or terms might cooperate in collective action. A term or concept is defined by its synonyms, by specifying to what it is equivalent or identical.

A common function of definition is what I call the *preoperational* or *premeasurement* function. A definition serves this function by preparing the way for measurement. It does so by bringing to an end (by deciding or settling) whatever conceptual disputes or uncertainties are present so that measurement and other forms of inquiry that depend on it can proceed.

The search for proper definition is often a utopian search, the search for purity in an impure world, for precision in a world defined by its absence, for stasis amid dynamism, for a deity who does not play dice with the universe. But definition is only one element of conceptual analysis, and the act of definition is sometimes forced or persuaded to take on more tasks than it can legitimately carry. Some conceptual problems must await the results of observation or experiment. They cannot be resolved by definition. When there is a large investment in measurement or adherence to a particular view of science (that it be cumulative), there is always considerable pressure to resolve all of the conceptual difficulties associated with a term at the definitional stage. Of course, this means that subsequent empirical work will have little chance of clarifying the meaning of the term. One will not be able to go back and say after many studies—without awkwardness—that one's fundamental understanding of the term was incorrect and that therefore one must define it differently. It is acceptable for empirical research to redefine and explore different antecedents and consequences, but not to change the definition of the concept or construct being studied—at least in one version of the proper way to do science. But the clarity of definition demanded by measurement cannot always be satisfied, *nor should it be,* because the conceptual issues that are involved cannot be resolved by stipulation. They are, and must remain, a retrospective achievement, the product of inquiry and not its precondition.

The next function of definition is what I call an *orienting* or *contextual* function. This purpose of definition is to locate a term within a particular theoretical, scientific, or intellectual tradition that serves as its *natural habitat.* This habitat orients the reader to the kinds of troubles, predicaments, battles, and assumptions that are associated with it. That is not to say that the term cannot be found outside of its natural habitat, but that it is where one should look first, and where its distinctive competence and incompetence are most likely to be found.

To serve an orienting function, a definition need not be precise. There need not be complete consensus about what the concept includes and excludes, implies or does not imply. In the conversations that this book reports, groups often began with a working definition. Perhaps concepts such as identity and identification only have working definitions: They help a group get on with its work because their precision is sufficient for the task at hand. They orient and provide direction (strategic intent) rather than give a precise location.

Knowledge of a concept's habitat means knowing who its neighbors are (some habitats are densely populated, others are not), what the history of their relationship has been, and what issues inevitably surface when they interact. To distinguish identity from image or reputation, for example, is to engage in a conversation about the social self, about authenticity and sincerity, and, ultimately, about the management or mismanagement of the discrepancy between what is public and private, intended and perceived. These issues are simply part of the natural habitat of the identity concept. The orienting function of a definition serves as a beginning map of the landscape of concerns that is typically associated with the concept. Thus, the term *self* in the definition of identification evokes the term *ego,* which suggests the domain of psychoanalytic theory as part of the natural habitat within which the concept "identification with" is located. The orienting function of definition identifies the characteristic questions that surround a concept, some of which, like fireworks, will dazzle but then fall harmlessly to the ground, while others will ignite sustained inquiry and lead to new discoveries.

One measure of the geography encompassed by a concept's habitat is the list of references that the authors have assembled, and just as the serious writer will sometimes buy a book and enter its habitat because of the elegance of a single paragraph, I suspect that readers of this volume will seek out many of the references listed at the end of each chapter as scientific and intellectual terrain worth exploring or revisiting.

The final function that definitions serve is a *generative* or *revelatory* one. A definition should open up rather than to close down inquiry; it should find the problems associated with the term to be defined and to go public about them, rather than to attempt to settle or resolve them, often prematurely. To be generative is to give rise to and, like a magnet, attract clusters of questions. The chapters in this volume offer ample evidence of the generative power of the concepts of organizational identity and identification. Indeed, I think that is what is truly special about the chapters that follow: They sparkle with new ideas and interesting paths to follow. That identity and identification have no one precise meaning or definition is part of their strength as concepts. Indeed, if these concepts have value, perhaps it is because they contain *the requisite degree of ambiguity*. Moreover, just as one person's footnote may be another person's life's work, sometimes, an offhand comment or a conversational aside can redirect the central focus of one's own thinking. When Marlene Fiol said about organizational identity, "The distinctiveness issue is only one of two. There is both similarity and distinctiveness always occurring simultaneously, and the meaning is located in the tension between the two" (Chapter 3), I came to understand the relation between identification and identity in a more complex way than I had previously. Although the term *identification* usually refers to the relation of an individual to an organization, what an organization consists of is, in part, the set of similar organizations with which *it* identifies. For example, since 1993, corporate boards have been required to publish a list of comparable firms that will allow stockholders to assess the quality of their management. This statement of peer group is part of their identity. Processes of identification can therefore occur at multiple levels: An individual can identify with a firm, a firm can identify with an industry, and so on. That a firm's reference group is part of its identity is not surprising until one wonders about how the section of this book that deals with identification would be altered if identification were seen as part of organizational identity, rather than being separate from it. Of course, the reverse is also true: An organization's identity is (or can be) part of the answer to the question of identification: *With what* is he or she identifying?

The generative function of definition highlights rather than conceals whatever vagueness or ambiguity is part of the term. A concept is defined by its irremediable and distinctive confusion and imprecision as well as by whatever it manages to express with clarity. Thus, by using the term *self* in the definition of identification (rather than the term *individual*), one signals that whatever problems exist in the definition and measurement of the self will find their way into a discussion of identification. A definition written to serve a generative or revelatory function washes all of a concept's dirty linen in public. Such definitions seek complexity; they do not hide it with oversimplifications; they highlight family resemblances; they do not claim uniqueness; they note rather than disguise difficulties of measurement; they wear this difficulty proudly as a distinguishing mark of identity, proof that quality is not quantity.

Although all scientific concepts have troubles associated with them, not all concepts are troubled in the same way or to the same degree, and not all troubles are, or should be, part of the definition of the concept. Still, some troubles are part of the concept itself and cannot be eliminated without eliminating the concept itself. Indeed, a term or concept may be indispensable precisely because it defines a certain kind of ambiguity, just as the invention of probability was a way to render precise that which was not.

To define identification with an organization as "oneness" with an organization (Ashforth & Mael, 1989) uses a vocabulary that will make the positivist uneasy because it evokes the domains of religion and metaphysics, which were supposedly banished from the scientific Eden centuries ago. But it is precisely the metaphysical overtones of an individual's need to embrace and possibly merge with a larger world that is at the heart of what is meant by identification. Identification is defined, in part, by the kinds of metaphysical quagmires that one chooses to engage. Nor can one discuss the concept of identification without at some point running into all of the difficulties surrounding the concept of self. A definition serving a revelatory function does not hide these troubles because a term is defined by the troubles that are part of its nature. Lear is Lear because of the troubles that surround him and that comprise his nature. The essays and conversations in this volume will give the reader a better sense of these troubles, which, of course, is all to the good because science demands both ignorance and difficulty as twin conditions that make for full employment.

Definition in the generative mode looks for the presence of paradox, irony, and internal inconsistency—consistent with theories that find an appreciation of paradox to be among the higher stages of thought and ego development. An example in the case of identification is the contradictory impulse to both transcend one's limits and yet not threaten the boundaries of the self that are needed for sanity. A definition highlighting the generative function might include a phrase such as "subject to the following pathologies of over- and underidentification" as part of, rather than separate from, the definition of identification (see Chapter 7).

In summary, by a metadefinition, I mean a statement or definition of the nature, purposes, and functions of a definition. Is a definition provisional, that is, a working definition, or is it a final and definitive one? Should a definition be a matter of prospective stipulation, or must it remain a retrospective achievement, the result of empirical analysis, observation, or experiment? Which conceptual issues can be settled by definition, and which cannot? When is vagueness or ambiguity or the use of language from another domain of human experience, such as religion, a necessary part of the meaning of a term or concept, and when does it signal imperfect or faulty understanding: Which imprecisions are resident and present by definition, and which are removable? A cloud has fuzzy boundaries. Should the fuzziness of these boundaries be part of or separate from its definition? Which parts of the concept, term, or relationship can be allowed to change over time, and which cannot without altering the meaning of the term, and should—and can—this question be decided in advance? Can the concept be represented by a variable, which is the assertion that a change in quantity is not a change in quality, that a little love is still love and not simply affection, and that a lot of love is still love and not obsession? Variables are enormously complex and intricate things. A definition, insofar as it explicitly opens the door to quantitative matters, is usually a proposal to treat a concept as a variable or bundle of variables. The extent to which a definition intentionally suggests a ready operationalization in terms of variables is a metadefinitional decision. To use the term *oneness* as part of a definition of identification resolutely makes the claim that simple quantitative scales will have a difficult time capturing important qualitative aspects of the concept, whereas a definition phrased in terms of *the degree to which* an organization is seen as expressing the values of the self throws up no such barriers to scaling.

With these comments about definition in mind, it should be clear why I cannot define more completely the concepts of identity or identification: In a sense, that is the task of this entire volume.

IDENTITY LINKS MULTIPLE
LEVELS OF ANALYSIS

The concept of identity has the advantage of being a concept, construct, or question that can be studied or posed at any level of analysis—individual, group, organization, or industry—because, in a certain sense, the question of identity is at the heart of the idea of level. How an organization is different from the groups or individuals that comprise it is what is core and distinctive about the organization qua organization. As Ashforth and Mael (1996) write:

> There are few conceptual bridges for linking macro- and micro-level structures and processes (House, Rousseau & Thomas-Hunt, 1995; Staw & Sutton, 1993). We believe that the concept of identity provides one such bridge (Kramer, 1993; Whetten, Lewin & Michel, 1992). Identity has been researched at the level of the individual (particularly in the fields of developmental psychology, social psychology, symbolic interactionism, and psychodynamics), group (particularly social identity theory and various perspectives on genre, racial, ethnic, and national identities), and more recently, the organization. We see many parallels across these levels in the conceptualization of identity dynamics. (p. 4)

Cross-level questions abound: How is personal identity linked with the identity of the organization(s) in which one is a member? How does individual identity come to inform and shape organizational identity (e.g., the influence of the founder), and so on. The concept of identity, whether at the individual or organizational level, is germane to questions of action and performance. Predictions about the road taken may be less a matter of assessing the comparative incentives of each path than of understanding the identity of the person or organization making the choice. How one acts may depend more on who one is, who others think one is, and who one aspires to be than on any objective assessment of the opportunities and costs associated with a given direction.

As many of the chapters display, conversation is a fine vehicle for revealing theoretical insights and a useful antidote to the sometimes impoverished minimal-ism of the Euclidean blueprint: assumption, hypothesis, method, proof. After all, science is, at its core, a dialogue, a particular kind of rule-governed conversation with nature (whether fabricated or found). We pose the questions—sometimes shaped by forces that we do not discern or understand—and nature supplies the answers, sometimes rejecting our questions as ill-formed; unanswerable; or not yet, or perhaps never, worthy of a reply. The "question" or "hypothesis" is for science what "thinking" was for Descartes; evidence of its essential being, a part of its identity. And sometimes, of course, the unanswerability of a question (perhaps akin to undecideability in logic) is its defining feature and hence the property that systems of measurement must register, display, and disclose.

PAST, PRESENT, AND FUTURE

The writing of contemporary history is fraught with dangers, and so what I offer is simply a series of conjectures about why the topic of this book seems to have emerged at this time.

Each of the chapters in this volume contains its own introduction, so let me make only some general comments about the current interest in identity and identification. Whether in the social sciences or in literature, the term *identity* (and by implication, the process of identification—which always raises the question, "Identification with *what*?") is part of the current cultural-historical scene. Part of the reason is that organizations are undergoing rapid change. Geopolitically, the loss of the former Soviet Union as an adversary also reduces the clarity of national self-definition. Old relationships between organizations and employees are also changing. Globalization and changes in technology are forcing a rewriting and rethinking of the organizational landscape, and as a result, fundamental questions emerge with new urgency. If an employee's identity is closely bound up with the organization of which he or she is a member, what happens to that identity when the organization downsizes? Or from the organization's perspective, faced with new competitive threat, how does it determine strategy without considering what the organization is or wants to be? And, of course, there is the recognition that the millennium is not special, except perhaps as a commercial opportunity, which raises anew the questions, What matters? What actions should we pursue to what ends? What is the defining nature of the organizations in which we spend so much of our lives? What should be our relationship to these organizations?

Identity is closely tied to recent interest in the study of *affect* and *emotion*. Identity, whether personal or organizational, as well as processes of identification and disidentification are intensely affect-laden questions. Dave Whetten, in a talk at the 1997 Academy of Management meeting, referred to identity as having the properties of an onion, not merely because it is multilayered (and perhaps has only a virtual center that, with quantum irony, vanishes when reached), but because an onion produces tears. One does not consider matters of identity, identification, or disidentification dispassionately. These topics often engender intense emotions: anguish, pride, anxiety, security sought and secured, and so on (see Celia V. Harquail's chapter: Organizational Identification and the "Whole Person": Integrating Affect, Behavior, and Cognition). Paul Godfrey (personal communication, October 1997) believes that identity may open the way for a discussion of alternatives to economic views of organizations, that the depth of the identity question will require a move from the most obvious, literal, material understanding of organizations to something more akin to their essence or spirit.

The study of identity and processes of identification has also emerged, I conjecture, because these processes are best described in narrative and qualitative terms (e.g., see Chapter 5) and are therefore linked to and legitimated by studies of narrative and by the continuing development of qualitative approaches. An answer to the identity question requires a narrative, not a number, a sentence, not a phrase. To answer the question "Who am I?" requires subject, object, and verb together with all of the modifiers and digressions that must be added if the answer is to do justice to the question.

Some scientific problems are less problems than predicaments, less to be solved than to be engaged. At a given moment, one may succeed in clarifying, proving, reinterpreting, synthesizing, or making relevant some feature of what is considered problematic or unknown. But some problems are not solved, certainly not once and for all—the need for foundational imagery and irreversible forward progress notwithstanding. Rather, I propose that problems of identity and identification are enduring dilemmas. At a certain point, other problems will replace them, for any number of reasons. But one reason we can exclude in advance: The study of identity and identification will fade from view not because the problems posed by these concepts have been solved. And we can be certain that the concepts of organizational identity and identification will, after a time, reemerge with full force, because these concepts, or something like them, are unavoidable. The issues they present, the questions they pose, and the functions they serve are, in some important sense, core, distinctive, and enduring.

At a certain point in time, a topic heats up; there is excitement in the air, new ideas surface, connections are made, and those present know that progress is being made. Although I am a partisan, such is a time in the study of organizational identity and processes of identification.

REFERENCES

Albert, S., & Whetten. D. (1985). Organizational identity. In L. L. Cummings & B. M. Staw (Eds.), *Research in organizational behavior* (Vol. 6). Greenwich, CT: JAI.

Ashforth, B. E., & Mael, F. (1989). Social identity theory and the organization. *Academy of Management Review, 14,* 20-39.

Ashforth, B., & Mael, F. (1996). Organizational identity and strategy as a context for the individual. In J. A. C. Baum & J. E. Dutton (Eds.), *Advances in strategic management* (Vol. 13, pp. 17-62). Greenwich, CT: JAI.

House, R., Rousseau, D. M., & Thomas-Hunt, M. (1995). The meso paradigm: A framework for the integration of micro and macro organizational behavior. In L. L. Cummings & B. M. Staw (Eds.), *Research in organizational behavior* (pp. 71-114). Greenwich, CT: JAI.

Kramer, R. M. (1993). Cooperation and organizational identification. In J. K. Murnighan (Ed.), *Social psychology in organizations: Advances in theory and research* (pp. 244-268). Englewood Cliffs, NJ: Prentice Hall.

Staw, B. M., & Sutton, R. I. (1993). Macro organizational psychology. In J. K. Murnighan (Ed.), *Social psychology in organizations: Advances in theory and research* (pp. 350-384). Englewood Cliffs, NJ: Prentice Hall.

Whetten, D. A., Lewin, D., & Michel, L. J. (1992, August). *Towards an integrated model of organizational identity and member commitment.* Paper presented at the annual meeting of the Academy of Management, Las Vegas.

PART I

What Does Organizational Identity Mean?

2

From Individual to
Organizational Identity

DENNIS A. GIOIA

Identity is arguably more fundamental to the conception of humanity than any other notion. That is a strong statement, but consider some of the key questions that we might use to assess the reach of the concept: What other issue is quite so important than answering the nebulous question, Who am I? What other concern is quite so captivating than dealing with the ongoing, lifelong project of assessing identity and figuring out how one relates to others and the surrounding world? What other question so influences understanding and action so heavily (if perhaps out of conscious awareness)? I can think of no other concept that is so central to the human experience, or one that infuses so many interpretations and actions, than the notion of identity.

Therefore, it should come as no surprise to find that the concept of identity, which is so germane to conceiving what it means to be human, also is central to the conceptualization of one of the most complex and fascinating of human creations, the work organization. Perhaps the minor surprise is that it took until 1985 for the first major articulation of identity as an organization-level construct to emerge through the insightful and articulate work of Stu Albert and Dave Whetten.[1] Their ideas continue to stand as a point of departure for further exploration, for continuing debate, and for the introduction of alternative conceptualizations of organizational identity.

I would like to begin this overview chapter on the identity of organizations at the beginning, by briefly acknowledging our debt to early philosophers and psychological and sociological thinkers in their musings about personal identity—mainly to demonstrate the focal position and longevity of the idea of identity. Then, I would like to devote a few pages to an admittedly selective and unquestionably subjective overview of some of the conceptual and empirical work inspired by Albert and Whetten's elevation of the identity notion to the macro level. Next, I would like to segue into a brief overview of three different "lenses" for conceptualizing and studying organizational identity. The discussion of these lenses provides some stage-setting and foreshadowing of the framing for the conversation about the identity of organizations (and the many ways of conceiving and studying it) that constitutes the subject of the following chapter.

THE PATH FROM INDIVIDUAL
TO ORGANIZATIONAL IDENTITY

Individual Identity

The concern with identity is literally an ancient one. Socrates, Plato, and Aristotle all considered the conundrum of personal identity in one philosophical guise or another. Who is a person? What is her or his place in the world? Plato's *Republic* articulates in metaphorical form the first statement of belief that each of us possesses a true self, a holistic identity that is the basis for our character, and his dialogues contain many passages dealing with identity and the question of how one can know oneself. For Plato, identity is a form that exists metaphysically and instantiates differently in each person; Aristotle's portrait of the self provides an early hint of the view that there can be many different identities housed within an individual. We can also note that Pericles's funeral oration can be viewed as the first documented statement of collective identity (i.e., what it means to be Athenian).

In style and belief, these ancient Greeks were the harbingers of objectivism in their views of identity; for them, identity is real. Their thoughts echo forward in time and supply the foundations for the modern positivist views of identity that found fuller manifestation in the still reverberating thought of Descartes ("I think, therefore . . ."). In fact, the examination of identity is woven throughout the history of philosophy, often occupying dense passages from many of the great thinkers of the post-Renaissance period.

That tradition of concern with identity is as pronounced in the 20th century as it was in the fifth century BC. The early Wittgenstein was following the objectivist trail in a larger sense by trying to find the ideal logical links that would accurately describe the world "out there." Along with Russell and Whitehead, among others, his project was to perfect philosophy as an investigative means for understanding the objective world. The question of identity was folded into these larger concerns, but was assumed, almost without question, also to be objective in character as well.

Of course, we now know that the later Wittgenstein famously concluded that there is no objective world that can be perfectly described—that the social world is contextually bounded and socially invented. His personal conclusion implies that he must therefore discount his own brand of positivism as an inadequate approach to understanding social phenomenology. The implications for identity are similarly profound, and his treatment of family resemblances is essential to understanding identity. Pursuing related lines of thought were Husserl and Schutz, who took an eminently phenomenological view in portraying identity as a constructed phenomenon. Sartre's existentialist writings also should be included in 20th-century explorations of identity. Taken as a historical concern, identity, especially on an individual level, is obviously of abiding interest to many of our great thinkers.

On the social science historical front, we see such writers as James (1918), Cooley (1902), and Mead (1934) laying early groundwork for the consideration of identity. James's musings about the "real me" and his further elaboration of the idea of multiple identities set the psychological stage for identity studies. Goffman (1959), Erickson (1964), and Gergen (1985), among many others, wrestled to articulate a workable definition of identity in the social domain. All of these writers converged on a definition that initially appears nonintuitive to a lay person—that identity is most usefully viewed as a general, if individualized, framework for understanding oneself that is formed and sustained via social interaction. They all argued that individuals learn to assign themselves socially constructed labels through personal and symbolic interactions with others. Therefore, identity is fundamentally a relational and comparative concept (Tajfel & Turner, 1985).

Implicit and important in these writings as well is the key idea that identity really is what makes a person a person. Identity constitutes what is somehow core to my being, what comprises the consistently traceable thread that is "me" over time, and what somehow distinguishes me idiosyncratically from a myriad of other people.

Social identity theory as applied to individuals tells us that people construct themselves as having some set of essential characteristics that they cite as defining their self-concepts, and that they engage in interpretations and practices intended to affirm the continuity of those self-concepts over time and place (Steele, 1988). Social identity theory also tells us that people tend to fixate on their distinctiveness, to emphasize their distinctiveness vis-à-vis others (Tajfel & Turner, 1985). They not only see themselves as distinct but also act as if they *are* distinct. Any reasonable observation would suggest that individuals who distinguish themselves along such fine-grained lines are actually more similar to their comparison others than they are distinct, but people manage consistently to pull off the legerdemain, and those around them willingly participate in the charade as a tacitly agreed-upon game of face-saving (Goffman, 1959). It all involves some wonderful deception and suspension of disbelief, but it also all seems to work quite well in practice.

Tajfel (1982) made some similar points concerning groups, arguing that group identity is maintained primarily by intergroup comparisons, and that groups seek positive differences between themselves and other reference groups as a way of enhancing their own self-esteem. Tajfel's work provides a strong hint that identity constructs have an apparent robustness about them and suggests a good basis for building bridges from individual to organizational conceptualizations of identity.

Erickson (1964) made the important observation that identity not only constitutes a way of seeing or classifying myself that distinguishes me from other people, but it also simultaneously allows me to see myself as similar to a class of individuals with whom I most closely associate myself or with whom I would like to be associated. There is a bit of a fine balancing act contained in individuals' wishes to have it both ways, to be both distinctive and nondistinctive, to be a member of a class of people, but set off from those people. Maintaining the balance between similarity and difference is one of the most challenging and interesting issues for the understanding of individual identity (as it is for understanding organizational identity). Despite these observations that tend to be fairly specific and definitive about the nature of identity, the ascription of individual identity in a social environment is at best an ambiguous process (see Weick, 1995)—one that does not lend itself well to precise definition or description (witness the somewhat vague and encompassing basic definition above). Yet that is just the way most people prefer it. Maintaining a certain optimal amount of ambiguity in defining myself grants me some latitude over time and context to harbor a wide range of opinions, beliefs, and values; to engage in many varied actions; and to see myself as an adaptive individual. Maintaining that ambiguity allows me a self-perception of complexity—or at least enough complexity to cover multiple, paradoxical, and even contradictory beliefs. Fostering ambiguity in my self-definition also gives me the latitude to change my self-image and my public presentation, typically in an incremental, evolutionary fashion. Although individuals might not themselves tolerate ambiguity very well in many social situations and change contexts, they nonetheless seek a tolerance for ambiguity from others where self-presentation is concerned. And it is all for the best; it allows the wiggle room or social lubricant necessary for us all to be together and work together in collective enterprises.

Such ambiguity results in something akin to multiple personalities (or at least multiple facets of a complex personality)—each one best suited to a specialized role or context (my professor persona, my father persona, my public speaker persona, etc.). This observation echoes James's (1918) early challenge to the conventional assumption of a holistic identity when he argued that a person has many different "social selves" appropriate for different audiences (capturing both multiple identity and the social nature of identity in his provocative statement that "A man has as many social selves as there are individuals who recognize him" [p. 294]).

Organizational Identity

These important features of individual identity supply the basis for the extension of the notion to organizations. As a first approximation, the leap to organizational identity is hardly a leap outward over a conceptual chasm; rather, it is a more straightforward leap upward in level of analysis. Most of the multilevel parallels are straightforward, but there are a few interesting twists when one imputes identity to an organization. As problematic as it might be for theorists and researchers to identify a collective organizational identity, and as much as this notion might be little more than a comprehensive construction by upper-echelon executives, by a relatively small subset of organization members, and/or by observing theorists and researchers, the notion is nevertheless metaphorically and analytically revealing. Certainly, we can observe that organizational leaders frequently invoke a collective identity as a means of imputing or maintaining the sense of organizational coherence and cooperativeness. Given the plausibility of the concept, we might ask questions like: How is organizational identity similar to individual identity? Are there subtle or significant discontinuities between individual and organizational identity? What do we think we know about organizational identity as a macro-level concept?

Albert and Whetten (1985) characterized organizational identity as "a self reflective question" (p. 264). (Who are we anyway, as an organization?) Identity captures the essential (in the phenomenological sense) features of an organization. Albert and Whetten concluded that those features could be summarized in three major dimensions: Organizational identity is (a) what is taken by organization members to be *central* to the organization; (b) what makes the organization *distinctive* from other organizations (at least in the eyes of the beholding members); and (c) what is perceived by members to be an *enduring* or continuing feature linking the present organization with the past (and presumably the future). Organizations, like individuals, decide who they are by employing some classification scheme and then locating themselves within that scheme. As is evident, these dimensional features are directly parallel to those noted for individuals, differing mainly in their collectively-shared character.

Similarly, organizations maintain identity through interaction with other organizations by a process of interorganizational comparison over time (Albert, 1977). In a sense, we can envision a kind of socialization at the macro level of organizations into an industry, a cooperative or competitive group, or other social or economic class that influences the development and evolution of organizational identity. Thus, the extension of the idea that identity is relational and comparative works nicely at the organization level as well.

Also, organizations clearly engage in the practice of appearing similar to a chosen group of other organizations while attempting to distinguish themselves from the other members of that class along some finer dimensions. Claims of distinctness or uniqueness are rife, even if they do not seem to hold up very well to comparative scrutiny (Martin, Feldman, Hatch, & Sitkin, 1983). As Dutton, Dukerich, and Harquail (1994) note, however, whether claims of distinctive collective identity are actually true is much less important than the fact that organization members believe that they are distinct and therefore engage frequently in efforts to foster the shared idea of a distinct, collective identity.

Like individuals, organizations can be viewed as subsuming a multiplicity of identities, each of which is appropriate for a given context or audience. Actually, at the organization level, the notion of multiple identities is perhaps a key (if subtle) point of difference between individuals and organizations. One has a markedly easier time making the case for the simultaneous presentation of multiple "personalities" because organizations are acknowledged to be complex entities with distinct components; they are expected to display different identities to different audiences. Thus, organizations can plausibly present a complicated, multifaceted identity, each component of which is relevant to specific domains or constituents, without appearing hopelessly fragmented or ludicrously schizophrenic, as an individual might. Rather than manifesting these multiple identities according to gender, race, role, and so on, as individuals do, organizations instead develop and manifest them mainly according to core values, practices, and, most visibly, products and services.

Another point of conceptual difference between individual and organizational identity concerns the stability or endurance of identity. At the individual level, personal identity often appears stable over time; I can easily trace elements of my identity to my youth. The same core set of values, perceptions, and attributes seems to prevail, so that when I look, I see constancy. Yet other elements of my values and perceptions clearly have altered over the years, so that when I look, I see change. I am a paradox, even to myself. I am both immutable and mutable (but I also have a kind of dynamic consistency to my mutability).

Organizations appear to operate in a similar fashion, but with a twist. The twist is that organizational identity is much more fluid than individual identity (Gioia & Schultz, 1995). Although individuals and organizations both display central features of identity that are both stable and unstable, what is core about organizational identity can change at a much more rapid pace than individuals can reinvent themselves. Toffler's (1970) thesis that change is occurring at a rate beyond an individual's capacity to cope with it might be truer of individuals than organizations, mainly because organizations have the capacity to alter aspects of identity more easily than do individuals.

Organizational environments shift rapidly these days. New contextual and competitive features appear and supplant old ones, products and services undergo extraordinarily rapid change, and so on—all of which has an immediacy of impact that requires rapid reconstruction of identity so that the organization can maintain a light-on-its-feet flexibility (or, as Gioia & Schultz, 1995, put it, an "adaptive instability" in identity) that allows the organization to cope. Although individual identity is not exactly immune to these contextual trends, individual identity is socially constructed with the balance shifted toward a centering stability; organizational identity is constructed with the balance shifted toward adaptive instability.

The underlying issue here really is one of attempting to balance stability and fluidity. For organizations, living in a world increasingly dominated by image and reputation, the issue often becomes transformed into one of balancing the *appearance* of stability and fluidity. Even more subtly, it also is a matter of managing the appearance of stability and order so that change can be managed while still retaining essential features of core identity (an observation that conjures up the line from di Lampedusa, 1960, in *The Leopard*: "If we want things to stay as they are, things will have to change" [p. 40]). Like individuals, who engage in interpretations and practices intended to maintain the continuity of self-concepts over time and place, organizations work at the appearance of consistency in value and action; paradoxically, they also work at maintaining an aura of adaptability (witness the periodic updates of the "Betty Crocker woman").

For these reasons, organizations also display tendencies for maintaining some ambiguity in their identities; this tendency, which mirrors the observation made about individuals, arguably is amplified when extended to organizations. If the organizational identity is not precisely pinned down, it can accommodate many different presentations and actions; it can accommodate many complex pursuits; and it can engage in planned and unplanned change without appearing to violate its basic (and ostensibly enduring) values. Yet it is this ambiguity that presents the most challenge to the maintenance of a view that can be labeled as "organizational identity."

THE EMPIRICAL ARENA

Given the apparent explanatory power of the concept of organizational identity, there is still relatively little organizational research on the topic. I would like to focus on three selected studies that have contributed empirical credence to the existing theoretical works and given more prominence to the organizational identity concept. First, Dutton and Dukerich (1991) employed the notion of organizational identity in their study of the New York/New Jersey Port Authority's attempts to deal with the problem of homeless people frequenting their facilities. They fingered identity as *the* key concept that provided an organization with a viable framework for understanding and action. They also demonstrated that identity simultaneously filtered, constrained, and ultimately shaped the Authority's interpretations and actions of an important issue over time.

In addition, Dutton and Dukerich related organizational identity to its first cousin, organizational image, defining identity as the way insiders see the organization and image as the way insiders believe outsiders see the organization.[2] They then argued that the perceived deterioration of image was also an important impetus for action. They were able to specify the attributes of the Port Authority identity in some detail and then did a convincing job of showing how interpretations and actions changed over time as the context for assessing image and its possible implications for identity changed. Overall, these researchers showed that identity influences the meaning of events and even influences (some might say governs) the set of possible actions considered to be within the realm of possibility. (Which are acceptable? Which are legitimate?, etc.) Identity also supplied the criteria for deciding the success, failure, effectiveness, or value of actions and outcomes.

Elsbach and Kramer (1996) investigated the responses of the top administrators of universities to the rankings published biennially by *Business Week*. These researchers explored how the administrators of eight highly ranked business schools dealt with the perceived threat represented by a ranking that challenged their own self-perceptions. The study is noteworthy because it demonstrated that rankings that threatened valued dimensions of identity produced clear effects on sensemaking strategies. Most notably, the administrators of schools who suffered in comparison to other peer schools chose more selective comparison categories that emphasized dimensions of evaluation that *they* preferred, but that were not given prominence in the formal rankings (e.g., public schools emphasized their rankings among other public schools; schools that emphasized teaching downplayed comparisons with research-oriented universities). This strategy allowed them to retain positive perceptions of their institution's identity in the face of putatively disconfirming evidence that triggered "identity dissonance."

The Elsbach and Kramer study provides evidence that organization members seek to affirm and maintain organizational identity perceptions (cf. Steele, 1988). When such perceptions were threatened by the *Business Week* ogre, they actively sought alternative categorization schemes that allowed them to emphasize their good standing according to *some* viable criteria. In this fashion, top managers did not need to surrender their chosen dimensions of identity and could continue to look good in their own eyes. Perhaps most importantly, the study portrays top organization members as actively engaged in identity management.

Gioia and Thomas (1996) also showed that identity and image were critical organizational perceptions that influenced interpretation and action during strategic change at a university. The change context is particularly interesting for the consideration of the nature of identity. If change is at issue, what changes? If it is substantive, strategic change, some aspects of identity must, of necessity, change. Gioia and Thomas's evidence suggested just that. Furthermore, their evidence indicated that the main driver of changing identity was changing image. The members of the top management team of the university they studied concentrated almost exclusively on pursuing the "future image" of a "mythological university" on the assumption that attempts to change the current image would foster desired changes in the identity.

On the basis of their findings, Gioia and Thomas took some issue with Albert and Whetten's rigorous rendering of the definitional dimensions of identity—in particular, they held that the assertion that identity was enduring and distinctive in any strict sense was conceptually problematic. Modern organizations find themselves in the position of having to change almost constantly to some greater or lesser degree, thus raising the question concerning the actual durability of identity at the organizational level. Even Albert and Whetten found themselves in the somewhat gymnastic position of arguing that durability was a key attribute of organizational identity, and yet they presented organizations as shifting between normative and utilitarian identities over time. Is identity really durable, or is it mainly another illusion preserved for the purpose of appearing stable and consistent over time for internal and external consumption? Of *course* identity is not durable in any absolute sense. It changes while maintaining a dynamic consistency. The more relevant issue is (again) one of balancing change and stability while maintaining some connection with past conceptions of who we are.

On empirical and practical grounds, Gioia and Thomas also raised the issue of the actual degree to which distinctiveness was a defining characteristic of organizational identity. Their evidence suggested that the current rage for benchmarking and within-industry emulation was diluting the actual distinctiveness of many organizations. Furthermore, the strategy of emulation frequently appeared to be intentional, thus calling into question the idea of distinctiveness as essential to the definition of organizational identity in the modern (and postmodern) era.

These kinds of issues, the ones that question even the definitional dimensions of identity, are healthy signs of an underdeveloped but high-potential concept. They engage the debate about the nature of identity at the macro level (and keep the question alive about whether identity is an appropriation of a psychological term inappropriately applied to a different sort of concept). On balance, however, the attributes of centrality, distinctiveness, and durability remain as useful dimensions for conceiving identity, even though they might need to be employed with a certain wink of the eye. Not only do distinctiveness and durability have some necessary malleability associated with them, as will soon be evident, even the notion of "central" features is assailed by postmodernists. Nevertheless, they serve as useful organizing and analytical concepts, and we will use them just that way in the next chapter.

THREE LENSES FOR UNDERSTANDING ORGANIZATIONAL IDENTITY

Albert and Whetten (1985) noted that statements of identity by organization members could conceivably be compatible, complementary, or even contradictory, depending on the circumstances that elicit the identity statements. A similar observation holds true for outsiders trying to discern the identity of an organization. In the case of organization theorists and researchers trying to analyze organizational identity, however, the potentially differing statements arise from differing paradigmatic assumptions about the nature of organizations. When we start with differing assumptions about the ontology and epistemology of organizations, we can end up with sometimes convergent, sometimes complementary, and sometimes profoundly different or contradictory views. We also can end up with views that either cover territory not accounted for by other ways of seeing or entail insightful observations that are simply uninteresting from another perspective.

At the Identity Conference in Sundance, Utah, we soon discovered that members of our group held markedly different paradigmatic views, even about the fundamental character of organizational identity. Our conversations revealed that the differences in our conceptions of organizational identity in fact provoked a much deeper and more comprehensive understanding of the concept. They also produced the potential for expanding the ways in which the field thinks about identity. Therefore, we decided to take advantage of our differences and organize a key part of the conversation around our disagreements.

In our conversation, we have chosen to consider the discussion of identity from three different perspectives—a functionalist perspective, an interpretive perspective, and a postmodern perspective. Of these, the functionalist perspective is most well known in the organizational literature and in fact tends to dominate current conceptualization and research; thus, it probably requires less descriptive summary than the others. The interpretive perspective, although steeped in tradition and perhaps even the recipient of a certain admiration because of the richness of the writing and production of insights, is still not widely known in our literature. The postmodern perspective, despite its widespread impact in Europe, has had a much rougher time making inroads into North American ways of understanding organizations. Actually, the more radical versions of postmodernism have sparked some rather heated resistance among social scientists and organization theorists—postmodernists are nothing if not provocative.

Without trying to steal any thunder from the conversation that follows, part of which is intended to explore some key similarities and distinctions among these ways of understanding organizational identity, I would like to offer a little foundational overview of these three perspectives. Some of this overview derives from my work with Evelyn Pitre a few years ago (Gioia & Pitre, 1990) and from the work of Burrell and Morgan (1979), Hatch and Schultz (1997), Hatch (1997), and also from Rosenau's (1992) literate attempt to explore postmodernism in understandable terms (no small feat!). The key point to keep in mind here is that entertaining different ways of thinking about identity in fact changes the character of identity itself. In that sense, the conversation that follows might serve to break a little new ground in organizational analysis.

The Functionalist Lens. Functionalism, as has been noted ad nauseam, is predicated on the notion that approaches to the study of social science phenomena are appropriately based on variations of natural science models (Burrell & Morgan, 1979). The underlying assumption, of course, is that physical and social phenomena are essentially similar enough that they can be described according to similar "laws." Functionalism in its most common forms is almost relentlessly realist and objectivist in its ontological assumptions (i.e., identity is best treated as something that exists and is available for study); functionalism also presumes that constructs are reasonably stable over time, so they have an enduring quality that allows comparisons over time. Identity is presumed to be relatively stable—changeable perhaps, but not easily so.

Functionalism typically proceeds via deduction, using research observers who are detached, independent, and ostensibly impartial to the investigation. There is a clear distinction between researcher and researched; researchers make no pretense of getting close to the subjects under study, because such a stance would subvert the detachment and independence necessary to render objective observational judgment. The study of identity is often treated as the study of something someone or some organization has; it is thus rendered as understandable to an interested observer and usually is conceptualized in fairly dispassionate, theoretical terms.

Hallmarks of the functionalist approach to the study of identity include specification of appropriate variables; hypothesis testing; concerns with reliability, validity, and generalizability; the search for relationships and regularities in the representation of identity; and, perhaps especially, the attempt to establish causal relationships among identity-related constructs and variables. The heart of the functional approach in organization study is the verification or (more importantly) falsification of a proposed hypothesis (Popper, 1959). The understanding of organizational identity progresses incrementally as more and more studies build on the evolving literature.

Some of the above characteristics imply that identity is treated as a variable to be manipulated (often for the purposes of predictability and controllability) to better manage an organization and its presentation to internal stakeholders as well as concerned external constituencies. For that reason, functionalism has sometimes been accused of overemphasizing managerial interests in comparison to employee interests. Functionalist studies present us with general, testable constructs that can be compared across time, industries, and organizations and that allow us to characterize identity along comparative dimensions (e.g., what is central, distinctive, and enduring).

The Interpretive Lens. Interpretivism traces its roots to the hermeneutic tradition (deriving from the mythological Hermes, the messenger in his role as interpreter of messages). If functionalism is relentlessly objectivist, then interpretivism is incorrigibly subjectivist (i.e., identity is a socially and symbolically constructed notion intended to lend meaning to experience). Interpretivism blurs the distinction between researcher and researched; in fact, in "pure" interpretivism, the project of the researcher becomes that of faithfully rendering the constructions of the informants studied and accurately representing *their* interpretations. (This point often is misconstrued: Many readers seem to presume that because all researchers engage in interpretation, by definition, everyone is an "interpretivist"; the key difference in hermeneutic interpretivism is that the prime interpreter is presumed to be the informant, not the researcher.)

The main project of interpretivist approaches is the description and insightful explanation of identity, with the intention of understanding the meaning system employed by organization members and other relevant constituents. Interpretive researchers tend to emphasize the views of insiders. They revel in getting as close to the action as possible, often teetering on the edge of "going native" (i.e., unquestioningly adopting the informants' views) in trying to adequately represent how organization members construe their identity. The best of all situations for a dyed-in-the-wool interpretivist is to "live the experience" of the informants, so there is a heavy dose of participant observation characterizing interpretive research. That is one reason that the research is so often held to a standard of being "adequate at the level of meaning of the informant." Sometimes, the research is treated at two levels: (a) a first-order level that meets this criterion by attempting to represent identity in the actual words and symbols used by the informants themselves; the first-order level, then, is the informants' level of representation; and (b) a second-order level that attempts to build a grounded, theoretical explanation for the patterns observed in the informants' words, symbols, and representations of their identity. At this more abstract level, conceptual explanations, frameworks, or models are constructed; the second-order level, then, is the researchers' level of theoretical representation (see Gioia & Chittipeddi, 1991, for an example of research that progresses from first- to second-level representation).

Interpretive approaches typically proceed via induction; actually, they come across as essentially opposed to deduction, preferring instead to maximize the opportunity for discovery. The focus often is on the ways that members organize and develop conceptualizations and practices that employ identity as both a facilitating and constraining concept in conducting their organizational lives. Interpretive accounts are usually rendered in narrative form, so another hallmark of interpretive work is that it often tells an interesting, readable story, one that has depth and richness, producing informative insights, but at the expense of demonstrable generalizability (which is an issue of minimal concern to many interpretivists).

The Postmodern Lens. Whereas functionalism and interpretivism lend themselves fairly easily to direct comparisons with each other, postmodernism's project of radicalizing most (all?) current ways of understanding identity means that it does not easily subject itself to a comparative template. Because postmodernism's assumptions and positions have not yet made substantial inroads into organization theory, its typical stance requires a bit more elaboration.

Fundamentally, postmodernism wants to challenge or at least suspend judgment on most current ontological, epistemological, and methodological assumptions in favor of questioning the basis for all belief and study, including its very own (Rosenau, 1992). Postmodernists are subjectivists in the extreme. Authors of "texts" (and, by extension, the usually revered founders and designers of organizations) are accorded no special status; indeed, their intended values, beliefs, and so on are discounted in favor of "other readers'" meanings. Meaning, although an important notion, is up for grabs. Postmodernists prefer indeterminacy in lieu of determinism, attend to diversity and fragmentation rather than integration, focus on differences rather than similarities or syntheses, and invoke complexity at the expense of simplicity (Rosenau, 1992). This short section is far too brief a forum for articulating the large scope of postmodernism's challenge to current organization theory, so I will focus mainly on several points that relate directly to identity and its study.

First of all, identity as a concept is a big problem for postmodernists. They question the existence of a rational and coherent identity, not necessarily disagreeing with interpretivists that identity is socially constructed, but arguing that because of that very construction, identity becomes a myth or, to use the favored term, an "illusion" (Baudrillard, 1983; Derrida, 1978; Edelman, 1988). A directly parallel idea therefore extends to the notion of organizational identity; identity becomes an invention for the (often sinister) purposes of parties in power. Postmodernists locate the source of social phenomena in language and treat personality and personal identity mainly as a product of language and linguistic convention (that is, the construction of a person's identity is not only enabled but also produced only by the use of language). It is not much of a reach, then, to conclude that organizations and any conception of organizational identity also are merely linguistic manifestations. Organizational identity is frequently construed as, at best, a fiction perpetrated by dominant parties.

In a related vein, postmodernists virtually dismiss the idea of a constellation of "central" traits or features that might constitute an individual person. Actually, among the group that Rosenau (1992) has termed the "radical postmodernists," individuals are accorded very diminished status, mainly because they "get lost in the flood of structures that overpower the individual" (p. 46). Again, the extrapolated consequences for the notion of central characteristics for organizational identity are also fairly dismissive. On the other hand, despite the dismissal of human agents with unified identities in favor of conceptions emphasizing their multiple, contradictory characters, postmodern thought easily accommodates the idea of an organization consisting of multiple, often contradictory identities (as long as no one attempts to nominate any one of those identities as more central). Fragmentation, ambiguity, and indeterminacy are inherent in any human systems, including organizations—and perhaps especially organizations.

If anything, postmodernists might be described as antihumanists because of the pervasiveness of the argument that larger systems (e.g., culture) predominate so extensively in shaping personalities. Curiously, organizations can be viewed as one of those larger systems, particularly in contemporary society, which implies that organization theory is arguably ripe for postmodern analysis (see Hatch, 1997, for an excellent treatment from this orientation, and Kilduff and Mehra, 1997, for a discussion of the possibilities). The role of identity in such analyses, however, becomes somewhat problematic if one accepts postmodernism's conclusions about the mythological nature of identity.

Postmodernism rejects so many notions deemed to be important by many organization theorists that the more extreme versions constitute a turn-the-world-upside-down assault on the normal way of seeing and studying organizations. Postmodernism is problematic, even threatening, for many scholars because of its project to abolish individual identity. The implications are apparent for organizational identity (although curiously, for the reasons noted above, there might be more room for organizational identity in postmodern thought than for individual identity).

Rosenau (1992) divides postmodernists into "radical" and "affirmative" camps. The affirmatives would seem to have a good deal to offer and contribute to expanding and revamping many of our views of organization. The radicals, although provocative and insightful, seem to offer visions that ultimately are nihilistic and anarchic—the very opposite of organization. My own reading of radical postmodern thought is that postmodernists just might be accurate in many of their skeptical and cynical readings of social and organizational phenomena. Much of what we do as organization members and as organization scholars *is* predicated on illusion. Yet it is a workable illusion. So far, the alternative illusions offered do not seem to be significant improvements on this one. Little is offered to replace what would be destroyed. So, one reasonable strategy I might propose is to acknowledge the radical postmodern position and then actively ignore it as a matter of pragmatism, while trying to accommodate the contributions of the affirmative postmodernists.

As is evident from this overview, and as will become even more evident from the immediately following chapter, we have come some good distance in chasing the notion of organizational identity, but things are still unsettled and undecided. Far from that being a discouraging observation, it is rather a sign that the investigation of organizational identity is still an embryonic area of some significant potential for understanding how and why organization members think and act as they do. It is an area that is personally intriguing (when you study identity, you learn something about yourself, too) and organizationally fascinating (it leads to a deep consideration of the nature of organization). Given those two characteristics, in addition to the fact that it is a ripe area for further theoretical work and a wide open domain for research, I invite all interested readers to join vicariously in the following conversation and in the larger exploration.

NOTES

1. I was particularly struck by Dave Whetten's memorable little anecdote at the first working conference on organizational identity in which he related the triggering event that led Stu Albert and himself to apply the idea of an organizational identity. He told the story of the over-the-top reactions of administrators and faculty at his former university responding to some relatively minor budget cuts in the early 1980s. In describing the intensity of the reaction to a cut that amounted to only a minuscule one half of 1%, he made the observation that the "screaming-to-pain ratio" (a wonderfully evocative phrase) was all out of proportion to the actual size of the cut and to the reactions he had seen in downsizing businesses as a result of much larger budget cuts. How to explain such an overreaction? Their mutual discussions led them to conclude that the university possessed a hybrid identity, the strong normative aspects of which were threatened by the symbolics of the perceived budget crisis.

2. Dutton et al. (1994) later applied the more formal and precise, but notably more awkward, labels "perceived organizational identity" and "construed external image" to these concepts.

REFERENCES

Albert, S. (1977). Temporal comparison theory. *Psychological Review, 84,* 485-503.
Albert, S., & Whetten, D. A. (1985). Organizational identity. In L. L. Cummings & B. M. Staw (Eds.), *Research in organizational behavior* (Vol. 7, pp. 263-295). Greenwich, CT: JAI.
Baudrillard, J. (1983). *Simulations.* New York: Semiotext.
Burrell, G., & Morgan, G. (1979). *Sociological paradigms and organizational analysis.* London: Heinemann.
Cooley, C. H. (1902). *Human nature and the social order.* New York: Scribner.
Derrida, J. (1978). *Writing and difference.* London: Routledge & Kegan Paul.
di Lampedusa, G. (1960). *The leopard* (A. Colquhoun, Trans.). London: Pantheon.
Dutton, J., & Dukerich J. (1991). Keeping an eye on the mirror: Image and identity in organizational adaptation. *Academy of Management Journal, 34,* 517-554.
Dutton, J., Dukerich, J., & Harquail, C. V. (1994). Organizational images and membership commitment. *Administrative Science Quarterly, 39,* 239-263.
Edelman, M. (1988). *Constructing the political spectacle.* Chicago: University of Chicago Press.
Elsbach, K. D., & Kramer, R. M. (1996). Members' responses to organizational identity threats: Encountering and countering the *Business Week* rankings. *Administrative Science Quarterly, 41,* 442-476.
Erickson, E. (1964). *Insight and responsibility.* New York: Norton.
Gergen, K. J. (1985). The social construction of the person: How is it possible? In K. J. Gergen & K. E. Davis (Eds.), *The social construction of the person.* New York: Springer-Verlag.
Gioia, D. A., & Chittipeddi, K. (1991). Sensemaking and sensegiving in strategic change initiation. *Strategic Management Journal, 12,* 433-448.
Gioia, D. A., & Pitre, E. (1990). Multiparadigm perspectives on theory building. *Academy of Management Review, 15,* 584-602.
Gioia, D. A., & Schultz, M. (1995, August). *Adaptive instability: The inter-relationship of identity and image.* Paper presented at the annual meeting of the Academy of Management, Vancouver, BC, Canada.
Gioia, D. A., & Thomas, J. B. (1996). Identity, image and issue interpretation: Sensemaking during strategic change in academia. *Administrative Science Quarterly, 40,* 370-403.
Goffman, E. (1959). *The presentation of self in everyday life.* New York: Anchor.
Hatch, M. J. (1997). *Organization theory: Modern, symbolic, and postmodern perspectives.* Oxford, UK: Oxford University Press.

Hatch, M. J., & Schultz, M. (1997). Relations between organizational culture, identity and image. *European Journal of Marketing, 31,* 356-365.

James, W. (1918). *Principles of psychology* (Vol. 1). New York: Henry Holt.

Kilduff, M., & Mehra, A. (1997). Postmodernism and organizational research. *Academy of Management Review, 22,* 453-481.

Martin, J., Feldman, M. S., Hatch, M. J., & Sitkin, S. S. (1983). The uniqueness paradox in organizational stories. *Administrative Science Quarterly, 28,* 438-453.

Mead, G. H. (1934). *Mind, self, and society.* Chicago: University of Chicago Press.

Popper, K. (1959). *The logic of scientific discovery.* New York: Basic Books.

Rosenau, P. M. (1992). *Postmodernism and the social sciences.* Princeton, NJ: Princeton University Press.

Steele, C. M. (1988). The psychology of self-affirmation: Sustaining the integrity of the self. In *Advances in experimental social psychology* (Vol. 21, pp. 261-302). New York: Academic Press.

Tajfel, H. (1982). *Social identity and intergroup relations.* Cambridge, UK: Cambridge University Press.

Tajfel, H., & Turner, J. C. (1985). The social identity theory of intergroup behavior. In S. Worchel & W. G. Austin (Eds.), *The psychology of intergroup relations* (Vol. 2, pp. 7-24). Chicago: Nelson-Hall.

Toffler, A. (1970). *Future shock.* New York: Bantam.

Weick, K. E. (1995). *Sensemaking in organizations.* Thousand Oaks, CA: Sage.

3

The Identity of Organizations

Parties to the Conversation:
Hamid Bouchikhi, C. Marlene Fiol, Dennis A. Gioia (moderator),
Karen Golden-Biddle, Mary Jo Hatch,
Hayagreeva "Huggy" Rao, Violina Rindova, and Majken Schultz

With Shadow Partners and Co-Conspirators[1]
Charles J. Fombrun, John R. Kimberly, and James B. Thomas

We begin our conversation within the context of Albert and Whetten's (1985) definition of organizational identity as that which members believe to be central, enduring, and distinctive about their organization. Although these key elements of the definition arguably have some conceptual limitations under some conditions (e.g., strategic change), this definition gives us a good first approximation and a good point of departure for a conversation that further explores the identity of organizations. To begin, we would like to examine a number of issues pertaining to the character and definition of organizational identity. Our stance here is perhaps an unusual one compared to the typical writing on organizational identity, in that we maintain that one's understanding of identity depends on the perspective one takes in approaching it. The answer to the question "Who are we?" as an organization, it would seem, very much depends on the assumptions we make about *how* we understand ourselves as an organization. Similarly, "Who are they?" as a question asked by those of us trying to understand the identity of organized others also depends on the assumptions brought to bear on the question itself. We hope to articulate this case in an interesting way at the outset of our wide-ranging conversation.

Although there are multiple possible perspectives that we might entertain, for the sake of some semblance of clarity, we are going to confine ourselves to three general orientations that can illustrate our overarching point that identity differs according to ways of seeing organizations and conducting inquiry about them. This point is key, if perhaps somewhat disconcerting; for many, it constitutes a wholly different way of thinking about identity. We do see our group as breaking a bit of new ground here. We see identity as a highly variable concept—not only by those expressing their own identity, but also by those who purport to get a grip on the expressed identity of others (i.e., we theorists and researchers).

We have identified our three demonstrative perspectives with the potentially provocative working labels: *functionalist* (which has blatantly objectivist overtones); *interpretivist* (which has unabashedly constructivist underpinnings); and *postmodernist* (which derives its impact from relentlessly contesting prevailing assumptions). Despite these competing stances, which tend to encourage freewheeling discussion and debate, we are going to try to explore the differences in viewpoint in a somewhat more structured fashion.

We propose to discuss alternative approaches to organizational identity in terms of (a) the central problem or the main questions about identity that concern each perspective, (b) the basic (albeit often tacit) assumptions that each perspective employs in conducting inquiry, (c) the putative purpose for inquiry concerning identity from these various perspectives, (d) representative metaphors that bring identity to life within each perspective, (e) the data that theorists and researchers employ in investigating identity, and (f) some of the consequences and implications of the views furthered by each perspective. At some point, we will try to present a workable definition of organizational identity from each perspective, although it is important to recognize that part of the value of adopting our approach to the concept of identity is that it is not necessarily easy to pin down a precise definition of this rather imprecise and multifaceted notion. For instance, think about Albert and Whetten's frequently cited "definition" of identity—see the first sentences of this chapter—as that which members believe to be central, enduring, and distinctive about their organization. This phrase seems like a workable working definition, but perhaps we should ask just what *is* the referent for the sly phrase "that which"? In other words, what is the "that" to which the definition refers? As will become apparent from the discussion, the intrigue around specifying the identity of an organization only deepens as we consider our set of six questions.

To facilitate our conversation, we have agreed to a kind of metalevel position about organizational identity to try to establish some tentative common ground; our agreed-upon position is that identity in some general sense addresses the question, "Who are we as an organization?" Despite the possible questions about Albert and Whetten's suggested dimensions for understanding organizational identity, we will nevertheless also share the common ground of trying to link our exposition to the focal ideas of centrality, durability, and distinctiveness. For the record, we conducted a semiscripted conversation that we tape-recorded and transcribed; we then moderately edited the transcription for clarification of the ideas and to remove a few of the more troublesome discontinuities of natural conversational language.

Representing the functionalist view are Violina Rindova, Hamid Bouchikhi, and Huggy Rao. Representing the interpretive perspective will be Marlene Fiol and Denny Gioia. Representing the postmodernist perspective will be Mary Jo Hatch, Majken Schultz, and Karen Golden-Biddle. Generally, one person from each perspective (Violina, Marlene, and Mary Jo, respectively) will articulate the positions agreed upon by the dyads or triads. Denny will act, in some loose sense, as a moderator.

Later sections of this chapter are devoted to the articulation of several models pertaining to organizational identity that a number of our members have been constructing in collaboration with our shadow partners. Also, we have inserted several additional "sidebar" commentaries on a number of key topics that arose in the course of the conversation. These commentaries were written after the fact to elaborate several important issues that were only tacitly dealt with in the conversation or else received only passing notation. These have been inserted in the text in appropriate locations. Okay, are we ready to roll?

The primary issue before us is to address the question, "What is organizational identity?" We will start with the functionalist perspective and ask, "What is the key problem or main question as framed by the functionalist perspective as it relates to organizational identity?"

⠿

Violina: The central problem from a functionalist perspective is the question of how identity affects actions. More specifically, this approach focuses on how identity affects cognitions of organizational members and how these in turn affect actions at the individual and organizational level.

Marlene: From the interpretivist perspective, we would suggest that the central problem is the question of how organization members collectively construct an understanding of "Who are we?"

Mary Jo: From the postmodern point of view, one needs to problematize the notion of identity itself. That might mean that we accept fragmented, multiple identities; it might mean that we deconstruct the whole notion of identity and suggest that such a thing does not exist.

Denny: OK. Those are pretty tightly stated positions. Can we consider the assumptions that undergird those statements?

Violina: The key assumption that the objectivist, functionalist perspective makes is that identity is *a social fact*. As such, it can be managed and changed for different purposes. As a result, the actions that identity affects can also be managed and controlled.

Marlene: The interpretive perspective argues strongly that identity is inevitably socially constructed. We have one other basic assumption, and that is that people in social groups have a need for some stability of meaning. Social groups always will be striving toward some level of convergence about meanings around their identity.

Mary Jo: Postmodernism differs from the other two perspectives quite a bit here; it makes key assumptions such as the indeterminacy of meaning, that identity is an accidental collection of forms clustering in moments of time, and that identity takes on a paradoxical form.

Denny: Well, I'm foxed now. Can you elaborate . . .? [Laughter.]

Mary Jo: I was afraid you were going to say that! Help me out here, Majken.

Majken: I think that it might help to think of it as a kind of garbage can full of meanings. That you have a lot of streams of identity that could be formed; it could be fragments of sent meanings, it could be statements, it could be names, it could be logos, and they are very much like garbage can processes. They may condense and vary in moments of time . . .

Denny: And the paradox is that they are all held together at the same time?

Majken: The paradox is that they are held together all the time, although they may not have consistently emerged within the organization. But these fragments of meaning are nonetheless competing for dominance, yes.

Mary Jo: It should also be noted that postmodernists would probably resist the frame here, beginning with resisting or problematizing notions like "key assumptions."

Denny: Okay. Purpose of inquiry . . .

Violina: Given the assumptions of the functionalist perspective, that identity exists objectively as a social fact and the central problem that it can be used to shape actions, the purpose of inquiry is to uncover that identity, to describe it, to measure it, to manage it where necessary, and ultimately, from a managerial point of view, to be able to put it to a productive use.

Marlene: Given the basic assumption that identities are not objective and easily manipulable, the interpretivist perspective's purpose of inquiry is to discover the meanings and meaning structures that are negotiated among organizational members.

Mary Jo: Two purposes of postmodern inquiry might be stated as provocation and reflexivity. By this we mean that postmodernists might take the approach of provoking a sense of identity and then reflecting upon it in order to produce a statement about identity.

Denny: That is what reflexivity is, thinking about your own identity?

Mary Jo: In this context, yes. But the notion of a perspective having a purpose is a bit problematic . . .

Denny: OK. We'll leave at that for now. Let's consider the differences in representative metaphors that might capture some of these differences in lay terms that organization members might use.

Violina: A functionalist metaphor of identity will probably represent identity as an object with a form, color, functions, and other characteristics with varying degrees of usefulness to an organization. That is why identity is also thought of as an asset, as a resource, as something that can be used to shape members' cognitions and actions.

Marlene: From the interpretivist perspective, there is probably less concern about identity's ultimate usefulness. Interpretivists might use the metaphor of a theater in which there are rules and actors on a stage. The actors are . . . what's the word I'm looking for . . . improvising. They are improvising and constantly defining their roles and their interactions, but within some larger set of theatrical rules.

Denny: I would like to add one more metaphor. That is a holographic metaphor, which recognizes that knowledge and constructions about identity are distributed among the members of the group in a fashion that is essential to the culture of the group or organization.

Mary Jo: Recognizing that postmodernists would probably not accept any particular metaphor, we nonetheless offer the metaphor of the collage, which is built on ideas of momentary constructions of identity that are fragmented. What we are suggesting with the notion of collage is that there are many possible forms that could come together to fit the metaphor of a collage—in the sense that collage is a juxtaposition of unexpected elements that leads to a new sense of something: A moment of surprise, an unanticipated excitement . . .

Denny: We certainly are being concise, and I am sure there are multiple metaphors that we might entertain for each perspective. Nonetheless, let's continue in our pattern of provocative conciseness and ask what each perspective might construe as data for studying identity.

Violina: Conceptualizing identity as an existing, objective element of organizations suggests that studying identity also focuses on the objective characteristics of organizations. Examples of such characteristics include (a) organizational demography as an antecedent of members' beliefs, (b) patterns of past decisions and actions from which identity can be inferred, and (c) statements of members (and especially of top managers) assumed to reflect an existing underlying identity. The appropriate methods of investigation are those that can measure or represent objectively dimensions of this existing identity, such as psychometric instruments and cognitive mapping techniques.

Marlene: Given the fundamental assumption of the interpretivist point of view that it is the meanings that people accept and construe that define their identity, the data that researchers believe would be most important in pursuing this line of research would be forms of symbols—anything that has meaning for organizational members, whether that be language, or artifacts, or mannerisms, etc. There also might be second-order forms of data that become important in this line of inquiry. One of those is the cognitive schema or worldview; it is basically schemas or interpretive schemes that members use to make sense of those symbols; the other form is our own schemas as researchers making sense of what we see.

Mary Jo: Okay, reflecting the linguistic turn that is part of postmodernism, we suggest that appropriate data for studying identity from a postmodern perspective would include language and discourse, and, furthermore, would focus on ruptures and absences in the discourse.

Denny: Good. Now to culminating definitions . . .

Violina: A functionalist definition will focus again on the reality-like quality of identity. We talked about identity as institutionalized beliefs about who we are that have taken-for-granted, reality-like status. These beliefs manifest themselves in other objective characteristics of an organization, such as its core business, operating principles, structures and systems, patterns of decisions, and a variety of artifacts.

Marlene: Again, from the interpretivist perspective, the definition that would embody the above would be that it is the continuously renegotiated set of meanings about who we are as an organization.

Mary Jo: From the postmodern point of view, we took a stab at this and said that identity might have to do with attending to the momentary and fragmented statements about who we take ourselves to be.

Denny: OK. How about entertaining some of the implications of these varying views?

Violina: We have a long list of implications about the properties of identity as that which is enduring. We discussed the property of enduring identity from two perspectives: an adaptation perspective and a more deterministic perspective. From an adaptation perspective within the functionalist approach, we would argue that if organizational identity is a variable, we can then manipulate it for strategic purposes. Therefore, it becomes a strategy implementation variable that is managed and adjusted with changes in an organization's strategy. On the other hand, the object-like quality of identity is likely to make it a constraint and a limit to change. In fact, we suggest that we can turn Thompson on his head. Thompson (1967) argued that in dealing with uncertainty, organizations protect their technical core. However, from a strategic change and adaptation perspective, firms may feel more pressure to deal with ideological uncertainty related to the importance and the consequences of the change. In this case, organizations will buffer their ideological core, which is their identity. Therefore, identity may be what organizations preserve when they adapt to change. In that sense, an organization's identity may be "enduring." Enduring, however, does not mean a "no change" condition. Enduring should be thought of as referring to the time and costs necessary for some beliefs about the organization to change.

The idea of buffering the ideological core is also related to the question of centrality of organizational identity. What firms choose to change and what they choose to preserve alludes to the centrality of these systems, businesses, key principles, and values—that is, elements defining identity. Not only beliefs about what is enduring but also about what is central to an organization may set the limits to change. Like the dominant logic of a top management team (Prahalad & Bettis, 1986), identity may determine what organizational members find to be acceptable and what they find to be an unacceptable strategic direction. Therefore, identity might be some sort of a truce: Up to a point, the organization will be willing and able to go along with a change; beyond this point, change might become catastrophic. Such a threshold point may demarcate the central elements of an organization and its modus operandi (at least as they are perceived by its members). In this sense, identity enables organizations to make choices and to distinguish what they are willing and able to do.

As for distinctiveness, a functionalist approach to identity will focus almost entirely on what the sources of distinctiveness are, where they exist, and how they can be managed. However, the question of distinctiveness may be one of both inclusion (what we are) and exclusion (what we are not). Thus, organizational taboos may be as defining of an identity as organizational accents. The problem of inclusion and exclusion is also related to the role and place of various members of the organization. Top management and management in general are inside the identity, inside the whole, and see only pieces of the whole. As a result, they may perceive some parts as distinctive when, in fact, the organization as a whole is not distinctive (which brings back the "uniqueness paradox"). Also, objectively, organizations may be pretty generic, but members may need to construct and maintain a sense of distinctiveness (Dutton, Dukerich, & Harquail, 1994). In that sense, researchers might be better off by focusing not so much on the differences in identity but rather on the identities of difference. Which puts us right into the interpretivist domain.

Marlene: From the interpretivist perspective, given the basic assumption that social groups strive toward some level of convergence about meaning, we believe that the implication for the enduring dimension of identity is that it will endure only to the extent that the social context affirms the projected identity. The other point to be made about identity endurance is that even as an identity might be in flux, there is a need for it to appear stable in terms of people's construction of meaning for themselves. And again, this notion goes back to a very basic assumption that we started with, which is the need for stability of meaning in our organizational lives.

Denny: The way I think of it is that because of the continuous construction and reconstruction processes, identity appears stable, even though it is actually in a state of flux.

Marlene: OK. A restatement would be that because of the continuous renegotiation, it is, in fact, in flux. But because of the need for stability, there is the need to make it appear to be stable. So, I think we are putting the two together very nicely there.

Mary Jo: You are drifting toward a sort of postmodernist view.

Denny: Well, not really. It just seems that way because the postmodernists steal from everybody.

Marlene: We have simplified the centrality dimension of identity in a way, saying that it is what members agree is central, and so again it depends very much on members' own definition of what is and is not central.

Denny: Yes. A very important point is that the locus of identity is with the members, not with observers like us researchers, who are inclined to impute attributes to the organization or its members.

Marlene: The locus is with the members, that's right. On the distinctiveness dimension, again going back to the fact that we are located and primarily focused on members' meaning-making, we are looking at the assumption that meaning derives from both what is different and what is the same. So, if an organizational member understands that we are a low-cost producer as a basic identity, that would derive meaning only based on comparisons to other low-cost producers and comparisons to high-quality, high-cost producers. So, it is "located." The distinctiveness issue is only one of two. There is both similarity and distinctiveness always occurring simultaneously, and the meaning is located in the tension between the two.

Denny: Great. Okay. Jo, are you ready? . . . Not with that sucker in your mouth, you're not.

Mary Jo: Okay, okay, I'm ready . . . back to postmodernists. As far as the implications of the notion of identity being central, we believe a postmodernist stance would be that identity is constantly shifting. It revolves around the decentering of the subject, so there can be no stable, steady point, no central essence that could be described as identity. With respect to the dimension of enduring, we would argue that identity is impermanent; it is subject to being continuously deconstructed and reconstructed. With respect to distinctiveness, identity, we feel, is defined with respect to so many others that fragmentation is a necessary condition.

Majken: And that distinctiveness is a major aspect of identity that would be represented in the postmodern view. In fact, taken to the extreme in the postmodern, because you are highlighting the whole postmodern notion of games at the marketplace and how you try to state yourself and differentiate yourself in the marketplace.

Mary Jo: Yes, the focus would turn to the uses of identity talk to construct organizational selves.

Denny: Good. Thanks. We seem to have a reasonable summary of the basics. We would now like to entertain a few comments about an additional dimension that seemed to emerge as a common interest in our subgroup discussion—power. Let us just briefly get some brainstorming from the functionalist perspective.

Huggy: From the functionalist perspective, power is simply a reality in the sense that there are power holders and power challengers. What complicates changes in identity and increases the costs of organizational change stems from political tussles in organizations. The observations made earlier about the speed of reorganization, the duration of the change effort, and so on are largely shaped by, on the one hand, the diversity of political interests, and on the other, the diversity of issues facing the organization. The more diverse the interests and issues in an organization, the greater are the reorganization costs, the longer the adjustment lags, and so forth.

Marlene: From an interpretivist perspective, power is also an interesting issue because meanings are often shaped by those who are powerful in organizations. The question of whose meanings these are becomes central.

Denny: It is a matter of managing meaning. There are at least two ways to look at the interpretive perspective where power is at issue. One is concerned mainly with the status quo, and then it becomes primarily a question of entrenched power holders unobtrusively reproducing the prevailing construction of the power structure. But if we include the critical theorists within an interpretivist perspective (and I think that we should), then power becomes a more contested issue, because a problematic question then becomes explicit: "Whose interests are served in the current construction of the power structure?" Usually, the interests of those in managerial positions are best served; that raises the larger issue of whether lower-level employees within the power structure are aware of the reality being created for them, and how much they accept the power structure, and how much it defines their sense of organizational identity. That, in turn, raises the specter of false consciousness and its role in identity construction, which shades toward a postmodernist perspective. Yet there is a long history within critical theory perspective about people being trapped in psychic prisons that are partially of their own construction because they accept the power structure as given by the powers that be.

Mary Jo: One aspect of the way in which critical postmodernists often think of power is in terms of absence or silence, which means, to give a simplified example, if you have a bunch of powerful, white, male managers defining identity, then the voices of females, blacks, and others will tend to go unnoticed. Postmodernists always look for those who are not present, not given a voice, because critical postmodernists would very likely expect that talk about organizational identity expresses somebody's will to dominate others.

Majken: The postmodernists are saying we want to give voice to those who are absent in a de facto sense.

Hamid: I think that this is where this group is making an interesting contribution to the discussion of identity, because in the literature about organizational identity, this power and politics aspect is hardly noticed. I think the framing of identity should account for or integrate them.

Majken: But it is much more than just a power struggle over whose identity perceptions prevail, because that takes for granted that we all have conscious awareness of it. It is also the much more subtle struggle for power. And that's a much more fundamental way of thinking of power than the way postmodernists normally think about it.

Karen: Somewhere in here we ought to acknowledge the issues of plurality and multiplicity. The other thing that is running through my mind is the conversation that we had just a minute ago—the idea of taking issue with the normally accepted political structure. It is not just top management that has the power; for example, if the union wants the power that top management has, that sets off an identity contest. One implication of the interpretivist and postmodern views is that it is not a matter of replacing one person in power, or one group with another, it's a matter of taking issue with the whole structure of power.

Denny: We seem to have reached a point where we are beginning to explore the wider ramifications of different approaches to studying and understanding identity. Let's see if we can make a segue for the benefit of people (our other colleagues in this conference, as well as future readers) who are not directly involved in this conversation. Perhaps this is a good time to introduce our discussion of various models of identity and its nomological net?

[NOTE: The dimensions and major points of the foregoing discussion are summarized in Table 3.1]

ORGANIZATIONAL IDENTITY
AND ITS NOMOLOGICAL NET

Identity, like most other concepts in organizational study, is a relational notion. It is difficult to discern or decide identity without being able to consider it in relation to a network of other concepts. For that reason, we as a group found ourselves talking in terms of using a "nomological net" as a way of exploring aspects of organizational identity and its ramifications. Not surprisingly, a number of our group members (in collaborative efforts with close colleagues whom we have labeled as our "shadow partners" in this conversation) have been working on models involving organizational

TABLE 3.1 Three Perspectives on Organizational Identity (OI)

	Functionalist	*Interpretive*	*Postmodern*
Central problem	How OI shapes actions and cognitions	How do we collectively construct who we are?	To problematize identity, often with an eye toward disclosing and disrupting existing power relations
Definition	1. Institutionalized beliefs about who we are 2. Objective dimensions (people, core business, operating principles, organizational purpose)	Continuously renegotiated set of meanings about who we are	Momentary and fragmented reflections about who we take ourselves to be
Key assumptions	OI is a social fact OI is observable and manipulable	1. Human beings have a need for some stability of meaning 2. Identity is a socially constructed phenomenon 3. Social groups strive toward some level of convergence around meanings of identity	1. Indeterminacy of meaning 2. Identity is an accidental collection of forms clustering in moments of time 3. Identity takes on paradoxical forms 4. Plurality, multiplicity
Purpose of the inquiry	Uncover Describe Measure Put to use (manage)	Discover/disclose the meanings and the meaning structures that are negotiated among organizational members	Provocation Reflexivity Give voice to silences Point to absences
Data	Observe actions to infer OI Study statements Study demography Psychometric instruments	1. Data important to members: Variety of symbols 2. Data important to researchers: a. symbols b. member interpretive schemes c. researcher interpretive schemes	Language and discourse Ruptures Absence

identity and its relationship to other notions. These models all provide specific insights into the character of organizations in general, and organizational identity in particular. Therefore, we decided that framing a major part of our conversation

TABLE 3.1 *Continued*

	Functionalist	*Interpretive*	*Postmodern*
Implications	1. Centrality: Core values and beliefs are touted	1. Centrality: Identity is meanings that members agree are central	1. Central identity is constantly shifting (it revolves around decentering the subject)
	2. Enduring: Hard to change (but not immutable)	2. Enduring: Only to the extent that social context affirms the projected identity	2. Enduring: Identity is impermanent, a subject to be deconstructed and reconstructed
	3. Distinctiveness: Distinctiveness is assumed and managed	3. Distinctiveness: Identity derives both from similarity with and difference from	3. Distinctive identity is defined with respect to so many "others" that fragmentation is a condition; distinctiveness is the defining moment
Metaphor	Object	Brain: holographic property (identity is distributed)	Collage: juxtaposition of unexpected elements
	Asset		
		Improvisational theatre	

around a discussion of these models would provide a good basis for a discursive exploration of identity. They range from grounded theory investigations to deductive theoretical models to analogical derivations from practice to postmodern perspectives. We had some good intellectual fun distilling our own models down to less than 10 minutes of (we hope) coherent description for the benefit of the tape recorder—and, by extension, you, the reader. We then edited the transcriptions for the sake of clarity. We have elected to present these descriptions to include the voices of our shadow partners, where appropriate.

Denny Gioia with Jim Thomas as Shadow Partner: It seems to us that this notion of a nomological net primarily covers relationships among identity, image, reputation, culture, and similar ideas that spin off from those. We thought we might go first simply because we have developed ("discovered," in the Glaser and Strauss sense, is probably a better term) a bona fide grounded model. Ours is somewhat of a serendipitous model, in that we actually did not start with the intent of studying image and identity. We began our research project with the simple intent of trying to understand how the members of a top management team in a university inter-

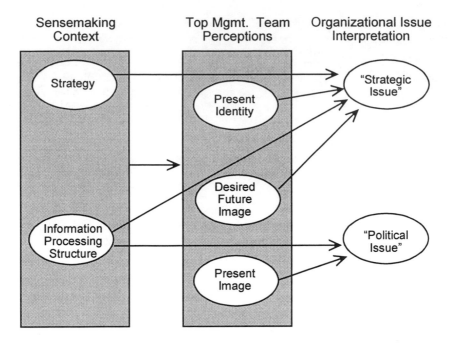

Figure 3.1. Emergent Model of Sensemaking in Academic Administration

preted issues of importance to them in the face of a dramatically changing academic environment. This team had implemented a strategic change effort a few years earlier (common enough practice in business, but relatively unfamiliar territory for universities at the time), and they were actively trying to sustain the momentum of that change effort. Perhaps our most important finding was that identity and image constituted the "interpretive screens" that these team members used to understand the issues they were confronting.

We have depicted the boxes-and-arrows version of this grounded model in Figure 3.1. To summarize it, we found that (a) the strategy the top management team was currently pursuing and the information processing structure they were using most influenced their sensemaking activities; (b) their perceptions of organizational identity and image (both current image and hoped-for image) constituted the major "lenses" through which the team members interpreted issues; and (c) these issues were not conceived in the usual "threat/opportunity" categories seen in business organizations, but in terms of more general categories of "strategic" and "political" issues (see Gioia & Thomas, 1996, for the complete story). Of these findings, those concerning organizational identity and image are most interesting and relevant to us and this conversation.

The thing we most want to emphasize here is the importance of the change context, for two reasons: first, because change is virtually a given in the environments of organizations these days (even, heaven forbid, in academic organizations); and second, for organizations to change substantively implies that something pretty basic has to change. Does that include something as fundamental as identity? You can see the main conceptual issue: Taking organizational change seriously might have some serious implications for the way we conceptualize identity.

Through repeated interviews with the managers in our study, we discovered an unequivocal presumption that identity was changeable. ("It *must* change; otherwise, how are we ever going to change this place?" as the president put it.) We also discovered, somewhat to our surprise, that the presumed path to changing identity was not via focusing directly on altering the existing identity (an approach that was assumed by the top management team members to be doomed to failure because of members' perceived resistance to change), but rather via focusing on trying to change organizational image. Furthermore, this process focused not on current conceptions of image, but rather on desired *future* image. Because of the close relationship between image and identity, identity was then assumed to be malleable. As another of the informants put it: "If we try to change identity, we probably won't get anywhere, but if we start by laying out an image that people want to achieve, that'll make it easier to move them off the current way of seeing themselves." Instead of the usual expressions of identity and image in terms of "this is who we are and how we are seen," these managers usually couched their identity in terms of "this is who we want to be and how we want to be seen *after* the change is accomplished." [A quick aside: These managers did indeed initially define identity as "who we are" and "how we think of ourselves" ("This is a stodgy institution"; "This institution has some hardening of the arteries"), but they did not stay on that definition very long; they talked consistently in terms of the future, and overwhelmingly in terms of future *image.*]

There are some fairly weighty managerial implications in these grounded findings. They suggest that a way for top managers to push the process of changing organizational identity along is to project an attractive future image that acts like a bandwagon for members to jump on. Once people are on board and have bought into the new image, that revised image serves as a catalyst for changing their identity. So image becomes the shaper of identity. The projection of a desired future image destabilizes existing identity and "pulls" it into alignment with the future image. The working logic here was that the desired image would motivate a change in identity that would produce a desire for quality improvements, thus facilitating changes and strategic adaptation to the changing environment. (Of course, there are also some obvious Orwellian possibilities in this sort of Madison Avenue approach to identity change, but those were understandably downplayed by our informants.)

There are also some intriguing theoretical implications for the study of organizational identity. For one thing, we cannot construe identity merely (or even mainly) as just an internal concept deriving from the founder's values and some insulated notion about preserving an organization's culture. Identity is an evolving, changing notion, developing over time in interaction with internal and external parties. This realization has some bearing on our basic conception of organizational identity. First, as noted, identity is typically taken as that which members consider to be central, enduring, and distinctive about their organization (Albert & Whetten, 1985; Dutton & Dukerich, 1991), but this study suggests that the notion of "enduring" at least needs to be tempered when change is at issue. The modern environment subjects organizations to forces that demand a shortening of time horizons for executing change, and such changes imply that identity probably is changing more dramatically than previous depictions suggest. Second, the findings also suggest that the bases for identity changes are often traceable to changes in image. For purposes of identity change, then, it would seem to be image that matters. And where do those images come from? Where else but from other successful organizations that you would hope to look like. Organizations try to emulate features of competing organizations (a process that seems to be increasingly prevalent in the academic industry). If that is really the case, and recent research suggests that it is (see LaBianca, Fairbank, Thomas, & Gioia, 1997; Porac, Thomas, & Baden-Fuller, 1989; Porac, Thomas, Wilson, Paton, & Kanfer, 1995), the implication is that organizations that are happily engaged in trying to copy each other will be become *less* distinctive from each other. To us, that is an interesting twist.

What does "enduring" mean when changing environments demand that even not-for-profit institutions engage in strategic change, thus encouraging the malleability of identity and image? What does "distinctive" mean when common practices augur for a loss of distinctiveness? These kinds of provocative little questions suggest that we do not yet have a firm handle on understanding organizational identity. That is probably a good thing. It implies that theorizing in this domain remains an intellectually exciting activity—one that could stand more voices contributing to the conversation.

Marlene: Well, pretty good. A mouthful in seven-and-a-half minutes! We'll hear next from Mary Jo and Majken. [The conversation continues on p. 52]

Sidebar Commentary #1

IDENTITY WITHIN AND IDENTITY WITHOUT: LESSONS FROM CORPORATE AND ORGANIZATIONAL IDENTITY

VIOLINA P. RINDOVA

MAJKEN SCHULTZ

With deregulation in the 1980s, the commercial bank J.P. Morgan reentered the investment banking industry, which the bank, or rather, its forerunner—The House of Morgan—had left involuntarily in the 1930s when the Glass-Steagall Act separated commercial and investment banking in the U.S. financial services industry. It divided The House of Morgan into J.P. Morgan—a commercial bank—and Morgan-Stanley—an investment bank. The return to investment banking was a big strategic challenge for J.P. Morgan; not only did the company need to find its position in a fiercely competitive industry, but it had to manage the tensions between it and its "tradition-bound lending side, oriented to relationship banking" (Fombrun, 1996, p. 345). One of the responses of the bank was to run a series of ads centered around symbols of tradition, such as bowler hats from the 1920s and steam trains. With these ads, the bank communicated about tradition, lasting relationships, trust, and long-standing expertise. It communicated about its core values that were to span both its investment and commercial businesses and to position it effectively within an industry where premier reputation is a key asset.

J. P. Morgan capitalized on its internally held beliefs about "who we are as an organization" by stating them in strong visual terms for the consumption of the marketplace. To put it in identity theory terms, it capitalized on its organizational identity through corporate identity. To the novice in the field, this can sound tautological: Why and how do organizational and corporate identity denote different things? Both concepts describe an organization's identity, yet they ask different questions and provide different answers. Some of the differences result from the origin of the two constructs in two different communities of practice and their key concerns. The construct of organizational identity has been developed by social scientists and management scholars to address belief systems and value orientations underlying organizational behaviors (Dutton et al., 1994). The construct of corporate identity was developed by practitioners in the area of graphics design, who sought to promote the idea of consistent and targeted visual presentation of an organization to observers (Olins, 1989).

Compared to the three theoretical perspectives on identity discussed in the dialogue, most of the literature within both fields belongs to a functionalist perspective (Martin, 1992; Schultz & Hatch, 1996). It posits the existence of core, defining characteristics of an organization and studies the consistent, shared perceptions of them by organizational members and observers.

The purpose of our comments is to highlight some of the differences between the two concepts, and to suggest a broader conceptualization of an organization's identity that incorporates both internally held beliefs and external expressions of these beliefs. We argue that the integration of the two concepts provides an understanding of the tensions between the internal and external aspects of identity, between substantive reflections and symbolic expressions. We claim that identity at the organizational level is constituted by these tensions because it is concerned with the boundary between an organization and its environment. The overarching construct of identity is distinguished by its focus simultaneously on issues of internal identification and external differentiation.

The introductory chapters of this book remind us that organizational identity has been defined as collective, shared understandings of the organization's distinctive, central, and enduring characteristics

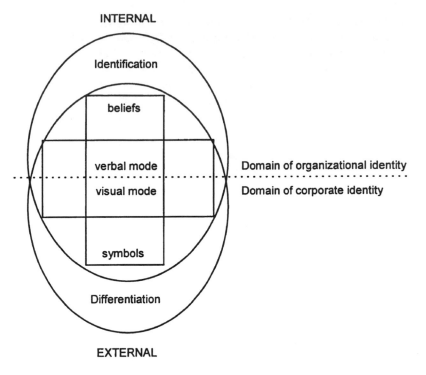

Figure 3.2. Levels of Identity

(Albert & Whetten, 1985). Thus, organizational identity defines the relationship between employees and their organization (Ashforth & Mael, 1989) and is embedded in organizational culture. Corporate identity refers to an organization's "central idea" (Olins, 1989) and the perceptions of it by various constituencies. It has also been defined as "strategically planned and operationally applied internal and external self-representation" (Birkigt & Stadler, 1986, as cited in van Riel, 1995, p. 32). The organization's self-representation is expressed through behavior, communication, and symbolism (van Riel, 1995, p. 32). Olins argues that a firm expresses its central idea through products, communications, behavior, and physical environment. Thus, the concept of corporate identity specifies the ways in which management expresses this key idea to external audiences and the interrelations between identity and the images held by various external audiences. Both approaches share a concern with the notions of centrality and distinctiveness in organizations. They also share an assumption about the existence of a consistent and somewhat harmonious notion of organizational "self" that has pervasive influence on all aspects of an organization's behavior and outcomes. At the same time, they express the inherent tension between internal and external and between self-reflection and self-representation. These oppositions are summarized in Figure 3.2. (Levels of Identity).

The figure shows that organizational and corporate identity are, in fact, an interrelated system of beliefs and symbols expressed both verbally and visually that trigger processes of identification and differentiation inside and outside an organization. We examine each of these elements in turn.

LEVELS OF MANIFESTATION:
BELIEFS VERSUS SYMBOLS

A firm's identity exists and manifests itself on several levels similar to the levels identified by research on organizational culture (Hatch, 1993; Schein, 1985). At its deepest, taken-for-granted level, an organization's identity is a set of beliefs. At the next level, an organization's identity is a set of symbols through which these beliefs are expressed and shaped. In addition, physical artifacts and overt behaviors are also related to identity; they are the most visible, but they are not directly interpretable as identity-defining or identity-expressing elements (Schein, 1985). Based on this framework, we can see that the divergent definitions of organizational and corporate identity in fact capture the different levels of an organization's identity. Organizational theorists have focused on the level of beliefs, whereas practitioners from marketing and design emphasize symbols and artifacts.

Like culture, however, identity encompasses all levels, and the simultaneous application of the two approaches is necessary to understand the construct. Without the understanding of the visual identity, organizational theorists miss some of the critical mechanisms through which identity is created, managed, interpreted, and changed. Without the understanding of the deeply seated beliefs and values of organizational members about "who we are as an organization," identity design practitioners miss the foundation that motivates firms' behaviors and that seeks expression through symbols and artifacts. Also, the interrelations between organizational and corporate identity raise the issue of representation: Do corporate symbols express deeply held beliefs of the organization, or are they accidental imitations that create a glittering organizational facade?

MODES OF EXPRESSION:
WORDS VERSUS VISUALS

Corporate identity is often called visual identity because of its use of visual forms. Organizational identity, on the other hand, is formulated and expressed through words. These different expression styles profoundly affect how the two identities are managed and experienced. Organizational identity (or an idealized version of it) often exists in official company documents, such as mission statements, codes of ethics, and newsletters. These statements surround organizational members and interact with their experiences in determining their beliefs about what the organization stands for (Kunda, 1992).

Corporate identity relies on visual means. The visual schools of corporate identity emphasize graphic design and management through official corporate symbols that focus attention on the strategic positioning aspects of identity (Balmer, 1995). Olins (1989) provides examples of the strategic use of symbols in companies like Shell Oil and Yves Saint-Laurent that make strong and consistent use of their corporate name, logo, and colors to create a monolithic image for their organizations. Yet "visual identity is a part of the deeper identity of the group, the outward sign of the inward commitment, serving to remind it of its real purpose" (Abratt, 1989, p. 68).

Visual cues, however, are a less direct mode of expression than are words and often operate at the unconscious level. As such, they are more likely to be perceived by members as a part of their immediate experience rather than as a part of the managerial perspective in an organization. Verbal statements often sound like slogans and acquire context from the organizational reality. To relate to verbal statements, organizational members may need to draw on their experience and may evoke images that contradict the idealized statement of the slogan. If such contradictions exist, members may discard identity-related statements. The visual cues by definition evoke an atmosphere and a context, which is implied rather than explicitly formulated. Thus, visual communication might reduce the potential for direct contradictions between members' experience and a managerial perspective on identity. At the same time, they might leave too much to the subconscious.

Thus, managers and design practitioners who combine the expression modes of both organizational identity and corporate identity may be more effective in achieving their communication objectives. However, the differences in expression modes might arise from the different ways of thinking of these two groups of practitioners. As a result, they might not be able to communicate with audiences who operate predominantly in one of the two modes. For example, CEOs think in terms of words and plans, and the media think in terms of pictures (O'Rourke, 1997). Graphic design experts think visually, but some of their audiences, such as financial analysts, may think in words. Sometimes, the very effectiveness of an organizational action may depend on the expression mode the organization uses to communicate about it. For example, Exxon spent billions of dollars cleaning up the *Valdez* spill but failed to secure visibility; the event carried no visual identification of Exxon, and its workers remained anonymous in the photographs taken by the media. The ability to shift between expression modes will help an organization to better communicate with various audiences.

RELATION TO ORGANIZATION:
IDENTIFICATION VERSUS DIFFERENTIATION

These two approaches to identity not only focus on different levels of manifestation of identity, but they also differ in their functional applications. Organizational identity has an internal focus on the beliefs of organizational members; corporate identity focuses externally—on the perceptions in the marketplace. From these different foci of attention, different forms of expression, emphases on action, and tools for management result.

Organizational identity creates a sense of identification among organizational members. The degree to which members identify with their organizations (Dutton et al., 1994) depends on the attractiveness of the perceived organizational identity, the consistency between individual self-concepts and organizational identity, and the distinctiveness of organizational identity. Members' identification with an organization enhances commitment and consistency of actions. Corporate identity creates emotional involvement with an organization in the marketplace that exceeds the functional relationships of buying or investing. Elements of corporate identity are often an integral part of a firm's positioning in the marketplace. They constitute the augmented product; they stimulate brand associations and help firms create strong brands. Thus, corporate identity enhances the process of differentiating a firm and its offerings, and it stimulates customer loyalty.

Differentiation in turn feeds into organizational distinctiveness, which might positively affect members' identification, because it has been argued that external images influence internal self-perceptions (Dutton & Dukerich, 1991; Fombrun, 1996). For example, the images and symbols that differentiate an organization in the marketplace often depend on its history and its organizational identity. Thus, each aspect of identity—the corporate and the organizational—is mutually dependent. Despite the differences in expression and platform, the two identities have a similar purpose—engagement of the self with an organization, except that this engagement is motivated differently for internal members and external observers. Managers and practitioners alike need to be aware of the interplay between identification and differentiation, between belonging and seduction directed both inwardly and outwardly.

In this brief comparison between organizational and corporate identity, we suggested that combining the two into one broader definition of identity enables us to understand better the underlying tensions in organizations between the internal and the external, between identification and differentiation, between the deeply seated and the expressed, between the desired and the actual. The differences between the two approaches to identity are, in fact, sources of mutual learning that can broaden the spectrum of managerial practices related to identity management. In combining the two approaches to identity into an integrated body of knowledge, thinking and practice can improve in both.

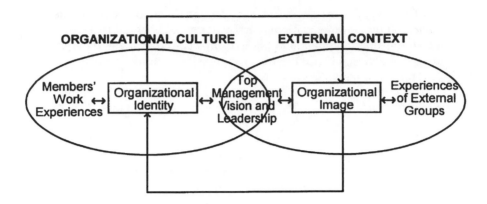

Figure 3.3. A Model of the Relationships Between Organizational Culture, Identity, and Image
SOURCE: Hatch and Schultz (1997). Reprinted by permission of MCB University Press, Ltd.

Mary Jo Hatch and Majken Schultz: The thing we immediately noticed in Denny and Jim's talk is that they elaborate the role of top management in a dynamic context. Denny and Jim focus on the right side of our model (Figure 3.3), which in our terms describes how visionary leadership acts as a communicative mediator between identity and image.

Our conceptualization of identity is influenced by conversations and collaborations with designers and consultants who are trying to affect and influence the identities and the images their clients project to various internal and external constituencies. Most recently, we have been conducting a case study of one of the world's leading companies in corporate identity consultancy. This company has defined organizational identity to include culture, vision, and image as interrelated aspects of identity (the present slogan says, "Culture and Image are One"). We have followed how they have struggled with the conceptual underpinnings of their work and with the organizational and managerial implications for their client companies. As such, it has been interesting for us to see how academics and practitioners alike are involved in similar constructions of new, cross-disciplinary, conceptual frameworks concerning organizational identity.

Compared to the other models of identity presented in this section of the book, we make three specific claims. First, we explicitly focus on the implications of boundary breakdowns between internal and external aspects of the organization. We argue that one of the primary challenges facing postindustrial organizations is a need to integrate values which were formerly considered either internal or external to the organization. Previously, organizations were able to disconnect their internal functioning from their external relations because contacts between insiders and outsiders were few. Top executives, marketing, purchasing, PR, and strategic planning departments handled external relations; mid- and lower-level managers, HRM, engineering, production, and accounting departments attended to internal issues. Now, however, the increasing levels of interaction between "insiders" and "outsiders" because of networking, alliances, and new service-driven organizational forms make it harder to maintain the difference between internal and external orientations. Simultaneously, the media-driven transparency of company behavior puts pressure on companies to articulate and express what they stand for. Where organizations were formerly able to conceal internal values from external constituencies, and even differentiate internal values from those presented to outsiders, the breakdown of internal-external boundaries creates a need for higher-level integration between organizational culture, identity, and image. Attempts to develop such integrated frameworks have been found in the communication of organizational values under labels like integrated communications, corporate communications, vision management, culture and image management, and corporate identity management.

Second, we point to the importance of organizational culture as a contextual framework for the managerial conceptualization and expression of organizational identity (Hatch & Schultz, 1997). Thus, we include the tacit patterns of meaning and behavior among organizational members in our model, emphasizing that organizational culture involves all organizational members and originates and develops at all hierarchical levels. This implies that the interdependencies between culture, identity, and image are defined as mutually circular processes that occur at all levels of the organization and are enacted among organizational members and customers as well as among top management and key stakeholders.

Finally, we put special emphasis on top management vision and values. The breakdown between internal and external boundaries poses new challenges to top managers because they must manage across boundaries that have been institutionalized in most organizations. For example, the core values inherent in the organizational culture must be reflected in the values guiding the attempts to influence external images. Here, the notion of vision is important as it serves as an evocative long-term guide, both internally and externally. Furthermore, managers themselves must cross the internal boundaries between divisions and departments, dealing with internal and external issues, respectively.

Our model illustrates both the internal and the external influences on organizational identity. The internal influences on identity are illustrated by the left side of the model, which depicts organizational identity as the nexus of influences from top management vision and leadership efforts, and from opinions and beliefs formed about the organization by its internal constituencies as they go about their daily work activities. Both sets of influence are interpreted within, and contextualized by, the organizational culture. We argue that when members of organizations express organizational identity, they use cultural artifacts symbolically to present an image that will be interpreted by others.

Thus, culturally aware organizational members can pick up the symbolic material from rich stories, everyday metaphors, and orchestrated rituals that already thrive within the symbolic world of the organizational culture(s) and use them in the reflection and communication of a much more focused organizational identity. Hence, culturally embedded organizational identity provides the symbolic material from which organizational images are constructed and with which they can be communicated internally and externally by top management and their representatives. Organizational identity is communicated to the various constituencies who form organizational images, at least partly in response to identity-based communication. Communicated identity, however, also can influence the interpretive processes of the organizational culture. The forms and means of communication might differ, ranging from unplanned appearances by top management in public media to a conscious strategy for corporate communication involving, for example, corporate identity programs, corporate advertising, and public relations. However, direct experience and interaction between internal and external constituencies are also strong forces in the image-formation processes. Direct contacts between insiders and outsiders are contextualized by the organizational culture, as everyday organizational behavior is assumed to be influenced by local sensemaking and interpretation. Thus, insofar as organizational members interact with "outsiders," there will be mutual influence of both organizational culture and identity on image beyond that carried by top management and other corporate spokespersons. Organizational images are then projected outward and absorbed back into the cultural system of meaning by being taken as cultural artifacts and used symbolically to infer identity: Who we are is reflected in what we are doing and how others interpret who we are and what we are doing. For example, a negative reading of organizational image by the press can affect organizational identity when news reports are perceived as genuine reflections of organizational activity or intent. The news message becomes a symbol to be interpreted and accepted or rejected; if accepted, it can affect the organization's definition(s) of itself. In this way, organizational identity is opened to the influence of opinions and reputations forged beyond the organization's direct sphere of influence, as happened, for instance, when Body Shop's image as a green retailer was attacked by allegations made in the business press. Anita Roddick's defense of Body Shop, we argue, was as much an attempt to protect organizational identity internally as it was an effort to avoid negative external images. Organizational image involves externally produced meaning-making about the organization, but, as noted above, this has an influence on internal processes of identity formation and maintenance. In our model, the arrows from organizational image to organizational identity and from organizational image through top management vision and leadership to organizational identity indicate these sources of external influence on organizational identity. Insofar as organizational members are also members of external groups, such as customers, environmentalists, and media watchers, image and identity will likely be compared; these comparisons will then be communicated within the internal symbolic context of the organization, leading to possibilities for synergy but also for cynicism. Also, the way in which organizational members are perceived by customers, competitors, and the like can influence organizational identity as members mirror themselves in the comments and complaints about the organization made to them by their external contacts. Thus, insofar as organizational members encounter organizational images as part of their lives, both inside and outside the organization, there is likely to be feedback from image to identity.

Finally, top management vision and leadership is opened to external influence via its concern for managing organizational image. Whenever this influence occurs, the statements, decisions, and actions top management directs to its internal audiences are influenced by these external concerns, with subsequent effects on organizational identity.

Thus, we argue that the relationships between culture, image, and identity form circular processes involving mutual interdependence. Organizational identity is a self-reflexive product of intertwined, dynamic processes, which includes both organizational culture and image. However, we stress that these circular processes are rarely processes of harmonious consistency. On the contrary, the understanding of these intertwined relations makes it possible to locate gaps that companies are facing, for example, between culture and image. As a recent example, we can point to the Danish audiovisual company, Bang & Olufsen, where a number of top and middle managers have recently emphasized the wide gap between a highly sophisticated, design-based international image and a very Calvinistic engineering culture with strong roots in Danish rural life. In their strategic process of building up their own distribution system with more direct links to the customer, this gap has emerged as a key issue in the ongoing reflections on what the company stands for to insiders as well as outsiders.

Hamid: May I venture a very quick comment on the first two models? My sense of both is that they probably give too much importance to top management in the identity process. In my view, and from what I can see elsewhere, identity is everyone's problem. Members at any level of the organization are receivers of the organizational image.

Denny: Guilty as charged. Yet I still think management exercises more influence over identity when you are trying to change identity.

Mary Jo: This is one of the questions that we are confronting as we move from our original model to one that more completely loses this boundary around the organization. In the past, this boundary between internal and external has afforded top management the ability to filter some information going across here. What happens when we collapse this distinction is that stakeholders in the organization (both the internal members and the external constituents of the organization) have much closer relationships with one another and begin to exchange information like crazy. So top management loses a lot of its authority to influence identity.

Denny: Nonetheless, I believe top management retains a privileged position. Let's hear Violina's and Charles's take on these issues. [The conversation continues on p. 59]

Sidebar Commentary #2

ORGANIZATIONAL CULTURE AND IDENTITY: WHAT'S THE DIFFERENCE ANYWAY?

C. MARLENE FIOL
MARY JO HATCH
KAREN GOLDEN-BIDDLE

We so often hear questions like, "What is the difference between identity and culture?" and "What does identity as a construct add to our understanding of organizations that culture studies have not provided?" The purpose of this essay is to comment briefly on the value-added of the identity construct in organizational research.

We first provide definitions of "culture" and "identity," highlighting the distinctions and overlaps between the two constructs. We then discuss differences in accessing the two phenomena as researchers. We end with a few comments about identity and culture as they relate to managing change in organizations.

CULTURE AND IDENTITY DEFINED

Organizational Culture

Organizational culture has been defined as a general system of rules that governs meanings in organizations (Fiol, 1991; Smircich, 1983). As such, an organization's or a subgroup's culture serves as an interpretive scheme that is historically developed and socially maintained (Geertz, 1973), although not necessarily shared, that individuals use both to make sense of and to structure their own and others' actions (Golden, 1992).

An organization's culture is defined by people's understanding of the social system to which they belong. It includes aspects and practices of everyday life (e.g., storytelling, joking, symbolizing of all sorts) of a group of people that define and help sustain what they consider normal and that support those things (e.g., production of objects, knowledge, activities) that they believe are necessary or valuable (Hatch, 1993). It is a symbolic field constituted by interpretation processes providing a context for meaning and sensemaking both about the organization and the "reality" it occupies.

Organizational Identity

An organization's identity is the aspect of culturally embedded sensemaking that is self-focused. It defines who we are in relation to the larger social system to which we belong. Identity is affected by organizational culture and also by other meaning-making systems with which the self interacts. For example, the identity of our business school is defined by the cultural values that it holds (e.g., research is

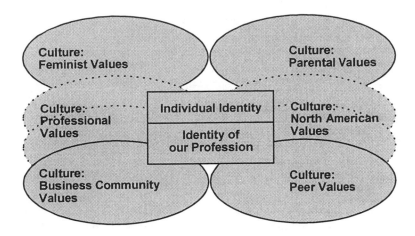

Figure 3.4. Identity and Cultures: Individual and Professional

valued above all else) and also by its place in the community, its size, its reputation, and so on. Each of these forces in and around the school forms impressions that are communicated back to the identity holder.

Although culture provides the system of rules that defines a social system, identity provides the contextual understanding of those rules that govern people's understanding of themselves in relation to the larger social system.

WHAT'S THE DIFFERENCE?

The difference between identity and culture, then, is one of perspective, not level of analysis. Identity exists at numerous levels, and at each level, it is defined in relation to existing cultures or to social systems of meaning around it. For example, as shown in Figure 3.4, (Identity and Cultures) we may define our identity as "professional women" in relation to (among other social systems) the professional culture in which we participate. Our profession defines its identity as "management" in relation to (among other social systems) the business community of which it is a part. Identity at these different levels of analysis may draw on similar cultural systems to define itself, as is shown in the overlapping circles in the figure. In all cases, identity answers the question "Who are we?" in relation to larger contexts of meaning.

HOW CAN RESEARCHERS ACCESS
IDENTITY AND CULTURE?

There has been much debate about what measures appropriately reflect an organization's culture. Do tangible measures such as myths, norms, and behaviors really capture the meaning system of an organization? If not, how does one access the values and normative beliefs that are often largely unconscious?

The subjective is very strong in culture work. Tangible measures are artifactual. Deeper levels of meaning (e.g., symbols, assumptions, values, beliefs) are known interpretively. That is, they must be inferred indirectly from the interpretations people make of their organizational experiences.

The identity construct might provide a way out of the dilemma. Because identity reflects how a social entity makes sense of itself in relation to the cultures it is a part of, it represents the essential linkage between observable manifestations of culture and the underlying meanings. By focusing on the language and behaviors that indicate how people define themselves in relation to larger systems of meaning or cultures, researchers may also gain better access to the systems of meaning themselves.

MANAGING CHANGE

It is here that the value-added of the identity construct is most apparent. Much has been written about the difficulty of changing organizational cultures. In fact, some would argue that it is impossible to "manage" a change in culture. This is because cultural values are deeply ingrained and often unconscious and are thus impervious to conscious manipulation (Krefting & Frost, 1985).

Identity is cultural meaning or sensemaking focused on itself. Self-conscious or self-reflexive processes tempered by feedback from related others constitutes the identity of an organization or any other social entity. Involvement of related others leaves identity more open than culture to "outside" influence. However, culture is also affected by the identity that contributes to it, so through identity change, culture may be altered as well.

Cultural change occurs relatively slowly, or at least at its own pace, and, according to Gagliardi (1986), it is only radical in content when a large number of organizational members change then it becomes questionable whether the same organization is even being considered. Otherwise, cultural change is either superficial (artifacts change, but not deeper meanings associated with them) or incremental (values and beliefs are added in such a way as to complement rather than alter existing patterns of values and belief).

In contrast, identity—how people understand themselves in relation to those values—is more conscious and more reflexive, and thus more amenable to change. Through self-reflection, organizations or organizational members are offered an organization-level, subjective experience capable of inspiring organizational transformations. Rather than changing organizations from the outside, a focus on organizational identity offers the opportunity to transform experience of the organizational self. The struggle with recognizing and acknowledging who we are permits and encourages self-criticism and self-knowledge, which can act as a fulcrum around which new patterns of communication can occur. Through these new patterns, altered structures and processes of organizing will emerge; that is, organizational change will occur.

Violina Rindova with Charles Fombrun as Shadow Partner: A very interesting question has been raised: What happens with organizational identity when stakeholders "exchange information like crazy"? We have been working on answering a similar question. Charles has been doing research on corporate reputations for several years, and I was interested in sociocognitive dynamics of market exchanges. Corporate reputations have a very intriguing duality: On the one hand, they are considered assets that are owned and managed by firms; on the other hand, they are perceptions of observers—perceptions over which firms have relatively limited control. Furthermore, observers develop these perceptions and evaluations in information-rich environments. In such environments, multiple voices express diverse opinions driven by diverse objectives. Can firms manage their reputations as assets in such environments? To answer this question, we engaged in an ongoing dialogue with managers in industries, as well as public relations and corporate identity practitioners, and supplemented this dialogue with insights from research and theory in economics, sociology, strategic management, and mass communications.

Obviously, there are two types of actors involved in reputation formation: firms and observers (see Figure 3.5). Observers also fall into two categories: those who control and exchange resources with firms and those who provide information and evaluations of firms to other interested observers. We call the first category "constituents," and the second, "institutional intermediaries." Firms attempt to influence both intermediaries and constituents by projecting certain images of themselves and developing relationships. Intermediaries refract the signals that firms send out: They transmit, distort, and add information about firms. Constituents observe, interpret, and select among these signals and form assessments of firms as exchange partners and as members of their organizational fields.

Identity and projected images. How firms interact with constituents depends on their strategic goals and on their identity beliefs (Barney, 1986; Eccles & Nohria, 1992). Identities shape business practices and relationships, which in turn shape images of firms. Because firms' actions often are not immediately observable, outsiders supplement their direct experiences with information provided by firms through advertising, press releases, and financial reports. This information supplies images that a firm's managers would like outsiders to hold (i.e., *projected* images). They constitute a corporate-level analog to self-presentations at the individual level. They call attention to certain attributes of firms and deemphasize others, providing

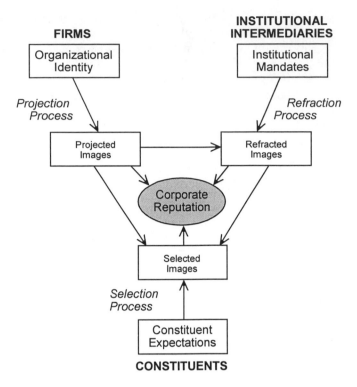

Figure 3.5. Mapping the Making of Corporate Reputations

frameworks that guide the perception and evaluation of outsiders (Tedeschi, 1981). Like self-presentations, projected images control information strategically and reveal only those aspects of a firm that are expected to trigger a positive response in a given situation.

Projected images reflect not only a firm's strategic objectives but also its underlying identity. Images that are consistent with organizational identity are supported by multiple cues that observers receive in interacting with firms. Images are not projected only through official, management-endorsed communications in glossy brochures because organizational members at all levels transmit images of the organization. Images projected to one constituent group often reach another because constituents frequently have overlapping roles (e.g., of customers and investors, of employees and investors) and vast access to information. Consistent images enhance each other, whereas contradictory images reduce the overall credibility of the communicator. Thus, the more closely a firm's projected images reflect its identity, the more credible and consistent across constituents and situations they will be.

Also, managers view projected images and identity as dynamically related. Like the informants of Denny Gioia and Jim Thomas, one manager told us: "The question of whether our image reflects our identity is inaccurate. They chase each other: Sometimes your image is ahead of your identity and sometimes your identity is ahead of your image." In fact, identity and projected images coevolve as organizations seek to ensure consistency between what they believe they are and what they communicate about themselves.

Institutional Intermediaries and Refracted Images. Regardless of how hard managers might try to impose a firm's attractive images on its constituents, constituents are subject to other social influences. Actors, such as the media, monitoring agencies, and constituents' organizations and associations, have institutional mandates to monitor and disseminate information about firms and act as institutional intermediaries of information. They not only transmit information, but they create new images of organizations. These are *refracted images:* They derive from the projected images, yet they acquire new content from the perspective of the institutional intermediaries who propel them. Refracted images often have higher credibility than projected images because they are created by third parties.

Nevertheless, institutional intermediaries process the projected images through the lenses of their own agendas, institutional mandates, or organizational identities. Organizations that attend to their relationships with intermediaries stand better chances of having refracted images similar to their projected images. For example, whether a press release will turn into a media story depends on the degree to which it satisfies the informational needs of the editor (Grunig & Hunt, 1984). Similarly, rating organizations give better ratings to organizations that cooperate and provide them with the information they need. A public relations practitioner told us a story of solving a client's problem with negative media coverage by organizing a meeting between the columnist and the firm's manager. Following the meeting, the newspaper made changes in the structure of its column and the firm made changes in its systems for providing information.

Selected Images and Corporate Reputation. Ultimately, reputations exist in the minds of constituents as cumulative perceptions and evaluations of firms acquired in repeated interactions. Interactions may include information from the projected and refracted images, as well as direct experiences from exchanges with firms. Interactions supply cues which constituents receive and retain selectively in the form of reputational schemas. Schemas originate from fragmented instances and become more abstract, complex, and organized with more experience (Fiske & Dyer, 1985).

As schemas, reputations make processing of new images dependent on retained past images; inconsistent information is discarded and schema change is deterred (Gioia, 1986a). Not only are reputations, as cognitive structures, resistant to change themselves, but they also create inertia in constituents' actions vis-à-vis an organization. This inertial property of corporate reputations provides firms that enjoy favorable reputations with a buffer in bad times. However, it also limits the manageability of reputations in the short run.

Identities and reputations are an outcome of a typification process through which social actors reduce complexity (first cognitively, and then behaviorally) and construct the reality they come to inhabit (Berger & Luckmann, 1966). In the case of identity, the typification process is internally directed, whereas in the case of reputation, it concerns others. Thus, identity and reputation increase the consistency and stability of interactions. At the same time, social actors seek to influence each other and to adapt to each others' changing demands through the various images they choose to project, refract, and select. Images reflect the inherent variation and experimentation in these interactions. Identities and reputations provide a frame of reference against which constituents evaluate and respond to social influence and change attempts. Overall, studying identity, image, and reputation together enables researchers to address the time dimension of these phenomena and, in particular, the problem of stability and change in interaction with constituents. [The conversation continues on p. 66]

Sidebar Commentary #3

THE EYE OF THE BEHOLDER:
THE ROLE OF CORPORATE REPUTATION
IN DEFINING ORGANIZATIONAL IDENTITY

VIOLINA P. RINDOVA
CHARLES J. FOMBRUN

I conclude, therefore, that the imaginations which people have of one another are the solid facts of society, and to observe and interpret these must be a chief aim of sociology.

—Cooley
(1902, p. 121)

Recently, management scholars seem to have taken Cooley's advice to heart; research on both organizational identity and reputation is growing rapidly. Research on organizational identity has focused on the "imaginations" that organizational members hold of their own organizations, and reputation research has focused on the "imaginations" of outside observers. Despite this similarity of interests, the two areas have developed in rather different directions. Rooted in the areas of strategy and economics, reputation research has been preoccupied with the performance effects of reputation; rooted in social psychology, identity research has focused on the development and maintenance of collective identities and their relationship to individual ones.

Identity and reputation, however, are inherently related. Reputations are interpretations and evaluations of identity, and identity incorporates reputational feedback. The purpose of this commentary is to explore the interrelatedness of identity and reputation. We draw on Cooley's (1902) "looking glass theory" of identity, according to which the self forms from an individual's understanding of how others perceive him or her, how others judge this perception, and how the individual feels about these imagined perceptions and judgments. Thus, the centerpiece of the theory is that social actors interact with each other based on perceptions—of themselves, of others, and of the perceptions of others of themselves. In the words of Cooley (1902):

> The man is one thing and the various ideas entertained about him are another; but the latter, the personal ideas, is the immediate social reality, the thing in which men exist for one another and work directly upon one another's lives. (p. 123)

Applied to organizations, this logic suggests that important strategic interactions between organizations and their various publics will depend on organizational identities and reputations, as well as the ongoing influence that they exert on each other. Because identity and reputation reciprocally affect each other, studies of one without the other may produce incomplete accounts.

FROM IDENTITY TO REPUTATION

At first glance, the relationship between identity and reputation is straightforward: Organizational identity affects the strategic choices an organization makes and the actions it takes. Constituents observe these actions and form impressions and evaluations of the organization. The aggregate assessments of constituents of an organization based on its past behaviors constitute its reputation. In reality, however, organizations take a variety of actions, some of which may not be immediately observable to outsiders. Different identities motivate organizations to take the same actions for different reasons. Organizations have different functional relationships with different observers and present "multiple selves"—just like individuals do. Finally, market interactions are characterized by information asymmetries; that is, organizations possess private information that they disclose selectively to outside observers. Given these complexities of the relationship between identity and reputation, how do outside observers come to know an organization's identity, and do they find some identities more attractive than others?

Organizations seek to reduce the complexity that faces their observers and supply them with descriptions and interpretations of their actions. In doing so, they also present themselves selectively and seek to predispose observers favorably toward the organization. In fact, in an organizational field, organization and constituents recognize each others' influences (DiMaggio & Powell, 1983). They participate in an interpretational web characterized by (a) a widespread exchange of information and interpretations among organizations and their constituents; (b) a multiplicity of interpretations, many of which are of a persuasive, self-serving nature; and (c) various levels of comprehensiveness and accuracy of the interpretations and evaluations of organizations. In this complex information environment, observers try to distill what defines organizations, what persists over time and across interactions, and what distinguishes them from other organizations in the field. Observers seek to grasp organizational identities as reflections of organizations' core, enduring, and distinctive characteristics. Because identity ensures consistency and continuity in organizational actions, identities are revealed in repeated interactions. Also, identity includes the various symbols and artifacts through which organizations express their beliefs (see Sidebar Commentary #1 in this chapter) and form direct perceptual input in the formation of reputations.

Reputations develop over time; they are the outcome of repeated interactions and cumulative experiences. In the minds of observers, reputations exist as schemas; observers organize and integrate discrete experiences into knowledge structures that become activated in all-or-none fashion (Fiske & Dyer, 1985). However, schemas not only store and organize experiences but also modify them. As Gioia (1986a, p. 346) summarizes, schemas maintain automatic information processing as opposed to active information search; they add schema-consistent information to what is actually observed and detract schema-inconsistent information; and they inhibit the use of inconsistent information. Thus, reputations become self-perpetuating, and reputation and identity can become decoupled.

The coupling of identity and reputation, however, is strategically important to constituents; they rely on corporate reputations to predict behaviors of others and to make decisions (Weigelt & Camerer, 1988). Therefore, they are likely to make efforts to maintain a close correspondence between an organization's reputation and its identity. Organizations that facilitate their efforts by making their identities clear are likely to be rewarded with more favorable reputations and to be treated with less backlash in times of crisis.

FROM REPUTATION TO IDENTITY

Unlike the connection between identity and reputation, the reciprocal relationship between the two is less evident. According to reputation theory, observers form reputations of exchange partners and other social actors to be able to better predict their future behaviors. Do those observed have similar incentives to respond to the reputations that observers ascribe to them? According to Cooley (1902), the answer to this question is a definitive "yes":

> The thing that moves us to shame or pride is not the more mechanical reflection of ourselves, but the imputed sentiment, the imagined effect of this reflection upon another's mind. This is evident from the fact that the character and the weight of the other, in whose mind we see ourselves, makes all the difference with our feeling. We are ashamed to be seen evasive in the presence of a straightforward man, cowardly in the presence of a brave one, gross in the eyes of a refined one, and so on. We always imagine, and in imagining share the judgments of the other one. (pp. 152-153)

Indeed, according to social identity theory, identity is a self-definition developed through the definitions of others (Schlenker, 1980). An individual's perceptions of the perceptions and judgments of others form the very core of his or her self-concept. At the individual level, the interrelatedness between outsiders' perceptions of an individual and the individual's own self-perceptions occurs through social learning and development of the self. According to Mead (1964), "The human self arises through its ability to take the attitude of the group to which it belongs" (p. 33). In doing so, the individual assumes the responsibilities that membership in the social group entails.

At the organizational level, identity derives from the strategic vision of founders and top managers (see the models presented by Gioia and Thomas, and Hatch and Schultz in the dialogue). However, for an organization to be successful, the vision of its top managers should encompass the expectations of constituents. Constituents judge an organization and its actions favorably or unfavorably to the degree to which the organization satisfies their expectations. The evaluative component of reputations distinguishes them from other cognitive structures of outsiders related to organizations. Corporate reputations are a mechanism through which outsiders externalize their expectations by signaling satisfaction or dissatisfaction with organizational actions and identity. Constituents have incentives to make these reputations explicit. Institutional intermediaries (for a discussion of their role, see our model in the dialogue) often undertake the task of making reputations explicit by presenting to the public various rankings and ratings. Although the production of rankings is itself a complex social process that creates distortions, rankings are manifest reputations and can be treated interchangeably.

Organizations also have incentives to monitor their reputations and align their identities. First, reputations signal to organizational members the attractiveness of their organization's identity to different publics. The attractiveness of organizational identity affects the degree to which members identify with their organizations and commit to organizational goals (Dutton et al., 1994). Individuals in organizations perceive personal implications of their organization's reputational standing and take actions to manage these impacts (Elsbach & Kramer, 1996). Second, reputations represent a form of performance feedback (Martins, 1997). As performance feedback, they summarize evaluations along multiple dimensions in a single indicator of the ability of an organization to meet (and exceed) the expectations of various constituents (Fombrun & Rindova, in press). By internalizing the expectations of various observers, organizations can better satisfy them. Third, reputational rankings make the status orderings in organizations' environments highly visible. Institutional intermediaries not only present them to multiple interested observers, but they do so in an authoritative manner. On one hand, they emphasize the research involved in producing rankings, thus giving them a veneer of objectivity. On the other hand, they make them public through social rituals laden with the imagery of winning. For example, awards ceremonies are, in fact, elaborately staged announcements of performance rankings. Organizations make these visible statements of reputational standing a part of their identity, thus increasing their attractiveness (and dependence on external validation).

In conclusion, identity and reputation depend on each other and feed off each other. Whether they are coupled in reality or not depends largely on the actions that different actors take to manage both their identities and their reputations (Rao, 1994). Understanding some of the connections we suggest prepares managers to interfere in the complex interpretational environment in which identities and reputations are defined and helps researchers study the invisible yet *solid facts* (Cooley, 1902, p. 121) of reputation and identity.

⁂

Denny: You covered a lot of ground in a short amount of time. How about you, Marlene? How do you see it?

Marlene: I am an acute care teaching hospital. My identity has long been rooted in the value of providing state-of-the-art health care, no matter what the cost. It has been easy for researchers to determine how I define myself, because any source they turned to provided similar information that was stable over time. Who I believed I was, how I wanted others to define me, and how others actually did define me were all congruent, grounded in a similar set of cultural and institutional norms. The theoretical model in Figure 3.6 describes the components that combine to shape and reshape organizational identities.

At the top of the figure are the cultural and institutional norms that have grounded my identity over a long period of time. They have, in fact, been so stable in my profession that we as insiders have simply taken who we are for granted, and outsiders have not challenged those assumptions. This led to minimal signaling between insiders and outsiders. The image projections and interpretations in the middle of the figure were not needed. Why would I spend my time signaling how I want outsiders to define me, when I am certain they define me as I define myself and nothing threatens that?

That was so, until old definitions of myself were challenged. When organizational definitions are challenged, internal and external actors begin to actively project images (which Violina and Charles have referred to as "projected images"), indicating how they want others to define the organization. Mediating agents, such as identity consultants (for insiders) and industry analysts (for outsiders), often get involved in the process to help project the intended images.

That is what is happening in our industry. Aspects of who I believe I am are being challenged: I hear that my costs are out of line, that there is not enough access to high-quality care, and that I am not monitoring results as I should. The old congruence between who I think I am and how others see me is breaking down. As a result, signaling between insiders and outsiders is becoming rampant. My administrative staff spends much of its time projecting images of how they want others to see me,

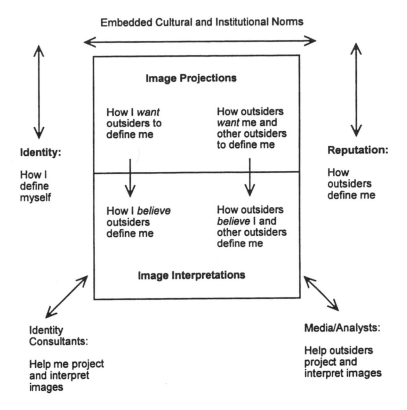

Figure 3.6. Identity-Image-Reputation Model

while outside actors are busily trying to persuade me and other outsiders that their view of me is correct. It's as though mirrors are being constructed that reveal multiple images, depending on where one sits. Maybe it's not such a bad thing that we are finally looking in the mirror. We've probably taken our identity too much for granted. But the conflicting images that the mirror is projecting are very confusing for us.

If that isn't bad enough, image projection is only half of the confusion. As represented in the lower half of the box in Figure 3.6, how each party interprets those images derives in large part from prior beliefs each one holds. Given the conflicting images out there about me and other health care providers, you can imagine the confusion this creates! How I believe outsiders should be defining me (based on my own views of who I am) is filtering how I see the images outsiders are projecting about me. That probably is resulting in my holding on to my old views of myself and not responding as quickly as I should to my external constituencies. What bothers me even more is that outsiders have similar ways of filtering what my staff is projecting about me. It seems that their beliefs about who I have become are causing them to interpret images of me in ways I did not intend or anticipate. For example, my staff released my operating costs to the general public recently, assuming that it would signal our identity of being good public servants. Instead of interpreting the signal as such, outsiders viewed it as yet another indication of my poor cost management.

To complicate matters further, outside parties increasingly seem to hold different views among themselves as to who I am. The deeply held, stable, cultural, and institutional norms that our identity and reputation were once so firmly rooted in no longer even hold outsiders' views together. Some of them seem to believe that I should be part of our government's identity; others believe that I should take on a corporate identity, with strict attention to profits!

Finally, we are not fighting our identity and reputation battles alone. Third-party "translators," which Violina and Charles referred to as "institutional intermediaries," are jumping into the arena to help each party win at the signaling game. So, I have hired identity consultants to help me interpret the multiple conflicting images of me out there; and I am told I need them to convince regulators, employers, and other key stakeholders that my signals are truthful and accurate. But of course, they have their own intermediaries who are fighting to establish their own views of me. I sometimes worry that intermediaries will end up shaping the future identities and reputations of organizations like me.

Who am I today? It's not as simple as it once was. My identity is no longer rooted in long-standing institutional traditions, and what I think I see in my mirror is not what seems to be reflected to outsiders. I am beginning to see that I must redefine my identity to be somewhat better aligned with other images of me out there. But that will be a slow and difficult process, because it is hard for me to view and assess those other images accurately.

My message to researchers today is this: You can no longer ask only me or look only inside of me to understand my identity. You can also no longer take a single snapshot of me at one point in time and believe that you have captured my identity. In these times of turbulence and change, you can only begin to understand who I am by focusing on the dynamic arena of image projections and interpretations. That is where my identity is being shaped and reshaped.

Hamid Bouchikhi with John Kimberly as Shadow Partner: Our interest in the concept of organizational identity emerged in the course of a research project on the internationalization of French firms. Our interest was stimulated by the realization that, while French firms had committed substantial resources abroad, little was known about the processes and outcomes of these investments.

As we began collecting data on a few cases, mainly from secondary sources, we were struck by what appeared to be a pattern. Some firms, it seemed, consistently approached foreign markets in a dramatic way, committing hundreds of millions of dollars to acquisitions within a very short time and with little or no prior experience with the target market. Other firms seemed to be more cautious, consistently approaching foreign markets in an incremental way. They might spend as much as several years experimenting with alternative ways to develop a market presence before committing substantial resources, either in the form of acquisitions or greenfield investments.

This observation led us to speculate that the behavior of firms with respect to internationalization might reflect some underlying, deeply rooted characteristics rather than being driven primarily by "rational," business-oriented calculations. This speculation subsequently led to our effort to conceptualize what we were encountering in terms of organizational identity and to look for opportunities to elaborate and deepen the perspective.

One such opportunity presented itself in the form of a field research project at Cement Corp., a French firm that has been involved in North America for four decades. The management of Cement Corp. was concerned by what they described as difficulties in integrating their North American operations within the parent company. Our mandate was to uncover impediments to integration and to make suggestions for improvement.

To carry out the assignment, we interviewed 30 of the most senior managers of Cement Corp., many of whom were involved in the North American operations from the earliest days. Throughout the interviews, we were struck by the continuity among key strategic moves and operating decisions made by successive management in four decades of expansion in North America and by the persistence of some serious management problems, some of which had emerged very early in the process but had never been resolved.

The more we observed at Cement Corp., the more we became convinced that traditional perspectives on organizations were limited in their ability to account for what we were seeing and hearing, and the more the nascent concept of organizational identity began to take shape. Cement Corp. provided a context where we could pursue our own sensemaking efforts in a relatively systematic fashion.

At this stage, it is important to explain why we thought that organizational culture was not enough for making sense of our empirical observations at Cement Corp. Organizational culture refers mostly to values, beliefs, and norms. While these are important and naturally involved in the internationalization of Cement Corp., other characteristics of the organization are involved too and fall outside the boundaries of what generally is meant by culture. The configuration of assets, for example, limits an organization's strategic options but is not part of its culture as conventionally defined. The technologies used by an organization are another example, as are the kinds of human resources employed by an organization, as well as its ownership and governance structure.

The concept of identity as we understand it incorporates not only the "soft side" but also the "hard side" of an organization. It is particularly revealing in extreme cases where the hard side (i.e., those dimensions that are difficult to change overnight) is at odds with the soft side (i.e., members' beliefs and values). The key French people interviewed at Cement Corp. all shared a strong commitment to internationalization, but the interviews also revealed an organization that has some serious difficulties in managing its international operations because of a number of deeply rooted attributes that we came to consider as elements of its identity (Bouchikhi & Kimberly, 1994).

A careful reading of the literature on organizational identity (Albert & Whetten, 1985; Ashforth & Mael, 1989; Dutton & Dukerich, 1991) suggested a distinct advantage in defining organizational identity in organizational terms because most of the work in this area approaches identity either in cognitive terms (identity as a construed image) or in psychological terms (identity as an identification process). Nowhere was it approached in organizational terms.

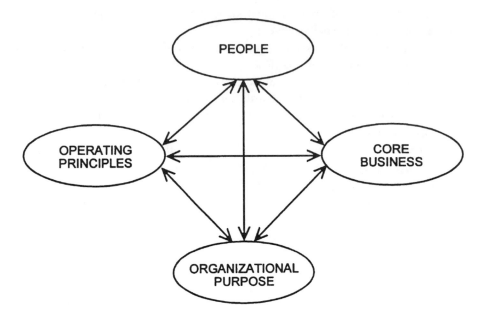

Figure 3.7. Organizational Identity as a Set of Interwoven and Mutually Sustained Dimensions

Therefore, we propose defining an organization's identity (Figure 3.7) as an idiosyncratic configuration of people sharing some attributes, pursuing a collective purpose through a given activity (core business), and using a limited number of operating principles. We believe that these dimensions profoundly shape the behavior of an organization and maintain its continuity and uniqueness.

The model presented in Figure 3.8 summarizes our understanding of the links between an organization's identity and members' actions. Organizational identity influences the premises which underlie members' choices regarding strategic, organizational, and operational issues (Dutton & Dukerich, 1991; Gustafson & Reger, 1995). These choices interact with other exogenous factors and yield some consequences in terms of profits, market share, competitive position, size, etc.

Members' interpretations of these consequences are also shaped by the organization's identity. A given level of performance is perceived as satisfactory or not depending on the organization's purpose and "normal" performance expectations in the core business. As long as members are either satisfied with consequences of their actions, can live with unsatisfactory consequences, or believe that marginal fine tuning of their actions can improve the consequences, they are inclined to keep working at the surface of the organization by reenacting familiar behavioral patterns. Throughout this process, they reinforce, although in an unconscious way, the underlying organizational identity and increase consistency among its dimensions.

It is only when they can no longer live with the consequences of their actions and they locate the causes in deeply seated, and so far unquestioned, attributes of the organization that members begin challenging its identity and trying to alter it. In so doing, they meet opposition from those members who are committed to the current identity of the organization. The subsequent evolution of identity will then depend

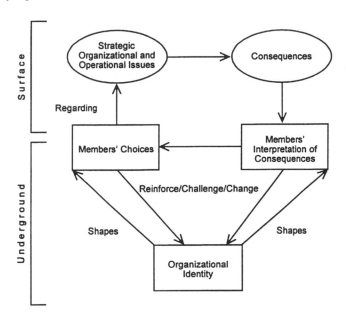

Figure 3.8. Organizational Identity as a Framework for Members' Actions and Interpretations of Consequences

on the balance between forces of convergence (status quo) and forces of divergence (change).

Huggy: All of the models and concepts that have been presented are interesting; they focus on related but different issues. I see all the models as having at least one quality in common, and that is realism. They are all the output of intensive fieldwork; combining them together might provide us with a generalized account of identity-related processes in organizations. The models also seem to have a nice progression about them and might be seen as complementary to the extent that they focus on different levels of analysis. Two of the models, Denny and Jim's and Hamid and John's seem to focus most on the organizational level, whereas the other models explicitly incorporate interorganizational structures, processes, and dimensions.

Together, the models also implicitly suggest that cognitive entrepreneurship by some key agents is crucial to the emergence, maintenance, and modification of organizational identity (whether those agents are top managers in one model or image consultants in another, etc.). More concretely, such agents are interested in projecting desired definitions of the organization to internal and external audiences and constituencies. Another intriguing commonality across the models is the role of contradiction. In Denny and Jim's model, contradictions are temporal—between current and future conceptions of identity and image that provide an impetus for change. By contrast, in the other models, especially Violina and Charles's, Marlene's, Mary Jo and Majken's presentations, the contradiction between the internal and the external environment provides the motive force for organizational change. One question all the models suggest is whether organizations can have multiple identities as a sort of hedging device in response to ideological uncertainty. A related point I would like to make centers around the impact of institutional norms on identity—in Marlene's model, for instance. Institutional norms constrain identity.

To my mind, institutionalized norms and beliefs are like building blocks for the construction of identity. Skillful entrepreneurs combine different norms, beliefs, and templates to communicate identity. For example, Joe Camel is used by a cigarette manufacturer as a way to communicate identity—as well as a way to persuade teenagers to smoke. Although I might personally find this disagreeable, the point is that cultural rules, norms, and icons are resources that can be manipulated by skillful entrepreneurs. By the same token, these cognitive entrepreneurs frequently push the boundaries of cultural constraints and thus produce a change in the institutional norms. There is not merely a one-way effect of these norms constraining what these entrepreneurs do; in a sense, they also change the rules.

We should also acknowledge that modifications to the institutional fabric over time can result in some interesting instances of hybrid identity. One quick example for me is that of the "corporate university," which blurs the boundaries between the world of education and the world of business; the institutional fabric of such organizations is arguably weakened and therefore requires continual construction. Similarly, the growth of the scientist-entrepreneur in biotechnology firms might also be seen as an outcome of the blending of business models and university models that have produced another hybrid identity. The overall point here is that we need to look at identity not only as that which is ordered and stable, but also that which can be disordered and changing.

Karen: Certainly, there are two broad points that I take away from our general conversations and models. First, it is surprising and interesting to see that we all view the relationship between culture and identity as really not problematic: Culture is the context within which identity is shaped, reshaped, negotiated, changed, decayed, and so forth. That doesn't mean that one is primary over the other. It does mean, however, that we need to look at all this in terms of interrelatedness. Further, at a more general level, the emphasis becomes interrelatedness between identity, culture, image, and reputation. We are used to thinking about our concepts in isolation, but the interrelatedness is the interesting part.

I would like to add a little bit about the highlights of the models, or at least some of the models, and I also echo what others have talked about from looking at the external more so than the internal in bringing out a certain aspect of this conceptual landscape or net. I look at the creation of reputation as really interesting, but what was insightful to me are the distinctions between targeted and shifting images, and the idea that there are some institutional intermediaries involved in this process. What I take away from other discussions is the whole identity and image projection and interpretation idea, as well as the interrelationships between identity, image, and reputation. Lastly, the interpenetration between the internal and external is still a little bewildering to me. How can that happen? That is a very interesting question to me.

Denny: Do we have a natural break point? Yes? Well, then, what shall we make of all these conceptual data?

Hamid: Perhaps at this point I could offer a two-by-two matrix as a way of understanding what we have. I think that what I really take away from this conversation is understanding how we can build different models, because we are dealing with different contexts. That is the real contribution of the models. This

Engines Dynamics of	Endogenous (Internal)	Exogenous (External)
Continuity	Bouchikhi & Kimberly	Rindova & Fombrun
	Hatch & Schultz	
Change	Gioia & Thomas	Fiol

Figure 3.9. Matrix

two-by-two (see Figure 3.9) helps me make sense of why these different models are interesting and appropriate for different contexts.

The first dimension is whether we are dealing with organizations that are changing or organizations that are just trying to maintain themselves in a kind of steady state. On the other side, we can say, well, some of us are more concerned with the internal dynamics of the organization and some are more concerned with the external dynamics and the consequences of the external world of the organization. This matrix at least helps me put some labels on the different things we have addressed. How you map the nomological net depends very much on how you answer questions like, "What are your priorities?" "What do you want to achieve?"

Marlene: Is it fair to say that to understand identity is to understand the intersection between internal and external? We may focus more on one or the other, but to me, explaining identity is not really about external forces. So in that sense, I disagree with that placement and with the two-by-two in general, unless the two-by-two is talking about "We are going to focus on this piece, recognizing that the context is one of internal/external interaction."

Hamid: Well, in the work I did with John Kimberly, we clearly have some places where we are dealing with external things and with change issues, but this is not the primary focus, so it's just a matter of where you put the emphasis.

Violina: It seems to me that your matrix actually brings another element to our nomological net: that of change or strategic state. It is something that we have been referring to intermittently, but certainly there are a lot of strategic considerations related to identity (which come out obviously in Denny and Jim's model).

Denny: I think it changes everything if you talk about "we're changing" as an organization. It has a whole different impact on identity and its status and uses.

Majken: What you are saying is that the issue of change actually highlights this tension between the internal and external. For me, the distinct contribution of the identity concept is the ability to facilitate the discussion between the internal and external. That is why we are seeing this merging between different strains of thinking; focusing on identity provides us the opportunity to have that kind of reflection.

Karen: It also allows the change-continuity issue to be brought up and made explicit. Rather than assuming that change is occurring, we are looking at how organizations construe whether change is occurring. In that way, it helps us remove a bias from the literature.

Denny: This is one of the intersections where we can get at the stability/ instability dimension and still think in terms of maintaining continuity.

Hamid: One more point about the change/continuity issue. In the steady state, there can be a lot of strategizing; stability doesn't mean that there is no strategy. We should remember that the strategy process is not always aimed at completely reorganizing or reorienting an organization.

Mary Jo: This issue gets us back to one of the paradoxes that we talked about on our first day together, which is that change and steady state are conditions that happen at the same time.

Karen: Regardless of whether organization members construe it more as change or as continuity . . .

Mary Jo: Does identity facilitate the ability of the organization to simultaneously change and stay the same?

Violina: This also brings us back also to the question of the enduring characteristics of identity; now we have a much more grounded understanding.

Denny: And therein is the basis for resolution of the endurance-of-identity question.

Karen: Right.

Majken: Another of the paradoxes we talked about was the tension between the striving for external distinctiveness while maintaining an internal need for belonging.

Denny: It is another one of the problematic aspects of the definition that can be resolved by considering the nomological net.

Karen: Yet there is also an external need to belong in the institutional environment.

Majken: And an internal need to be distinct. These two concepts can be flipped around, but they are both important in the constitution of identity.

Hamid: I have a quote from Erickson (1964) about continuity and change in identity that is relevant here:

> The key problem of identity, then, is, as the term connotes, the capacity of the ego to sustain sameness and continuity in the face of changing fate. But fate always combines changes in inner conditions, which are the result of ongoing life stages, and changes in the milieu, the historical situation. Identity connotes the resiliency of maintaining essential patterns in the process of change. Thus, strange as it may seem, it takes a well-established identity to tolerate radical change, for the well-established identity has arranged itself around basic values which cultures have in common. (pp. 95-96)

Denny: At the organizational level, the implication is that some of those basic facets of identity have to do with flexibility, fluidity, and orientation toward changing—incorporating that in the way we see ourselves as an organization.

Karen: There is also a need to recognize organizations that are based strongly in tradition, where culture change would not be talked about, but "customizing" would be. That is how they construe change. I am thinking of one Fortune 500 firm I studied whose managers really have reverence for past generations of managers and the practices they implemented. They do not talk change; it is not their language. They talk continuity, and yet they do, nevertheless, change.

Huggy: Whether you change or whether you are in a steady state, being in a steady state does not mean you are being inert.

Denny: I think that it is important to recognize that even those organizations that think that they are not changing, are changing.

Mary Jo: And that those organizations that think they are changing, are not changing.

Huggy: Yes!

Karen: I think identity as a concept helps us as researchers reflect back on our own lives and predispositions toward change while growing up, so that we can be critical or postmodern in the sense of reflecting back and saying, "What are our assumptions?" "What are we seeing?" "How are our biases influencing what we are seeing if people talk or don't talk about change by the organization?"

Marlene: We've talked about distinctiveness around this nomological net. We have talked about endurance and change. My sense is that, implicitly or explicitly, we are all recognizing the centrality of the identity concept for organizational members. It is something we did not raise explicitly in most cases, but it seems to me that there is a centrality about it.

Majken: To the extent that we defined "who we are" as the really key, central question for organizations, I think we do agree on some kind of centrality, because that has been a focal point in our discussions, both in theoretical perspectives and in conceptual mappings. Identity might best be viewed mainly as a central question that organizations are facing.

Marlene: That is exactly what I was referring to. We have defined identity as perhaps not an enduring or a distinctive feature of organizations, but certainly it defines that which people hold as central about their organizations.

Huggy: One of the nice things about the way that people are thinking about identity here is that there seems to be a tendency towards resisting a proliferation of different types of identity. To take an analogous example, the concept of capital has been subdivided into 9 or 10 types of capital, with the result that the boundary conditions of the term *capital* have been muddied. We don't seem to be proliferating 10 kinds of identity.

Denny: Oh, I would not agree with that statement, Huggy. I see a lot of different forms of identity. We are cutting each other a lot of slack to accept that we have different views of just what identity might be.

Marlene: I agree with him. I think we are all converging very much on what we mean by identity in each of these different perspectives.

Denny: How can we say that we are converging and simultaneously say that we are adopting three different views?

Majken: That was a starting point. Now we have moved beyond that. We had been thinking about identity as functional, interpretive, postmodern. Now we are moving toward some sort of convergence . . .

Denny: Well, I am going to run like hell, conceptually, if that is what you think we are doing.

Mary Jo: I don't believe that is true either, because I think what we agreed to do today was to go back to our original table and to think through using some specific examples of what those different perspectives bring. When we do that, we are going to see our diversity embedded neatly in here. So some of our agreement has to do with operating at this level. When we get to the specifics, we will bring out these differences.

Marlene: I am still not sure that means we are disagreeing about what identity is.

Mary Jo: We are agreeing and disagreeing!

Marlene: But the perspectives are more about the processes around which identity gets developed, maintained, changed, decayed.

Denny: I think that glosses over what we have done. Our tacit agreement is that we trying not to be incommensurable as we have defined things, but the possibility of incommensurability among our views lurks around every corner. We are not necessarily in agreement, but we are trying to accommodate many views. That's what all of us are doing. That also constitutes our main hope for the future readers of the transcript of this conversation—that they will see organizational identity in multiple ways and accept that although others might see it differently, their views can provide some different and useful insight and understanding.

EPILOGUE

In this preceding conversation from the almost-autumn of 1996, we assumed that Albert and Whetten's (1985) three key elements in defining organizational identity—centrality, endurance, and distinctiveness—constituted a workable initial definition of the concept. In places, we pointedly noted that each of these elements could be construed as problematic from various perspectives, but that they nevertheless provided a common referent and a point of departure for launching a spirited discussion about the nature of organizational identity.

We began with the initial premise that one's understanding of the concept of organizational identity depends on the perspective one takes in approaching it. For the purpose of managing the discussion and making it intelligible to an interested eavesdropper (you, the reader), we delimited ourselves to a discussion of only three perspectives from a universe of many other possible ways of seeing. We entertained a traditional and dominant functionalist view, a rather restrained but still provocative interpretive view, and a fairly radical postmodern view. We believe, however, that the conversation, even within this somewhat constrained subset of possible perspectives, nevertheless demonstrated the power and scope of our premise in the wideranging discussions that ensued.

When the lens is trained on those of us who are organizational theorists and researchers exploring fundamental questions like "Who are we as an organization?" the lessons and implications of these multiple views are important. What we learn and how we model organizational identity within its nomological network clearly depends on the ground assumptions we make about the way we understand organizations. Our differing assumptions came to life and were most provocatively presented when we prodded ourselves to consider our comparative answers to such basic questions as, How do we define our central problems when investigating organizational identity? What do we take to be the main purposes of inquiry? What evocative metaphors characterize our depictions? What do we even construe as "data"? And what are the consequences and implications of our perspectives?

Questions, of course, are at the heart of the academic endeavor. So, we are given to asking what the next set of questions might be in the continuing exploration of organizational identity. We could begin by first posing a metaquestion, such as, "What might the driving questions be if we were to meet again as a group, with the intent of extending our previous thoughts?" In other words, we could do a bit of group introspection and try to discern the questions that derive from, and enlarge upon, those asked during the course of this conversation. We might also pose a guiding metaquestion, such as, "What might constitute promising questions for research, perhaps especially for those younger scholars looking for high-potential dissertation topics related to the identity domain?"

A review and extension of this conversation suggests several big questions that seem to be as yet inadequately explored, and which could occupy us in a future meeting, such as:

1. What are the processes that facilitate or inhibit the evolution (or even transformation) of organizational identity?

2. What is the role of power and politics in the construction, maintenance, and alteration of identity? (And, relatedly, what are the implications of identity for power distribution in an organization and the implications of power distribution for identity?)

3. Will (and if so, how will) organizational identity tend toward hybrid identities as organizational environments become increasingly complex?

4. Which other perspectives might fruitfully be brought into the discussion of the nature of organizational identity?

For those interested in considering the ramifications of our conversation for the purposes of designing empirical research, perhaps the following questions might suggest some guidelines:

1. How does identity facilitate or hinder organizational change? (And as first cousins to this question, How is the character of identity affected under conditions of change? How does the projection of a "future identity" affect organizational change processes?)

2. What are the relationships between organizational identity and organizational performance?

3. What are the empirical relationships among identity and the concepts in identity's nomological net: image, reputation, culture, etc.?

4. Do emulation processes produce organizations that are less distinctive from each other? (And will distinctiveness be increasingly narrowly defined in a world of benchmarking practices?)

We should also note that our conversation generated some questions that also have clear practical relevance, such as:

1. What are the implications of gaps or discontinuities between identity, image, and reputation?

2. What are the implications of gaps or discontinuities between the perceptions of insiders and outsiders?

3. How are projected images modified by parties external to the organization and by interactions between internal and external representatives?

4. What are the implications of trying to manage both organizational and corporate identity?

In addition to these questions in these specific categories, we also generated a number of other questions of interest, some of which we considered, but they require further discussion. These include the following:

1. What are the processes by which organizational identity develops, maintains, alters, or deteriorates? (And in what ways do the forces of convergence [status quo] and divergence [change] affect the evolution of identity?)

2. To what extent is identity enduring? How do we resolve the paradox that identity is simultaneously stable and changing?

3. Should the definition of identity give more emphasis to the opposing question of "who we are not"?

4. What are the implications of asserting that identity is simultaneously an internal and an external concept?

These questions certainly constitute an ambitious agenda. The overarching message that derives from our ability to frame such questions, however, is that identity is a rich domain with huge potential for exploration. That exploration encompasses many voices representing many perspectives and approaches to theory, research, and practice. We hope our conversation, and your invited eavesdropping on that conversation, will serve as an inducement for you to join us in the continuing investigation of organizational identity.

NOTE

1. We have chosen to label as "shadow partners and co-conspirators" those scholars who were collaborators on some of the research projects prominently discussed in these conversations.

REFERENCES

Abratt, R. (1989). A new approach to the corporate image management process. *Journal of Marketing Management, 5,* 63-76.

Albert, S., & Whetten, D. (1985). Organizational identity. In L. L. Cummings & B. M. Staw (Eds.), *Research in organizational behavior* (Vol. 7, pp. 263-295). Greenwich, CT: JAI.

Ashforth, B. E., & Mael, F. A. (1989). Social identity theory and the organization. *Academy of Management Review, 14,* 20-39.

Balmer, J. J. (1995). Corporate branding and connoisseurship. *Journal of General Management, 21,* 24-46.

Barney, J. B. (1986). Organizational culture: Can it be a source of sustained competitive advantage? *Academy of Management Review, 11,* 656-665.

Berger, P. L., & Luckmann, T. (1966). *The social construction of reality.* Garden City, NY: Doubleday Anchor.

Birkigt, K., & Stadler, M. M. (1986). *Grundlagen, Funktionen und Beispielen* [Corporate identity]. Landsberg: Verlag Moderne Industrie.

Bouchikhi, H., & Kimberly, J. R. (1994, August). *How an organization's identity shapes its internationalization processes: A French perspective.* Paper presented at the annual meeting of the Academy of Management, Dallas.

Cooley, C. H. (1902). *Human nature and the social order.* New York: Scribner.

DiMaggio, P., & Powell, W. (1983). The iron cage revisited: Institutional isomorphism and collective rationality in organizational fields. *American Sociological Review, 48,* 147-160.

Dutton, J., & Dukerich, J. (1991). Keeping an eye on the mirror: Image and identity in organizational adaptation. *Academy of Management Journal, 34,* 517-554.

Dutton, J., Dukerich, J., & Harquail, C. V. (1994). Organizational images and membership commitment. *Administrative Science Quarterly, 39,* 239-263.

Eccles, R., & Nohria, N. (1992). *Beyond the hype: Rediscovering the essence of management.* Boston: Harvard Business School Press.

Elsbach, K. D., & Kramer, R. M. (1996). Members' responses to organizational identity threats: Encountering and countering the *Business Week* rankings. *Administrative Science Quarterly, 41,* 442-476.

Erickson, E. (1964). *Insight and responsibility.* New York: Norton.

Fiol, C. M. (1991). Managing culture as a competitive resource: An identity-based view of sustainable competitive advantage. *Journal of Management, 17,* 191-211.

Fiske, S., & Dyer, L. (1985). Structure and development of social schemata: Evidence from positive and negative transfer effects. *Journal of Personality and Social Psychology, 48,* 839-852.

Fombrun, C. (1996). *Reputation: Realizing value from the corporate image.* Boston: Harvard Business School Press.

Fombrun, C., & Rindova, V. (in press). Fanning the flame: Corporate reputations as social constructions of performance. In J. Porac & M. Ventresca (Eds.), *Constructing markets and industries.* Oxford, UK: Oxford University Press.

Gagliardi, P. (1986). The creation and change of organizational cultures: A conceptual framework. *Organization Studies, 7,* 117-134.

Geertz, C. (1973). *The interpretation of cultures.* New York: Basic Books.

Gioia, D. A. (1986a). The state of the art in organizational social cognition: A personal view. In H. P. Sims, Jr. & D. A. Gioia (Eds.), *The thinking organization* (pp. 336-356). San Francisco: Jossey-Bass.

Gioia, D. A. (1986b). Symbols, scripts and sensemaking: Creating meaning in the organizational experience. In H. P. Sims, Jr. & D. A. Gioia (Eds.), *The thinking organization* (pp. 49-74). San Francisco: Jossey-Bass.

Gioia, D. A., & Thomas, J. B. (1996). Identity, image and issue interpretation: Sensemaking during strategic change in academia. *Administrative Science Quarterly, 41,* 370-403.

Golden, K. (1992). The individual and organizational culture: Strategies for action in highly-ordered contexts. *Journal of Management Studies, 29,* 1-21.

Grunig, J. E., & Hunt, T. (1984). *Managing public relations.* New York: Holt, Rinehart & Winston.

Gustafson, L., & Reger, R. L. (1995, August). *Using organizational identity to achieve stability and change in high velocity environments.* Proceedings of the Academy of Management meeting, Vancouver, BC, Canada.

Hatch, M. J. (1993). The dynamics of organizational culture. *Academy of Management Review, 18,* 657-693.

Hatch, M. J., & Schultz, M. (1997). Relations between organizational culture, identity and image. *European Journal of Marketing, 31,* 356-365.

Krefting, L. A., & Frost, P. J. (1985). Untangling webs, surface waves, and wildcatting. In P. J. Frost, L. F. Moor, M. R. Louis, C. C. Lundberg, & J. Martin (Eds.), *Organizational culture* (pp. 155-168). Beverly Hills, CA: Sage.

Kunda, G. (1992). *Engineering culture.* Philadelphia: Temple University Press.

LaBianca, G., Fairbank, J., Thomas, J. B., & Gioia, D. A. (1997). *Image, identity, and industry structure: Cognitive isomorphism in an interorganizational emulation network* (Working paper). University Park: Pennsylvania State University.

Martin, J. (1992). *Cultures in organizations.* Oxford, UK: Oxford University Press.

Martins, L. (1997). *Organizational responses to reputational rankings: A strategic-issues interpretation approach.* Unpublished doctoral dissertation, New York University.

Mead, G. H. (1964). *Selected writings.* Chicago: University of Chicago Press.

Olins, W. (1989). *Corporate identity.* London: Thames & Hudson.

O'Rourke, R. (1997). *Reputation in good times and in bad times.* Address at the Conference on Corporate Reputation, Image, and Competitiveness, New York University, New York.

Porac, J. F., Thomas, H., & Baden-Fuller, C. (1989). Competitive groups as cognitive communities: The case of Scottish knitwear manufacturers. *Journal of Management Studies, 26,* 397-416.

Porac, J. F., Thomas, H., Wilson, F., Paton, D., & Kanfer, A. (1995). Rivalry and the industry model of Scottish knitwear producers. *Administrative Science Quarterly, 40,* 203-227.

Prahalad, C. K., & Bettis, J. (1986). The dominant logic: A new linkage between diversity and performance. *Strategic Management Journal, 7,* 485-502.

Rao, H. (1994). The social construction of reputation: Certification contests, legitimation, and the survival of organizations in the American automobile industry: 1895-1912. *Strategic Management Journal, 15,* 29-44.

Schein, E. (1985). *Organizational culture and leadership.* San Francisco: Jossey-Bass.

Schlenker, B. R. (1980). *Impression management.* Monterey, CA: Brooks/Cole.

Schultz, M., & Hatch, M. J. (1996). Living with multiple paradigms: The case of paradigm interplay in organisational culture studies. *Academy of Management Review, 21,* 529-557.

Smircich, L. (1983). Concepts of culture and organizational analysis. *Administrative Science Quarterly, 28,* 339-358.

Tedeschi, J. T. (Ed.). (1981). *Impression management theory and social psychological research.* New York: Academic Press.

Thompson, J. D. (1967). *Organizations in action.* New York: McGraw-Hill.

Van Riel, C. B. (1995). *Principles of corporate communication.* Hemel Hempstead, UK: Prentice Hall.

Weigelt, K., & Camerer, C. (1988). Reputation and corporate strategy: A review of recent theory and applications. *Strategic Management Journal, 9,* 443-454.

PART II

What Does Identity Imply for Strategy?

4

Organizational Identity Within the Strategic Management Conversation
Contributions and Assumptions

J. L. "LARRY" STIMPERT

LOREN T. GUSTAFSON

YOLANDA SARASON

The objective of this chapter is to serve as an introduction to the more conversational chapter that follows. To accomplish this objective, this chapter addresses two important sets of questions. The first set of questions asks, "What makes the concept of organizational identity compelling to the group of strategy researchers who gathered at Sundance last fall to share their research interests and participate in the conversation that appears in this volume?" and "Why have a number of strategy researchers developed an interest in this concept?"

For readers to understand and appreciate fully the conversational chapter that follows, this chapter must also describe and clearly delineate the assumptions, perspectives, and research paradigms that guide the thinking of the participants. So, this chapter also asks, "What are the common bases and fundamental assumptions shared by strategy researchers who are working with the concept of organizational identity, and what perspectives and research paradigms are guiding these researchers?" and "How does identity research differ from other types of strategy research?"

WHAT MAKES THE CONCEPT OF ORGANIZATIONAL IDENTITY COMPELLING?

The quest of strategy research is to understand the sources of sustained competitive advantage that provide business organizations with consistently high levels of performance. Indeed, the conversation recorded in the next chapter begins by describing the fundamental objective of strategy as a "theory of actions" that firms should take to establish a competitive advantage. Therefore, describing how the concept of organizational identity has come to be relevant and compelling for many strategy researchers is the aim of this section. We begin by describing how developments in the strategic management field have created a context that is favorable to research on organizational identity. We then assess the potential of organizational identity to provide firms with a sustained competitive advantage. The section then describes the relationship between organizational identity and other important strategy concepts. We then conclude this section by suggesting that organizational identity is uniquely helpful in addressing several important issues in the strategic management research literature.

Background

All strategy researchers are familiar with the field's traditional emphasis on industry structure. The most definitive statement of this emphasis on the relationship between industry structure and firm performance is found in Michael Porter's (1980) classic book, *Competitive Strategy*. Porter persuasively argued that firm performance is determined by the structural characteristics of the industries in which firms compete. For Porter, strategy involves either selecting the appropriate generic "formula" for altering industry structure or diversifying into more attractive industry environments.

The key limitation of Porter's conceptualization of competitive strategy is its implicit assumption of interfirm homogeneity. Although not directly stated, Porter's book suggests that all firms are equally able to implement competitive strategies, and his book does not address the significant differences in capabilities or resource endowments across firms. It is not surprising, then, that the emphasis on industry structure and the assumption of interfirm homogeneity was quickly balanced by a new interest in firms' own internal capabilities and resources. An early article by Wernerfelt (1984) was followed by several articles by Jay Barney (1986b, 1991), and they laid a foundation for what has come to be known as the resource-based view of the firm. A key premise of the resource-based view of the firm is the idea that competitive advantage is derived not only by firms participating in attractive or favorable competitive environments, but also from their access to and endowments of valuable capabilities and resources.

Thus, the resource-based view of the firm provides much needed balance in our understanding of how business organizations come to enjoy high performance. According to the resource-based view of the firm, Merck enjoys high performance not simply because it participates in the profitable pharmaceutical industry—after all, many other firms compete in the pharmaceutical industry, but their performance levels lag far behind Merck's. Resource-based theory suggests instead that high performance is a function of both favorable positions in attractive industries and endowments of valuable resources.

A second key premise of the resource-based view of the firm is that competitive advantage depends on asymmetry or uniqueness. Wernerfelt (1984), Barney (1986b), and other early proponents of the resource-based view argued that firms cannot maintain an advantageous position in their industries or enjoy a competitive advantage over their rivals without some sort of resource mobility barriers. The reasoning behind this important insight is quite simple: Once other firms determine how or why the leaders in their respective industries enjoy a competitive advantage, they will quickly seek to imitate the sources of the leading firms' competitive advantage. Thus, resource-based researchers have argued that competitive advantage is not only inherently asymmetrical but also intimately linked with the concepts of causal ambiguity and uncertain imitability, which prevent the rapid diffusion of the sources of competitive advantage (Lippman & Rumelt, 1982).

The ironic consequence of resource-based theorizing is that nearly all of the traditional "strategy levers" tend to fail this asymmetry test. Much strategy content, for example, is readily observable and easily imitated by competing firms. Most strategic initiatives receive attention in the business press, and others are easily detected in firms' publicly disclosed financial statements. As a result, firms aspiring to improve their performance levels are quick to imitate or adopt the strategies of their more successful rivals.

In short, many of the resources that are typically associated with performance are not, and cannot be, true sources of sustained competitive advantage. An outstanding manager can be lured away by an attractive compensation package. A new technology can be reverse-engineered and imitated. A firm can outspend its rivals on research and development. Thus, few strategies or the tangible competencies or resources that are associated with those strategies are likely to pass the tests of asymmetry or inimitability that are a necessary condition for competitive advantage.

Subsequent resource-based theorizing has sought to identify less easily imitated capabilities and resources that can be sources of sustained competitive advantage while also asking how the inimitability and causal ambiguity of any resource associated with competitive advantage can be enhanced. For example, Dierickx and Cool (1989) distinguished between "stocks" and "flows" of resources and emphasized that competitive advantage is most likely to result from the development of unique asset stocks that are built up through an ongoing process of resource accumulation over time. They emphasized the importance of several factors, including time, past success, interconnectedness, and ongoing investment, that not only lead to the development of valuable organizational capabilities and resources but also tend to make those capabilities and resources difficult for competing firms to duplicate easily or imitate successfully.

Mahoney and Pandian (1992) provided an early comprehensive review of the resource-based literature and sought to identify links between the developing resource-based theory and other literature streams, including mainstream strategy research, organizational economics, and industrial organization economics. They noted that the resource-based literature has always emphasized the importance of isolating mechanisms and other barriers to imitation that are necessary for meeting the criterion of asymmetry.

Furthermore, by the early 1990s, much of the resource-based literature had begun to focus attention on nontraditional strategy levers that are likely to be much more difficult to imitate. For example, Barney (1991) began to emphasize the importance of "nontradable" resources or resources that are "imperfectly tradable." Barney (1986a) had earlier examined the circumstances in which organizational culture could be a source of sustained competitive advantage. Similarly, Itami (1987) had described the importance of "invisible assets" that, by their very nature, would be more difficult for competitors to imitate. Schoemaker (1990) had similarly emphasized the potential for organizational processes, routines, and heuristics to contribute to competitive advantage, suggesting that, by their very nature, such firm-specific factors are difficult to imitate.

In empirical studies, Aaker (1989) and Hall (1992) surveyed corporate managers with the aim of developing lists of resources that managers see as contributing to their firms' successes. Most of the items that the surveyed managers identified included either intangible resources such as "know-how," or items like "reputation for quality," "customer service and product support," "name recognition," and "culture," which are outcomes or results of firms' own internal processes.

As a consequence, resource-based theorists and other strategy scholars have now begun to focus attention on a wide array of internal organizational processes and socially complex resources that are more likely than other resources to pass the asymmetry test. Barney (1992) defines these socially complex resources as

> resources that enable an organization to conceive, choose, and implement strategies because of the values, beliefs, symbols, and interpersonal relationships possessed by individuals or groups in a firm. Some examples of these socially complex phenomena include organizational culture, trust and friendship among managers in an organization, the reputation of an organization among its customers, teamwork among managers and workers, and so forth. (p. 44)

Because these socially complex resources and organizational processes are firm-specific, and because they must almost always be developed over time, they can be exceedingly difficult for competitors either to understand or to imitate. And, as a result, socially complex resources and organizational processes have now come to be viewed by many theorists as the most likely sources of sustained competitive advantage.

Surely an even more ironic twist in the development of the resource-based view of the firm is that what is largely regarded as an economic theory or paradigm has now come to focus most of its research attention on the importance of social or behavioral phenomena. Although many fundamental components of resource-based theory such as interfirm heterogeneity and barriers to imitation are grounded in economic thought, nearly all resource-based researchers are concluding that socially complex behavioral phenomena—rather than traditional strategy levers—offer the most likely sources of sustained competitive advantage.

Organizational Identity as a Valuable and
Socially Complex Resource That Can Be a
Source of Competitive Advantage

It is the strategic management field's search for difficult-to-imitate and socially complex resources that can be the sources of competitive advantage that has encouraged many strategy researchers to become interested in the concept of organizational identity. In their pathbreaking work, Albert and Whetten (1985) defined organizational identity as managers' beliefs about what is central, distinctive, and enduring about their organizations. The key issue for the strategy participants who gathered at Sundance was the relationship between organizational identity and strategic management, or, more specifically, the relationship between organizational identity and competitive advantage.

As the meetings at Sundance got underway, it became apparent that the participants in the strategy conversations had rather quickly developed a consensus that identity represents the shared beliefs that managers hold about their organizations. Notions of centrality, distinctiveness, and permanence were seen by all participants as important aspects of organizational identity, but also as aspects of identity that could vary significantly across organizations. To avoid the risk that the conversation become focused exclusively on definitional issues, the discussants adopted the working definition that identity is *the theory that members of an organization have about who they are.*

As the next chapter will reveal, participants in the strategy conversations brought with them a number of beliefs and understandings about the relationships among organizational identity, strategy, and competitive advantage. During formal and informal conversations, at least four different themes, points of view, and even emerging literature streams were well represented and articulated.

First, as suggested by Albert and Whetten (1985), identity describes the essence of an organization. Thus, identity becomes a major way in which firms and other organizations define or describe themselves to customers, employees, suppliers, and investors, and also the way customers, employees, and other constituencies develop an image of these organizations (Dutton & Dukerich, 1991). An identity that creates a distinctive and particularly attractive image in the minds of customers or other constituencies can have significant and positive reputational impacts that can be the source of sustained competitive advantage.

Second, identity helps to focus management attention on the most significant or important strategic issues. Studies by Dutton and her colleagues (Dutton & Dukerich, 1991; Dutton, Dukerich, & Harquail, 1994; Dutton & Penner, 1993) have shown that organizational identity influences which environmental stimuli are and are not noticed, and that identity can also play an important role in influencing organizational agendas. It is not that managers can ignore less central competitors and issues, but identity allows managers to focus their attention on a much more limited set of direct competitors and those issues that are most relevant. This ability to focus management attention may be important or even essential to organizational effectiveness.

For example, in their analysis of two railroads—one that was successful and one that failed—Barr, Stimpert, and Huff (1992) found that the managers of the successful railroad focused on *their own company's internal problems* and what they could do to overcome these problems. The managers of the railroad that failed, on the other hand, maintained a focus not only on their own company but also on *the unattractive characteristics of the railroad industry,* which were largely beyond their control, and did not acknowledge or address the problems unique to their own company until it faced financial calamity. Barr et al. concluded that this difference in identity focus had much to do with the very different fates of these two railroads.

Third, identity is a major influence on the resource allocation process, and understandings of identity can become tightly coupled with organizational processes, standard operating procedures, and fixed assets. For example, the firm that defines itself as a distinctive consumer products company will seek to build organizational processes and to accumulate the resources and skills that complement this identity. To the extent that the firm is successful in developing these processes and skills, it further reinforces its identity as a distinctive consumer products company. Together, then, organizational identity and any associated processes can form what Mintzberg (1978) has called an organizational "gestalt." Such a gestalt not only places a firm in a unique position vis-à-vis its rivals in the competitive environment, but it also provides that firm with a set of organizational competencies that supports or enhances its identity.

Finally, identity can be very motivational. A number of recent articles and books, including the best-selling *Built to Last* by Collins and Porras (1994), have emphasized the motivational aspects of concepts such as organizational identity and vision. Firms that have strong or powerful identities can provide managers and employees with a sense of meaning, purpose, and excitement, which can arouse commitment and even passion. Furthermore, many authors have concluded that a discrepancy between understandings of an organization's ideal identity and its current identity or image can motivate managers to improve or otherwise change their organization so that it is more closely aligned with its ideal identity (Dutton & Dukerich, 1991; Reger, Gustafson, DeMarie, & Mullane, 1994; Senge, 1990).

Thus, organizational identity can do much to enhance organizational effectiveness and performance. Furthermore, because organizational identities are socially complex phenomena, developed over time, and held in managers' cognitive beliefs and understandings, they are likely to be both unique and difficult for other organizations to imitate, and therefore potential sources of sustained competitive advantage.

Organizational Identity and Its Relationship to Other Important Strategy Concepts

Not only does the concept of organizational identity have the potential to pass the asymmetry test for competitive advantage, it also resonates with many strategy researchers who have been interested in other important, but perhaps inadequately defined, concepts. For example, Prahalad and Bettis (1986) coined the concept of dominant logic as the way managers conceptualize their firms, yet dominant logic remains a somewhat ambiguous term that has generated little empirical study. Likewise, Drucker (1994) described the importance of what he calls a "theory of the business," which includes beliefs that "shape any organization's behavior, dictate its decisions about what to do and what not to do, and define what the organization considers meaningful results" (p. 95). In his classic study of American liberal arts colleges, Burton Clark (1970) referred to the concept of organizational sagas that not only define organizations but also influence the behavior of their members. Abell (1980) has emphasized the importance of business definition, or how firms define or position themselves in their competitive environments. The popular business press has recently focused attention on the importance of vision (Collins & Porras, 1994).

The common characteristic that identity shares with these related concepts is its potential to provide both internal as well as external stakeholders with meanings and understandings of what is central and distinctive about their organizations. While researchers are probably far from agreement about the relationship between identity and terms like *dominant logic, theory of the business, organizational saga, business definition,* and *vision,* the considerable interest in these many related concepts may suggest an important new stream of thought in the strategy field. To the extent that the concept of organizational identity can serve as a locus for and generate momentum among researchers who are interested in these many related ideas, it can do much to add coherence and bring energy to common research efforts.

Growing interest in organizational identity and many other related concepts and terms may, in fact, be paralleling the interest in managerial and organizational cognition that developed during the past decade. In his review of the cognition literature, Walsh (1995) found that researchers had used more than 75 different terms to refer to knowledge structures and schemas. Instead of worrying that this multitude of related terms was an indication of theoretical imprecision, Walsh argued that a large number of similar concepts and terms is not unusual for new domains of inquiry and that it is an indication of promise and excitement.

Organizational Identity May Be Uniquely Helpful in Addressing a Number of Strategic Issues

Finally, although the concept of organizational identity may be only one of many possible sources of sustained competitive advantage, organizational identity does seem uniquely helpful for addressing a number of troubling issues in the strategic management research literature.

Explaining interfirm heterogeneity. The question of why a particular firm would choose a particular strategy when many viable options or strategies are available is one such problematical issue in the strategy field. The dominant theoretical frameworks have certainly helped explain firm differences in the aggregate. For example, industrial organization economists have shown how industry structure influences firms' strategies (Porter, 1980). Evolutionary economists have emphasized how variation in founding conditions, evolutionary paths, and organizational routines are helpful in understanding firm differences (Nelson & Winter, 1982). Resource-based theory describes how the accumulation of valuable resources and capabilities that are rare and difficult to imitate can lead to firm heterogeneity and differences in performance outcomes. Still, none of these theoretical perspectives explains how or why firms develop in their own unique ways.

A number of recent studies have shown, however, that the concept of identity can provide considerable insight into understanding firm choices and organizational differences. For example, Porac, Thomas, and Baden-Fuller (1989) studied the mental models of managers of Scottish knitwear firms and concluded that the understandings these managers held of their competitive arena limited the range of strategic possibilities that they would—or could—consider. More recent investigations of organizational identity and firm differences include Sarason's (1997) study of three Baby Bells. Despite initial similarities in internal and external environments, these organizations have diverged in different strategic directions. Sarason's study found that the Baby Bells had developed distinct identities and that these identities have been very influential in shaping their diverging strategic paths.

Organizational inertia, change, and renewal. Another troubling question—also deemed one of the fundamental issues in strategy (Rumelt, Schendel, & Teece, 1994)—is why the process of organizational change is so difficult for most firms. A number of strategy researchers have now employed the concept of organizational identity to shed much new light on the inertia that tends to characterize organizational change processes. Their studies have suggested that the inertial characteristics of organizational identity can significantly limit organizational effectiveness by constraining the strategies that managers will pursue. Studies have found, for example, that managers have difficulty noticing, interpreting, and appropriately acting on environmental changes that do not correspond with their firms' organizational identities.

The inertial nature of organizational identity suggests that, over time, many aspects of a particular firm's identity are likely to become obsolete. As industries evolve, and as the nature of competitive rivalry in those industries shifts, organizational identities will therefore need to be updated. The fact that some firms manage the change process so much more effectively than others suggests that, while enduring, identity is also at least somewhat malleable (Gioia & Thomas, 1996).

To better explain the relationship between identity and organizational change, Gustafson (1995) proposed and tested a normative model of organizational identity for firms operating in turbulent environments. His model distinguished between two types of identity attributes: *abstract* identity components that help to establish an organization's context and tend to be reflected in organizational culture and underlying values that transcend any particular product, process, time, or environment;

and *concrete* identity elements that are tied to a particular time and set of environmental conditions, such as products, strategies, and geographical scope.

Gustafson and his colleagues (Reger et al., 1994) also proposed that firms have both current understandings of organizational identity as well as desired or ideal conceptualizations of identity. They proposed that an identity gap exists when there is a cognitive discrepancy between these two identities. They also proposed that the existence of an identity gap can either facilitate or impede the strategy renewal process. Identity gaps that are too narrow or too wide can create cognitive inertia or opposition. Successful strategy renewal results from a moderate identity gap that will allow firms to discard some concrete identity attributes that no longer provide them with a competitive advantage, while simultaneously adding new, concrete attributes that elaborate on abstract identity attributes and offer the potential of new advantages.

Understanding patterns of corporate diversification and the relationship between diversification strategy and firm performance. Several years ago, in a significant departure from mainstream diversification research, Prahalad and Bettis (1986) suggested that managers' dominant logics are an important influence on the relationship between diversification strategy and firm performance. As noted earlier, dominant logic, with its focus on "how managers conceptualize the business" (Prahalad & Bettis, 1986, p. 490), is remarkably similar to the concept of organizational identity, which describes what is central, distinctive, and enduring about organizations. Together, these concepts can offer new and potentially insightful tools for studying corporate diversification.

For example, managers' dominant logics, or their understandings of identity, are likely to reflect their beliefs about how their diversified firms' businesses are related. Beliefs about relatedness, as well as the ability to articulate a coherent identity, may be especially important in the case of widely diversified firms that have business units operating in many different product markets that have no obvious linkages to each other. Developing an organizational identity for a diversified firm poses a number of challenges, however. Such an identity must be distinctive in order to differentiate a diversified firm from other diversified firms, but any identity must also be readily understandable by various stakeholders. A particularly novel identity might leave investors and other stakeholders confused, whereas a bland identity might provide neither distinctiveness nor direction for strategic decision making. Field research has found considerable variation in diversified firms' identities. Many top managers have reported that their firms' identities are very helpful in guiding diversification strategy, whereas the managers of other firms have indicated concerns about the effectiveness of their firms' identities, with one manager even stating that his firm had an "identity crisis" (Stimpert, 1992).

Barney (1992) has gone even further and suggested that distinctive identities can be a source of high performance for diversified firms. He concluded that diversification strategies based on economies of scale and scope are unlikely to contribute to high performance because these concepts are well-known and readily pursued by most diversified firms. More unique conceptualizations of identity and business unit relatedness may, however, contribute to high performance if they are not only valuable but also difficult for other diversified firms to imitate. These theoretical ideas suggest that relatedness may exist "in the eyes of the beholder," and managers may see and act on understandings of identity and business unit relatedness that have little to do with the conventional conceptualization of relatedness that is found in the diversification research literature (Stimpert & Duhaime, 1997).

Summary

Thus, considerable interest and research findings suggest that organizational identity may have an important, perhaps even a profound, impact on key streams of strategic management research. Research that has incorporated the concept of organizational identity into studies of firm heterogeneity, organizational change and adaptation, and diversification all suggest that identity provides the managers of firms with powerful understandings or theories of who they are. These under-standings guide subsequent resource allocation decisions so that organizations evolve in a particular way that results in interfirm heterogeneity or in particular patterns of diversification and various processes for managing diversification. Furthermore, managers' conceptualizations of identity can both facilitate and hinder the organizational change process. Research suggests that firms can grow and change in ways that are consistent with their identities, but a growing body of evidence also reveals that most firms find it almost impossible to change in ways that are inconsistent with their identities.

Nearly all of the strategy research studies incorporating the concept of identity have highlighted its social nature. The concept of organizational identity is closely tied to managers' own beliefs and understandings. The working definition—*identity is the theory that members of an organization have about who they are*—adopted by those participating in the next chapter suggests the highly social nature of identity. Thus, decisions about resource allocation that reflect an organization's identity will most likely be imbued with a deeper meaning. Sarason's (1997) research on the Baby Bells, for example, found that the managers of each of the companies held surprisingly strong beliefs or convictions about the correctness of their company's particular strategies, and that managers maintained these strong convictions even when expressing doubts about the appropriateness of particular policies or tactics pursued by their firms.

This social nature of identity also helps to explain the problems associated with organizational change and adaptation. Identity is very different from an aging product line that can be more or less easily retooled at low cost. Changing identity involves much more than economic costs; indeed, it can be argued that the costs of changing identity are largely psychological and social rather than economic. Firms thus find it very difficult to change in ways that are inconsistent with their identities because the managers of those firms find the social and psychological tasks of giving up old meanings and accepting new meanings so costly.

WHAT COMMON ASSUMPTIONS
AND THEMES ARE SHARED BY
STRATEGY RESEARCHERS WHO ARE
WORKING WITH THE CONCEPT OF IDENTITY?

Whereas the previous section sought to explain why many strategy researchers find the concept of organizational identity so intriguing, the aim of this section is to describe the broad themes and fundamental assumptions shared by the researchers who participated in the conversational chapter that follows. The rationale for including this section is to provide researchers from outside the strategy field and those strategy researchers who operate from an economics perspective or paradigm with the necessary background for understanding many of the points that will be made in the next chapter.

Readers should see that the researchers who came together at Sundance are bound together by a common set of intellectual beliefs and understandings that led them to focus on process issues and engage in behavioral and sensemaking research. Thus, in many respects, this section serves as a "statement of beliefs" of those strategy researchers who pursue their research interests from a more behavioral or sense-making paradigm.

Research Focus: Process Research
With a Behavioral Lens

The field of strategic management has long differentiated between content and process issues. Strategy content research has traditionally focused on "what" firms do, that is, how the choice of particular strategies leads to more or less optimal performance under varying environmental contexts. In contrast, strategy process research examines "how" firms do what they do, or the administrative systems and decision processes that influence the formulation and implementation of their strategies (Chakravarthy & Doz, 1992).

Using this distinction, most of the strategy participants who have joined in the identity conversation engage in process research, and most would readily subscribe to a number of assumptions underlying most process studies (Pettigrew, 1992):

- Process research requires an appreciation for the importance of temporal interconnectedness, or linkages across the past, the present, and the future.
- Process research involves recognizing the importance of multiple levels of analysis in order to capture the "embeddedness" of strategic processes, and that both managerial discretion *and* organizational and environmental context are important in understanding strategic processes.

In addition to their focus on strategy process, nearly all of the strategy participants at the identity conferences work primarily from a behavioral, rather than an economics, perspective. This behavioral perspective has its roots in the behavioral sciences, borrowing theories and constructs from the fields of psychology, sociology, and political science in developing an understanding of strategic management. For example, whereas strategy researchers working from an economics perspective would employ "objective" measures of industry structure to assess the levels of competition and rivalry in various markets, behavioral researchers draw on psychological theories and constructs to examine how and what managers think about their firms' competitive environments (Porac et al., 1989).

Ontological Affinity:
Sensemaking in Organizations

The group's members also share a common belief in the importance of sensemaking (Weick, 1995). Sensemaking includes the interpretive processes that allow individuals to understand and to share understandings about their organizations' missions, what their organizations do well and not so well, what issues and problems their organizations face, and how these issues and problems should be resolved (Drucker, 1994; Feldman, 1989). The idea of sensemaking is rooted in the interpretivist paradigm, which holds that environments are neither objective nor perceived; instead, the world is enacted through the social construction and interaction processes of organized actors (Daft & Weick, 1984; Smircich & Stubbart, 1985; Weick, 1979). Such a paradigm contrasts sharply with logical positivism, which has dominated both social science research in general and strategic management research in particular (Bettis, 1991).

Thomas, Clark, and Gioia (1993) have described sensemaking as "the reciprocal interaction of information seeking, meaning ascription, and action" (p. 240). Sensemaking research thus focuses on organizational actors and the meanings they construe as they interact with their environments. Nearly all sensemaking studies share several common features (Weick, 1995), and conversations at the identity conferences revealed that many of these same features are inherent in studies of organizational identity. These common features include the following:

- Researchers who work "in close" rather than "from the armchair." Because sensemaking research aims to capture actors' own definitions and understandings, researchers rely less on specified measures and more on actors' narratives (Barry & Elmes, 1997). Specific case studies that are described in the next chapter represent examples of researchers entering organizations and interviewing organizational members.

- Sensemaking research also tends to rely on a small number of cases rather than large cross-sectional samples and databases. In addition, investigators seek to understand both actors and their actions *and* their unique organizational and environmental contexts.

- Sensemaking research also draws on alternative research methodologies. Findings are often described in terms of patterns rather than hypotheses, and explanations are tested as much against common sense and plausibility as against *a priori* theories. Sensemaking researchers seek to mobilize a set of methodological tactics that will allow them to identify meanings, and the density of information and the vividness of meanings are as crucial as precision and replicability.

From Sensemaking to Action:
Seeking to Understand Action by First
Understanding How Managers Think

The interpretive, sensemaking process ultimately seeks to identify those theories of action that guide managers' decisions and behaviors (Hedberg, 1981). Thus, most sensemaking researchers, including most of the strategy researchers participating in the identity conversations, would argue that an understanding of organizational action requires an appreciation for and an understanding of managerial thinking (Weick, 1995). As summarized by Smircich and Stubbart (1985), "Rather than seeking a detached Olympian perspective on an industry or firm, interpretive research explores what strategists were thinking, why they acted as they did, what they wanted to accomplish" (p. 733). This perspective has resulted in a growing body of research examining links between managerial thought and action (Barr et al., 1992; Dutton & Dukerich, 1991; Gioia & Thomas, 1996).

Case Studies and Their Place
in Strategic Management Research

After reviewing these common assumptions held by nearly all of the strategy participants at the identity conferences, it should come as no surprise that most of their empirical studies on organizational identity have used the case study methodology. The advantage that case studies offer over other research methods is the opportunity to draw on the perspectives of organizational members while also understanding organizational contexts (Yin, 1994). Case studies of organizational identity not only allow researchers to interact with managers and other actors, but they also provide researchers with an appreciation of how context and history have both shaped, and been shaped by, individual beliefs.

Indeed, conversations among strategy researchers at the identity conferences were so meaningful *because* many of the participants had conducted case studies examining organizational identity. Several of these studies were either ongoing or recently finished and are referred to throughout the next chapter. These case studies provided anchors that helped to guide the discussion, and they were particularly valuable as the group focused on more abstract or complex issues and questions.

For example, the question of whether organizations could have multiple identities resulted in a highly energized discussion, with some participants arguing that the idea of multiple identities is not useful in understanding relationships between identity and strategy. As participants shared specific cases—one in which Allina Healthcare had combined three separate organizations and another describing how US West had merged three operating companies—that vividly illustrated the presence of multiple identities within a single organization, the larger group began to agree that the idea of multiple identities could be both relevant and useful. Thus, access to rich data provided by case study research allowed the group to engage in more meaningful conversations.

Most of the identity research that has been conducted to date is suggestive of an earlier era of strategy research. Case studies were the major research tool of early business policy scholars, but over the past two decades, strategy research has become more quantitative, adopting methodologies that require constructs and variables that can be both readily and reliably measured. Because the rich contextual information contained in case studies cannot lend itself to easy codification or measurement, this change in research approach meant that much of the richness of case studies was lost. By the late 1980s, Huff and Reger (1987) had already observed that

> the strategy field, up until ten years ago, was dominated by qualitative, comprehensive case studies. Narrowly focused, large sample size, quantitative studies were a welcome balance to these studies. But there is a danger in believing that statistically rigorous, narrowly focused studies are superior to the rich, complicated understanding that results from careful study of a few organizations. Just as broadly focused studies are often open to conflicting interpretations, the tight boundaries that must be drawn around research questions in order to study statistically the relationships between a few variables are artificial ones that may lead researchers to misleading conclusions. (p. 227)

Studies of organizational identity have sought to bridge these two important strategy research traditions, seeking to realize both the richness of the case study methodology while also pursuing a more scientific understanding of organizational phenomena that is typically associated with the more quantitative research tradition.

CONCLUSION

Important work is being pursued by scholars who are incorporating the concept of organizational identity into traditional as well as new streams of strategic management research. This work is generating excitement in the field and offering new insights. A few final observations about the potential contributions of organizational identity conclude this chapter and serve as an introduction for the chapter that follows.

First, the concept of organizational identity is useful for advancing strategic management research. Not only can identity be a potentially important source of sustained competitive advantage, but the concept of organizational identity seems uniquely helpful in addressing some of the more perplexing questions in the strategy field, including why organizations pursue unique patterns of resource allocation. Identity also appears likely to shed new light on understanding strategic change processes. Furthermore, organizational identity shares conceptual affinity with many other ideas and terms, all of which emphasize the importance of imparting meaning to organizations.

Second, like researchers studying managerial and organizational cognition, researchers incorporating the concepts of organizational identity, dominant logic, business definition, and vision into their studies are pursuing new and different ways to study organizations. Identity research is truly *behavioral research* in that it seeks to explain organizational outcomes by first understanding managers' beliefs about what is central and distinctive about their firms. Growing interest in the concept of organizational identity may offer the strategy field a catalyst for studying questions that have been generally regarded as significant yet widely viewed as difficult to study using existing theories and methods.

The aims of this chapter and the more conversational one that follows are to encourage other strategy researchers to build on and enhance early work on organizational identity. The participants in these chapters have followed a number of different paths that led them to the identity conferences that have culminated in the publication of this book. Each participant believes that the concept of organizational identity represents an exciting new lens for studying important questions in the field of strategic management. We will feel that our efforts have been worthwhile if these chapters convey this enthusiasm and encourage others to join in this continuing conversation exploring relationships between organizational identity and strategic management.

REFERENCES

Aaker, D. A. (1989). Managing assets and skills: The key to a sustainable competitive advantage. *California Management Review, 31,* 91-106.

Abell, D. F. (1980). *Defining the business: Starting point of strategic planning.* Englewood Cliffs, NJ: Prentice Hall.

Albert, S., & Whetten, D. (1985). Organizational identity. In L. L. Cummings & B. M. Staw (Eds.), *Research in organizational behavior* (Vol. 7, pp. 263-295). Greenwich, CT: JAI.

Barney, J. B. (1986a). Organizational culture: Can it be a source of sustained competitive advantage? *Academy of Management Review, 11,* 656-665.

Barney, J. B. (1986b). Strategic factor markets: Expectations, luck, and business strategy. *Management Science, 32,* 1231-1241.

Barney, J. B. (1991). Firm resources and sustained competitive advantage. *Journal of Management, 17,* 99-120.

Barney, J. B. (1992). Integrating organizational behavior and strategy formulation research: A resource based analysis. In P. Shrivastava, A. Huff, & J. Dutton (Eds.), *Advances in strategic management* (Vol. 8, pp. 39-62). Greenwich, CT: JAI.

Barr, P. S., Stimpert, J. L., & Huff, A. S. (1992, Summer). Cognitive change, strategic action, and organizational renewal. *Strategic Management Journal, 13,* 15-36.

Barry, D., & Elmes, M. (1997). Strategy retold: Toward a narrative view of strategic discourse. *Academy of Management Review, 22,* 429-452.

Bettis, R. A. (1991). Strategic management and the straight jacket: An editorial essay. *Organization Science, 2,* 315-319.

Chakravarthy, B., & Doz, Y. (1992, Summer). Strategy process research: Focusing on corporate self-renewal. *Strategic Management Journal, 13,* 5-14.

Clark, B. (1970). *The distinctive college.* Chicago: Aldine.

Collins, J. C., & Porras, J. I. (1994). *Built to last.* New York: HarperBusiness.

Daft, R., & Weick, K. (1984). Toward a model of organizations as interpretations systems. *Academy of Management Review, 9,* 284-295.

Dierickx, I., & Cool, K. (1989). Asset stock accumulation and sustainability of competitive advantage. *Management Science, 35,* 1504-1511.

Drucker, P. F. (1994). The theory of the business. *Harvard Business Review, 72*(5), 95-104.

Dutton, J. E., & Dukerich, J. M. (1991). Keeping an eye on the mirror: Image and identity in organizational adaptation. *Academy of Management Journal, 34,* 517-554.

Dutton, J. E., Dukerich, J. M., & Harquail, C. V. (1994). Organizational images and member identification. *Administrative Science Quarterly, 39,* 239-263.

Dutton, J. E., & Penner, W. J. (1993). The importance of organizational identity for strategic agenda building. In J. Hendry & G. Johnson with J. Newton (Eds.), *Strategic thinking: Leadership and the management of change* (pp. 89-113). Chichester, UK: John Wiley.

Feldman, M. S. (1989). *Order without design.* Stanford, CA: Stanford University Press.

Gioia, D. A., & Thomas, J. B. (1996). Identity, image, and issue interpretation: Sensemaking during strategic change in academia. *Administrative Science Quarterly, 41,* 370-403.

Gustafson, L. T. (1995). *The structure and content of organizational identity in hypercompetitive environments.* Unpublished doctoral dissertation, Arizona State University, Tempe.

Hall, R. (1992). The strategic analysis of intangible resources. *Strategic Management Journal, 13,* 135-144.

Hedberg, B. (1981). How organizations learn and unlearn. In P. C. Nystrom & W. H. Starbuck (Eds.), *Handbook of organizational design* (Vol. 1, pp. 3-27). New York: Oxford University Press.

Huff, A. S., & Reger, R. K. (1987). A review of strategy process research. *Journal of Management, 13,* 211-236.

Itami, H. (1987). *Mobilizing invisible assets.* Cambridge, MA: Harvard University Press.

Lippman, S. A., & Rumelt, R. P. (1982). Uncertain imitability: An analysis of interfirm differences in efficiency under competition. *Bell Journal of Economics, 13,* 418-438.

Mahoney, J. T., & Pandian, J. R. (1992). The resource-based view within the conversation of strategic management. *Strategic Management Journal, 13,* 363-380.

Mintzberg, H. (1978). Patterns in strategy formation. *Management Science, 24,* 934-948.

Nelson, R. R., & Winter, S. G. (1982). *An evolutionary theory of economic change.* Boston: Belknap.

Pettigrew, A. M. (1992, Winter). The character and significance of strategy process research. *Strategic Management Journal, 13,* 5-16.

Porac, J. F., Thomas, H., & Baden-Fuller, C. (1989). Competitive groups as cognitive communities: The case of Scottish knitwear manufacturers. *Journal of Management, 26,* 397-416.

Porter, M. E. (1980). *Competitive strategy.* New York: Free Press.

Prahalad, C. K., & Bettis, J. (1986). The dominant logic: A new linkage between diversity and performance. *Strategic Management Journal, 7,* 485-502.

Reger, R. K., Gustafson, L. T., DeMarie, S. M., & Mullane, J. V. (1994). Reframing the organization: Why implementing total quality is easier said than done. *Academy of Management Review, 19,* 565-584.

Rumelt, R. P., Schendel, D. E., & Teece, D. J. (1994). Afterword. In R. P. Rumelt, D. E. Schendel, & D. J. Teece (Eds.), *Fundamental issues in strategy* (pp. 527-555). Boston: Harvard Business School Press.

Sarason, Y. (1997). *Identity and the Baby Bells: Applying structuration theory to strategic management.* Unpublished doctoral dissertation, University of Colorado, Boulder.

Schoemaker, P. J. H. (1990). Strategy, complexity and economic rent. *Management Science, 36,* 1178-1192.

Senge, P. M. (1990). *The fifth discipline: The art and practice of the learning organization.* New York: Currency/Doubleday.

Smircich, L., & Stubbart, C. (1985). Strategic management in an enacted world. *Academy of Management Review, 10,* 724-736.

Stimpert, J. L. (1992). *Managerial thinking and large diversified firms.* Unpublished doctoral dissertation, University of Illinois at Urbana-Champaign.

Stimpert, J. L., & Duhaime, I. M. (1997). In the eyes of the beholder: Conceptualizations of relatedness held by the managers of large diversified firms. *Strategic Management Journal, 18,* 111-125.

Thomas, J. B., Clark, S. M., & Gioia, D. A. (1993). Strategic sensemaking and organizational performance: Linkages among scanning, interpretation, action and outcomes. *Academy of Management Journal, 36,* 239-270.

Walsh, J. P. (1995). Managerial and organizational cognition: Notes from a trip down memory lane. *Organization Science, 6,* 280-321.

Weick, K. E. (1979). *The social psychology of organizing* (2nd ed.). Reading, MA: Addison-Wesley.

Weick, K. E. (1995). *Sensemaking in organizations.* Thousand Oaks, CA: Sage.

Wernerfelt, B. (1984). A resource-based view of the firm. *Strategic Management Journal, 5,* 171-180.

Yin, R. D. (1994). *Case study research: Design and methods* (2nd ed.). Thousand Oaks, CA: Sage.

5

A Strategy Conversation on the Topic of Organization Identity

---

Parties to the Conversation:

Jay B. Barney, J. Stuart Bunderson, Peter Foreman,

Loren T. Gustafson, Anne S. Huff, Luis L. Martins,

Rhonda K. Reger (moderator), Yolanda Sarason,

J. L. "Larry" Stimpert

Rather than preface our conversation with a note focusing on themes and process, as requested by Dave and Paul, I think the best way to introduce our conversation is to assume the role of host and to introduce my fellow conversationalists. If you really want an outline, most of what you need to know about our approach, our questions, and our grounding in case research is found in the introductory section of the conversation.

When you join a conversation, you are not usually given a thematic outline, but rather your host provides short introductions so that you have some background from which to interpret everyone's comments. So, let me tell something about the participants in this conversation. They are all my friends, and remember, this introduction is entirely from my perspective.

In alphabetical order, I start with Jay Barney. Even though I know Jay well, I had always thought of him as an economist (with all the negative connotations that should evoke for someone who claims a psychological bent). I have to admit that I was concerned when I learned that Jay would be part of our conversation. I respected him enormously, but I worried that he would push us to be overly rational and needlessly objective. Jay really surprised me here: He talks of passion and morality, of meaning and stories! He also brought the best of economics and pushed us to be disciplined in our thinking, which was also a big plus. Now I think of Jay as a very smart theorist who happens to be well-grounded in economics. Oh yes, Jay is Mr. Resource-Based Theory of the Firm, and, no surprise here, that perspective came to color our conversation. Again, however, that was a big plus.

Stu Bunderson is studying health care organizations at the University of Minnesota and is working with Andy Van de Ven. I don't know Stu as well as most of the other participants, so it is harder for me to give a thumbnail sketch. I can say that, like the other doctoral students in the conversation, he added new perspectives and a fresh, exciting voice. Like everyone else in the group, I like Stu a lot, and I hope I have the chance to collaborate with him on future projects.

Peter Foreman is a doctoral student in organization theory at the University of Illinois. He worked with Dave Whetten researching agricultural co-ops before Dave left the subtle beauty of the prairie for spectacular Rocky Mountain vistas. Peter knows Dave's thoughts about organization identity in the very rich, nuanced way that only comes from hours together in a cold Illinois office, grappling together over real, live, fascinating cases and elegant, promising, but not-quite-there theory. Peter has a way of cutting to the nub of the matter. He brings a sociological perspective that is quite foreign to me, which makes talking with him especially interesting.

Loren Gustafson is an assistant professor of strategic management at Seattle Pacific University, his undergraduate alma mater. He completed his dissertation on organization identity under my direction at Arizona State University, and we have written several papers together. For us, this conversation is a 2-day slice in a multiyear dialogue. Like almost everyone who recently completed an excellent dissertation, Loren's tacit knowledge exceeds his explicit knowledge—he knows more than he knows he knows about organization identity. What is really interesting to me in the conversation that follows is to see how others in the conversation elicited new insights from Loren about topics we had discussed countless times before. It is true, you learn new things about old collaborators by watching them collaborate with others.

Anne Huff was my dissertation chair. I realize this is not the most important thing about Anne; surely, it is not central to her identity as a scholar. But it is central to my identity as a scholar, and I am making the introductions. What is interesting to me is that Anne chaired both my dissertation and Marlene Fiol's in the mid 1980s; we were all interested in managerial cognition. But as far as I can remember, the term *organization identity* never even came up in all those years when we were huddled together in Anne's basement office in Illinois. Yet here we are almost 10 years later, long since moved from Illinois and moving away from the topics we worked on together. Now, separately, we are energized by the promise of identity to help us find new answers to old questions. I could tell you any number of things about Anne, but the most important thing for understanding her role in this conversation is that Anne is the most thoughtful academic I know.

Luis Martins was a doctoral student at New York University working with Charles Fombrun on organization reputation at the time of this conversation. He recently accepted a strategic management position at the University of Connecticut. I did not fully appreciate it at the time of the conversation, but while editing the transcripts, I found that Luis made several truly insightful comments. I wish the group had followed up on more of them. At my suggestion, he wrote a comment on the conversation titled "Organizational Identity as a Strategic Buffer."

Yolanda Sarason is an assistant professor of strategic management at the University of New Mexico. I feel a special bond with her because she completed her dissertation under Anne's direction at the University of Colorado at Boulder. Marlene was a member of her committee. So, although I didn't know Yolanda very well personally, I immediately felt our common intellectual heritage. Her research on U S WEST is incredibly rich, and her understanding of the management of identity is wonderfully sophisticated. It is fun to watch her and Anne play off each other.

Larry Stimpert is an old pal of mine. He started the strategy doctoral program at Illinois just as I was finishing up, so we were not in residence at the same time. We have published together and continue to work together, but not on identity research. I am not quite sure how Larry got mixed up in this identity crowd, but he knows a lot about the management of diversification, has talked to a lot of managers about their thinking on diversification, and, of course, has a really great article on how managerial schemas affect change (Barr, Stimpert, & Huff, 1992). Larry teaches strategy at Colorado College.

Finally, about me. I came to the study of identity in a very odd way. More than a decade ago, I borrowed the methodology from George Kelly's personal construct theory (a theory of self-identity) to study strategic groups. In sort of the mirror image of how Jay is approaching organization identity, I took a cognitive psychologist's point of view to study what most people thought were economic issues. About 5 years ago, I became interested in what a firm must do internally to change its strategic position, to move from one strategic group to another. Right under my nose, I found Kelly's identity theory. More recently, I have been reading other psychological theories of self-identity. For me, it is hard to think about identity as anything other than a psychological construct.

I became the "leader" of this group because Dave called me up a couple of weeks before the meeting and asked me to do it. A rule that has served me well is "Never say no to Dave" because he always has really creative, fascinating ideas. Also, 15 years ago, he gave me my first job in teaching, and I was so bad I still owe him for not firing me. I was also intrigued by the whole idea of "leading" a scripted conversation—whatever that was!

As far as process goes, our group was extremely self-organizing. I, the appointed leader, was not even there the first evening when those who were in attendance formed natural affinity conversations that only loosely mirrored the carefully crafted groups Dave and Paul intended. I have heard lots of stories about the founding of our group, but interestingly, the stories conflict, except on two points. Everyone in the group was uncomfortable with the "practice of" label that Paul and Dave originally intended, and everyone had rich, firsthand accounts of identity in interesting organizations that they wanted to share. The latter, I think, was our natural affinity.

Over the course of 2 days, our nine disparate academics forged an identity, complete with intellectual, emotional, and moral bonds. And at a beautiful mountain resort high above Provo, we had a fun, lively, and quite satisfying conversation about identity.

From time to time, I break into this conversation, take you aside, so to speak, when I think the conversation might be hard to follow if you had not been part of the full 2 days. What follows is a transcript of our final conversation as a group. In it, we summarize the key ideas we discussed throughout the weekend. I have also done a little editing to improve the readability of the original, spoken language. Now, come join us.

Rhonda: Okay, this is the very beginning of . . .

Jay: . . . of Rhonda Reger's group. [Laughter.]

Rhonda: Of Rhonda Reger's group. Make it clear that this is *my* group. [More laughter.]

Peter: The Reger think-tank.

Rhonda: We have been thinking of ourselves as the strategy group, and our view is that we are bringing a third perspective on identity issues. We'll organize our conversation around seven questions.

Jay: Also, our conversation will be grounded in a number of case studies various members of our group have conducted on organizational identity. Some of these will appear as sidebars throughout our conversation.

Rhonda: That's right. Jay's studied Koch Industries, Yolanda's dissertation examined U S WEST, Stu studied Allina Healthcare, Loren's dissertation looked at Intel, Peter is looking at a number of agricultural co-ops, and Luis's dissertation examines business schools.

Peter: It is important to note we aren't just talking about profit-driven manufacturing firms. Koch Industries is privately held and is a quite diversified oil and gas company, U S WEST is a service firm in the telecommunications industry, Intel is primarily a semiconductor manufacturer, Allina Healthcare is partly for-profit and partly not-for-profit, and co-ops are purely nonprofit ventures.

Rhonda: And Luis has studied business schools that are part of public and private universities. What is interesting is that we have covered a wide range of organizational forms and settings. Everyone in this conversation has studied organizational identity in real organizations.

We will organize our conversation around seven key questions. The first four questions we will discuss cover some of the basics. First, so that everyone knows what we are talking about when we say things like "organizational identity" or "strategy," what are our working definitions? Second, given these austere definitions, can we describe organizational identity in greater depth so that others can study it? Third, how is identity created and articulated in organizations? And fourth, is identity a source of competitive advantage? Or more precisely, when is organizational identity a source of competitive advantage, and when is it a source of competitive *dis*advantage? Throughout the discussion of these four questions, we will talk quite a bit about the relationship between identity and strategy.

Once we lay that basic foundation, we will tackle three more questions. The fifth question is, "How does identity change?" This was such an important question to us that we will have two subgroups talk about change and identity. The sixth question is, "How are multiple identities managed?" We will end with the final question, "How is identity used to manage complexity?"

So, Jay, are we ready?

Jay: Oh, I think we're ready!

Rhonda: Our working definitions.

QUESTION 1: WORKING DEFINITIONS

Jay: It is my opportunity to talk about working definitions. Our primary task is to try to understand the implications of organization identity for management, strategy, and other practice questions within a theoretical context. But to do that, of course, one has to have definitions of these primitives in our analysis: things like "What is organization identity?" and "What is strategy?" Early on, on Friday evening, we agreed to adopt a couple of definitions. Throughout the weekend, we revisited these definitions. To summarize a long dialogue, we found these definitions to be quite fruitful and quite important and have illuminated a lot of our discussions.

The first definition is the definition of *organizational identity.* We defined that as *the theory members of an organization have about who they are.* Let's be clear by what we mean by the term *theory* here. The theory does not have to be always broadly understood, it does not have to be explicit. Sometimes, it is implicit, sometimes taken for granted, sometimes, there is disagreement among the individuals within a firm about what that theory is. But we like the notion of a theory because one has to tell a story about who one is and what one stands for in some sense. Building on that same logic, *strategy is defined as a theory of actions that the firm should take or can take.* Again, for our discussion, strategy is *members'* theory of action. So, we start with two agreed-upon definitions: the theory of action on the strategy side and the theory of who we are, the theory of identity, on the identity side.

Anne: Strategy is a theory of action—*to gain some desired outcome.*

Jay: Right, some desired outcome. The desired outcome, since this is a strategy group, is assumed to be competitive advantage. We will talk about that a fair amount later. There has been some discussion when we get together with the other two discussion groups about the viability of these working definitions. Certainly, some groups are spending much more time trying to unpack different definitions to understand their subtleties. There is certainly value to that.

We are taking a slightly different approach. We are going to stick a stake in the ground as to some definitions that we have found fruitful and practical that allow us to say what we think are interesting theoretical things about identity and strategy. This does not discount the value of the other approach, of spending more time on definitions. We are taking a more pragmatic view. We would like our definitions to be evaluated in terms of their fruitfulness, their ability to generate interesting insights. That would be the test we are looking for.

Rhonda: Any observations about these definitions before we move on?

Stu: We also have a working definition about image. An organization's image is the members' theory of what other people think of the organization. That was also woven into some of our earlier conversations.

Luis: As a theory, it is also very important to draw attention to the idea of identity and strategy as sensemaking. We are talking about how members of an organization make sense of their organization, their environment, their situation overall.

Rhonda: I also want to note that calling identity a theory of self isn't something we made up here at this meeting. The basic idea is theoretically grounded in cognitive psychology and theories about personal identity. When George Kelly (1955) wrote about personal identity, he described it as an individual's personal theory of self. Kelly's notion of "man-the-scientist" is very old. So, when we put our stake in the ground on these definitions of identity and strategy as members' theories of self and action, we are on solid ground. Again, I want to echo Jay, these theories can be highly articulated and thought about, or they can be implicit.

One last point on definitions—we recognize that many definitions of identity and strategy exist. Everyone at this table has done research on organizational identity, and our working definitions—our stakes in the ground, as Jay puts it—have allowed us to get moving. They have allowed us to conduct interesting, fruitful research.

Jay: We have our working definitions. We also recognize that these definitions are very odd, very austere, but they are useful. Next, we will have Rhonda talk about some of the dimensions on which these definitions can vary. Rowdy Rhonda!

QUESTION 2: HOW CAN WE DESCRIBE
ORGANIZATION IDENTITY IN GREATER DEPTH?

[There were several themes that came out over and over again in our conversations during the conference. First, as is clear from our definitions, we decided not to use Albert and Whetten's definition of organizational identity. Their definition of organization identity is that which members believe is central, enduring, and distinctive about their organization. It is not that we thought the definition was

TABLE 5.1 Dimensions of Organization Identity

1. Homogeneity: members of the organization share a common set of beliefs about the organization's identity
2. Intensity (Conviction): strength of belief and degree of positive affect toward the identity
3. Complexity: number of beliefs that comprise the identity and the number of identities
4. Abstractness: extent to which the identity is couched in abstract language
5. Content: what the identity is
6. Context: the internal and external context, identity is path dependent

wrong, but rather, we had two issues. First, central, enduring, and distinctive are characteristics or variables that could describe a firm's identity, but not the definition of identity per se. For instance, firms can vary in how distinctive members believe the fundamental nature of their organization is compared to other organizations. Second, from comparing our case studies, it became clear to us that central, enduring, and distinctive are not the only dimensions along which organization identity varies. The following are the dimensions that emerged in our group.]

Rhonda: Over the course of the last 2 days, I've kept track of the various characteristics of identity we discussed. These characteristics, summarized in Table 5.1, can be thought of as components or dimensions of identity. These six are not part of the definition of identity, but these are important ways that organization identity can vary.

The first dimension is *homogeneity*. Organizational identity varies in terms of the degree that it is shared by people within the organization. A second way identity can vary is how strongly the beliefs are held—the *intensity* or *conviction*. Intensity is the belief of, "Yes, this is our identity," and the second part of conviction is, "Yes, this is a good identity to have."

The third dimension is the *complexity* of the identity. Complexity can vary from either a simple set of beliefs to a highly complex set, or it can vary from a single, unified identity to multiple identities. All of these would add to the complexity of the identity of the organization.

The fourth dimension is what we call *abstractness*. This is something I've been working on with Loren. We don't think this is the best name, but we don't have anything better for the moment. In terms of abstractness, an identity can focus on specific, concrete things or on abstract, intangible ideas. For example, Koch was founded with a very concrete belief that they were an oil and gas company. Koch later moved to a more abstract identity—"We are a discovery company." The term *discovery* can have many more meanings than "oil and gas."

Koch Industries: Organizational Identity as Moral Philosophy

JAY BARNEY

This case illustrates organizational identity as a core competence uniting otherwise disparate businesses in a diversified corporation. This case also demonstrates that for very highly diversified firms, organizational identity, in order to act as a core competence, must be defined in very abstract terms, and one way that this can be done is to define organizational identity in terms of moral philosophy—a statement about right and wrong around which employees in a diversified firm can rally and a statement that can help determine their behavior.

ORGANIZATIONAL IDENTITY AT KOCH INDUSTRIES

Koch Industries is a diversified firm headquartered in Wichita, Kansas, operating in the oil, gas, oil and gas derivatives, and agricultural products industries. Koch Industries is the second largest privately held company in the United States. Eighty-five percent of Koch Industry stock is owned by Charles Koch, who is currently the CEO and chairman of the board. Since inheriting the company at the time of his father's death in 1967, Charles—as he is known to Koch employees around the world—has presided over a 100-fold increase in sales at Koch Industries. In 1966, Koch Industries had $177 million in sales; in 1996, they had more than $27 billion in sales. In 1967, Koch employed 650 people; Koch currently employs more than 13,000. An intensely private man, Charles Koch is also one of the wealthiest men in the world.

Charles attributes much of the success at Koch Industries to a management style he calls "market-based management." Market-based management, in turn, is Charles's solution to a fundamental conundrum. On one hand, the virtues of market capitalism—as an engine of progress, as a way to allocate scarce resources, and as a way to promote individual freedom—are impossible to deny. In an important sense, the collapse of the Soviet Union is irrefutable empirical evidence of the inherent superiority of market capitalism over other forms of economic exchange. On the other hand, even casual observation suggests that the simple market capitalism described by Adam Smith—with small shopkeepers and manufacturers responding to the "invisible hand" of supply and demand—does not exist. Instead, huge multinational corporations, some with sales in excess of the gross national products of many medium-sized countries, compete in global markets. The sheer size of these corporations suggests that much value creation in the modern economy occurs within managerial hierarchies and not across markets. And many of these managerial hierarchies are characterized by highly centralized decision making, a change-resistant bureaucracy, and uninformed and underappreciated workers—the very attributes of nonmarket economies that ultimately led to their competitive failure. Is it really possible to have market capitalism when markets are populated with inefficient, bureaucratic, centrally planned corporations?

Market-based management is Charles's answer to this question. Market-based management does not seek to recreate market exchanges within an organization. After all, as Williamson (1995) has shown, if it were possible to perfectly create market exchanges within a corporation, then these exchanges should not occur within the corporation but across a market. Rather, market-based management seeks to derive principles from the analysis of market efficiency and to adapt those principles in the context of an organization. Some of the key tenets of market-based management, derived from the analysis of market efficiency, include the following:

1. All decisions made in an organization should focus on maximizing the net present value of the firm.
2. Decisions should be made by those people in an organization who have the local knowledge necessary to make present-value-maximizing decisions, regardless of their rank or status.
3. Compensation should be directly tied to the ability of individuals in a firm to maximize the present value of the firm.
4. Management control mechanisms should focus on measuring those aspects of behavior that are most directly linked to maximizing present value (i.e., focus on economic value added, not accounting measures of performance).
5. Present-value-maximizing decisions need to be consistent with rules of just conduct to ensure that fair and appropriate decisions are made.
6. Success is only possible if employees are intellectually honest, humble, and respect the contributions made by unique individuals throughout the firm.

These principles lead to what many firms might conclude are unusual management practices at Koch Industries. For example, Koch invests heavily in training its employees. Much of this training focuses on microeconomic theory and net present value analysis—training that is given to managers, secretaries, and janitors at all levels. Koch's objective is that employees see their job in terms of how it affects the present value of the firm, no matter what that job is.

Koch has no budgets nor budget systems. Senior management at Koch decided to abandon budgets for several reasons. First, they concluded that budgeting, per se, makes no money for Koch. Second, they observed that budgets assume that all the critical information needed to make a decision is available at the time a budget is set in stone. That assumption is simply not true in most of Koch's markets. Rather than engaging in the fiction adopted by most firms—where budgets are set and then adjusted when new information becomes available—Koch simply does not have budgets.

Finally, budgeting is, according to Koch management, inconsistent with delegating decision-making authority to those people with the local knowledge needed to make a decision. Rather than constraining those individuals to budget targets, Koch expects its employees to constantly make decisions that maximize the present value of the firm. Indeed, the only way to ensure long-term employment at Koch is to demonstrate the ability to add economic value to the firm over the long run.

Finally, despite being highly diversified, Koch Industries has not adopted a multidivisional organizational structure. Rather, they have adopted a functional organizational structure, a structure that requires employees at Koch to coordinate with numerous other employees in numerous different functions in order to accomplish anything. This helps ensure the free flow of ideas that is necessary if Koch is to take full advantage of its economic opportunities and the skills and knowledge of its employees.

In the end, market-based management is more than just a management system derived from the study of market economies. As Charles says, market-based management is "a framework, a philosophy, a methodology." It is an organizational identity that employees can accept and believe in, something greater than their narrow self-interest, something that connects employees to each other and to Charles Koch. It is a statement of values and beliefs, and it helps define a moral code of behavior within the firm. Market-based management goes beyond describing an economically efficient way to manage a diversified corporation—it helps define the "right and wrong" of working in a modern corporation. The power of this moral philosophy is, perhaps, best revealed in a common answer to a simple question often addressed to Koch employees: "Why do you work so hard?" That answer is, more often than not, "I just can't imagine letting Charles Koch down."

ORGANIZATIONAL IDENTITY AND
DIVERSIFICATION STRATEGY

One way to think about organizational identity as moral philosophy is as a solution to an organizational control problem in a large, diversified corporation. In general, for a diversification strategy to be economically valuable, that strategy must realize economies of scope that outside investors could not realize on their own (Barney, 1997). Economies of scope can take many forms, including operating economies (e.g., shared activities in multiple businesses, shared core competencies that cut across several businesses); financial economies (e.g., efficient internal capital allocation); and anticompetitive economies (e.g., multipoint competition and mutual forbearance). In moderately diversified firms, it is usually possible to identify potential economies of scope and work toward realizing those economies through appropriate organizational control systems.

Suppose that a firm needs to pursue a highly diversified corporate strategy. This is the case in a privately held firm like Koch Industries. In most publicly held firms, most shareholders can hold a highly diversified portfolio of stocks, thereby reducing the firm-specific risk they would otherwise have to absorb. The owners of privately held firms may not have this option, because much of their wealth may be tied up in owning the firm. Thus, for the owner of a privately held firm to gain the benefits of diversification while maintaining ownership control, this type of a firm must engage in relatively high levels of diversification.

However, the management challenges for realizing economies of scope in highly diversified firms remain, despite the fact that it may be in the self-interest of the privately held firm to be highly diversified. How can economies of scope be realized in this high-diversification context? One tool for accomplishing this may be organizational identity. By possessing a clear organization identity, a firm can give guidance to employees in their decision making that otherwise would not be appropriate.

In this sense, organizational identity can be understood as a core competence in an organization, as the collective learning that links and is shared among the businesses owned by a diversified firm. Of course, as a firm becomes progressively more diversified, this unifying identity must become more abstract to include multiple businesses. Based on the principles of market-based management, Koch Industries has attempted to develop this kind of organizational identity. Using Charles Koch's language, Koch Industries sees itself as a "Discovery Company."

This identity as a "Discovery Company" has a profound impact on behavior inside Koch. One implication of this identity is that the Koch employees are not just supposed to efficiently execute established routines—they are constantly supposed to be discovering new routines, new ways of adding value to the firm, new businesses where their skills can be leveraged. Market-based management, by itself, would not necessarily lead to rapid growth. An organizational identity as a Discovery Company would not necessarily lead to high profitability. However, by combining market-based management with the identity of being a "Discovery Company," a clear message is sent: At Koch, all employees are expected to constantly search for profitable ways to grow the firm.

REFERENCES

Barney, J. B. (1997). *Creating and sustaining competitive advantage.* Reading, MA: Addison-Wesley.

Williamson, O. E. (1995). *Markets and hierarchies: Analysis and antitrust implications.* New York: Free Press.

The fifth dimension is something that we call *content,* but again, I don't think anyone is satisfied with that label. One aspect we are trying to capture here is internal versus external focus. We think it is important that organizations vary in how much their identity is affected by what others think of them, how much they pay attention to image, how much they are looking for validation from outsiders in terms of their identity.

Yolanda: Could you elaborate on what you mean by "content"? I'm not sure we are being clear about everything we mean.

Rhonda: Well, this is the area where our earlier discussions were fuzzy. To elaborate, let me back up to our most primitive question. We began our conversation with a simple question: "What is identity?" The answer from our group is equally simple, yet quite powerful: Organization identity is a member's theory of who the organization is. In that definition of organization identity, we don't make any assumptions about the content of the identity. Members of organizations can answer the question "Who are we?" in very different ways, and it will still be identity. Having said that, we ask if there are systematic ways that content varies across organizations. And can these systematic differences in content differentially provide competitive advantage? One key factor we were able to tease out was abstractness, and I made that a separate dimension in Table 5.1. Another factor is this notion of internal versus external—how much does the organization monitor and react to what others think? Luis's dissertation research provides a good example.

Luis: Two business schools I studied extensively were Harvard and Wharton. As you know, Harvard has been considered the undisputed number one business school in the world for a long time. But when *Business Week* published its ranking of best business schools in 1988, Harvard ranked number two, and by 1994 had dropped to number five. Wharton, on the other hand, also long considered a top business school, has risen from the number four spot in *Business Week*'s rankings in 1988 to number one in 1994. The rankings can be considered "reputation"—what others think about the organization. I studied the identity of Harvard and Wharton and whether their identities were affected by the reputational rankings. Interestingly, both of these business schools appear to be similar on all the other dimensions listed in Table 5.1, but yet Harvard was very slow to change in response to the reputational ratings—both in terms of the reputation affecting their identity and in terms of the rankings affecting their actions.

Wharton has been much more responsive to the rankings. I think the difference is in their identities. Harvard seems to be internally focused: "Our identity, which we are happy with, is we are an educational institution, we are the experts with all the answers." This aspect of the content of Wharton's identity is quite different: "We are a responsive organization, we respond to external constituencies." Because of that content, Wharton has been much more responsive in changing its strategies, its actions. For example, by the time Harvard made a decision to change its MBA curriculum in 1994, Wharton had already instituted massive changes in curriculum that helped vault it to the number one spot in the rankings.

Rhonda: There are other aspects of content that are also important, so we'll just leave the label "content" for now.

Finally, there is another factor important to understanding identity. I'm not sure we think of it as a variable, but it is an important characteristic of identity. It cuts across everything we've said: Identity is within a context, both an internal context and an external context. Part of context is the idea that identity is path and time dependent.

Peter: So we have the ultimate disclaimer, everything's context-dependent? [Laughter.]

Jay: No . . . everything depends, though. [More laughter.]

Anne: This is a point that bothers our colleagues who are only convinced by large-scale studies. When we say identity is context and path dependent, we are saying it is important to understand quite a bit about the specific circumstances of every organization we study. I like to see work that approaches an issue from many different perspectives, and surely there is room for large-scale correlational studies in identity research. But the point here is that the antecedents, consequences, and effects of identity are different for every organization. When we say "path dependent," we mean what happens at founding matters, and the history of the organization matters. But it doesn't mean identity can't be changed, or that current context doesn't matter. Sometimes, the researcher might want to look historically at what the organization's identity has been in the past; for other purposes, it is more informative to let current members tell you their interpretation of what the organization's past identity was.

Rhonda: Another aspect of the time dimension has to do with the future. What do members think are the future possibilities for the organization? What do they think is ideal? Obtainable? These kinds of questions haven't been asked much in the strategy literature, but they are vital for understanding why some firms seize opportunities and other firms seem not to even notice them.

Now that we have our definitions and the components of identity that emerged during our earlier conversations, we can move on to some of the interesting implications of organization identity for action and performance.

###

QUESTION 3: HOW IS IDENTITY CREATED AND ARTICULATED?

###

Luis: As a theory, it is important to note that sensemaking is extremely important when you talk about identity, so identity is a product of a process of sensemaking.

Anne: But, in fact, Weick (1995) argues that you cannot make sense without some sense of who you are, and I think that's important.

Luis: Would it then be an emergent process of going back and forth between identity as a precursor and product of sensemaking?

Anne: Right. In order to exist, you have to act, and to act, you have to have some sense of who you are and some sense of what you are trying to do. So, both identity and strategy, as we have defined these terms, are sensemaking activities. Identity may be not very well articulated, it may not be in the forefront of consciousness, but the notion is that sensemaking does depend upon having some sense of self.

Luis: I agree, and organization identity, a theory of the self, is what you are calling a sense of self. And as you said, it might be shared or not shared.

Rhonda: In terms of how identity is created in the first place, there is very wide variance in the founders' heedfulness. Some organizations are founded with an extremely conscious, deliberate sense of identity. For example, the founders of the

SUNDANCE

The History of
SUNDANCE

Centuries ago, the Ute Indians retreated to this canyon to escape the summer heat and hunt the abundant game. By the beginning of the twentieth century, the Stewarts, a family of Scottish immigrants, had settled the canyon. While the first generation were mostly surveyors and sheepherders, the next generation of Stewarts opened Timphaven, a local ski resort which boasted a chair lift, a rope tow, and a burger joint named
Ki-Te-Kai-Maori for "Come and get it!"

In 1969, Robert Redford bought Timphaven and much of the surrounding land from the Stewart family. Redford says his newly acquired land is an ideal locale for environmental conservation and artistic expression.

As with most experiments, there were a few early setbacks. A dinner/movie night was abandoned when waiters repeatedly collided in the darkness. A mountain man rendezvous never saw past the first year because the deafening roar of musket and cannon competition sent both wild and domestic animals scrambling for the Wyoming border.

Years of experimentation and refinement have ultimately resulted in what we now call Sundance. The Sundance Institute, the spectacular skiing, the stunning natural scenery, and the tasteful excellence of the accommodations combine to make Sundance dynamically unique. It is the blending of process and place which puts Sundance in uncharted waters, on a steady course of its own.

Our community should represent who we are and what we believe in. Sundance is an arts community, a recreational community, a community of people who appreciate the beauty of nature and feel responsible to preserve it.

For years, we knew that without overnight accommodations, the Sundance experience was incomplete. To miss the brilliance of the rising moon, and sunny calm of morning is to miss the subtle moments which make Sundance so special. The simplicity of space and the integrity of the original landscape were guiding principles during the development of the cottages.

We want to help you find those elements of the Sundance experience which will most likely fulfill your needs. As you'll see, Sundance has many shapes, many moods, and many possibilities. Somewhere in our community awaits an experience which belongs to you, and we are committed to helping you find it.

Figure 5.1.

United States were quite thoughtful about what kind of institutions they were creating and what they stood for. On a more mundane level, the Sundance Resort, where these meetings are being held, is another good example of heedful attention to identity at founding. When Robert Redford bought this property, he had very definite ideas about the values he wanted to preserve. Things like respecting the environment and keeping this a beautiful, peaceful place (Fig. 5.1).

On the other hand, organization identity might not be on a founder's mind at all. She may just be thinking, "I just know I hate my job, so I'm starting my own company."

Jay: Which is an identity.

Peter: An anti-identity, actually, is what it is.

Rhonda: Almost an anti-identity, but not . . .

Jay: We're not x.

Rhonda: "We're not x" could be a heedful identity. There is also a less conscious approach. It could be that the entrepreneur doesn't think about identity at all. They could say, "We're just a firm and we're doing these things" or "We are just a bookstore" or "We're just a whatever," without really thinking through these notions. Many owners are very tied up in action and performance and survival. In these cases, it could be that identity is later created through reinterpretation of actions taken or because of stress or crisis. Only then do you think: "Wait a second, we have been acting, but mindlessly acting. We need to decide, in a very purposeful way, who we are and why we do things."

Larry: There are two points that are important to me in this discussion of the unfolding of identity. One is the notion that while stress forges and really creates identity, there can also be long periods of taken-for-grantedness. We need to make it explicit that during times of taken-for-grantedness, there can be decay in identity, as we've seen with the co-ops case. Another linkage that is implicit in our thinking is the linkage between identity and strategy. You have to know who you are before you can take action. What we have seen in some of our cases is that once companies answer that question of who we are, once companies have asked that question, it is very easy then to say what we must do. The theory of what we should do follows pretty quickly from the theory of who we are. At the same time, the downside is, once you lose that understanding of who we are, it can become paralyzing for a company.

Anne: It is also true, though, that a company can start out with a clear theory of action, and then the theory of who we are develops out of that action.

Peter: Or, in the process of attempting to respond to a strategic threat and form a theory of action, the members of a corporation have to ask themselves: "Well, wait a minute. We really didn't question who we are."

Loren: Another assumption is that when one exists, one acts. Existing is acting. The theory of action then requires a corresponding theory of identity. You start to see the reciprocal interdependence. The reciprocal interdependence is graphically displayed in Figure 5.2. You start to see the path dependence.

Another point is the fact that although there are multiple entry points for managers to intervene to influence identity in a heedful way, it does not necessarily imply that management should or needs to or will choose to intervene at all of these points. There may be selective intervention.

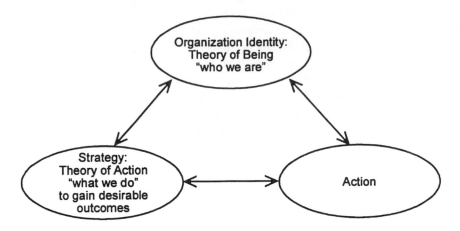

Figure 5.2.

Jay: Or there may be no intervention.

Loren: Or no intervention. So it may be that management is involved every step along the way. Management may be very active in attempting to shape the creation, the articulation, or the altering of identity. On the other hand, managers may simply interpret or attempt to make sense out of some of the stress that is occurring from one or more various sources, and the new identity will emerge relatively automatically.

Rhonda: These ideas on the interplay of identity and strategy, thought and action, are great. I know we will elaborate on them more when Stu and Anne talk about approaches to managing and changing identity. But before we get too far down that path, I want to summarize our thoughts on how identity is created and articulated, and make sure we address the fourth question about competitive advantage.

To summarize, Figure 5.3 shows, on the left side, the options at founding. Entrepreneurs can be quite heedful, quite purposeful in articulating a positive identity at founding. By positive, I mean the founders are thinking about attributes they want the organization to have, they are thinking about creating a particular type of organization that stands for certain things, that has certain values, perhaps. Or, they can consciously have an "anti-identity" in mind: "We aren't sure who we are and what we stand for, but we definitely are not like this other organization." In the case of Sundance, Redford could have said, "I don't know what I want Sundance to be, but I definitely don't want it to be another Aspen." That's an *anti*-identity, and not as powerful as having a positive sense of who the organization is and why it exists. But maybe better than nothing. Finally, many companies, maybe the majority, seem to be founded without much conscious thought to identity.

Second, we articulated a linkage between strategy and identity, between a theory of action and a theory of self. The things I've said about identity could be said about strategy. For instance, at founding, the firm could have a heedful identity, but no articulated strategy, or an articulated strategy, but no conscious identity.

Jay: Or neither.

Rhonda: Or neither.

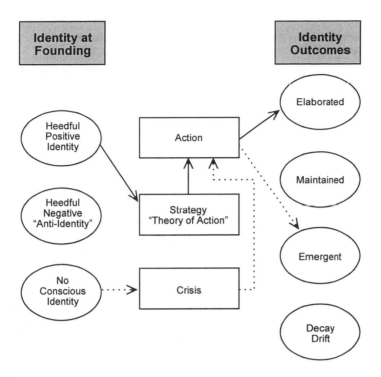

Figure 5.3.

The relationship, as Loren pointed out, starts with "existing is acting." I think one overarching point is that firms *vary* on this chicken-and-egg question; sometimes, the theory of who we are comes first, sometimes, the theory of action comes first, and sometimes, action without theory comes first. In the last case, identity and strategy emerge out of action. Paul pointed out to me that maybe identity and strategy are like pencils linked by a rubber band. At any point in time, they don't have to correspond exactly. But if one gets too far removed from the other, stress is created.

Larry: That analogy fits nicely with the stress model Anne will present later.

Peter: It also fits with Rhonda's "gear model." If there is lots of slack in the system, strategy and identity don't have to mesh very closely. Slack would be how long the rubber band is.

Rhonda: To finish out Figure 5.3, there are a number of things that can happen to identity after founding. I've indicated just two of the many possible paths identity formation can take in an organization's history. First, there can be a heedful positive identity at founding. Following the path of the solid arrows in Figure 5.3, identity can become better articulated and refined in relationship to the firm's theory of action. The theory of action leads the firm to take action. Identity becomes elaborated through this process. In the second case I've included in this figure, a firm can start out from a "no conscious identity" founding. Following the dashed lines, identity can develop in response to a crisis. The crisis evokes action and experimentation, and an identity emerges from that. We will talk much more about crises later when we talk about changing identity. I want to stress that many other paths are possible.

Finally, for Figure 5.3, are the notions of identity maintenance, decay, and drift. Even if an organization has a conscious, well-articulated identity at founding, it doesn't mean it will maintain the identity or that the identity will naturally evolve in ways the management desires.

Are we ready to talk about the next question?

QUESTION 4: IS IDENTITY A SOURCE OF COMPETITIVE ADVANTAGE?

[In this section, the conversation ranges over various roles that identity can play in an organization. Most of the comments address the role of identity in shaping the outcomes of the strategy-making process. Here, identity is alternatively viewed as a generator of strategies, a screen, a constraint, a filter, an enabler, and an influence on strategy. Other comments relate to the role that identity plays in the relationship of the firm with its environments. In this case, identity is variously conceptualized as an interpretation device and a buffer.

Given the diversity of roles, identity can be a source of competitive advantage under certain conditions. Sometimes, identity is merely neutral or provides competitive parity. But there is also what we called "the dark side." Identity can be a source of competitive disadvantage because it is dependent on the past and can be more difficult to change than some other resources. In this situation, identity can be a source of inertia in thought and action that can be problematic when the environment changes. However, as discussed below, inertia is not always a bad thing.]

Jay: Let's tell some stories about how a particular identity can affect the strategy-making process. And let's tell the stories in relationship to the analytic straw man we teach in MBA classes. First, it may be the case, given your organizational identity, that you would not even be able to conceive of certain options, options that would be readily apparent if you did not have that identity in place.

Rhonda: Bill Starbuck would call that "selective noticing."

Jay: Of course, this isn't always a bad thing because identity constrains the firm to think only of options that it can actually implement. The other story that I want to tell here, based on the conversation at last night's dinner, is a simple story. You have a firm that does a standard resource-based analysis and says, "Based on my analysis of my resources and capabilities, I have five strategic options, and all of them are viable." What organization identity does, sometimes, is say, "I cannot do three of those because they are inconsistent with who I am." Identity does not tell you necessarily which of the two remaining you will actually choose, but it does act as a constraint on strategic options. In constraining, it also then turns around and becomes a source of competitive advantage. It keeps you from choosing an option the firm can't implement.

Loren: So you are saying identity is not simply a screen, it is also a source of competitive advantage. It constrains our thinking of options in the first place. It helps prevent the firm from attempting to implement a strategy it is incapable of doing well with. But I'd go a step further, Jay. Identity might also allow you to conceive of options and to see opportunities that someone without that identity can't see.

Anne: It is an interpretation device, a source of options.

Yolanda: It is what we have to contribute to the resource-based view of the firm. Identity is a tacit resource.

Jay: It is a classic, socially complex resource.

Yolanda: Well, yes, you can put it that way, but identity gives me, as a researcher, an understanding of why certain firms do certain things at certain times. I can make that link better with understanding identity than I can with just saying resources that are socially complex.

Larry: I just remembered a great story from my dissertation research which goes right along with this topic that Jay has been talking about and the point that you made, Yolanda. And that is, I was talking to a CEO and he said, "Now that we know who we are, we have a tremendous competitive advantage over our competitors because we can make decisions so much faster." And he told this great story about how they had an internal policy that they would never make an acquisition over a third of the size of the company because they did not want to cause what he called "an indigestion problem." Along comes the perfect acquisition opportunity in keeping with who they were. The problem was, it was almost the same size that they were. He said, "We knew that if we did not buy it, somebody else would. We made the decision immediately." He called it "the best decision we ever made." It overruled all their internal policies about how big an acquisition could be, but it fit perfectly with who they were.

Jay: That is a sweet example. . . . Identity is an enabler of sorts . . . in Larry's case, an enabler of quick, decisive decision making. Then, because of the path-dependent characteristic, because it can be idiosyncratic, it can be a source of competitive advantage. We do have to be careful. We did talk briefly about the notion that . . .

Rhonda: The dark side?

Jay: No, there will be a dark side to talk about in a minute, but first I want to tell a slightly different story—when identity is only a neutral. My firm may have a unique organization identity. But there may be strategically equivalent organizational identities. These firms are also unique, but their identities are substitutes for my organizational identity. One firm might have the unique-in-the-industry organizational identity, "We are a low-cost firm." Another firm might have the also-unique-to-the-industry identity, "Whatever we do, we are the best." Those two firms have different, unique identities that are path dependent, socially complex, and have all those standard valuable resource attributes consistent with resource-based theory. But if those two firms interact in an industry where, in order to be a winner, you have to be a low-cost producer, they are going to generate exactly the same strategies. And so, those two identities, because they are strategically equivalent, would not be reflective of a source of competitive advantage.

Loren: To elaborate the notion just a moment, of whether or not identity acts as a screen for strategy, or as an enabler, or a creative force, I think we're talking about strategic alternatives that apparently have the same net present value, in terms of their returns. In that case, and I guess I am stating a proposition here, organizational identity would function more as a screen. In the case where there may be more variance in the present value of these different strategic alternatives, I would suggest that, in fact, identity may function not just as a screen, but also as a generator.

Yolanda: This is the Koch example. Because of their identity, they were able to push those resources even further than anybody else did.

Jay: The way I see Koch is, because of their identity and how it diffuses throughout the organization, Koch is able to do things strategically that its competitors think are impossible. Competitors think "you cannot do it; it is impossible; it cannot be done." But Koch is doing it because they believe *they* can do it. . . . That is both a generator and a screen.

Luis: I would like to bring up the issue of identity as a buffer. I am particularly interested, in my work at least, in the impact of the environment on organizations in terms of stakeholder pressures and the like. Identity, by telling you what you can do, what you will do, and what you will not do, can buffer you from various fads and fashions.

Rhonda: Now we get to the dark side of identity. The buffer can be good, but the buffer also represents one aspect of the dark side. Because identity can buffer the organization from the environment, it can be a source of competitive *dis*advantage.

Identity can also be a disadvantage when it blinds the firm to what should be obvious options. That's a key lesson in the Greyhound story. In the early 1960s, Greyhound was essentially a bus line, the largest in the U.S. Their identity was "a mover of people from city to city." They knew the bus business was in an endgame decline, so they investigated railroads and airlines as alternative ways to move people between cities. Pretty quickly, they rejected rail and air for sound reasons. Not seeing any options relating to their identity, they chose to pursue totally unrelated diversification.

What is interesting about this story is that in the early 1960s, Greyhound was the leading package express company. But of course, there was no FedEx or UPS, and Greyhound didn't think of themselves as being in this business. According to their V.P. of corporate planning, they never considered aggressively pursuing the package express business at all. This was something they did with excess baggage space, not part of who they were, and therefore, not a business to pursue.

Anne: Identity was the source of inertia of thought as well as action. That leads directly into Table 5.2. To preface this table, we realize that identity is not the only source of advantage or the only resource available to the firm. Identity is attractive

TABLE 5.2 The Relationship Between Identity as a Resource and Competitive Advantage

1. Identity can be a negative resource: A source of competitive disadvantage
2. Identity can be a neutral resource: Contribute to competitive parity, but a source of neither competitive advantage nor disadvantage
3. Identity can be a positive resource: A source of competitive advantage by
   - allowing the firm to do something competitors cannot do
   - allowing the firm to do something better than competitors
   - preventing the firm from succumbing to fads

as a competitive resource because it has aspects that potentially are strategically and operationally relevant to the firm, in terms of the firm's performance. As a resource, it can take on three potential values vis-à-vis competitive advantage.

First, identity can really undercut advantage. That is what Luis said earlier about Harvard in the university setting. It also fits with the General Mills example we discussed yesterday. Because General Mills thought of themselves as a mill, they held on to their milling operation long after it made no strategic sense. They had a sense of themselves that was not really viable to the economic environment.

Rhonda: We also discussed Greyhound in this context. By 1990, the bus lines had been a drain on profitability for 20 years in this now highly diversified firm. But they couldn't bring themselves to sell the bus lines or rename the company. Management thought the Greyhound name was valuable somehow, even though, pardon the pun, it was a real dog. They also didn't want to give up the stock symbol "G" because somehow they were convinced a single letter stock symbol was prestigious. I've told this story to many audiences, and no one outside of the company can offer any explanation of why they thought this. At any rate, they did finally sell the bus lines, and for a short time they used the corporate name "Greyhound Dial." Now, of course, they are simply the Dial Corporation. The point is, being the Greyhound Corporation and owning the bus lines were integral parts of their identity, something they couldn't give up easily, even though both had ceased to be a source of advantage many years before.

Loren: This is part of Burgelman's classic take on Intel getting out of the memory business. They delayed the decision to exit memory several years past when they "objectively" should have, because they thought of themselves as a memory company. After all, they had invented memory chips. Interestingly, most people at Intel remember thinking "It's about time" when they exited memory. It was really top management who still held that identity, not the bulk of the company.

Anne: A second possibility for identity as it affects resources is that, in some cases, it just contributes to competitive parity. For example, a firm may identify with others in its environment. Members might think about what the others are doing and incorporate some of that into their own sense of identity and theory of action. The upside is that the firm may learn about some of the competitive necessities in this environment and do those things well. It is a resource, but it's not gaining the firm competitive advantage. The downside of this approach is that all you can hope to achieve is competitive parity. This is the classic railroad example. Firms in the industry thought of themselves as "railroads" and looked to each other for strategies to mimic.

Rhonda: Jay's story of strategically equivalent identities fits here as well.

Anne: The last possibility is that identity provides a competitive advantage by allowing the firm to do something that competitors don't do, or allowing them to do it better.

Yolanda: Or, as Luis pointed out, preventing the firm from doing something other firms *are* doing. Yesterday, our subgroup talked about conditions under which the firm would be susceptible to fads, and when it wouldn't be. Identity cuts both ways. We talked about how sometimes it is good that the firm changes with the environment, but other times, it is better not to try to respond to every change in the environment. "Inertia is bad, flexibility is good" is too simplistic.

Rhonda helped us pull together a set of propositions about how changeable identity is in relationship to the attributes of identity. We talked about how variance along the attributes affects how changeable identity is. For example, in terms of intensity, we suggested that the greater the conviction of how deeply people felt about the identity, the more inertia. Koch and Sundance are good examples—they feel the intensity to their core, which contributes to their inertia. But inertia is a good thing here—you don't want these firms responding to every new trend in their industries.

[We discussed potential propositions for several minutes, but the conversation is difficult to follow. Building on this conversation, I attempted to formalize some of our thoughts on when identity is likely to be a source of competitive advantage and when it will be a source of competitive disadvantage. These appear in Table 5.3 as a list of propositions, but these by no means capture all the potential propositions about identity and competitive advantage.]

Jay: You know, there is a fundamental insight here that we haven't talked about yet. We are talking about gaining competitive advantage. We have talked about the competitive advantage that stems from a particular identity given the conditions of the industry environment. But another story to tell is, maybe there is a competitive advantage in the ability to *manage* identity.

Larry: I want to build on this observation. Let's not lose this insight. In the strategy field, we have seen an important movement or evolution in thinking. At first, we thought competitive advantage must lie in some easy-to-find strategic lever.

TABLE 5.3   Propositions Linking Identity, Competitive Advantage, and Change

In a relatively stable environment, organizational identity is likely to be a source of competitive advantage when

> homogeneity is high (members agree on the identity)
> intensity is strong (they believe it strongly)
> conviction is high (they believe it is the right identity)
> complexity is low (the identity is simple and unified)
> abstractness is low (the identity is concrete)
> content fits with the environment.

In an environment that is changing in ways that require new strategies from the firm, identity is less likely to be a source of competitive disadvantage when

> homogeneity is low (members disagree about the identity)
> intensity is weak (they are not sure what the identity is)
> conviction is low (they are not sure it is right, or even think it is wrong)
> complexity is high (the identity has many aspects, or there are multiple identities)
> abstractness is high (abstruse terms allow for multiple interpretations)

unless:

> content includes ideals favoring change, innovation, and risk taking.

Identity will be relatively easier to change when

> homogeneity is low
> intensity is weak
> conviction is low
> complexity is high
> abstractness is high
> content is focused on the external environment.

We evolved then to the view that it is not so much the lever itself but it is the management of the lever. Now, one aspect of identity that is exciting is that it takes us to the next level. It isn't simple levers that bestow advantage. We need to look more at socially complex resources, like identity, as the source of competitive advantage. In the future, we may get to a point where we realize it is not so much the identity itself, but it is the ability to manage the identity that provides competitive advantage.

Peter: Just the ability to manage identity might be the source of competitive advantage.

Rhonda: I'm hesitant to go too far on the road of "advantage comes from the management of identity" for a couple of reasons. I realize I wrote an *AMR* [*Academy of Management Review*] piece with Loren and a couple of other colleagues on how identity can be managed, and I believe it can be influenced by management. But, and this is a big but, one of the things Loren learned at Intel is, even if the firm devotes considerable resources to the management of identity, it doesn't mean they will always be as successful as they would like.

⁜

Intel Corporation

LOREN GUSTAFSON

DESCRIPTION AND BRIEF HISTORY OF INTEL[1]

Intel Corporation is the largest and most profitable semiconductor company in the world. Intel invented the microprocessor, making possible the handheld calculator and personal computer. Although Intel's major business is microprocessor design and manufacturing, the company also produces other semiconductor products, such as embedded controllers, flash memory, and motherboards for original equipment manufacturers (OEMs); network and communications products, such as personal conferencing products; and massively parallel processor supercomputers. The company operates chip fabrication plants, or "fabs," in California, Oregon, Arizona, New Mexico, Ireland, Israel, and Malaysia.

Intel was founded in 1968 by Gordon Moore and Robert Noyce, two former Fairchild Semiconductor founders who had invented the integrated circuit. The company was founded as N M Electronics (referring to Noyce and Moore), but the name was quickly changed to Intel (from the first syllables of "integrated electronics"). Soon, Moore and Noyce were joined by Andrew Grove, another former Fairchild engineer. Grove was Intel's president and CEO from 1987 until he was named chairman in May of 1997.

Moore and Noyce started Intel with the belief that large-scale integrated (LSI) semiconductor memory could quickly replace the existing magnetic core memory technology. This approach quickly led to the introduction of a dynamic random access memory (DRAM) chip in 1970 and, more significantly, the 1971 introduction of the world's first microprocessor, the 4004 chip. In 1974, Intel introduced the 8080 chip, the first true general purpose microprocessor. During the next several years, Intel continued to develop and improve 8- and 16-bit microprocessor designs. A watershed event occurred in 1980, when IBM chose an Intel chip for its personal computer, making Intel's chip architecture the de facto standard for much of the personal computer industry. During this same period, Intel introduced several other important innovations. One of these innovations was the erasable programmable read-only memory (EPROM), which originally had little functionality, but ultimately proved useful in testing microprocessors. Peripheral controller chips, such as math coprocessors, were another major Intel development.

In 1982, Intel introduced the first of its x86 chips, the 80286, which quickly became the dominant chip in the PC market. The 286 was followed by the 386 in 1985, which, for the first time, provided the speed and power for PCs to run multiple software programs at the same time. The 486 chip was released in 1989. *Business Week* called the 486 a "mainframe on a chip" (Brandt, 1991), offering power more than 50 times that of the original microprocessor in the IBM PC. Intel's fifth generation chip, the Pentium processor, was introduced in 1993. Whereas the original IBM PC chip contained 30,000 transistors, and the 486 contains 1.2 million transistors, the Pentium contains 3.3 million transistors, with up to five times the speed of the 486 (Sherman, 1993). Intel introduced the Pentium Pro processor, with 5.5 million transistors in 1995. In January of 1997, Intel released the Pentium MMX™ chip with enhanced multimedia performance.

During the 1980s, Intel moved from being a semiconductor company with a fairly wide range of products, such as EPROMs and DRAMs, to being a more focused microprocessor company. In 1985, the company made a decision to get out of the DRAM business because of low margins and falling market share that resulted from stiff international competition. However, Intel also began new businesses that supported its microprocessors, such as producing PC motherboards for its chips, as well as entire PCs. Intel also builds supercomputers using massively parallel processing technology.

Intel has grown rapidly, from 12 employees at its founding to 15,000 in 1980 to more than 48,500 at the end of 1996. Intel's financial results have been equally impressive. Although it is now 29 years old, Intel continues to grow like a new venture. The company topped $1 billion in net income in 1992 after the start of the "Intel Inside" marketing campaign. In 1996, Intel had revenues of $20.8 billion and net income of $5.2 billion. Intel's microprocessors now power more than 80% of the world's PCs (Kirkpatrick, 1997).

INTEL'S CORPORATE MISSION AND VALUES

Intel Corporation's published mission statement is as follows: "Do a great job for our customers, employees and stockholders by being the preeminent building block supplier to the computing industry worldwide." This mission highlights Intel's strategic intent to provide the most important and technologically advanced components for personal computers. This mission is built around several characteristics that make up Intel's espoused ideal organizational identity. These characteristics are summarized in a booklet given to new employees titled, *What Makes Intel Intel?* This booklet has the stated goal of describing what makes Intel unique, and it highlights five organizational characteristics. The first element listed is technology leadership. Innovation is considered a cornerstone of the company's success. Second, Intel claims to possess a uniquely motivating environment. This environment is described as demanding and characterized by constructive confrontation of issues, providing a mix of individual responsibility and collaborative decision making within an atmosphere of professional discipline. Third, Intel strives to create a can-do atmosphere. This atmosphere includes empowered people who assume responsibility for problems and their solutions. Open communication, an open-door policy, and the absence of executive perks are also part of this environment. The fourth espoused characteristic is the measurement of performance in almost every possible way. Aggressive, benchmarked goals are established, and continuous improvement is stressed for all performance dimensions. Measures include customer feedback from the Vendor of Choice program, the culture survey,

and departmental employee perception surveys. Fifth, Intel promotes the
sharing of successes through a meritocracy-based compensation system,
including cash bonus and stock purchase plans, sabbaticals, and community
involvement. Although all of these organizational characteristics can be found
at other companies, Intel is quick to point out that they have a unique
combination and implementation of these elements.

Intel supports its mission and organizational identity with six espoused
corporate values. These values, to the extent they are achieved, represent
behaviors consistent with top management's stated ideal organizational
identity for the company. The six values are discipline, results orientation, risk
taking, great place to work, customer orientation, and quality. The company's
description of these values are provided in the table.

INTEL'S IDENTITY-BUILDING EFFORTS

From the beginning, Intel management has attempted to create and foster a
unique organizational identity and culture. When the company was small, top
managers held informal weekly lunches with employees as a means of
communicating their values and receiving feedback. As the company grew,
new methods were developed. Today, Intel uses a variety of methods to
implant and cultivate shared values. For example, every new Intel employee is
required to attend an extensive orientation. This orientation includes sessions
on the company culture and values taught by senior managers. The company
also has produced a series of videotapes on the espoused values that is shown
to new employees and to managers who request them. Additionally,
performance appraisals are structured around the employee's performance
with respect to the six company values. These assessments concern how well
employees practice the Intel values, and they are used in coaching,
counseling, determination of merit increases, bonuses, promotions, and
terminations.

One major means of values development is the Intel Quality Award. This
award is given to up to three organization subunits annually. To apply for the
award, units are required to achieve a minimum score on a self-assessment
using the Malcolm Baldrige Quality Award criteria. Applicants for the award
are judged on a self- assessment of performance to Intel's values. To win,
applicants must show demonstrable and continuous improvement over time
on multiple performance measures. Intel believes that the real value of the
Intel Quality Award is the self-assessment and feedback on how units can
become more competitive.

Another major effort in value assessment and feedback is the
companywide culture survey. This extensive survey is conducted every 2 or 3
years and gives every employee the opportunity to assess the current state of
both the company's culture and their unit on the Intel values. The results of
these surveys are extensively analyzed, reported directly to all managers, and
summarized in the Intel newsletter for all other employees. Top management
takes the results of these culture surveys very seriously and, in the past, has
made significant changes in response to the reported results.

CHANGES AND CHALLENGES
TO INTEL'S IDENTITY

At Intel, a widely shared perception exists that Intel identity currently is not at the ideal. This gap is exactly the perception that top management desires. Intel's CEO, Andy Grove, is well-known for his statement, "Only the paranoid survive" (Schlender, 1995). Top managers at Intel repeatedly attempt to adjust the identity gap to create strategic change and innovation. For example, Intel has successfully defended its CISC chips' market share against significant inroads by RISC chip competitors. Responding to the strong perceived threat from Motorola and its PowerPC chip, Grove said, "We needed a little threat, a good target. The juice is flowing." It has been a poorly kept secret that Intel recently has been spending a significant amount of capital and effort on developing its own RISC-based chip. Faced with the strong perceived threat from the PowerPC chip, Intel has announced that the architecture for its forthcoming P7 chip will be a RISC design. However, this radical shift is only the latest of several successful changes in strategy for Intel. Other examples include the company's well-documented shift from memory to logic chips and the production of motherboards and personal computers.

The well-publicized "Pentium flap" also represented a challenge to Intel's identity. Prior to the discovery of this flaw in Intel's then-premier chip, Intel employees typically believed that technological leadership and excellent customer service were inherently incompatible, with technology being the more important value. In fact, Intel had no mechanism for accepting or responding to end-customer complaints prior to this incident. Predictably, the company initially responded arrogantly to end-customers who wanted their flawed chips replaced, insisting that Intel would decide which customers merited replacement chips. The resulting customer outrage was a major public relations fiasco for Intel, leading to a reversal of policy and the replacement of chips for all customers making requests. As a result of the flap, managers at Intel began to focus on customer service while maintaining the existing emphasis on technological superiority.

NOTE

1. This section draws extensively from the Intel Corporation 1996 Annual Report (1997) and Gasbarre (1995).

REFERENCES

Brandt, R. (1991, April 29). Intel: Way out in front, but the footsteps are getting louder. *Business Week,* pp. 88-89.

Gasbarre, A. D. (1995). Intel Corporation. In P. Kepos (Ed.), *International directory of business histories* (Vol. 10, pp. 365-367). Detroit, MI: St. James Press.

Intel Corporation. (1997). *1996 annual report.* Santa Clara, CA: Author.

Kirkpatrick, D. (1997, February 17). Intel's amazing profit machine. *Fortune,* pp. 60-72.

Schlender, B. (1995, July 10). Why Andy Grove can't stop. *Fortune,* pp. 88-98.

Sherman, S. (1993, February 22). How Intel makes spending pay off. *Fortune,* pp. 12-15.

COMPANY DESCRIPTIONS OF ESPOUSED INTEL VALUES

Discipline

The complexity of our work and tough business environment demands a high degree of self-discipline.

We strive to:

Conduct business with uncompromising integrity and professionalism.
Clearly communicate intentions and expectations.
Make and meet commitments.
Properly plan, fund, and staff projects.
Pay attention to detail.

Results Orientation

We are results oriented.

We strive to:

Set challenging goals.
Execute flawlessly.
Focus on output.
Assume responsibility.
Confront and solve problems.

Risk Taking

To succeed, we must maintain our innovative environment.

We strive to:

Embrace change.
Challenge the status quo.
Listen to all ideas and viewpoints.
Encourage and reward informed risk taking.
Learn from our successes and mistakes.

Great Place to Work

A productive and challenging work environment is key to our success.

We strive to:

Be open and direct.
Work as a team with respect and trust for each other.
Manage performance fairly and firmly.
Recognize and reward accomplishments.
Maintain a safe and neat workplace.
Be an asset to the community.
Have fun!

Customer Orientation

Partnerships with our customers and other business partners are essential to our mutual success.

We strive to:

Listen to our partners well.
Communicate mutual intentions and expectations.
Deliver innovative and competitive products and services.
Make it easy to work with us.

Quality

Our business requires continuous improvement of our performance to our Mission and Values.

We strive to:

> Set challenging and competitive goals.
> Do the right things right.
> Practice Intel basics.
> Continuously learn, develop, and improve.
> Take pride in our work.

Jay: Dick Rumelt has a funny concept. I call it the Infinite Regress Problem. Dick Rumelt said once, "In the next century sometime, we'll probably have papers that are titled 'Learn How to Learn How to Learn How to Learn.'" [Laughter.] But at some point you stop, because from a practical reality, the infinite regress doesn't help you manage your company any better. I do think that the leverage, the ability to change these things and manage these things, is critical.

Stu: I do not know if it has been clearly emphasized, but Jay made the comment a couple of times in our multiple identity subgroup. The ability to manage identity may be the true source of competitive advantage; particularly, the ability to manage multiple identities may be crucial. Allina, for example, may, in fact, have an advantage over a very similar vertically integrated health delivery system that has the same set of identities to grapple with, simply because Allina has the ability to manage multiple identities, and the other does not.

Anne: Yes, I see your point. But I think we do not want to come down too strongly on the side of "the management of identity is more important than the content of the identity" because we do not want to be on that same road as "you can manage culture." Maybe the advantage of identity is more than simply the management of identity. It is an influence on decisions, yes. But I also think there is an advantage to just being peaceful about what the firm is. To be conscious of it and aware of it can be a source of advantage.

Rhonda: Right. I don't think it is possible to radically revolutionize the identity of a company, certainly not a large one. I am thinking of a large hospitality company, like the Holiday Inn chain or something, coming to Sundance and saying, "Aha, we see the identity of something like Sundance. We will decree that identity within our organization, and then change our organization very quickly." You can't do that kind of thing. If we talk too strongly about the ability to manage identity, you will see managers trying to decree a new identity over a weekend.

Yolanda: Well, if we back off from the focus on the *management of* identity and say, the *understanding of* identity, that notion is powerful for our understanding of strategic behavior. Then we are on shared ground. We have felt the need for a new way of thinking about organizations. That is what brought us together here as a group. It is part of *our* identity.

Anne: Yes. That is part of our shared identity as a group. But our group also clearly has a point of view that management can influence the firm's identity.

Jay: Let me build on your Holiday Inn example: I would propose [said with irony], and this is a very radical observation, if Holiday Inn came up and built a hotel in this valley, it would not be the same experience for us. [Laughter.] That's a radical observation, but what it tells me is that identity is at work. In fact, Holiday Inn sees itself in a particular way; it has a theory of who it is. Sundance's theory of who it is is fundamentally different. It is very difficult to close those gaps in a short term. I don't see how it can be done.

Anne: What it means is that they cannot do the same things.

Jay: They cannot play the same games.

Peter: Yesterday, somebody evoked Hansen. Hansen PLC acquires businesses but leaves them alone to continue to operate as they have in the past. That is part of Hansen's theory of action. I think I could argue that if Hansen bought Sundance, it would stay just like it is . . . if Hansen buys them and leaves them alone.

Rhonda: I'm skeptical, Hansen comes through and cuts costs . . . [Laughter.]

Jay: They fire people . . .

Rhonda: Later, we will talk more about identity in mergers and acquisitions. Maybe we should move on now.

U S WEST Inc.

YOLANDA SARASON

U S WEST was officially born on January 1, 1984, a result of a settlement between the Bell System and the U.S. Department of Justice. The agreement called for the company to divest the Bell Operating Companies (BOCs) that provided local telephone service. The spin-off resulted in the creation of seven Regional Bell Operating Companies (RBOCs), which came to be known as the Baby Bells. U S WEST is one of the seven and at that time primarily provided local telephone service in 14 western states.

Since divestiture, U S WEST has stood out among the Baby Bells. It has been the most active and widest diversifier, venturing into many unregulated activities. Initial efforts after divestiture were focused on diversifying into real estate and financial services, but subsequently, the company exited these industries. Since 1989, the company has diversified into the cable and entertainment industries.

U S WEST provided an appropriate case to anchor a discussion of strategy and identity. One reason is that at divestiture, U S WEST had to create a new identity separate from the Bell System. Tunstall (1985) has the following description of the impact of divestiture on the employees of these new organizations:

> There was a corporate identity crisis of sorts immediately after the divestiture experience. A collective voice could almost be heard to say: "I know the old Bell System, its mission, its operation, its people, its culture. And I knew my niche in

it. In that knowledge, I had identity and confidence about my company and myself. Now I work for a new company . . . with only a partial history and no track record. With the loss of our mission and the fragmentation of telephone service, I find myself asking, Who are we? Who am I?" (p. 152)

Another reason to reflect on U S WEST's history in discussing our growing understanding of organizational identity is that it is also an organization that had to deal with conflicting subidentities. At divestiture, the company was made up of three underlying Bell Operating companies—Northwestern Bell, Mountain Bell, and Pacific Northwestern Bell. One of the challenges for senior management was to provide the mechanism to move the organizational members from thinking, "We are Mountain Bell of AT&T" to "We are U S WEST."

This mini-case description draws upon a larger research project by the author, which investigates the link between identity and strategy (Sarason, 1996). The subsequent discussion highlights key strategic and identity episodes in U S WEST's history.

SUMMARY IDENTITY STATEMENT:
U S WEST IS NOT A TELEPHONE COMPANY

The initial period for U S WEST marked an initial convergence of an identity. It was during this time that key decisions were made surrounding the question, "Who are we?" A theme throughout this period reflected a moving away from an identification with the traditional Bell System. It was as if the collective voice exhibited a desire *not* to be a telephone company. This identification away from the Bell System can be seen in a number of actions. One of the first was the choosing of the company name. The company was the first RBOC to select a name after the divestiture. The name—U S WEST—did not include the familiar and widely recognized "Bell." This came as a surprise to those watching the divestiture process, because allowing the RBOCs to use the Bell name was a concession Judge Greene had given to the RBOCs. Other RBOCs, Bell Atlantic, Bell South, Pacific Bell, and Southwestern Bell, chose to keep the familiar "Bell" in their name. However, U S WEST was moving in new directions and wanted its name to reflect that movement. One former U S WEST executive pointed out, "We felt that retaining the 'Bell' label would be a liability rather than an asset as we chose to further diversify."

Further evidence of U S WEST not seeing itself as a telephone company can be seen in the adoption of the mission statement: "U S WEST's mission is to provide quality products and services to customers in responsive and innovative ways in order to create the highest possible value for our investors, through long term growth and profitability."

It is notable that the words "telephone" or "telecommunications" are missing from the mission statement. The following statement by Jack MacCallister, first CEO and president of U S WEST, provides further elaboration on how the senior management team saw the company:

This commitment to serving shareowners is the overriding consideration in every decision we make, and is the nucleus of our management philosophy, organizational structure, and vision of the future. More than anything else, they describe the character and content of our organization. They are also the basis for our claim that U S WEST is not a telephone company. (Schlesinger, Dyer, Clough, & Landau, 1987, p. 194)

The major strategic initiative during this time was a decision to aggressively diversify into real estate and financial services.

SUMMARY IDENTITY STATEMENT:
U S WEST IS AGGRESSIVE AND COMPETITIVE

By the end of 1988, the company's identity had better coalesced. There was a growing sense that senior management wanted U S WEST to aggressively compete in the competitive marketplace. This richer and more affirmative identity gave the foundation for the strategic changes that occurred in the next period of U S WEST's evolution.

For example, a concern of the executives during the second phase of identity development was how to bring the three operating companies together to be a more cohesive group. The managers at each of the three operating companies of U S WEST had unique sets of identities for their respective companies. The senior executives deliberately organized U S WEST events to facilitate the process of changing managers' mindsets. When managers asked themselves, "Who are we?" the senior executives wanted the answer to be U S WEST. Ottensmeyer and McGowan (1991) have the following description of an event that facilitated a coming together of a shared identity at U S WEST:

There were 120 people from all over the company in one room. . . . There were nine slide projectors going, the music from *Chariots of Fire* was playing, and at one time or another, the face of every person in the room was on the screen, then the words, "We are U S WEST and we can do it." It really fired us up and we left feeling like something had begun. (p. 40)

An example of a strategic move that was atypical for a telephone company at that time was U S WEST's change in organizational structure. During this phase, the company decided to change its organizational structure from one that focused on geographic territories, the traditional Bell approach, to one that focused on customer groups. This change resulted in U S WEST becoming the first Baby Bell to dissolve the underlying operating companies and legally become one entity.

Also during this period, executives began to reevaluate some of the strategic decisions that had been made immediately after divestiture. Senior management began a series of planning activities that were designed to solicit information to be used in a strategic planning retreat. This retreat was to be held in an off-site facility that became known as "The Cottage." One U S WEST executive had the following description of the preparation for this event:

Before we started the cottage team, we had a larger group of leaders—about 45 or so—who were engaged in exercises in which we tried to determine what our beliefs were. Is the industry going to be regulated or not regulated? Is the industry going to converge? Is the industry going to be global? Are we better off being an information company or a network company? We went through about three-and-a-half sessions where we sorted that all out and then getting a consensus around beliefs. Once we did that, then the cottage team had a good foundation from which to assess strategic alternatives. Had we just gotten a small group of people and said go figure out your strategy, without having done the belief alignment, I don't think that it would have been effective.

After this preliminary work was accomplished, a group of senior managers met at The Cottage. The participants at this event articulated the core beliefs they shared about the industry and opinions about U S WEST's next strategic moves. Another executive gave the following description of the event:

We designed a methodology to go through and essentially launch what came to be the foundation of our strategy, which is to really kind of come to grips with our beliefs. What were our basic beliefs? We used a variety of tools and technologies to make that happen. . . . Now out of that, I think, very importantly, came the process of taking this group of people or winding that group of people's viewpoints back into the senior management team and then winding those viewpoints into the Board of Directors back into The Cottage.

The impact of the cottage team facilitated a reevaluation and refinement of U S WEST's identity and strategy in U S WEST and set the stage for the next phase in U S WEST's evolution.

SUMMARY IDENTITY STATEMENT:
U S WEST IS A MULTIMEDIA COMPANY

The work at The Cottage coalesced into the shared belief that U S WEST should be a player in the emerging multimedia industry. The cottage team helped the company to begin to see itself as a multimedia company. The company changed its mission statement to "U S WEST is a leading provider of integrated communications, entertainment and information services over wired broadband and wireless networks in selected local markets worldwide."

There were then a series of strategic changes that followed this realignment. The company divested itself of its real estate and financial holdings and began to aggressively invest in cable and entertainment companies. In 1993, U S WEST announced that it would buy 25% of Time Warner for $2.5 billion. At the time, it represented the largest joint venture between an RBOC and a cable and entertainment company. Subsequent to the passage of the 1996 Telecommunications Act, U S WEST announced the purchase of Continental Cablevision. This union was the largest-ever combination of an RBOC and a cable TV firm. *Fortune* magazine had this to say about the company's strategy:

U S WEST has bet its future on cable TV—investing more than $14 billion in systems outside its 14-state region. The idea is to turn these systems into mini-informational highways able to carry phone calls, movies on demand, Internet traffic and other dishes of the digital feast. . . . While U S WEST was reaching toward the horizon, most of the Baby Bells were settling on strategies closer to home, both geographically and conceptually. (Kupfer, 1996, p. 144)

Reflecting upon U S WEST's history provides insight into organizational identities and how they evolve. Understanding the evolution of U S WEST's organizational identity provides a rich, socially complex framework that helps explain the company's strategic actions.

REFERENCES

Kupfer, A. (1996, October 14). Even Telco cowboys get the blues. *Fortune*, pp. 144-148.
Ottensmeyer, E., & McGowan, R. P. (1991, Jan/Feb). U S WEST: The architecture of corporate transformation. *Business Horizons*, pp. 35-42.
Sarason, Y. (1996). *Identity and the Baby Bells: Applying structuration theory to strategic management.* Unpublished doctoral dissertation, University of Colorado, Boulder.
Schlesinger, L. A., Dyer, D., Clough, T. N., & Landau, D. (1987). *Chronicles of corporate change.* Lexington, MA: D. C. Heath.
Tunstall, W. B. (1985). *Disconnecting parties: Managing the Bell System break-up.* New York: McGraw-Hill.

"Slaying the Chimera?"
Threats to the Survival of Agricultural
Cooperatives as Multiple Identity Organizations[1]

PETER FOREMAN

In Greek mythology, there is the tale of the Chimera—a fire-breathing monster with a lion's head, a goat's body, and a serpent's tail. The polygenic creature terrorized the cities of Caria and Lycia until Bellerophon, riding on the winged horse, Pegasus, outwitted and slayed her. Over time, the creature's name came to represent an incongruous composition or unlikely union of multiple parts. In particular, botanists use the term chimera to describe plants in which genetically different tissues co-exist, typically as a result of grafting or mutation.

Albert and Whetten (1985) used another botanical term, hybrid, to describe organizations with dual identities. Like chimeras, hybrids contain the genetic information of more than one (typically two) species. However, in a hybrid, the genes of the two parents are combined to form a third unique species. In a chimera, on the other hand, the various tissues are combined and coexist, yet they maintain their genetic distinctiveness. The analogy of a chimera seems to better capture the phenomenon of multiple-identity organizations, where any number of distinct, and often incongruous, identities are embedded and maintained in a single entity.

Agricultural cooperatives are one type of organization that, like a chimera, has multiple natures or identities. Like universities, hospitals, and family businesses, cooperatives have historically embodied a plurality of missions, goals, and values. One widely used definition of a cooperative states: "A cooperative is a group of persons pursuing common economic, social, and educational aims by means of a business" (Groves, 1985). Embedded within this definition is the "genetic code" of a *chimerian* organizational identity. More specifically, as this case will describe, co-ops can be seen as "businesses" created to redress farmers' lack of market power, "communities" established to support and advance rural life and values, and "unions" designed to increase farmers' political clout and protect their interests. Although this plurality contains incongruities, there has been a corresponding plurality of social, cultural, and legal forces that have supported and maintained the multiple identity nature of cooperatives. However, changing demographics and economic forces are creating sweeping structural changes in rural society, affecting people's values, preferences, and expectations. As a result, the cooperative's long-standing chimerian identity has come under attack. Indeed, co-ops are seen by many agricultural economists as an anachronistic symbol of a bygone era of farm life and thus must either redefine themselves or face extinction. This case study will provide a historical overview of the chimerian identity of agricultural cooperatives, describing their founding, growth, maintenance, and decline. In addition, we will look at one particular cooperative, the Farm Credit System, as a striking example of the challenges involved in maintaining multiple identities in an organization.

AGRICULTURAL COOPERATIVES:
A UNIQUE ORGANIZATIONAL FORM

Agricultural cooperatives are one class of an organizational form that includes such well-established entities as consumer co-ops, mutual savings and loans, credit unions, and mutual insurance companies. What makes a cooperative a distinctive form of organization is that the members are both the owners and the patrons. Like other cooperatives and mutual organizations, agricultural cooperatives have been granted special legal status by state and federal statutes, including exemption from all taxes and relief from antitrust legislation. In return, agricultural cooperatives must adhere to several unique guidelines, including (a) members must provide all equity capital for the business, thus becoming shareholders; (b) business with nonmembers is strictly limited (the most liberal allowance is 50%); (c) net proceeds must be shared as patronage refunds, based on a member's volume of business and not equity; and (d) governance is one-member-one-vote, regardless of a member's equity position.

There are three main types of agricultural cooperatives: marketing, supply, and service. Marketing co-ops facilitate the marketing of agricultural products, including activities such as price bargaining, shipment and delivery, packaging, and branding. Many marketing co-ops have become household names (e.g., Sunkist, Ocean Spray, Land-O-Lakes, and Sun Diamond). Supply co-ops are organized to purchase and deliver agricultural inputs (e.g., seed, fertilizer, chemicals, etc.), whereas service co-ops encompass a broad range of related services (e.g., irrigation, power, insurance, and credit).

THE CHIMERIAN IDENTITY OF COOPERATIVES

Cooperatives have historically embodied social, political, and economic identities. In fact, the earliest co-ops were founded primarily for social and political purposes. In 1867, the first of several general farm organizations, The Order of Patrons of Husbandry (commonly called the Grange), was organized as a self-help association for the social and political needs of farmers. In the first decade, more than 20,000 local Granges were formed, and many of these began serving as business enterprises as well as social and political organizations. Northern European immigrants brought with them experiences in forming consumer cooperatives, and as a result of their influence, the Grange formally established a policy in 1875 supporting the development of cooperatives.

The Grange movement declined in the 1880s as a national force, although there are many successful "relics" of the Grange, including the large supply cooperative Agway. The social and political agendas of the Grange were taken up by two other national farmers' groups, The Farmer's Alliance and The Farmers Educational and Cooperative Union of America (the Farmers Union). These and other national farm organizations were active in lobbying for farmers' concerns and in promoting agricultural education. They were, for example, intimately interconnected with the Agricultural Extension Service and the burgeoning land grant colleges. Thus, in the Grange, we see the founding of co-ops on social and political identities, the addition shortly thereafter of an economic identity, and then the beginnings of an erosion of the political (and also social) identities as other organizations took on these goals.

The major growth and expansion of cooperatives, however, occurred in the 1890s and 1900s, largely as a response to economic pressures. After the recession of the late 1880s, many of the small farm supply firms were out of business, and the majority of the trade in inputs was controlled by large industrial trusts. In response, many local supply cooperatives were formed for countervailing this adverse market power. A similar lack of bargaining power in the northeastern dairy industry led to the founding of the Dairymen's League (Dairlea) and then many other dairy marketing cooperatives throughout the country. Shortly thereafter, Aaron Sapiro was organizing regional marketing cooperatives among California fruit and nut growers in order to stabilize production and prices in these wildly fluctuating industries. Meanwhile, rising farm prices and the lack of reliable and economic sources of credit for farmers led to the Farm Loan Act of 1916 and the establishment of the Farm Credit System.

Thus, in a relatively short span of 30 years, supply, marketing, and service cooperatives were formed in response to various adverse market or economic conditions. By the 1920s, cooperatives had become a critical force in the organization of virtually all aspects of the farm sector, and the number of foundings and total organizations peaked in 1921. The subsequent depression of the 1920s and its corresponding economic pressures caused a steep decline in the number of both farms and co-ops. However, in the face of this decline, the number of memberships in co-ops continued to increase through the 1950s. In fact, during this period, the cooperative form was repeatedly chosen as the means for doing business in rural America. For example, the federal government greatly expanded the Farm Credit System and established rural electrification and telephone cooperatives to bolster the depressed rural economy of the 1930s.

It is important to note that during the 1930s and 1940s, cooperatives were founded less and less for political and social purposes and more and more for economic purposes. The chimera was already beginning to lose part(s) of its identity. The "union" identity, although critical in the early stages of the 1880s and 1890s, was never again as prominent as the "community" and "business" identities. The social and educational missions associated with a "community" identity were important to co-ops through the postwar years, but by the 1960s and 1970s, the size and scale of both farms and co-ops had increased dramatically, and co-ops were increasingly viewed as big businesses. Furthermore, the grain embargoes of the late 1970s and the farm credit crisis of the early 1980s put enormous economic pressure on the agricultural sector and further accentuated the importance of the "business" identity.

THE CHIMERIAN IDENTITY OF
THE FARM CREDIT SYSTEM:
IDENTITY CONFLICTS AND IDENTITY DRIFT

The Farm Credit System (FCS) is a service cooperative—a nationwide network of cooperatively owned banks that provide credit for farmers, farmer cooperatives, rural homeowners, agribusinesses, and rural utilities. Currently, there are more than $60 billion in FCS loans outstanding, representing one fourth of the agricultural credit market. Over the years, the FCS has exhibited the trifold chimerian identity of cooperatives. Its very purpose as a financial lending institution is obviously economic in nature, yet at the recommendations of several government commissions in the early 1900s, the FCS was designed to be a cooperative, owned and controlled by its member-borrowers. The history of the FCS has been characterized by an ongoing tension among its multiple identities, and the degree to which they have been successfully combined has varied. Most recently, in the past two decades, the FCS banks have gradually "drifted" (Albert & Whetten, 1985) from their initial state of identity plurality to a narrower focus on their economic, utilitarian characteristics.

Hoag (1976) notes that the relative emphasis on cooperative principles in the FCS has varied over time and geographic location. In the early years, there was considerable disagreement over whether farm credit needs should be met via a cooperative system, such as FCS, or by some other, more traditional mechanisms. Many early FCS leaders did not see the system as being part of the larger cooperative "family," viewing it instead as a government program. Furthermore, some FCS bank presidents clearly preferred a "banker" image to a "co-op" image.

But the FCS was being called upon by many to assume a broader leadership role in cooperative development. For example, the Cooperative Research and Education Division operated as part of the FCS in the 1920s and 1930s, and its activities helped other co-ops identify with FCS and vice versa. Through this division, the FCS was responsible for distributing circulars, bulletins, and magazines, covering a wide range of topics in cooperative education. Gradually, the FCS banks, because of their ongoing work in assisting cooperatives, assumed a stronger co-op identity, began joining state and national cooperative associations, and became accepted as co-ops by their peers. By the 1950s, if not sooner, the entire FCS was seen as a vital part of the agricultural cooperative community.

Perhaps the most critical factor in the relative emphasis of a plural, chimerian identity has been the leadership of the FCS. Whereas the 1920s were a period of identity conflict, characterized by the fierce debates over the "commercial" versus "cooperative" focus of FCS, the 1930s were a period of strong reaffirmation of FCS's plural identity, largely because of the influence of a few key individuals. The first Commissioner of the Bank for Cooperatives, F. W. Peck, made an especially strong pronouncement in one FCS circular, in which he said,

> While we are primarily concerned with the business side of operating cooperatives, there is more to cooperation than just doing business. There is involved the creation of attitudes of mind that vitally concern a way of living as well as a way of doing business. (Peck, 1935, p. 5)

In the same bulletin, Peck proclaimed that some of the "poisoning influences" affecting the health of cooperatives included an "overemphasis on price consciousness" (economic identity), the dissemination of anticooperative "propaganda" (political identity), and "throat-cutting" competition between cooperatives (community or social identity; p. 13).

Perhaps the most important FCS leader was W. I. Myers, governor of FCS from 1933 to 1938 and a key advocate of its cooperative nature. In one FCS circular, Myers (1936) stated,

> Confidence on the part of farmer-borrowers themselves in their ability to meet their common problems through united action has always been the backbone of cooperative credit. To doubt that ability would be to lose faith in the cooperative movement—to lose faith in democratic government itself. (p. 4)

This kind of ideological rhetoric was no doubt a key factor in building and strengthening the normative cooperative identity of the FCS.

However, in spite of the strong emphasis on the cooperative nature of the FCS in the 1930s through the 1960s, in the 1970s and 1980s, FCS banks began "drifting" from their plural, chimerian identity toward a narrower focus on an economic-utilitarian identity. For example, the relative emphasis on cooperative education was diminished when the Cooperative Research and Education Division was removed from FCS in the late 1950s and made into the Agricultural Cooperative Service, under the direct auspices of the USDA.

Meanwhile, utilitarian concerns were brought to the forefront via a growing consensus that diversifying risk was critical to the long-term health of the FCS. As a result, a series of legislative acts, beginning with the Farm Credit Act (1971), broadened the lending authority of FCS banks. The system now makes loans to rural homeowners, rural and agricultural businesses, aquatic and timber firms, rural development projects, and rural utilities. FCS banks have also expanded their scope of services—perhaps the most dramatic example of this aggressive diversification is the system's recent joint venture with American Express, whereby FCS banks now contain American Express "mini-offices," offering a full range of personal financial services.

But the most important factor in FCS's identity drift was the farm credit crisis of the late 1970s and early 1980s, which put a severe financial strain on the system and precipitated significant changes in their policies and procedures. A particularly vivid example of these changes can be seen in FCS's expansive lending criteria and long-standing tradition of forbearance with distressed farmers. In 1935, Congress commissioned FCS to provide special assistance to "young farmers," most of whom had insufficient collateral or earnings to qualify for a loan. In a 1935 circular (Arnold, 1935), the FCS policy on foreclosures states,

> Our rule is that we will not foreclose in cases where the borrower, first, is doing his honest best; second, is taking proper care of his property; third, is properly applying the proceeds to the payment of taxes and mortgage installments; and fourth, is capable of carrying a reasonable burden of debt under normal conditions. (p. 9)

This tradition of forbearance continued throughout the 1950s, 1960s, and 1970s. In 1975, FCA Governor Malcom Harding stated, "Thus, whether it be in today's or yesterday's context, the System's policy of forbearance remains unchanged. The FCS will stick with a farmer-borrower so long as there remains hope of his being able to work out of financial difficulties—so long as you can see light at the other end of the tunnel" (Hoag, 1976). In fact, in the period 1945 to 1975, FCS land banks made only 840 foreclosures on 1,298,000 loans, preferring to stick with a farmer rather than call his loan.

But excessive loan losses in the 1980s, reaching more than $3.6 billion in 1986, coupled with additional losses because of loan pricing policies, forced the government's hand. The Agricultural Credit Act (1987) mandated much stricter and more conservative lending policies and more aggressive handling of distressed loans, either through restructuring or foreclosure (Farm Credit System, 1987). Evaluations of creditworthiness now stress the adequacy of the borrowers' earnings, their willingness to make payments, the adequacy of their collateral, and the ability to realize proceeds from the sale of secured assets. Loans now have more conservative terms, including higher down payments, shorter maturities, more aggressive repayment plans, and risk-adjusted rates. These strident policies are a far cry from the expansive guidelines of FCS's earlier years.

This "drifting" from the cooperative identity is evident in the local FCS banks as well. There is little mention of the cooperative identity in FCS bank communications. An advertising campaign conducted in the Midwest in the early 1990s took pains to demonstrate how "different" the current FCS banks were from "the old Land Banks and PCA's." Newsletters and mailings rarely note the cooperative structure or character of FCS. A recent case study of a local FCS bank assessed the local organization's relative identity emphasis (Foreman, 1995). The interview responses of managers and employees were marked by a preponderance of a "business" rhetoric, using terms such as "customer," "investor," and "market share." When asked, "If someone walked in here without any knowledge of FCS, what would signal to them that this is a cooperative?" virtually all respondents admitted that customers would never know until they applied for a loan and were asked to "buy stock" in the bank as part of their loan fees.

In summary, the history of the Farm Credit System illustrates the difficulties and tensions in founding and maintaining a multiple identity organization. The degree to which all of the facets of the organization's chimerian identity were emphasized or supported, versus simply a traditional single identity, varied based on leadership, interorganizational ties, and environmental munificence. The overall trend, however, has been a gradual "drifting" from its chimerian identity roots to a stronger identification as a typical bank. Although FCS has maintained the capitalization and governance structures of a cooperative, its policies, activities, strategies, and values no longer possess the "central, enduring, and distinct" character of a cooperative. Have we seen the death of the chimerian identity of agricultural co-ops? Given that other chimerian identity organizations, such as universities and hospitals, are under serious pressure as well, what does this case tell us about the ability of organizations to embody and maintain multiple and competing identities?

NOTE

1. Most of the historical information included in this case study was gathered from several texts on agricultural cooperatives (Barry, 1995; Barry, Ellinger, Hopkin, & Baker, 1995; Hoag, 1976; Knapp, 1969).

REFERENCES

Albert, S., & Whetten, D. (1985). Organizational identity. In L. L. Cummings & B. M. Staw (Eds.), *Research in organizational behavior* (Vol. 7, pp. 263-295). Greenwich, CT: JAI.

Arnold, C. R. (1935). *Agriculture buys its credit cooperatively.* Farm Credit System circular A-1. Washington, DC: FCS.

Barry, P. J. (1995). *The effects of credit policies on U.S. agriculture.* Washington, DC: American Enterprise Institute.

Barry, P. J., Ellinger, P. N., Hopkin, J., & Baker, C. (1995). *Financial management in agriculture* (5th ed.). Danville, IL: Interstate.

Farm Credit System. (1987). *Farm Credit Administration annual report.* Washington, DC: Author.

Foreman, P. (1995, August). *The contextual nature of organizational identity.* Paper presented at the annual meeting of the Academy of Management, Vancouver, BC, Canada.

Groves, F. W. (1985). *What is cooperation?* UCC Occasional Paper #6. Madison, WI: University Center for Cooperatives.

Hoag, W. G. (1976). *The Farm Credit System: A history of financial self-help.* Danville, IL: Interstate.

Knapp, J. G. (1969). *The rise of American cooperative enterprise.* Danville, IL: Interstate.

Myers, W. I. (1936). *The farmers' stake in cooperative credit.* Farm Credit System circular A-7. Washington, DC: FCS.

Peck, F. W. (1935). *The cooperative way.* Farm Credit System circular A-2. Washington, DC: FCS.

TABLE 5.4   Alternative Models of Identity Change (based on Van de Ven & Poole, 1995)

Change Theory	Logic of Change	Role of Manager	Examples
Life-cycle	As organizations age, grow, and mature, their identities naturally evolve and change. The transition from one developmental stage to another may result in a crisis of identity.	Intervene at key developmental points (i.e., during an identity crisis) to facilitate the transition to a new stage or state.	U S WEST, agricultural cooperatives
Evolutionary	*Variations* in organizational identity occur naturally as members/stakeholders are exposed to alternative self-definitions. Some variations are *selected* and *retained* by (a) managerial intervention (top-down), (b) member validation (bottom-up), and/or (c) the influence of the market.	Introduce promising variations in the organization's identity, and intervene to influence managerial selection processes.	Koch
Teleological	Identities change as managers heedfully and purposefully create, nurture, change, and/or refine their organization's identity to achieve specific organizational goals.	Shape and mold the identity of the organization through vision, mission, and stated values as well as through the careful management of key symbols (Pfeffer, 1981).	Intel, Koch
Dialectical	Identities change when an existing identity (thesis) is confronted with an alternative identity (antithesis). The conflict that results from this interaction can result in (a) the maintenance of the old identity, (b) the overthrow of the old identity by the alternative, or (c) the creation of a totally new identity through synthesis.	1. Facilitate the creation of a synthesis through creative reframing (Bartunek, 1984). 2. Act as an advocate supporting a specific, favored identity.	Allina, agricultural cooperatives

QUESTION 5: HOW DOES ORGANIZATIONAL IDENTITY CHANGE?

[On Saturday, two subgroups separately attacked the question of how and when organizational identity changes. The first group, led by Stu Bunderson, applied organizational change models as explicated by Van de Ven and Poole (1995). The second group, led by Anne Huff, applied a stress and inertia model originally developed by Huff, Huff, and Thomas (1992) to explain strategic repositioning. This model was conceptually applied to identity by Reger, Gustafson, DeMarie, and Mullane (1995). The conversation here assumes a familiarity with these works, but goes well beyond them.]

⁂

Rhonda: Stu will talk about what his group came up with to help us understand change in identity.

Stu: The general mandate for our group was to develop ways of thinking about changes in organizational identity. More specifically, our discussion focused on the question, "How and why do organizational identities change?" In order to answer this question, we found it useful to apply a framework introduced by Van de Ven and Poole in a recent *AMR*. Based on a review of literature dealing with change and development, Van de Ven and Poole identify four ideal-type theories of change that underlie most attempts to understand change and development in social systems. Each of these ideal types provides a somewhat different explanation for why identity changes occur and what drives them. The four ideal types include a life-cycle model, an evolutionary model, a teleological model, and a dialectical model.

I'm referring to the "Logic of Change" column of Table 5.4.

The life-cycle model is based on a metaphor of organic growth and assumes there is a natural developmental progression as an organization matures. In the case of identity, this model would suggest that identities naturally evolve and change as organizations mature. And, perhaps organizations, like individuals, pass through "identity crises" as they move from one stage to another. We tried to apply this idea of evolving identities and identity crises to the specific cases we have been considering. We felt that Koch is going through a midlife crisis. The cooperatives are in some sort of a geriatric crisis. U S WEST might be viewed as being in an adolescent stage of development. Intel was in its aggressive and arrogant 20s, driving around in their sports car. We were not sure where Allina is—possibly in infancy—although we thought that the infancy stage might be more appropriate for a startup firm like Tom's of Maine.

Rhonda: Interesting. For those of you who were at the first Identity Conference, you remember the CEO and founder of Tom's of Maine, who spoke with us. It was a new, small, entrepreneurial company in a very heedful identity stage.

Stu: The second model is an evolutionary model and argues that change in organizations occurs through a process of variation, selection, and retention. In the case of identity, this model would suggest variations in organizational identity occur naturally as organizational stakeholders explore alternative definitions. Certain of these variations in possible identity are selected either by internal or external selection pressures. External selection pressures might result from the influence of the market. That is, some identities may be more viable given market contingencies. Internal selection pressures might result either from management intervention (management supports or fails to support certain identities) or from member validation (members support or fail to support certain identities). In other words, we felt that selection pressures can come from either above or from below.

Peter: The variation can be naturally occurring in the environment. The example you have listed is the co-op. Or the variation can occur from within. In the case of Koch Industries, they actually created their own variation and acted on it. Is that correct?

Stu: That is correct. And if it is selected, an evolutionary model would argue that it can continue as a viable identity.

The third model is a teleological model in which change occurs as purposeful actors set goals, pursue their goals, and monitor process toward goals. This model would suggest that identities change as organizational leaders consciously and heedfully nurture certain identities which they view as superior or desirable. In terms of our different cases, we felt that Koch Industries fits this model fairly well since there is a conscious effort to nurture and maintain a specific identity and to build on and elaborate existing identities in that organization. Intel's six official values and employee training efforts were also viewed as consistent with a teleological model of changing identities.

Rhonda: Intel's top executives, starting with Andy Grove and Craig Barrett, are very conscious that they want to create a particular identity, and they are consciously trying to manage the process. They are not 100% successful, but they definitely have that intention.

Anne: In both of those organizations, there is a very strong effort to let new employees know what the identity is. So both of these organizations have this very strong . . .

Rhonda: Maintenance of identity . . .

Anne: . . . and socialization process. People who are coming in understand what the identity is.

Stu: The fourth and final model is a dialectical model where organizational change occurs as a result of conflict between a thesis and an antithesis. This conflict results in the preservation of the thesis, the overthrow of the thesis by the antithesis, or in a new synthesis which somehow incorporates aspects of the two. In the case of identity, this model would suggest that there are more options than one when it comes to identity—that there are often multiple, alternative, and competing identities—and that conflict between these alternative identities can produce some sort of change (either through the overthrow of an old identity or through a synthesis which produces a new identity).

Examples from our five cases include Allina Health System and the co-ops, where there were clearly multiple, conflicting identities that led the organization in different directions.

Anne: It is also interesting that at U S WEST, management tried to *force* the belief that their identities were in conflict to some extent. They created the notion that there was a dialectic there.

Loren: I would also add that before the Pentium flap at Intel, the identity "technological leadership" was typically viewed as being in conflict with the officially sanctioned "customer service-oriented" identity. The Pentium flap gave top management an opportunity to bring this conflict out into the open more and allowed Intel to begin to synthesize two beliefs which were previously considered to be conflicting.

Stu: Those are good examples because they show that the source of the dialectic can be internal, as in the case of U S WEST, or external, as at Intel.

Peter: There's something else that is important to recognize. In the case of Allina—well, I'm extrapolating a little bit based on what we found in our health care studies of other organizations that are in a similar situation as Allina. Working with Mike Pratt and Shankar Nair, I found that previous to managed care, health care companies like Allina had multiple identities. These multiple identities were in conflict. But they were kept fairly separate. The doctors just had to do their business and hospitals did their business. Everything was fine. It is when you bring the conflict to bear *within the physician* that identity may have to change. The physician himself or herself has to reconcile conflict between the existing criteria of the health alliance plan, the medical plan that says that you can only treat these kinds of things, the hospital, the patient, the doctor's professional code, and so forth. Then you have the dialectic. Previous to that, doctors saw the conflict, they recognized the conflict. The tension had been around, but it was not a big deal. Now, though . . .

Rhonda: Because previously you had slack, you did not have the pressure saying "we cannot do all of these things."

Peter: Because of the slack, there we go.

Yolanda: I think, Anne, what you were saying about U S WEST is they purposely used the conflict to help answer the question, "Who are we?" To do so, they sent a message throughout the organization that these three underlying operating companies are now competing for the same resources, and we need to start working together. Therefore, we need to stop thinking of ourselves as three different organizations with three different identities. They sharpened the conflict between the three identities so that everyone could see that it didn't make sense to try to keep all three. They wanted to force everyone into thinking of a new identity for U S WEST that was different from the identities of the three operating companies.

Larry: Yolanda's comment brings out an important theme that has not emerged from this discussion of change models. That is this notion that managers can have an influence. A particular manager or a particular top managing team can make a difference. We saw that with U S WEST. Yesterday, we talked about what happens when a key empire builder, a top manager, or a CEO of a large, diversified firm goes away. The person who has really been the driving force in shaping the company's identity.

Stu: Larry's point brings up the second part of our discussion. So far, we've been talking about the "logic of change" column of Table 5.4. the "role of manager" column focuses on the managerial implications. As a manager, your theory of change, or how you believe identity changes, will influence how you think you can manage changes in identity. It will impact the kinds of actions you take to attempt to change identity. For example, under a life-cycle model, a manager's role would be to intervene at key developmental points. The manager would be constrained by the life-cycle, but a savvy manager would say, "Okay, I am going to intervene to help my organization negotiate this midlife crisis."

Peter: Or stop geriatric decay, or whatever . . .

Stu: Right. And we have the co-ops and U S WEST as examples of management intervention that are consistent with the life-cycle model.

Moving on to the next approach, under an evolutionary model, a manager's role would be to create variations in identity—to put up some trial balloons related to alternative identities—and then to see what is selected out by the market or through internal selection pressures. We thought Koch did some of this by suggesting issues on the radar screen and then inviting people to think about how their identity should evolve and change to meet this changing set of circumstances.

Rhonda: In Koch's case, are they creating variations in the identity, or are they creating variations in actions?

Jay: Well, based on our earlier discussion, . . . I think Koch was trying to create variations in identity that would then have impact on actions. The variation in actions would then help clarify the identity, so there is the reciprocity we talked about earlier.

Anne: The key part of that story is when Charles Koch says, "We are a discovery company." That is a pretty empty box. Then people put variations in the box. Well, it is not just variations. Some were elaborations about what "a discovery company" might mean. But of course, these variations and elaborations were not all consistent.

Jay: In a different way, by defining your company as a discovery company, and keeping that vague, what you do is you enhance the probability that discovery will actually occur.

Rhonda: We talked about that, about how abstract identities provide room for greater interpretation, greater variation, more experimentation. These variations, internal variations, can come from top management, but if they do, they still have to be validated by the organization. And if a variation comes from the bottom of the organization, it still has to be validated by top management through giving it resources.

Anne: That is what happened at Ford. People in various parts of the organization tried variations around quality, but the variations were just isolated experiments until the efforts were validated by top management.

Jay: Quality efforts bubbled up, and eventually, quality became part of Ford's identity: "Quality is job one."

Stu: Moving on, under a teleological model of identity change, the manager has the most active role in setting the vision and managing symbols that will help to achieve and nurture a particular identity. Under this model, the manager's degrees of freedom in changing the organization's identity are the broadest since he or she is not constrained by life-cycle stages, selection pressures, or processes of conflict. The teleological model seems to capture our mainstream notions of how identity should be managed. It is a teleological dynamic.

And finally, under a dialectical model, one role of a manager might be to somehow facilitate the process of creative synthesis by bringing opposing identities together. We also thought that perhaps a manager could intervene in favor of one or the other of two conflicting identities and that, although a synthesis would not result, the tension would be resolved.

Jay: It strikes me that the dialectical is the only model where you do not have an example written down. Is that an omission, or can you think of an example? This is going to come up later when we talk about managing multiple identities. This notion that management brings conflicting identities into interaction with each other, and magically, a better identity will spring up. It seems to be almost a false promise.

Loren: It might be rare, but here's an example. Prior to the Pentium flap, Intel recognized that including greater customer awareness and orientation in its identity was something that its customers desired. However, top management clearly made a choice, because they, perhaps unconsciously, viewed technological leadership and customer service in opposition. They clearly made a choice to go with technological leadership, almost in an arrogant sense believing, "Where else are the customers going to go?"

Anne: So customer orientation was a voice, but not a strong voice.

Loren: Yes, they were not equal, equivalent voices. But during the Pentium flap, management had to confront the conflict and more fully integrate their thinking about customer orientation into their thinking about Intel's identity. For the first time, a lot of people at Intel understood that they had to be—and could be—good at technology and good with customers.

Rhonda: It wasn't exactly magic, but it was an epiphany.

Jay: Certainly, that will come up as part of our discussion of merging multiple identities, what happens when there are two equally strong, profound voices.

Anne: Mason and Mitroff's early work is an example of trying to engineer that within the organization (Mason & Mitroff, 1981). They were talking about using a dialectic to manage strategic choices, and not identity, but you could draw on that work.

Peter: I know we need to finish up the first group's answer to Question 5, but there is another point that hasn't come out yet. Stu helped remind me that these four models are the motors that drive change, but there are also certain mechanisms that could be used with multiple motors. I am thinking about concepts like reframing and some of the strategies that we will talk about in managing multiple identities. He helped me realize that the concept of reframing doesn't really fit in any of these models. But yet you could reframe, as a consequence of a teleological motor, you could reframe . . .

Jay: Reframing fits in all of them.

Anne: Even the life-cycle model. To move on in the life-cycle requires some reframing; it requires that people understand that the organization has moved to a different life stage.

Peter: Yes, I guess I did not articulate my point very clearly. The point I'm trying to make is, let's not mix the motors with the actual mechanisms.

Jay: Is there any way, beyond what we talked about before, to begin to tease out the empirical? Under what conditions would life-cycle be more likely the driver, the motor of change than evolutionary or teleological? Has anyone thought about that at all?

Stu: We could, for example, make some predictions that in a merger situation, you are going to have conflict, and dialectical is going to be a likely scenario.

Jay: You also could make an argument that it is going to be teleological because the people who put the merger together have something in mind, typically.

Luis: Also, we've talked about heedfulness and mindfulness, and that might determine which of these models will explain a particular situation.

Jay: Say more, I do not understand.

Luis: Well, when you are actively managing your identity, then maybe a teleological explanation might be more appropriate than when, for example, your identity is driven by external factors, such as reputational rankings.

Jay: But we've just said that management can intervene under any of these models. So, potentially, the manager can affect the life-cycle, or he can create variations under an evolutionary model. He can use the teleological, and the dialectical . . .

Anne: There is another important variable—time. Under the life-cycle and the evolutionary models especially, there is a notion that accumulation of time is going to have certain consequences.

Jay: That's right, that's right.

Anne: And maybe under the evolutionary model is an interaction between different systems. Evolution advances when, for example, there is a change in climate, and so you have certain characteristics of life forms becoming more important, more useful.

Jay: That begins to work because you could argue—between those two, for example, one proposition might be "firms that are facing significant changes in their competitive environment would often manage change through an evolutionary process." Maybe the life-cycle model fits better when firms are facing relative stability in their environment, when the environment evolves very slowly over long periods of time.

Anne: In the latter case, the firm might be facing, for example, an increasingly experienced customer group. The firm will have to make changes in its identity because of that.

Jay: As opposed to the evolutionary approach.

Peter: So, for the evolutionary model, very explicitly, we could say, "The degree to which there is more variation in the competitive niche or the industry, there will be a greater preponderance of evolutionary motors of identity change."

Jay: [said with irony] And for the M&A story, we could have dialectical unfriendly takeovers and teleological friendly takeovers! [Laughter.]

Larry: I can see ways in which all of these approaches might come to the fore at different times. For example, a firm operating in a declining industry might very much be in a life-cycle mode. Or, management might take a more teleological approach and say, "We have to do something about this." The acquisition that they might make in response could introduce both a dialectical and an evolutionary approach to identity.

Stu: So, there is no reason you cannot combine these four models in order to more fully explain and manage changes in identity. In fact, we will probably not observe these four ideal types acting in isolation. The real action will often be found in the interplays and interactions that occur between these four developmental motors as they complement each other, substitute for one another, or counteract one another. Similarly, attempts to manage these different change processes will usually involve some combination of efforts to consciously nurture an identity, encourage variations, negotiate transitions, and manage conflict.

Jay: You know, if there is a competitive advantage in the ability to manage identity, we can really start to think in interesting ways. What is fun about that is, one way you can gain advantage is to manage using a different model than the rest of the industry. Let us imagine that all firms in an industry are managing identity through a life-cycle model. The key entrepreneurial insight that gives a firm competitive advantage could be, "We are not going to do it life-cycle, we are going to do it teleological from now on." The insight that results from just the change in the way the company strategizes might be a source of competitive advantage in managing.

Anne: Or, building on the path dependency issue, your company could have had three top management teams that tried a teleological approach. The firm might respond better, and gain some advantage, by trying something new: "Let's try a dialectical."

Stu: I think another interesting thing here is that in at least two of these models, identity is not some unitary, agreed-upon thing. In the evolutionary and dialectic models, change happens because there is some disagreement about identity. Members perceive an option to the existing identity. There is at least a potential option to the existing identity. That can be powerful.

Peter: There is variation.

Stu: There is variation in the evolutionary view, and in the dialectical, there is an antithesis. So, identity is not this one, unitary thing that is monolithic in an organization. This can be good, especially if you are hoping to change.

Rhonda: Yes, and underlying the notion of change and identity is an old identity and a new identity, so you have that tension.

Peter: But Stu, doesn't Andy [Van de Ven] suggest that the life-cycle and evolutionary models are significantly out of the bounds of managerial control, and teleological and dialectical are more in the bounds of managerial control?

Rhonda: We are suggesting that all four are within the manager's influence.

Jay: I would like to point out that, in fact, they are not. You can either speed up or slow down the evolutionary process. You cannot either speed up or slow down the life-cycle process.

Rhonda: Wait, it is not in your *control,* but it is within your *influence.* Where a firm is within a life-cycle isn't an objective phenomenon. Management can influence whether the rest of the organization thinks of the company as new, or adolescent, or middle age.

Peter: But the degree of influence is different. In a life-cycle model, management can impede death or speed maturity but cannot take major quantum leaps in identity.

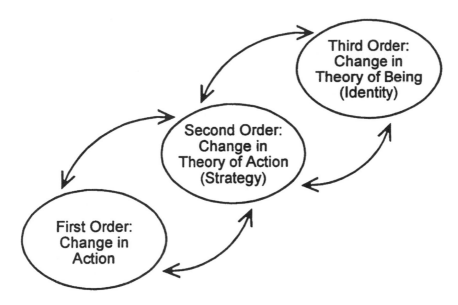

Figure 5.4.

Anne: I think there is an important additional thing to say around dialectic; we talked a little bit about it yesterday when talking about AT&T. At AT&T, we see how difficult it has been to move from one theory of action to another. We talked about how often there is a dialectic in the organization. In order to get the company to accept the new, management has to make it clear how the new is different from the old. But you also have to have a bridge from the old to the new. The mere fact of moving from one identity to another, and particularly trying to have an influence on the movement, ultimately involves the firm in a dialectic. They have to understand how the new is different from the old.

Loren: Without so completely discrediting the old that no bridge is left. The work I'm doing with Rhonda is trying to address these ideas—how to create a new identity while keeping the psychological health of the organization intact.

Anne: Bob Tannenbaum, who used to be at UCLA, has this wonderful paper on death and dying. He said one of the failures that we have had in change efforts is that we have not helped people figure out how to let the old die. The new manager comes in and thinks, "The world begins today, here is the new theory."

Rhonda: Stu Albert has a fascinating paper on the algebra of change. He suggests additions to organizational identity are easier than subtractions, because subtractions result in a loss of something that at least some members value.

Jay: Where is the mourning?

Anne: Exactly. Where is mourning? Where is grief? Where is the shock of, "Surely the doctors made a misdiagnosis. I do not have cancer!"

Peter: "Surely Andersen Consulting is wrong. We do not . . . " [Laughter.]

Yolanda: Let's move on to the next group.

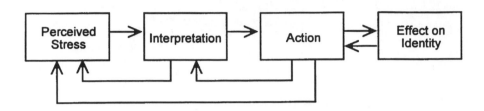

Figure 5.5.

Rhonda: One last point before we move on, and I was thinking of this in terms of people wanting to do identity research using these models. One way of looking at these four perspectives is to try to figure out which is the right way of looking at identity change, and when does it occur, and under what conditions. But another way of looking at the four perspectives is as multiple lenses. Research like Allison did on the Cuban missile crisis. It would be interesting to see a disciplined case study that applied all four of the perspectives. These are different perspectives that highlight different parts of an incredible complex process. So I could see comparative case study research to get added richness.

Jay: That is right. One story is, these are alternatives. The other is that they exist simultaneously.

Anne: Or at different points in time.

Loren: The one thing that I would like to add is in regard to the magnitude of change that is possible for a particular organization. We had some discussion about the fact that you do not automatically throw out your theory of who you are. On the other hand, that may be necessary in order to survive. In our subgroup, we talked about three qualitatively different magnitudes of change. If you will let me, I will introduce Figure 5.4. First-order change is changing action within the firm's existing theory.

Jay: Of who we are.

Loren: The firm's existing theory of *who* they are and *what* they are. It is new action, but not new theory. Then we talked about a second-order change where the firm changes the theory of what they do. Second-order change is change in the theory of strategic action, but no change in the theory of who they are.

The third-order change is where the firm changes their theory of who they are. This model suggests that it is easiest to change action, moderately easy to change strategy, and difficult to change identity. But in fact, it may be that the stressor is so dramatic that we move immediately to third-order change.

Jay: And it is not a linear accumulation . . .

Rhonda: You do not have to go through each loop to get to the third one.

Anne: So, if you have a competitor that comes out with a product at 50% of its old price, you could perceive a problem that is going to mean you have to be somebody new.

Rhonda: While we are on the subject of stress, I think this is a good time to see how Anne's group answered the same question about organization identity changes.

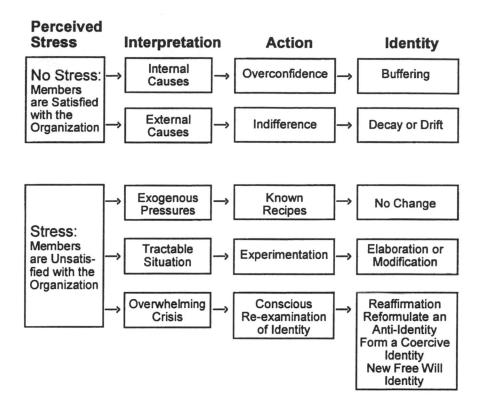

Figure 5.6.

Anne: One summary of our subgroup's discussion can be found in Figure 5.5. Here, we started with the situation that members of the organization perceive stress. Organizations vary widely in terms of their perception of stress; it is not an objective assessment. When members of the organization think things are not going well, they interpret the situation. They interpret the source of the stress and whether it is a short-term event or a permanent change. They interpret whether their company can effectively meet the challenge posed by the stress. Both perceiving the stressors and interpreting them are essentially sensemaking activities. Then the firm acts. (Of course, we recognize that sometimes the firm acts, then interprets.) What actions they take depends on their perceptions and interpretations. Action can change perceptions and interpretations, as we've indicated with feedback loops. Finally, the action and members' interpretation of the effectiveness of the action may affect identity. We've drawn this as a linear model, but clearly, all the steps are interactive and recursive. Echoing our discussion summarized in Figure 5.1, we've drawn double-headed arrows between action and identity to highlight that recursive relationship.

To flesh out this general model, we explored some of the relationships among these variables for U S WEST, Intel, the co-ops, business schools, Allina, and Koch. We tried to relate their identity, as we understand it, to some of the stressors in their environment. Figure 5.6 starts on the left-hand side with a notion that, at any given point in time, members of an organization can have a sense that things are right or they are not right, everything is great or not. Not all members have to share this sense of stress, the collective can be large or small.

First, looking at the top left-hand corner of the figure: There are alternative scenarios for times when there is a sense in the organization that things are going well. Implicit in this sense of well-being is often a belief that we know what to do, we are who we are, and we feel good about that. If you look at organizations like, perhaps, Harvard, one practical outcome can be an overconfidence, a lack of attention to cues, that can have negative implications for competitive advantage. Another possibility, if there is a sense that things are going pretty well, is that it may seem that it does not matter who we are, or it does not matter what we do. This can lead to decay or drift, and that is a part of the co-op story. In all these cases, the organization does not feel any stress, at least not enough to make them seriously question their identity or strategy. They believe things are going reasonably well.

If there is a sense that things are not going well, as shown at the bottom of the chart, there are at least three different possibilities, different interpretations the organization can have. One is the interpretation, "It is not going well, but these are exogenous pressures on us, it is not possible to really influence them." The consequence for action is often to continue with known recipes. I think universities in many cases are doing that. They are holding tight, waiting for current problems to go away. If pressed, they make percentage reductions across the board. They are not calling upon new sensemaking.

Loren: This would be first-order change—a change in action, but no change in the organization's theory of strategy or identity.

Anne: If there is, instead, a sense that this is a more tractable situation, there is stress that means—potentially—people within the organization will become dissatisfied with their theories of action. Then you see efforts to come up with new theories of action, often after some experimentation and sensemaking around new actions.

Luis: This could be Wharton. The identity "we are a responsive organization" doesn't change, but the strategic actions, the curriculum, does change.

Anne: Part of this second possibility is that there might be alterations in identity; there might be elaborations, or minor fine-tuning. Loren's example of the effects of the Pentium flap on Intel seems to fit here. It isn't a completely new theory of action nor a completely new theory of self. We see in the Intel story an elaborated theory of action: "We are going to do everything we did before, but we fixed this one thing. We are now going to add that we have to be responsive to the customer, to the end customer, which we haven't emphasized before."

Rhonda: Consistent with Albert's algebra of change, these kinds of additions to strategy and identity should be relatively easy for people in the organization to handle.

Anne: The third possibility is that people in the organization feel overwhelmed. Folks feel the need to come up with new theories of action, the kind of sensemaking that is really stressing. If, under this kind of stress, an organization comes up with new theories of action, there are a number of possibilities for identity. We've tried to categorize some of the possibilities and then think about what the potential implications are for competitive advantage. One possibility is that there is a reaffirmation of the existing identity: "We are who we thought we were." Though we didn't expand upon this example in great depth, I think IBM is an example of this possibility. They just recently reaffirmed that they are a mainframe company. Now they're thinking about mainframe in terms of something that sounds to me like servers, but apparently to them, it is the same identity they've had all along. It is possible that even after you go through a fundamental sensemaking effort, that you don't come down that far from your old theory, even after it has been reexamined.

Loren: Yes, as a matter of fact, IBM uses the term "server" now. However, when IBM says "server," IBM means "mainframe."

Anne: Interesting. Not what a Sun would mean by the term "server."

Another possibility in reformulating a new theory of who we are is what we have called an anti-identity. The firm will decide "we are not x" without yet having a sense of who they are now. That's one of the things that's interesting about the early U S WEST story. Their clearest early identity is that they are *not AT&T.*

Yolanda: They're not the Bell System. The plus of an anti-identity is that it can lead to a contrarian strategy. A contrarian strategy can win in the marketplace. But the negative is the sense of self is defined by somebody else. I think the anti-identity is unlikely to lead to competitive advantage in the way that we understand it now.

Anne: Another similar possibility, as shown on Figure 5.6, is that a firm can decide "we are who we *have* to be." Allina Health Care System is an example of this. With a coercive identity, the company is sensitive to the environment, which is a plus, but again, there is an external referent that makes company identity ultimately problematic.

Rhonda: The notion of free will and choice is missing. The element of coercion can undermine commitment to the identity.

Anne: Our final possibility is more likely to lead to competitive advantage. This is an identity that arises out of deciding to be who we *want* to be. Koch provides one of the more interesting examples. Out of the stress of a changing world, and acquisitions, and so on, Charles Koch said, "Maybe we can be who we want to be." That's a powerful position to be in. It is a stronger sense of self. But there is risk of self-delusion, that the identity is so strong that you end up telling yourselves a lie.

Rhonda: Which leads you back to the top of this figure—the position of Harvard—thinking everything is great when it isn't.

Anne: That's our overview of how we see identity changing in relationship to stressors. The additional point to make is that there are multiple points where management can potentially intervene in this sensemaking activity.

Peter: One way I look at Figure 5.6 is that it is an agglomeration of organizational pathologies and responses to organizational pathologies. Anne has mapped out a very complex system of responses. It is very inclusive and I think makes a great summary map of our entire discussion to this point.

Rhonda: Does it make a good road map for future research? Someone reading this book, are they seeing, "Here is a place where research is needed"?

Jay: Certainly, to do that, we would have to add some additional content. For example, we have talked about alternative ways of developing a new identity. It would be very interesting to see under what conditions firms choose one of these alternatives versus another alternative. I don't know the answer to that question; that's an interesting question.

Yolanda: I think an interesting area for research is the conditions of stress; what causes stress, and when and how it leads to changes in identity. We can look at our cases to examine what forms of stress caused them to make these decisions. In every case, there was a gap between two schemas, two theories. Rhonda and Loren's work is helpful here. For example, there is the gap between identity and reputation, between who they thought they were and who other people thought they were.

That was the Harvard example, and Harvard chose not to deal with the gap. Although recently, they appear to be making changes, at least in their theory of action, if not their identity.

Then we talked about the difference between who a company wanted to be and information that they were getting of who they actually were. This would be a gap between ideal identity and image. That was the Intel example. Then we talked about the difference between how a firm thought of themselves and who they chose as their referent. In the U S WEST example, there was growing gap between who they saw as their competition and how they thought of themselves. Over time, they began to understand that the companies they were comparing themselves to were doing different things than they were now doing.

Rhonda: I think that was true with the co-ops as well.

Yolanda: Right. And then we also saw cases where the significant gap was the difference between the firm's identity, their sense of who they were, and their performance. Over time, they said, "We should be performing better than we are performing now, and how do we deal with that?" Figure 5.6 summarizes some of the ways a firm could choose to deal with that performance gap.

Jay: Most of those are exogenous forces—stress from the environment. There is also the endogenous change agent, which was prominent in the Koch example. Charles Koch said, "We are going to create the stress because that makes us better."

Yolanda: Right. That was a purposeful action from management that said, "I *like* putting the organization through stress and through change."

Loren: That's a big part of the Intel story. Andy Grove likes to create stress—paranoia, he calls it—because he believes fear of poor future performance keeps the organization on its toes. He wants the organization to continuously question their theory of action, and, I think, to a certain extent, their identity.

Rhonda: That's what Jack Welch says he did at GE, also. He took a high-performance organization and created the stress to change from the inside. He didn't wait until the environment created the stress. I'm not very close to the GE case, however, so it isn't clear to me if he really created a new identity, or simply new expressions of the existing identity.

Luis: We also talked about the amount of slack in the system. Slack can determine whether there is enough stress on the system to change.

Yolanda: Right.

Anne: The point is that there is a link between theory of who we are, and the theory of action, and the context.

Rhonda: Those need to mesh. When you have little slack, they have to mesh more closely. But when you have a lot of slack, there can be more slippage.

Yolanda: More slack will hinder efforts to change the identity; it will lengthen the time needed to change.

Anne: Slack will also make it less likely that sensemaking happens at all.

Rhonda: That's got to be part of the story at Harvard. They have huge resources, a huge endowment. They didn't feel the pressure to change.

Larry: This is the important entry point for management, too. The juggling, maintenance, and adjusting of these variables is one way management manages identity. They raise the heat or lower the heat by providing interpretations to the organization.

Loren: What Denny Gioia calls "sensegiving." Andy Grove can say sales are soft this quarter due to a mild correction in the PC market, or he can say the fundamental nature of computing, communications, and entertainment is changing, and we need to rethink our identity as a building-block supplier to the computing industry.

Larry: I'm also reminded that we should talk about the "Use it or lose it" notion of identity. Components of identity, if they are not used, if there is not strategy applied, if they don't explain good performance, can be lost. We saw that in the co-op case, where a political identity was part of the original sense of self. But co-ops moved away from political causes. Other organizations took over this function for co-op members. Then, when co-ops were threatened by for-profit corporations, they didn't think about, or know how to use, political strategies to combat the threat.

Loren: One point I want to make, drawing at least on a physiological sort of model, is that a moderate level of stress is beneficial and necessary. I'm not just talking about the minimal level of stress that keeps the organization alive. I am talking about a level of stress beyond that. The minimal level may allow you to maintain some level of heedfulness, to help the organization avoid drift or decay. But perhaps minimal levels aren't really enough. Related to the "use it or lose it" idea may be the notion that pretty high levels of stress provide an impetus for investment in organization identity. Without this impetus, management may not choose to invest in the maintenance of and the elaboration of identity.

Anne: It is important to note the enormous variance in the capacity of organizations to do this. Some organizations are able to operate successfully with what other organizations think is a disruptive amount of stress. Some firms have a theory of who we are and a theory of action that allows them to handle what looks like enormous amounts of stress. How an organization will react to a stressful event, or even that it will interpret something as stressful, is very much grounded in context.

Allina Health System[1]

STU BUNDERSON

Allina Health System is a not-for-profit, integrated health care system based in Minneapolis that operates in Minnesota and western Wisconsin. Allina was formed by the 1994 merger of HealthSpan Health Systems Corporation and Medica Health Plans. HealthSpan was a diversified delivery system with hospitals, clinics, nursing homes, and ambulance services, whereas Medica was a health plan provider with managed care products and preferred provider networks. At the time of the merger, HealthSpan had $1.05 billion in assets and revenues of $970 million (40% from HMOs/PPOs), whereas Medica reported revenues of around $890 million.

The merger between HealthSpan and Medica was motivated by an emerging interest in the Twin Cities marketplace and legislative community in "integrated service networks," or ISNs. An ISN is a coordinated system of doctors, hospitals, and health plans that has joined together to manage the full continuum of health care for a defined population under joint financial accountability. Proponents of ISNs argue that the integration of all components of the health care system with joint financial accountability is the only way to align incentives so that all parts of the health care system work together to address the health needs of a specific community of patients (Shortell, Gillies, & Anderson, 1994).

Traditionally, doctors, hospitals, and health plans have operated under conflicting incentives that work at cross-purposes with one another as well as with the goal of managing population health. For example, hospital revenue is maximized when there are large numbers of (very sick) patients who can fill hospital beds. Health plan revenue is maximized when large numbers of plan enrollees pay premiums but do not use system services. And primary care physician revenue is maximized when large numbers of patients continue to see their doctor for routine checkups so that they can stay out of the hospital. Under this incentive system, one part of the health care system benefits at the expense of the others (e.g., health plans make money when hospitals and doctors don't see patients). The goal of an ISN is to operate all three of these health care components under one revenue stream (i.e., capitation) so that the three work together to deliver high-quality health care as efficiently as possible.

Although the legal integration of doctors, hospitals, and health plans took place at Allina in 1994, the creation of a common identity and purpose is still being worked out. Each of the organizations that joined together to form the Allina system maintains its own identity in the marketplace (e.g., Medica Health Plans, River Valley Clinic, Abbott-Northwestern Hospital) as well as its relationships with outside providers and payers. As a result, Allina units are frequently rewarded for behavior that hurts other parts of the Allina system or that compromises the ability of Allina to establish itself as a single organization with a focused identity.

Furthermore, physicians and managers at Allina are not always in agreement about the kind of organization they want to create. Differences of opinion relate to different occupational orientations (e.g., health plan manager, hospital executive, primary care physician, hospital physician) and organizational affiliation (e.g., clinic, hospital, health plan). At least four different models for the Allina organization are emerging from this debate: (a) a *system* model, which emphasizes internal efficiency and system integration; (b) a *market* model, which emphasizes market share and industry competitiveness; (c) a *physician* model, which highlights quality health care and physician autonomy; and (d) a *community* model, which emphasizes the system's responsibility to improve health in the local community. The arguments for each of these models are strong and well-supported.[2]

When Allina first began to advertise in the Twin Cities community, the following slogan was selected to communicate the system's commitment to integrated health care: "*Allina Health System:* Doctors, Hospitals, and Health Plans." This slogan highlights the current management challenge at Allina—to integrate three historical adversaries under one corporate banner such that the combination means something more than the sum of the individual parts.

NOTES

1. This short case is based on research undertaken by Andrew H. Van de Ven, J. Stuart Bunderson, Shawn M. Lofstrom, and David N. Grazman at the University of Minnesota. For further reference, see Bunderson, Lofstrom, and Van de Ven (in press).

2. Bunderson et al. (in press) note that each of these models has deep roots in an existing theoretical tradition: (a) system = bureaucracy literature, (b) market = strategic management literature, (c) physician = professions literature, and (d) community = social responsibility literature.

REFERENCES

Bunderson, J. S., Lofstrom, S. M., & Van de Ven, A. H. (in press). The Allina Medical Group: A division of Allina Health System. In W. J. Duncan, P. M. Ginter, & L. E. Swayne (Eds.), *Strategic management of health care organizations.* Cambridge, MA: Basil Blackwell.

Shortell, S. M., Gillies, R. R., & Anderson, D. A. (1994). The new world of managed care: Creating organized delivery systems. *Health Affairs, 13*(5), 46-64.

QUESTION 6: HOW DO ORGANIZATIONS MANAGE MULTIPLE IDENTITIES?

[In this section, Stu introduces four strategies for managing multiple identities that his subgroup had discussed earlier. Anne later proposes a fifth strategy, create a new identity. Loren suggests that we hadn't considered the option of simply ignoring the problematic identity to allow it to naturally decay. I've included all six of these options in Table 5.6.]

TABLE 5.5. Characteristics for Comparing Alternative Organizational Identities

1. Articulable: Can the identity be clearly articulated?
2. Energizing: Does the identity capture the imagination of organizational members?
3. Robust: Can the identity survive the market test?

Rhonda: We are running out of time. Let's move on to the next question: how to manage multiple identities.

Stu: Yes. Yes, let's. The whole concept of multiple identities was a major disagreement initially for our group. There were several who believed there is no such thing, that identity is that which integrates multiple perspectives . . .

Jay: But they changed their minds. [Laughter.]

Stu: But they changed their minds. Then there were those who believed you can have multiple identities without any meta-identity. These folks also shifted.

That was in the large group. In our small group, when we got together to talk about managing multiple identities, we found it useful to examine the components of an identity that might influence whether it will conflict with another identity. We identified three components of an identity that would cause it to conflict with another identity: (a) It can be articulated, (b) it captures the imagination, and (c) it survives a market test. These are found in Table 5.5.

We believe if the identities or the subidentities of units within an organization are high on all three of these dimensions, then you have what we have termed a multiple-identity organization. If all three characteristics are high, then you can expect significant conflict between the different units that hold these different identities.

Anne: Stu, I wonder if we are losing the feeling of, "This is me." Is that part of your three components of identity? Maybe that is within your notion "captures the imagination." "This is me, this could be me, has to be me"—that is an important part of identity. I'm referring to the topic of the *identification with* group.

Stu: Yes, that is part of what we mean by "captures the imagination."

On one hand, if subunits have identities that are high on all these three, you are going to have some conflict. On the other hand, if the firm can find some higher-level identity, a corporate-level identity in the case of a multidivisional organization, that is also high on these three attributes, then it would provide the ideal way of resolving the conflicts inherent in a multiple-identity organization. The higher-level identity would have to capture the imagination of all of the subgroups, it would need to be articulated in a way that encompasses the subgroups, and also survive the market test in order to provide the integration. That is a pretty tall order, but necessary to settle the conflict.

We came down on the side that multiple-identity organizations are a nonequilibrium condition. Often, they are created by major changes, such as a merger, or a major change in strategy. The equilibrium condition is where there's some integrating meta-identity.

Peter: I would voice some dissent. I know of cases where multiple, conflicting identities are held in an equilibrium state. In the terms we are using, I want to make clear that if any one of these three conditions is not met, the company can be in an equilibrium state even though they have multiple, conflicting identities. This is certainly true of co-ops, and universities, and other organizations. This is where Jay helped reconcile the two opposing views of our discussion group. Jay pointed out to us that it's only when these three conditions hold true that it becomes problematic to have multiple identities.

Stu: Yes. That's a good point. If these three conditions hold, there is a question as to whether the organization can continue as a single entity.

Peter: In that situation, it is a nonequilibrium. Yes, right.

Stu: That is a good clarification. Okay, then we went on from there to say, "Okay, let us say we have an organization. It has multiple identities that vary on these three dimensions. What are strategies that managers can use to manage this multiple-identity organization?" Pete, do you want to talk about these, or do you want me to?

Peter: As a group, we came up with four strategies to resolve conflicts in multiple-identity organizations. We gave them cute names. The four options are (a) Swallow (one identity subsumes the others); (b) Chop It Off (where you get rid of one or more of the troublemaking or problematic identities); (c) Endure the Pain (you try to live with the conflict; find the best way to work it out; create a negotiated-order, coalition model of the firm); or (d) Find a Higher Level of Meaning or Abstraction (look for a meta-identity, multivocality).

There is a lot of research in sociology in the past few years on a notion of multivocality and robust action. Robust action is basically, from Eric Leifer, a notion of being able to take action which is clear enough to accomplish short-term goals and meet the immediate situation at hand, and yet does not lock oneself, either an individual or an organization, into long-term commitment. It keeps multiple long-term options open. That is robust action.

Yolanda: Would you say the co-ops are examples of "Endure the Pain"?

Peter: Well, we did not go through the strategies and attach specific cases to them yet. But, yes, some co-ops would probably be in the Endure the Pain strategy. Currently, there are co-ops that are actually engaging in all four. There are co-ops that have swallowed. They have become, within the bounds of legal prescriptions, as much of an economic entity as possible, and basically just swallowed up the social part. Others have actually divested. They have changed their charters to become for-profit, investor-owned firms. They got rid of the social part, they are really no longer a co-op. Enduring the pain? Yes, you are right. A lot of co-ops are trying to live with the conflict, make the best of it, and they are not doing too well. Other co-ops are following a path similar to what Rhonda and Loren's paper says. They are reframing it and trying to find a different identity and image that placates traditionalists in the constituencies who want to remain socially conscious and yet still make strategic moves that are much more economically aggressive.

Stu: I just want to speak to the Allina situation. I would say, right now Allina is looking for a higher level of abstraction. They want to create a seamless, integrated system of doctors, hospitals, and health plans. They are finding, however, that this meta-identity may not be powerful enough to capture the imagination of all the subgroups, and so right now, they are enduring the pain. They realize, I think, that enduring the pain isn't a good long-term solution for them.

Jay: And it is also problematic about whether or not Allina's new identity will survive the market test.

Stu: Right now, the jury is out. Allina is agreeing to disagree until they can either find a higher identity that integrates, or the pain becomes so intolerable that they pursue one of the other two strategies.

Peter: This brings up the three meta-identities we talked about. We thought of them as three metaphors that managers at these organizations are trying to make work as meta-identities in their problematic, multiple-identity organizations. Allina uses the metaphor of seamless service, Koch uses the metaphor of discovery, and GE has been very successful with using the notion of "boundarylessness." Boundarylessness is so purposely vague, nobody really knows what it means. But it's been a powerful tool for Jack Welch to go in and be Neutron Jack. For him to fire a whole bunch of people under the guise of boundarylessness. Now, Yolanda has more to say about U S WEST.

Yolanda: U S WEST is an example of a company that switched strategies over time. Early on, they chose to swallow. They used a swallow tactic by integrating the three underlying operating companies that they had and attempting to get rid of the separate identities. They did some very purposeful things. They tore down the organizational structure, they moved people around, and they developed lots of new symbols to, hopefully, tie people into this idea. They wanted people to think "we are no longer Mountain Bell, Pacific Northwest Bell, and Northwestern Bell. We are U S WEST." Think about it. U S WEST was a completely new entity, it had no identity, it had no meaning to people. So, as they faced divestiture from the AT&T system, they said, "We do not want our employees to think of themselves in these three different identities. We want to somehow figure out a way to swallow them and merge them into one."

Peter: Did they swallow, or did they merge? It sounds like you might be describing an effort to create a meta-identity.

Yolanda: I do not think they created a meta-identity. They did not say, "Let's take what we are doing and put a new level of abstraction above that." They said, "We are doing away with all of the existing identity associated with the three operating companies." In fact, people in the organization were not allowed to talk about Mountain Bell, Pacific Northwestern Bell, and Northwestern Bell.

Anne: U S WEST highlights why time is so important. Creating the new U S WEST identity was the first step. Then, 7 years later, they are trying to find another new identity. This strategy is a fifth strategy to add to your list. This time, they are trying to create an identity that is not tied to its Bell identity. They are trying to deal with the merging of the communication, information, and entertainment industries. The question they have posed for themselves is, "Our industry, our environment has

TABLE 5.6. Strategies for Managing Multiple Identities

1. Swallow: One identity subsumes the other(s).
2. Chop It Off: One identity (not necessarily one unit) is eliminated from the organization.
3. Endure the Pain: Proponents of alternative identities agree to disagree.
4. Find a Higher Level of Meaning or Abstraction: Create or discover a meta-identity that accommodates each of the alternative identities.
5. Create a New Identity
6. Downplay the Conflict: Allow one or more identities to decay.

changed such that our identity won't meet the market test in the future, so, how do we create an identity that fits within that merging technology?"

Peter: That is an example of meta-identity that can encompass multiple identities.

Anne: Well, they aren't talking that way; I don't think they see it that way. Another thing that is interesting is they were more aggressive than some of the other Baby Bells in swallowing the old identities, and they have been faster off the mark in creating this new identity.

Yolanda: Because they confronted the challenge of multiple identities early on, they have this option now. Other Baby Bells endured the pain of multiple identities for a longer time, and they aren't prepared to take the next step. Other companies do not have this option.

Peter: That is interesting. So, these five ways of changing identity may be interrelated and interactive.

Anne: Over time. That is part of this path-dependent notion that we really need to bring out.

Luis: Other aspects of context also matter. For example, look at the case of the business school rankings. In reputational rankings of business schools and universities, the criteria used in the rankings make certain issues salient, which make certain identities salient. So, that could guide which strategy you use for managing multiple identities.

Jay: Just a quick observation. The options for responding to multiple identities are in Table 5.6.

Stu: Then we developed a few tentative propositions. Someone might want to write a commentary on this part to more fully develop these ideas. These are really just the beginning of ideas to get people thinking. For instance, let's say a firm has three identities, and one of those identities fits all three of the properties: It is well articulated, it captures the imagination, and it has survived market tests. But the other two do not meet these tests. Then, we predict, the first identity will swallow the others.

Rhonda: It would be interesting to see if that is a natural process, or if management has to intervene. Would the prediction be that swallowing would always occur in this situation, or just that successful firms will use this strategy? It goes back to what Larry said. Management has a role in these processes.

Peter: Interesting. Another proposition we explored was the situation where management could find a meta-identity for every identity but one. Like at U S WEST, they had three identities to manage. If they found a meta-identity that would placate two of the three regional Bells, but not the third, we predict the firm will divest themselves of the third. We thought of this as the black sheep or the problem child.

Jay: Divest the third identity or the business?

Peter: It may or may not be divesting the business. At a minimum, you would divest the identity. At GE, businesses have to be number one or two in their industries. If they aren't, they get divested. So, if you are the management team of one of the divisions that doesn't have this "be number one or two" identity, you either have to divest your identity and adopt the GE corporate identity, or risk being divested by GE.

Then, a third case we thought about was if you have to have all three identities. The perfect example is Allina. They must be professionally identified because they work with doctors. They must be economically driven because their health plan has to make money. They cannot afford to swallow or divest either identity. At a minimum, they just endure the pain. You do the best you can to endure the pain. This is presuming that you have not been able to find a meta-identity that satisfies it.

The final case we thought about was what would happen if the market test results are unclear. If, for instance, the identities are articulated, they capture the imagination, but it is unclear if this is viable for the future. I think part of the Allina story is, members of the organization are not 100% sure that this meta-identity will survive the market test. Then, we predict, the firm will endure the pain.

Stu: So, we are not sure, so we will endure the pain until we are sure, and then we may adopt one of the other strategies.

Jay: We may swallow. We may divest. We may synthesize. We may create a new identity if we become convinced the existing identities are not viable.

Loren: Are you assuming that management's reframing efforts have not been successful?

Peter: It is in the process. The ideal is, management would either be able to find a higher-level meta-identity or would be able to reframe the situation such that you would make all the parties relatively happy. But if you cannot, then you are left with the other three options: swallow it, cut it off, or live with it.

Rhonda: I'm worried that we are oversimplifying the firm's options. My bias is that multiple identities are the usual case. Different units in the organization will develop subidentities and will also have different beliefs about the identity of the overall organization. This is part of what Loren found at Intel, even though they work very hard to maintain a singular, common identity.

All organizations have multiple stakeholders who bring their claims against the organization. To a larger or lesser extent, there will always be conflict. There will be tensions driven from the outside around this. Maybe it is a place for more research. There are strategies for managing those kinds of tensions; strategies like decoupling, keeping different parts of the organization separate, and so on. Multiple, conflicting identities are not a bad thing to manage away if the environment makes multiple, conflicting demands on the organization. I guess I'm on a tangent here: We don't have time to develop that now.

Peter: But that is a good point.

Rhonda: It is a place, I think, for more research on how to successfully manage change. We talked about universities as well as health care as two very fruitful places to look at multiple identities that seem irreconcilable.

Anne: There are at least three other places to look at multiple identities. First, when you have an agglomeration of firms, no matter what the situation is, there is going to be a period where you have multiple identities. This could be mergers, acquisitions, the initial Baby Bell situation. Second, when firms make a significant change in strategy. When the theory of what to do has implications for the theory of who you are, there is going to be a period that is unclear. You likely will have the old and new identities competing. Third is when environments change radically, as they are for U S WEST and the arena they want to play in. It is very hard for U S WEST, and all the other firms who are trying to make sense of this very ambiguous environment, to sort out who they want to be, who they need to be. In the third situation, it is really the environment that is making it difficult to say, "What is a viable theory of who we are?"

Loren: I think two unspoken assumptions underlying the four strategies for managing multiple identities is that the identities are held with strong conviction, and they are pervasive throughout the organization or the subunit. If these conditions aren't met, there is at least one other option. For example, if one of the identities is less intense or less pervasive, a sixth alternative would be to ignore it.

Peter: Which is a divest strategy.

Loren: It is a form of divest, but less formal. Less active. Management just allows it to decay. They avoid bringing the conflict out into the open.

Stu: This is a good point. You are right. Our strategies for managing multiple identities are based on the presumption that there is a conflict in the identities, which creates a problem for the organization. There have been differentiated identities in health care for decades, but the conflict wasn't as much a problem because there was little attempt to integrate the different players or manage them tightly. In the co-ops example, people initially had no cognitive conflict between being both a social community and an economic entity. But as Jay suggested, the social community identity no longer survives the market test, and it no longer captures the imagination of people the way it used to because of changes in rural society, so now you have a problem.

Rhonda: Maybe we are back to the notion of slack. One way to manage multiple, conflicting identities would be to create slack. But we really must move on.

QUESTION 7: HOW DO ORGANIZATIONS MANAGE COMPLEXITY THROUGH IDENTITY?

[In this final section, we intended to talk only about a very old question in strategic management: How do you successfully manage diversification? Larry makes a couple of very insightful comments on this subject. Then Jay and Anne very quickly took us to two points that apply much more widely than just to managing diversity. It is a nice place to end our conversation. I hope these don't seem like afterthoughts to our discussion, because I believe these are possibly the most important and powerful ideas expressed in the entire conversation.]

Rhonda: We have talked about many of the things we had planned to say here. But there are a few important ideas about diversification that we haven't covered. The question is, "How is identity used to manage complexity?" In strategy, the most common source of complexity is diversification. Larry has done quite a bit of research on diversification. Can you start us off?

Larry: I think, actually, where we just left off is a good place to pick up this discussion because we might think of "What would an ideal identity be?" Of course, it would have to pass the market test. It would be compelling and have emotional buy-in. It would be something that could be fairly easily articulated. Then, what we would also like to see is an identity that would be a helpful guide to action.

It might be easy to argue that you could expect to see this most often in the entrepreneurial firm, where the firm itself is almost an extension of the entrepreneur. The entrepreneur's identity very often transfers to the organization's identity. At least, start-up is one time when a strong individual can have a powerful influence on identity.

One of the issues that we have been talking about is, What happens as the firm grows in complexity and size? What happens when it diversifies? One of the ways organizations may cope with this is by adopting more flexible or more abstract kinds of identities. The gain is that in moving toward a more abstract identity, more activities can be subsumed under that identity. There is greater flexibility in terms of what characteristics the organization can take on. The downside is, we risk losing the emotional buy-in. We risk losing the ability to easily articulate the identity, and we risk losing identity as a guide to strategy and action.

The organization that can manage this transformation has a better chance of being successful. If it can move toward a more abstract identity and, at the same time, maintain this emotional buy-in, the ability to be widely held and be easily articulated within the firm, this can be a very powerful identity.

Jay: We have a specific hypothesis about how that could be done. It has to do with the content of the identity. It is not the only way it can be done. The identity must become more abstract so that it encompasses the broader range of activities and actions the firm is engaging in. But how do you do that without losing some of the buy-in, some of the emotional content?

One way it can be done, and we have seen it happen, is for the identity to pick up moral dimensions. The reason this is important is that the moral dimension is something that is very real and tangible. It is something that the people can really relate to. It informs their life and their decisions. We have a couple of examples.

Let's look first at Koch Industries, which is a very widely diversified firm. The identity is not just, "This is the way we manage" or "This is who we are." But the identity is also, "This is the morally right way to manage a highly diversified organization. This is the *right* thing to do and not just *a* thing to do." That seems to capture the dimension of right and wrong for employees and managers in the organization.

We also talked about the moral dimension in terms of a university. The university is an enormously diversified operation with lots of different, multiple, competing identities and constituencies and on and on and on. How do you define an organization identity in that context? One that people throughout the university community can relate to and understand and identify with. One specific example of the moral dimension is the possibility of defining the university's mission in moral terms. Not defining it in mundane terms of research, teaching, or service, because that understates what the university actually does. Rather, to define the university's mission in terms of its role in maintaining a free society.

Then, all of a sudden, instead of, as Rhonda said it so eloquently yesterday, instead of teaching people accounting, what we are doing is teaching people how to be a part of the process of maintaining and creating free society. That sounds silly, but in fact, accounting has a role in maintaining a free society. Suddenly, by putting a moral dimension on this identity, we ennoble the organization and the people who are associated with it, and we value them, and we see a greater purpose in what we are doing.

Rhonda: Identity creates meaning for people.

Jay: Right, right.

Anne: Another thing that is interesting to me is that it is often a story that makes identity compelling. So, if you are the president of a university and you say, "We ought to think of ourselves as supporting a free society," you may have cynical professors respond, "No way." Instead, you can use stories to make your point. As often happens, the president has students writing letters about how they are the first in their family to come to the university. Even cynical professors respond to the appeal of these letters because the stories have a compelling moral dimension. But it becomes real because of the story, it isn't just moralizing.

Jay: This fits nicely with how we previously discussed the process of how an identity forms and is articulated. You repeat the stories, and the stories define a range of themes. After a period of time, you begin to label the themes as those things that we do in the university that have the effect of maintaining and creating a free society. I think storytelling is the only way to do it, especially in this context, where cynicism is the assumed condition of most of the people associated with the university. You really have to be very subtle about how you bring in the moral dimension. On the other hand, it is no different than the Koch problem.

Anne: Tell the Koch secretary story, because that is one of my favorite stories.

Jay: The Koch secretary story. A friend of mine goes to work after leaving a university position. First day of work at Koch. He is a former professor. He decides he needs to make some copies of some articles. So he takes the copies and goes to a Xerox machine, which is what you do at the university. He is about to make a copy, when his secretary comes up and says, "Excuse me, what are you doing?" He says, "I'm making copies." She responds, "Well, let's think about this for a second. Your opportunity cost for making these copies is about $170 an hour, because if you look at your direct income, benefits, and everything, that is about how much you cost to be employed by Koch. My opportunity cost, on the other hand, is about $50 an hour if I include all those different things. So it seems to me that since my opportunity costs for making copies are substantially lower than your opportunity cost to make copies, that I should be making these copies. You need to go back to your office and figure out how you can add value to Koch in excess of $170 an hour." Now that is a very profound and highly diffused moral sense of how one is actually supposed to work in an organization.

Anne: She had a strong sense of "who we are," and she helped him have it, too.

Jay: And trained him to do that. He tells that story with admiration. This was not a power play. This was not an agency thing. This was, "I learned a lot from my secretary that day."

I tell that story and then I talk about agency theory. [Laughter.] Agency theory is only relevant when people in an organization have not identified with and internalized the moral.

[We end the group's conversation here. It wasn't the actual end of the conversation, but it is an appropriate stopping place. I hope that a little bit of the energy, excitement, and, yes, fun of the group has come through in this transcript. And I especially hope that Dave and Paul can think of some other good academic excuse to get us all together again at Sundance for Identity IV.]

EPILOGUE

A year after the conference, Dave Whetten and Paul Godfrey asked me to suggest topics emerging from my group's conversations that I would like to see addressed in dissertation research. Before I do that, I want to take this opportunity to suggest that the best dissertation topic is the one about which the student is passionate. So my best advice is to find a topic about which you care deeply. Crafting and framing a topic to which you are committed in order to "sell" it to journal reviewers is much easier (and rewarding) than devoting years of your life to something about which you are indifferent but that you think might be interesting to others.

When choosing a dissertation topic (or any research for that matter), you can be theory driven, problem driven, method driven, or data driven. In the hierarchy of management research, theory-driven research is usually given the highest status, regardless of subfield. I could not agree more. The ultimate aim of any excellent dissertation should be to develop new theory or to extend existing theory. But purely theory-driven research can be quite sterile and runs the risk of irrelevance.

In general, strategy research derives its greatest strength from being problem driven. In problem-driven research, the researcher identifies the real-world problem he or she wants to address (maybe even solve!) and is driven by the problem to find the theory, methods, and data that best fit the problem. The seven areas for research I discuss below are all problem driven. But I also think they provide the greatest opportunities to discover and extend theory about organization identity.

There are many exciting directions for future research. I've chosen to focus on seven topics that arose from our conversation on strategy and identity. The first two are tracing identity paths and managing identity. The next five I subsume under the heading of problematic situations: mergers and acquisitions, joint ventures and alliances, industry evolution and turbulence, crisis, and temporary organizational forms. Because these situations are problematic for organizations, identity is likely to be surfaced and possibly challenged, and these are the times when management is most likely to attempt an active hand at managing identity. Underpinning these topics are several processes: formation, maintenance, decay, change, and conflict of organization identity. Overlaying the topics are the questions of competitive advantage and disadvantages associated with managing a socially complex, often tacit, and organizationally pervasive resource such as organization identity. In addition to these substantive subjects, these areas also provide fruitful ground for methodological contributions. In the rest of this epilogue, I briefly comment on each of these.

Tracing identity paths. Much of our conversation focused on ideas that reflected our belief in the path dependence of organizational identity. Although we also believe that managers can take actions to influence identity at particular points in time, an organization's identity is dependent upon actions taken at founding and at crucial defining moments in its history. Without pushing the analogy to individual-level identity too far, I believe the notion of "life course" developed in the self-identity literature might be a promising way to think about the path dependence of identity. Dissertations that historically trace the evolution of identity in a limited number of organizations, perhaps three or four within a single industry, could make significant contributions to our understanding of path dependence. To do this effectively might require the use of historical and biographic methods coupled with identity elicitation methods from psychology. Dissertations that take these approaches could also make significant methodological contributions.

Managing identity and heedfulness. In our conversation, we talk many times about the limits to manageability that identity presents. We do not want to lead researchers into the dark forest of much of the culture research; therefore, we are cautionary. Identity, like culture, is a socially complex, often tacit, and organizationally complex characteristic of organizations. Individuals and groups within an organization are likely to disagree about the nature of the organization's identity (even while holding the beliefs with strong conviction). Still, all of us involved in the conversation have conducted research in organizations where managers were heedful about creating, maintaining, or changing identity. As industries evolve and companies move into new competitive arenas, executives seem to be intuitively aware of the powerful advantages bestowed by an appropriate identity and the equally powerful disadvantages associated with an inappropriate identity.

There are opportunities for dissertation research that addresses the limits of managerial discretion in shaping identity at founding, during crisis and other change events, and in "normal" times. Research that focuses on the *process* of identity management and change is especially needed. This work is probably best done using intensive case studies and participant observation methods from anthropology. Work is also needed that develops underlying theoretical rationales for typologies of situations and the characteristics of identities that provide advantages or disadvantages in these situations. Here is an area where large-scale, cross-organizational research might be most useful.

Problematic Situations

The following situations are interesting because they create special challenges to organization identity. They are fertile research sites because the unique pressures they exert will tend to make identity both salient and problematic for the organizations. The normally tacit, taken-for-granted nature of identity is most likely to surface in these situations.

Mergers, acquisitions, and spin-offs. The SmithKline Beecham (A) case written at INSEAD provides a detailed description of two firms that merged as equals and the combined management's attempts to forge a single, new identity for the resulting organization. The process was difficult and time consuming, and it is not clear if it was entirely successful. In acquisitions, employees of the acquired firm often complain about a loss of personal identity as the acquiring firm's identity overwhelms the identity of their organization. Practices and ideals that were valued previously are now devalued. Executives of firms that have grown through a series of acquisitions, such as AlliedSignal, often find they have a collection of units with very different identities and no sense of a common corporate identity. Finally, spin-offs, especially spin-offs of long-held and previously core business, present the challenges of loss of corporate identity and the need to forge a new identity appropriate for the changed circumstances.

Even in the face of a decidedly mixed performance picture for merger, acquisitions, and spin-offs, these events are occurring at historically high rates. Understanding the unique challenges they pose for organization identity and developing ways that managers can better manage identity during these periods would be important and interesting contributions to both the organization identity and the corporate strategy literatures.

Joint ventures and alliances. Similarly, joint ventures and alliances pose interesting challenges and opportunities for organization identity research. The joint venture literature suggests that up to 90% of all joint ventures are dissolved within 10 years. Some of these are clearly not failures, but rather alliances formed for a particular purpose that was fulfilled and the venture disbanded. Researchers in this area suggest, however, that the vast majority are failures in which one or both parties were unable to achieve the goals they set for the alliance. Because identity brings deeply held, but usually tacit notions of who we are, why we are successful, and the right way to do things, it might be an underlying cause for difficulties in managing joint ventures and other interorganizational relationships. The need to develop trust is becoming a prominent concern in alliance research. Similarity of values and alignment of other aspects of identity might provide important clues for understanding the challenges posed in choosing alliance partners and managing the process. These might also provide important answers to managers intent on increasing the success rate of alliances.

Industry evolution and turbulence. Organization identity is resistant to change. This can provide important stability and continuity to a firm. But if key elements of the identity prevent the organization from seeing environmental change, interpreting it correctly, and acting appropriately, then identity can be a source of competitive disadvantage in changing environments. Telecommunications and other digital industries, health care, higher education, and many other industries are undergoing fundamental changes in industry structure and the bases of competitive success. There are at least two critical issues here. First, how can an organization mutate its identity fast enough to keep pace with these changes? Second, are there substantive elements of identity that help some firms thrive in these environments?

Crisis. Dave Whetten is fond of saying that you do not know what a firm's identity is until "you see them cry." Although I disagree that identity only becomes salient in crisis, I agree that crisis provides unique opportunities to study identity. As in mergers, crisis may make identity more explicit. The crisis forces members to think about what is really most important to them, and, it is hoped, to take action consistent with these values. Sometimes, crises lead organizations to take actions inconsistent with identity. I believe this was the case with Marriott when it spun off its bondholder debt to a new company, Host Marriott, in 1992. The executive who engineered the deal no longer works for the company, and current management agrees that the spin-off could have been handled better if it had been handled in ways more consistent with the corporation's identity.

Additionally, crises are character-building events in the lives of organizations. They precipitate questioning of taken-for-granted beliefs and can become identity-defining moments in which identity is changed, sometimes in subtle, sometimes in radical ways. Of greatest interest to me is not how the organization acts in crisis, but how it processes and interprets its actions once the crisis has passed. What actions do they take to return to core values or to develop new ones? What lessons did they learn? In what ways are they wiser, stronger, or perhaps weaker because of the crisis? It is my belief that organizations that heedfully develop and maintain value-based identities are more likely to avoid crises, are better able to weather crises, and, most importantly, are most likely to rebound stronger than ever in the aftermath of crises. Other than popular books such as *Built to Last,* there is scant evidence to support my intuition. This, then, is a promising area for research.

Temporary organizational forms (and workers). In our conversation, we assumed long-lasting organizations. We talked about agricultural co-ops, universities and business schools, the Baby Bells, Intel, health care organizations, and so on. These are very different organizational forms operating in diverse environments. This diversity enriched our ideas and hinted at the potentially wide generalizability of the identity construct. However, we did not give attention to temporary organizations, such as project consortiums and motion picture film crews. We also did not speculate on the effects that large numbers of temporary and contract workers might have on organization identity. These types of organizations are becoming more common. For example, DuPont recently contracted its informational technology function to Andersen Consulting. Several thousand former DuPont workers still report to the same job locations and do the same jobs, but their paychecks, evaluations, and career paths are now controlled by Andersen. Many other workers in similar situations work for temporary agencies and labor next to permanent workers who enjoy better pay and benefits. These changes in work have to have an effect on the identity of the organizations involved. As far as I know, no one has investigated these situations.

CONCLUSION

In this epilogue, I have suggested seven areas of research that I believe could yield important and interesting (and doable) dissertations. As you can see from the range of topics, the field has only just begun to explore the intersection of strategy and identity. There is much exciting and groundbreaking work to be done. The topics I outlined are just some of the ones that are personally interesting to me. But as I said at the beginning of the epilogue, the best dissertation topic is the one about which the student is passionate.

REFERENCES

Barr, P. S., Stimpert, J. L., & Huff, A. S. (1992, Summer). Cognitive change, strategic action, and organizational renewal. *Strategic Management Journal, 13,* 15-36.

Bartunek, J. M. (1984). Changing interpretive schemes and organizational restructuring: The example of a religious order. *Administrative Science Quarterly, 29,* 355-372.

Huff, J. O., Huff, A. S., & Thomas, H. (1992). Strategic renewal and the interaction of cumulative stress and inertia. *Strategic Management Journal, 13,* 55-75.

Kelly, G. A. (1955). *The psychology of personal constructs* (Vols. 1 & 2). New York: Norton.

Mason, R. O., & Mitroff, I. I. (1981). *Challenging strategic planning assumptions.* New York: Wiley.

Pfeffer, J. (1981). *Power in organizations.* Marshfield, MA: Pitman.

Reger, R. K., Gustafson, L. T., DeMarie, S. M., & Mullane, J. V. (1994). Reframing the organization: Why implementing total quality is easier said than done. *Academy of Management Review, 19,* 565-584.

Van de Ven, A. H., & Poole, M. S. (1995). Explaining development and change in organizations. *Academy of Management Review, 20,* 510-540.

Weick, K. (1995). *Sensemaking in organizations.* Thousand Oaks, CA: Sage.

PART II

How Do People Identify With Organizations?

6

To Be or Not to Be?
Central Questions in
Organizational Identification

MICHAEL G. PRATT[1]

Naturalism in its most naive manifestation made a blunt distinction between the "individ-
ual" and the "environment," hence leading automatically to the notion that an individual's
"identity" is something private, peculiar to himself [or herself]. . . . [Psychologists] discov-
ered accurately enough that identity is not individual, that a man [or woman] "identifies
himself [or herself]" with all sorts of manifestations beyond himself [or herself], and they
set out to "cure" him [or her] of this tendency. It can't be "cured," for the simple reason
that it is normal. . . . Thus, in America, it is natural for a man [or woman] to identify himself
[or herself] with the business corporation he [or she] serves.
—Burke (1937, pp. 263-264)

Whereas identity is often concerned with the question, "Who am I?" identification
asks, "How do *I* come to know who I am in relation to *you*?" As the quote that opens
this chapter suggests, the "you" that "I" use to define myself is often the organiza-
tion(s) in which I participate. In this chapter, I will review some of the central
discussions regarding organizational identification. The first of these central questions of
identification is, "*Who* identifies?" Following Burke (1937), I will begin with the assumption that identification is a process inherent to social animals such as ourselves.
That is, I posit that we all identify. I also argue that identification is a fundamental task of
organizations: Organizations must engender identification to facilitate their functioning
(cf. Cheney, 1983a, 1983b). Recognizing that identification is a rather ubiquitous
process, however, does not necessarily add much to our understanding of what it
means to identify with a social group, such as an organization. The purpose of this

chapter, therefore, is to provide an overview of the other central questions of organizational identification.

Chapter Overview:
An "Incomplete List"

At the University of Illinois, we recognize outstanding teachers in an "Incomplete List of Excellent Teachers." The list is incomplete because there is an explicit recognition that there are many fine teachers who may not have made it to the list (e.g., never had students fill out evaluations, or their excellence was not captured in their teaching ratings), yet who exist nevertheless. This "incomplete list" is a good metaphor for this chapter on organizational identification. Because we are social animals, the topic of identification with others has a long intellectual history that dates back to early philosophical questions about the fundamental relationships between self and other, and self and society. Thus, although this review will discuss many treatments of identification in such diverse fields as psychology, social psychology, communication, and sociology, it will, nevertheless, be incomplete. Two considerations were used to narrow the focus of this review. First, I have limited my review to those ideas that are most relevant to the topic of identification within organizational settings (i.e., organizational identification). Second, I have concentrated most on those ideas and theories that will be touched upon later in this book. Special emphasis has been placed on reviewing social identity theory because this theory has tended to dominate much current thinking on organizational identification (see Ashforth & Mael, 1989; Dutton, Dukerich, & Harquail, 1994).

I have started this chapter by addressing the question, "Who identifies?" The rest of this work will integrate various theories as they inform our understanding of the remaining central questions of organizational identification, namely, "*What* is identification?" "*Why* do people identify (and why do organizations encourage it)?" "*When* are individuals most likely to identify?" and "*How* does identification occur?" As these central questions are being addressed, I also raise many of the *unanswered* questions of organizational identification. Although several scholars have addressed the topic, organizational identification remains an exciting and fertile area for future research.

WHAT IS ORGANIZATIONAL IDENTIFICATION?

There are some differences in how identification has been defined, but most conceptualizations agree that identification involves an individual[2] coming to see another (individual, group, object) as being definitive of one's own self. A summary of some of the more influential definitions of identification can be found in Table 6.1.

Building on these definitions, I suggest that *organizational identification occurs when an individual's beliefs about his or her organization become self-referential or self-defining.* That is, organizational identification occurs when one comes to integrate beliefs about one's organization into one's identity. Several aspects of this

TABLE 6.1   Definitions of Identification

Author(s)	Definition
Aronson (1992)	"[Identification] is a response to social influence brought about by an individual's desire to be like the influencer" (p. 34).
Ashforth and Mael (1989)	"Social identification, therefore, is the perception of oneness or belongingness to some human aggregate" (p. 21).
Cheney (1983a)	"Identification—with organizations or anything else—is an active process by which individuals link themselves to elements in the social scene" (p. 342).
Dutton, Dukerich, and Harquail (1993)	"When a person's self-concept contains the same attributes as those in the perceived organizational identity, we define this cognitive link as organizational identification" (p. 239).
Tajfel (1983)	"In order to achieve the state of 'identification,' two components are necessary . . . a cognitive one, in the sense of awareness of membership; and an evaluative one, in the sense that this awareness is related to some value connotations" (p. 2).

definition are worth noting. First, it focuses on *beliefs*. Most treatments of identification talk about identifying with people *or* ideas. For example, Cheney (1983b) distinguishes identification with people from identification with values, goals, and objects: "As an individual response to the divisions of society, a person acts to identify with some target(s), i.e., persons, families, groups, collectivities; and to a lesser extent, values, goals, knowledge, activities, objects" (p. 145). Similarly, in organizations, members have been argued to identify with a wide range of targets, including organizational leaders, symbols, mission statements, products, and so on. However, it is not clear that identifying with individuals is any different, in theory, than identifying with things that are not individuals (e.g., values). In fact, in all of these cases, the target of identification is beliefs. If I identify with my boss, for example, what does this mean? With what about my boss am I identifying? I would argue that it is my beliefs about who my boss is (or what he or she represents) that I see as self-defining.[3] Alternatively, when beliefs about a person change (e.g., "I realize I never *really* knew this person"), identifications can change.

Second, unlike other concepts that deal with how individuals relate to or attach themselves to organizations, organizational identification explicitly refers to the social aspects of a person's *identity* or *self-concept*. As will be elucidated upon later in this chapter, although identification is often used as *one* explanatory mechanism underlying related concepts, such as organizational commitment and person-organization fit, these latter concepts often draw upon literatures that have little relevance to identity theory (e.g., economics or organizational selection) in order to explain individual-organization relationships.

Third, this definition leaves open the possibility of two different ways or *paths* to identification: through the recognition of an organization deemed similar to one's self, or through changes in one's self to become more similar to an organization. Most conceptualizations of identification involve some sort of perception of value congruence between an individual and an organization. However, such perceptions of congruence do not necessarily entail radical changes in individual values. Rather, congruence can also be perceived when individuals join organizations that they believe reflect their own values (cf. Judge & Bretz, 1992; Schneider, 1987). Each of these two "paths" highlights different meanings of identifying.

For example, one meaning of identifying is "to recognize." This meaning is made salient when individuals identify with an organization that they believe has values and beliefs that are similar to their own. In this case, we use organizations that we see as similar to ourselves to refer to ourselves (e.g., although not an employee, I can identify with Ben and Jerry's Ice Cream because we both value the environment). This path is what I will refer to as identification through *affinity,* where "like seeks like": In this case, individuals seek similar organizations. Affinity identification is similar to what Schneider and his colleagues refer to as "attraction" because it denotes that individuals are drawn toward organizations that they perceive as similar to themselves (Schneider, 1987; Schneider, Goldstein, & Smith, 1995). Identification, in this sense, may not involve identity *change*; however, it does involve using the identity as a means of understanding one's relationship with the organization. That is, I argue that this path to identification involves using one's own identity *as a means of determining* that there is a kinship between, or a unity of, self and organization. As a result, it conforms to Ashforth and Mael's (1989) contention that although identification involves a "feeling of oneness" with an organization, it does not necessarily involve changes in individual values or beliefs. Moreover, it supports their later findings, which suggest that individuals who perceive themselves to be similar to an organization are more likely to identify with that organization (Mael & Ashforth, 1995).

Identifying can also refer to "the act making the same (or identical)." This meaning of identifying makes salient the second "path" to identification: identification through *emulation*. Here, we identify with organizations when we incorporate organizational beliefs and values into our own identities.[4] For example, in my own work on Amway (Pratt, 1994, 1997a, 1997b), I examined how some individuals' self-concepts began to change as they started to define themselves in terms of other Amway distributors. This conceptualization is similar to that of Tajfel (1982), who sees social identification as occurring when one's membership in a group becomes part of one's self-concept. In his work on social identity theory, Tajfel implies a process whereby one changes one's view of self by incorporating his or her beliefs about a social group (Tajfel, 1981, 1982; Tajfel & Turner, 1979). Similarly, Aronson (1992), borrowing from Kelman (1961), sees identification as involving the adoption of the beliefs and values of a person or persons whom an individual desires to be like.

A fourth aspect to the definition of identification that I propose is that individuals need not become organizational members in order to identify with an organization. As illustrated when describing the affinity "path" to identification, one may identify with an organization such as Ben and Jerry's Ice Cream from a distance. Although studying phenomena such as "organizational groupies" has remained largely outside of the scope of research on organizational identification, it is clear that this aspect of identification may become increasingly important as our notion of what an "organizational member" is becomes broader and the boundaries between organizational insiders and outsiders becomes more diffuse (e.g., customers as members, or as electronic "members" of virtual organizations).

In sum, organizational identification is the process whereby an individual's beliefs about an organization become self-referential or self-defining. The act of "becoming" identified seems to involve either (a) evoking one's self-concept in the recognition that one shares similar values with an organization (affinity), or (b) changing one's self-concept so that one's values and beliefs become more similar to the organization's (emulation). These two paths, I believe, help to make sense of some of the controversies and confusions surrounding the concept of organizational identification. It is to these controversies that I now turn when discussing "what identification is not."

What Identification Is Not

Despite some similarities across definitions, controversy exists over what identification is—and perhaps most importantly, what identification is not. Specifically, identification is most often confused and/or equated with three related concepts: internalization, organizational commitment, and person-organization fit. In the following sections, I recount and elaborate upon much of the extant work on the relationships among identification and these three concepts.

Organizational Identification Versus
Internalization of Organizational Values and Beliefs

One of the biggest confusions regarding identification with an organization entails the degree to which it involves the adoption of organizational values (i.e., internalization). Although the two concepts are often treated separately, the line between identification and internalization is somewhat fuzzy and difficult to distinguish conceptually. Two of the more influential definitions of social/organizational identification highlight this conceptual ambiguity and tension. Tajfel (1981, 1982), for example, defines identification as part of an individual's self-concept. An individual's self-concept, he argues, is composed of a social identity (or identities) and a personal identity. A personal identity is that part of the self that is composed of idiosyncratic attributes (e.g., about one's personality and abilities). One's social identity, however, involves defining oneself in terms of the groups to which one belongs (i.e., social categories). It is "that *part* of the individuals' self-concept which derives from their knowledge of a social group (or groups) together with the value and emotional significance of that membership" (Tajfel, 1981, p. 255). Because the incorporation of social identities involves a change in the self-concept, Tajfel's conceptualization of identification involves some degree of internalization (see Ashforth & Mael, 1989). Ashforth and Mael (1989), however, try to clearly distinguish identification from internalization by defining identification as a perception of unity or "oneness" with the organization that does not necessarily entail the adoption of organizational values. But in a later article (Mael & Ashforth, 1995), they note that in "identifying with the organization, people often internalize these attributes as their own" (p. 312).

Although the line between identification and internalization is sometimes difficult to distinguish, there have been attempts to help resolve the problem by ordering the terms in "conceptual space." One of the oldest and most popular ways of distinguishing identification from internalization is to view them as differing in degree, permanence, and motivation. In his original work, Kelman (1961) distinguished identification from compliance and internalization (see also Aronson, 1992, and O'Reilly & Chatman, 1986, for similar treatments). Borrowing from Kelman (1961), Aronson (1992) suggests that compliance, identification, and internalization are all responses to social influence. Compliance occurs when the individual follows the dictates of an individual or group because of valued rewards. Identification is motivated by attraction and involves adopting some of the values and beliefs of others. Internalization also involves the adoption of values and beliefs but is motivated by a need to be right rather than to be liked. Moreover, internalization is associated with embracing others' values and beliefs more deeply than in identification, thus resulting in more permanent and fundamental changes within an individual. In sum, for Kelman (1961) and those that adopt his typology (e.g., Aronson, 1992; O'Reilly & Chatman, 1986), identification and internalization are seen as differing in magnitude (strong vs. stronger), permanence (less vs. more permanent), and motivational drives (attraction vs. being right).

Another way to view the identification versus internalization "debate" would be to adopt the arguments that I have mentioned above about the two paths to identification. Using this conceptual scheme, the internalization of values *after* one becomes an organizational member becomes one way for identification to occur[5]— the other involving the recognition of similar values. That is, internalization becomes necessary for identification through *emulation*. (But note that internalization of values takes place prior to organizational involvement in affinity identification.) Positing that the internalization of organizational values occurs in some forms of identification (e.g., emulation) and not others (e.g., affinity) is consistent with other definitions of organizational identification, such as the one recently posited by Dutton et al. (1994). These scholars define identification as a cognitive connection that occurs when "a person's self-concept contains the same attributes as those in the perceived organizational identity" (p. 239). Both emulation (via internalization) and affinity could lead to the outcome where there are similar attributes in one's self-concept and in one's beliefs about the organization's identity.[6]

Organizational Identification
Versus Organizational Commitment

Organizational commitment, broadly defined, refers to a psychological bond that a member forms with his or her employing organization that is characterized by behavioral, emotional, and cognitive consistency on the part of the member (Pratt, 1994). Similar to organizational identification, the focus of organizational commitment is the relationship between an individual member and the employing organization. Implicit or explicit in particular conceptualizations and measures of commit-ment—specifically attitudinal, affective, or "value congruence"[7] conceptualizations—is the equating of organizational commitment with organizational identification.

The conceptual overlap between organizational commitment and organizational identification resides in how they are defined and measured. For example, one of the most frequently used conceptualizations of commitment can be found in the Organizational Commitment Questionnaire (Mowday, Porter, & Steers, 1982; Mowday, Steers, & Porter, 1979; Porter & Steers, 1973; Porter, Steers, Mowday, & Boulian, 1974). According to Cook, Hepworth, Wall, and Warr (1981), the OCQ defines commitment as the

> strength of an individual's identification and involvement in a particular organization, and is said to be characterized by three factors: a strong belief in and acceptance of the organi-zation's goals and values; a readiness to exert considerable effort on behalf of the organi-zation; and a strong desire to remain a member of the organization. (p. 84)

Explicit in this definition is the notion that identification is a large part of organiza-tional commitment.

Similarly, other scholars have viewed identification as being integral to the commitment process (Dutton et al., 1994). For example, Buchanan (1974) sees identification as one of three "components" of organizational commitment, along with loyalty and job involvement. More recently, O'Reilly and Chatman (1986) have adopted Kelman's (1961) typology (compliance, identification, and internalization) and have used it to describe the different bases of organizational attachment. However, Vandenberg, Self, and Seo (1994) note that O'Reilly and Chatman's (1986) measure of identification is "conceptually redundant" with the OCQ. Finally, Meyer and Allen (1991) define *affective commitment* as "the employee's emotional attachment to, identification with, and involvement in the organization" (p. 67). Affective commitment, and thus identification, is seen as one of three components of commitment, along with continuance and normative commitment.[8]

Despite their similarities, some researchers have attempted to make organiza-tional identification and organizational commitment more conceptually distinct. Ashforth and Mael (1989), for example, try to differentiate identification and commitment (as defined by the OCQ) in two ways. First, they note that the two terms differ in their specificity. Because many organizations have similar values and goals, and organizational commitment simply involves a strong belief in those values and goals (and not the organization per se), organizational commitment need not be organization-specific. Organizational identification, however, must be or-ganization-specific because it is a specific organization that is seen as being self-defining. Second, they posit that the OCQ does not measure an individual's "feelings of oneness" with the organization and thus is conceptually distinct from their measurement of organizational identification.

Moreover, organizational identification is clearly distinct from some conceptu-alizations of organizational commitment.[9] For example, identification has not been posited to be important to assessments of "side-bet," continuance, or calculative commitments (Farrell & Rusbult, 1981; Hrebiniak & Alutto, 1972; Meyer & Allen, 1984; Rusbult & Farrell, 1983; Sheldon, 1971). These conceptualizations of commitment tend to focus on the economic reasons for staying with or leaving an organization. Specifically, they focus on individuals' investments and calculations of losses and benefits as explanatory mechanisms for commitment. As such, they tend to be more similar to Kelman's (1961) notion of compliance than to identification.

In sum, those who favor attitudinal conceptualizations of commitment tend to see identification as being either identical with or part of organizational commitment. Those who view commitment in more economic terms, such as those who advocate calculative or continuance models, see identification as being very different from organizational commitment. What both of these views lack, however, is a deeper understanding of the differences between organizational identification and organizational commitment. Perhaps the most salient distinction is that identification explains the individual-organization relationship in terms of an individual's self-concept; organizational commitment does not. As such, the two seem to ask very different questions. Organizational commitment is often associated with, "How happy or satisfied am I with my organization?" Consequently, it is sometimes viewed as a measure similar to, but more global than, job satisfaction, and it is often used to predict turnover and absenteeism (cf. Mowday et al., 1982). Organizational identification, by contrast, is concerned with the question, "How do I perceive myself in relation to my organization?" This is not to say that individuals who identify strongly with the organization do not experience satisfaction; rather, satisfaction in identification is more "ground" than "figure"; that is, it is not central to the concept. The differences are clear when you consider that attitudinal measures of commitment are equated with the "acceptance" of organizational values and beliefs (Meyer & Allen, 1991), whereas identification is equated with "sharing" or "possessing" organizational values and beliefs.

Organizational Identification
Versus Person-Organization (P-O) Fit

Scholars examining person-organization fit attempt to assess the compatibility of an individual with an organization (Chatman, 1989; Judge & Ferris, 1992; Kristoff, 1996; Lovelace & Rosen, 1996; O'Reilly, Chatman, & Caldwell, 1991; Tsui, Egan, & O'Reilly, 1992). Similar to commitment, some conceptualizations of person-organization (P-O) fit are conceptually similar to that of organizational identification. For example, Chatman (1989) defines P-O fit as "the congruence between the norms and values of organizations and the values of persons" (p. 339).

However, many researchers see P-O fit as being much broader than what is normally considered organizational identification. For example, in her review of the P-O fit literature, Kristoff (1996) defines person-organization fit as "the compatibility between people and organizations that occurs when (a) at least one entity provides what the other needs, or (b) they share similar fundamental characteristics, or (c) both (pp. 4-5). The relationship between organizational identification and P-O fit is most evident in her second condition, that of similarity of fundamental characteristics.

Moreover, according to Kristoff (1996), P-O fit can be either *complementary,* whereby the individual adds distinctive characteristics or values to the organization in an attempt to make the organization more "whole," or *supplementary,* in that an individual possesses values and characteristics that are similar to those of other organizational members. In this conceptualization scheme, organizational identification may be viewed as one assessment of a supplementary fit. Thus, similar to the relationship between identification and commitment, P-O fit seems to be a broader concept than organizational identification.

This additional conceptual breadth is also evidenced by the fact that organizational identification is very dissimilar to some notions of fit that are categorized under the rubric of P-O fit. For example, person-situation (a.k.a. person-job) fit attempts to assess the match between an individual's skill qualifications and organizational job requirements (Kristoff, 1996; O'Reilly et al., 1991). Such conceptualizations do not necessitate any form of identification in the analysis of fit.

The differences between organizational identification and P-O fit, however, are not best captured by measurements of breadth. As with organizational commitment, the biggest difference between the two concepts lies in the fact that identification is an identity-based theory of organizational attachment, whereas P-O fit is not. Identification is concerned with understanding the fundamental *nature* of the individual-organizational relationship ("Who am I in relation to the organization?"); it is not necessarily an assessment of the potential *costs* or *benefits* of that relationship. P-O fit, by contrast, seems to be more instrumental: It involves calculations about whether or not an individual would provide some gain or advantage to an organization, or vice versa. Thus, although the two concepts speak to the individual-organizational relationship, they appear to be interested in explaining different aspects of that relationship.

What Organizational Identification Is:
A Summary and Commentary

To summarize, organizational identification is said to occur when an individual's beliefs about his or her organization become self-referential or self-defining. Identification has been posited to be related to, but conceptually distinct from, notions of internalization, organizational commitment, and person-organization fit. I have also noted that the boundaries between and among these concepts are not always clear. As Albert will point out in a later chapter, there are numerous complexities involved in defining the concept of identification.

I have also suggested that there may be two paths to identification. The first involves recognizing an organization as one that has values and beliefs that are similar to those in one's own identity: identification through affinity. The second involves changes in an individual's values and beliefs so that they become more congruent with their organization's: identification through emulation. Inherent in both of these paths are rather simplistic assumptions about individuals with clearly delineated self-concepts identifying with relatively "monolithic" social groups. However, it is clear that individuals must manage multiple identifications and that organizations themselves have multiple identities that can be the target of identification (see Cheney, 1991; Pratt & Rafaeli, 1997). In her chapter on identification, Elsbach probes more deeply into some of the intricacies of the individual-organizational bond and explores how individuals may be embedded in constellations of identifications. Moreover, she asks how individuals identify with organizations that have fragmented identities.

While attempting to answer many questions about the construct, this review of identification raises others. For example, although most treatments of the term recognize the cognitive aspects of identification, they do not explore in detail the emotional aspects. This is not to say that affect has been completely ignored by identification researchers. Ashforth and Mael (1989), for example, refer to identification as a "feeling", and Tajfel (1982) refers to the "value and emotional significance of that membership" (p. 24) as being central to social identities. In my own work on Amway distributors (Pratt, 1994; Pratt & Barnett, 1997), for example, I found that emotions played a large role in inducing organizational identification. Specifically, emotions play a large role in breaking old relationships (and identifications) and creating new ones. Despite these conceptualizations, however, there has been very little work exploring the emotional side of identification. Harquail begins to address this shortcoming in her discussion of organizational identification with the *whole* person.

An emphasis on beliefs in identification research also suggests the importance of sensemaking and interpretation in identification (Weick, 1995). Many accounts of identification involve several of the characteristics that Weick (1995) sees as central to sensemaking: Identification, at minimum, is grounded in identity construction; it involves the extraction of cues; and it is social, retrospective, and ongoing. For example, given that identification is based on subjective beliefs, ascertaining whether or not one is "congruent" with an organization is likely to involve retrospective interpretations of one's own values as well as those of the organization. This process, in addition, is likely to involve more than a simple "matching process" considering that individuals and organizations have multiple and sometimes conflicting identities. Thus, sensemaking may be needed in order to determine which aspects of our individual identity we feel need to be congruent with specific organizational identities.[10]

Why Organizational Identification?
Potential Outcomes for
Individuals and Organizations

One theme that threads through the discussion of "what identity is" is why people identify with others in the first place. For example, Kelman (1961) partially distinguishes identification from internalization on whether the person wants to be needed or wants to be right. Similarly, Cheney (1983a, 1983b) sees identification forming because social divisions cause individuals to feel disconnected and alone. Here, I discuss some reasons for why people identify with others, in general, and to organizations, more specifically. I then discuss why organizations attempt to foster identification in members. Thus, I change perspectives from what individuals gain by identifying to what outcomes organizations gain by this identification.

Identification: Why Individuals Identify and What They Hope to Gain

As the quote opening this chapter suggests, many theorists view identification as a basic human function. However, such assertions do little to illuminate what benefits individuals hope to gain through identification. In this section, I discuss the relationship between identification and the fulfillment of four types of individual needs: safety, affiliation, self-enhancement, and holistic needs.

Identification and Safety Needs

It appears that all social animals engage in some form of identification. Some of these tendencies are "hardwired" in genetic codes, such as the case of imprinting, where a young animal, such as a duckling, is programmed to identify a target as an object of learning (Lorenz, 1937). (For those who have taken courses in psychology or ethology—Lorenz is often pictured with a group of ducks following him around. He is the person who noticed that ducklings would "imprint" on the first moving object that they noticed within 2 days of being born.) Although it is unclear whether we could refer to the duckling as "identifying" with a parental figure, imprinting is suggestive of a need of animals to seek out others as a source of information about what kind of creature one is (even if that information is false—as in the case of Lorenz and the ducks). Moreover, such behavior is likely to have an adaptive or protective function that facilitates the survival of the species.

In humans, the need to identify may be as much for psychological safety as physical safety. For example, Erez and Earley (1993) note that self-efficacy and self-consistency are primary motivators in the development of the self. Feelings of safety and trust underlie both of these needs as individuals attempt to experience some control over their environment through perceptions of competence or through perceptions of redundant and predictable patterns. Organizational literature linking identification with safety needs is scant; however, some indirect evidence does exist. For example, Bullis and Bach (1989) note that identification is likely to occur during particular turning points in the mentor-protégé relationship. Such identifications may be prompted by feelings of vulnerability or uncertainty, thus explaining why identification in these instances is associated with protégés asking for more advice from their mentors. Ashforth and Mael (1989) suggest that threats from *external* groups may increase identification with one's own group, whereas Pratt has found that identification (Pratt, 1994, 1997a) and individual change (Pratt & Barnett,

1997) may result from members trying to resolve tensions or ambivalences raised *within* the organization by organizational elites. In the latter case, identification serves as a kind of coping mechanism that members use to resolve inconsistent cognitions and emotions.

Finally, identification motivated by safety concerns may occur in situations where individuals feel some coercion to become or remain as organizational members. This situation would be analogous to, but less intense than, the "Stockholm syndrome," in which hostages come to identify with their captors (Pilevsky, 1989). Organizational members may feel that their choices about being an organizational member are restricted when (a) they have few employment options and therefore feel compelled to remain with an organization, or (b) they are "strongly encouraged" to join a new organization because of a merger, acquisition, or partnership. To illustrate, a colleague and I are currently examining rural doctors who have been "bought out" by a larger managed care firm (see Nair & Pratt, 1997). In all of the interviews conducted, physicians expressed a feeling of being "trapped" by the managed care organization. Physicians often described the "inevitability" of managed care and how they needed to join the managed care organization to survive. Despite resentment among these doctors, however, some have come to strongly identify with the managed care organization. Perhaps their identification is similar to a type of "Stockholm effect." Future research on reluctant organizational members may shed light on the protective function of identification.

Identification and Affiliation Needs

One of the most frequently discussed reasons for identification concerns needs for belonging and affiliation. Kelman (1961), for example, posited that liking a person or group is an important motivator for identification. Moreover, Aronson (1992) notes that behavioral change due to identification occurs because "it [identification] puts us in a satisfying relationship to the person or persons with whom we are identifying" (p. 34). Thus, identification seems to be related to individuals' social needs. These social needs are also suggested in Ashforth and Mael's (1989, p. 21) view of organizational identification. As noted in Table 6.1, they see identification as "the perception of oneness with or belongingness to some human aggregate." Thus, they seem to see belongingness as being central to organizational identification.

Scholars trained in the tradition of communication and rhetoric forcefully argue that the purpose of identification is to help organizational members overcome social isolation. Cheney (1983a, 1983b), building on Burke (1937), states that identification with organizations is a natural response to the sense of "separateness" that workers feel in today's organizations. According to Cheney (1983b), "As an individual response to the divisions of society, a person acts to identify with some target(s)" (p. 145). Specifically, organizational identification is seen as the remedy for the alienation experienced by workers because of the division of labor. Thus, needs to belong are at the heart of the drive to identify with an organization or other corporate body.

Identification and Self-Enhancement Needs

A central tenet of many theories of identity is that individuals seek to have a positive view of themselves. Identification can serve to fill this self-enhancement function (Erez & Earley, 1993). Psychoanalysts have long discussed this use of identification. Termed an "ego-defense mechanism," identification is said to occur when one tries to enhance one's sense of self by modeling oneself after someone who is respected or admired. Thus, a barely competent middle manager may try to increase his sense of self-worth by copying the behavior of the company's CEO.

In terms of identification with social groups, social identity theory (see Hogg, Terry, & White, 1995; Tajfel, 1981, 1982) suggests that identification is driven by needs for self-enhancement. Specifically, they note that individuals are driven to perceive groups in which they are members (their ingroups) as being more positive than those groups in which they are not members (their outgroups). Similarly, Cheney (1983b) notes that "corporate" identities may enhance feelings of self-worth by providing status and prestige. Finally, Dutton et al. (1994) suggest that organizations with attractive images and identities are likely to induce identification in members. Attractiveness, they argue, is partially determined by assessments of self-enhancement. Specifically, attractiveness is partially determined by how much an organizational identity makes people feel distinctive or special, as well as the degree to which the identity enhances an individual's sense of self-esteem. In sum, this research suggests that individuals may identify with organizations as a means of enhancing their own sense of self-worth.[11]

Identification and Holistic Needs

Some scholars suggest that individuals may seek to identify with an organization in order to find meaning or a sense of purpose in one's life. Organizational members are increasingly faced with the uncertainty and anxiety that come with global competition, rapidly changing market environments, organizational downsizing, work-family tensions, and other organizational changes. Because of these changes, members are coming to feel that their lives are more fragmented and often more meaningless. As a result, they are seeking to find deeper meanings that help reorder and perhaps even simplify their lives. This need is sometimes referred to as self-actualization, a holistic need, or even a spiritual need.

Organizations associated with a particular vision (Collins & Porras, 1991), social cause, or worldview (Greil & Rudy, 1983, 1984; Lofland & Stark, 1965) may be successful in fostering identification because they cause individuals to feel complete in a way that is more profound than denoted by affiliation or self-enhancement needs. Amway distributors, for example, often deepen their identification with Amway through the adoption of religious values (Pratt, 1994, 1997b). Moreover, Amway provides a worldview that integrates individuals' family, social, work, and spiritual lives (Pratt, 1994). Although the role of "meaning seeking" has been largely unexplored in organizational research on identification, these issues have been addressed elsewhere. Lofland and Stark (1965), for example, suggest that an individual is more likely to identify with a cult if he or she is a religious *seeker* "searching for some satisfactory system of religious meaning to interpret and resolve his [or her] discontent" (p. 868). More recently, Neck and Milliman (1994) suggest that individuals seek organizations where they can enact "one's set of deeply held personal values" (p. 9). Thus, individuals who are feeling incomplete may sometimes seek to identify with organizations in an attempt to feel whole.

Why Do Organizations Foster Identification?

When reading the extant literature on identification, especially the work on identification rhetoric (Cheney, 1983a, 1983b), it is clear that organizations can greatly benefit from inducing identification within their members. The motivation for why organizations try to foster identification is summed up quite succinctly by Cheney (1983b): "In short, fostering identification is the 'intent' of many corporate policies, for with it comes greater assurance that employees will decide with organizational interests uppermost in mind" (p. 158).

Researchers have posited several outcomes of organizational identification that indicate that "organizational interests" are likely being met. To illustrate, identification has been linked to greater employee compliance, lower attrition, lower ingroup conflict, and an increase in behaviors congruent with the organization's identity (Aronson, 1992; Dutton et al., 1994; Mael & Ashforth, 1995; Tajfel, 1981, 1982). Moreover, identification has been found to affect member decision making and sensemaking (Cheney, 1983a; Pratt, 1997a, 1997b) in that identification causes members to think and act in ways that consider organizational values and beliefs. In his review of identification theory, Cheney (1983a) provides a long "laundry list" of organizational benefits that are derived from member identification:

> Organizational identification has been linked either theoretically or empirically to each of a variety of work attitudes, behaviors, and outcomes—including motivation, job satisfaction, job performance, role orientation and conflict, employee interaction, and length of service. The study of organizational identification can aid us in explaining the impact of a variety of organizational policies and activities, including socialization (both formal and informal); personnel selection, training, promotion, and transfer; internal organizational communications; and public relations. . . . The study of organizational identification can help us better understand the basis of "referent power" in organizational settings. (Cheney, 1983a, pp. 343-344)

The message given by Cheney (1983a) and others is clear: Organizational identification helps organizations retain control over members. This control comes, in part, from workers who are satisfied with their work and are committed to their organizations because of their identifications.

Some downsides, however, have been posited to follow from fostering identification within organizational members. Schneider et al. (1995) imply that organizations that foster high degrees of identification may not be able to adapt to changing demands from constituents and from exogenous crises. They argue that as organizations come to have increasing numbers of people who have values and beliefs similar to the organization, the resulting homogeneity will cause the organizations to implement strategies that do not match environmental conditions. Thus, organizations with highly identified workers may be more likely to fail. Similarly, Tajfel and others (Hogg et al., 1995; Tajfel, 1981, 1982) argue that increased identification with a particular ingroup may lead to stereotyping and degrading outgroup members, thus leading to conflict. Finally, Ashforth and Mael add that high degrees of identification among organizational members can sometimes lead to overdependence on and overconformity to organizational dictates; antisocial, unethical, and even tyrannical behaviors; decreased creativity and risk taking; and the loss of an independent sense of self (Ashforth & Mael, 1996; Mael & Ashforth, 1992). Moreover, they add that high identification can damage self-esteem if the target organization becomes stigmatized.

Why Identification?
A Summary and Commentary

I have argued that the motivation for identification by individuals and organizations is the fulfillment of needs. Individuals seek to identify with social groups, such as organizations, in order to feel safety, belonging, or self-esteem, or to satisfy a search for transcendent meaning. What was left unaddressed, however, was the possibility that identification, in and of itself, could be a human need. Glynn discusses in detail the possible differences in individuals' needs to identify with organizations later in this book.

I have also argued that organizations try to foster member identification in order to gain more control over members[12]—control that occurs, in part, by making members more satisfied. Although organizational identification seems like a panacea for both individuals and their employing organizations, *some* dangers of high identification have been identified.

Clearly, more work needs to be done on the potentially negative effects of organizational identification. One only needs to look at the tragedies of the People's Temple, Branch Davidians, and Heaven's Gate to realize that one can identify with an organization too much. Moreover, it would be interesting to explore what role, if any, overidentification may have played in the problems of IBM and Apple in the 1980s and 1990s. Both of these companies were known for creating high degrees of organizational identification (O'Reilly, 1989), and both had problems adjusting to environmental demands. Although it is too simplistic to view their problems simply in terms of identification, it may be worth exploring the role of overidentification in organizations that are undone by their own success (Barnett & Pratt, 1997). In short, much more is known about the positive side of identification than about its dark side. To help remedy this imbalance, the dark side of organizational identification is addressed in the next chapter in the discussion by Dukerich, Kramer, and Parks.

Examples such as the People's Temple and Heaven's Gate also highlight another underdeveloped area of organizational identification: that of disidentification. If members are prone to identify with organizations (even when such identifications can be dangerous), what can cause members to break an identification? The question of disidentification raises several important questions for organizational scholars. For example, do individuals disidentify when their needs are not being met by the organization? If so, how might such assessments be made? What role might multiple identifications play in the process of disidentification? We also need to ask ourselves under what conditions might an organization *want* members to disidentify with the organization? More problematically, if managers highly identify with their organizations, might they be able to even recognize those conditions in which organizational disidentification is desirable?

Questions about the cost of identification and the causes of disidentification are now being addressed by organizational scholars. Ibarra (1996), for example, illustrates both the benefits and costs to professionals who adopt "inauthentic selves." Moreover, Pratt (1997a) discusses how processes of "seekership" and "encapsulation" can lead to positive identification, disidentification, ambivalent identification, or deidentification. The topic of disidentification is addressed in the next chapter in the sections by Elsbach and by Dukerich, Kramer, and Parks.

WHEN DO INDIVIDUALS IDENTIFY? ANTECEDENTS OF IDENTIFICATION

Although the answer to when individuals identify may be closely related to why they do so in the first place,[13] the problem of defining the antecedents of identification is not an easy one. To begin, antecedents of identification vary depending on whether one views identification as a process of affinity or emulation. If identification occurs because individuals believe that the organization has values similar to them (affinity), then identification would occur when individuals perceive their values and beliefs to be similar to that of the organization (cf. Dutton et al., 1994; Judge & Bretz, 1992; Judge & Ferris, 1992; O'Reilly et al., 1991; Schneider et al., 1995). Thus, individual experiences and biodata would be useful predictors of identification to organizations possessing strong and coherent sets of values and beliefs (see Mael & Ashforth, 1995).

However, if identification occurs through emulation and the internalization of values, then other predictors need to be postulated. Barker and Tompkins (1994), for example, suggest that identification is more likely to occur the longer you are on the job. Similarly, Hogg et al. (1995) argue that identification can occur once members engage in and enact organizational roles. Most of the currently postulated antecedents of organizational identification, however, follow directly from social identity theory (e.g., Ashforth & Mael, 1989; Dutton et al., 1994), and to a lesser extent, social categorization theory (Tsui et al., 1992).[14] Before explaining these antecedents, I will briefly review these two theories.

Social Identity Theory

Broadly defined, social identity theory (SIT) is about how social categories serve as "a system of orientation which helps to create and define the individual's place in society" (Tajfel, 1981, p. 255). More specifically, SIT is about how individuals incorporate knowledge of their group memberships into conceptions of their self-identities. In SIT terms, the defining characteristics of the social categories with which an individual feels membership (e.g., one's profession, nationality, bowling team) comprise an individual's *social identity* (Hogg, 1996; Hogg et al., 1995; Kawakami & Dion, 1995; Tajfel, 1981, 1982; Tajfel & Turner, 1979). Social identities differ from personal identities in that the former are consensual and shared by group members, whereas the latter are seen as idiosyncratic.

In terms of organizational identification, at least three aspects of SIT are important. First, categorization is viewed as a basic cognitive process. According to SIT, group members need not interact or even feel strong interpersonal ties (i.e., feel strong cohesion) in order to perceive themselves as a member of a group. In a variety of experiments in the "minimal categorization" or "minimal group" paradigm (see Tajfel, 1982, for a review of these studies), several scholars demonstrated that simply being assigned as a member of a group on a random basis is enough to create an ingroup bias. Thus, in response to "When do individuals identify?" SIT suggests that identification is a fundamental human process that occurs whenever individuals perceive themselves to be a member of a collective.

Second, social identification has clear perceptual and behavioral outcomes. When a specific social identity is salient, members tend to perceive and act in ways that conform to the norms and stereotypes of that social group. Thus, perceptions of differences among ingroup members become minimized. In contrast, ingroup members come to perceive outgroup members in stereotypical (and sometimes in derogatory) ways, and differences between ingroup and outgroup members are maximized. As a result, SIT traditionally has been used to explain intergroup behavior and conflict (Hogg, 1996; Hogg et al., 1995; Oaker & Brown, 1986; Tajfel, 1981, 1982; Tajfel & Turner, 1979).

Third, SIT assumes that individuals are motivated to achieve "positive group distinctiveness." That is, groups tend to make comparisons with other groups that "protect, enhance, preserve, or achieve positive social identity for members of the group" (Tajfel, 1982, p. 24). Because social identities are seen as self-evaluative (Hogg et al., 1995), members are motivated to make comparisons with other (out)groups that are favorable. Thus, individuals will often engage in various strategies for maintaining a positive view of their group.

SIT Antecedents to Organizational Identification

SIT posits two underlying processes of identification: *categorization* and *self-enhancement*. Categorization involves clarifying ingroup/outgroup boundaries, whereas self-enhancement involves making favorable ingroup comparisons. Borrowing on

SIT, organizational scholars have developed a set of six main antecedents to organizational identification. Three of these hypotheses deal with categorization, whereas the other three deal with self-enhancement. Each hypothesis is listed below.

Categorization Antecedents

Categorization antecedents all deal with making the distinctions between the ingroup and outgroup clearer. To illustrate, the following SIT-related hypotheses have been posited to lead to greater organizational identification:

1. Organizational identification is more likely to occur in distinctive organizations than in organizations that are not distinctive (Ashforth & Mael, 1989; Dutton et al., 1994; Mael & Ashforth, 1992).
2. Organizational identification is more likely to occur when outgroups are salient than when they are not salient (Ashforth & Mael, 1989; Mael & Ashforth, 1992).
3. Organizational identification is less likely to occur when there is intraorganizational competition than when there is the absence of such competition (Mael & Ashforth, 1992).

The first hypothesis deals with organizational distinctiveness. Organizations (or ingroups) that are seen as more unique are more easily separated from other organizations (or outgroups) and thus would enhance categorization and, ultimately, identification. Similarly, outgroup salience also reinforces the perceived differences between one's organization and those in the external environment.[15] Just as external threats make groups more cohesive, one's own identification with an organization becomes stronger when one's competition becomes more salient. Finally, when there is competition within one's organization, cohesion and identification are likely to suffer. Ingroup differences, as opposed to similarities, are more likely to be made salient. As a result, identification is less likely to occur.

Self-Enhancement Antecedents

Self-enhancement antecedents all predict that organizational identification is more likely to occur when organizational membership increases members' feelings of self-worth. To illustrate, the following SIT-related hypotheses have been posited to lead to greater organizational identification:

1. Organizational identification is more likely to occur when organizations have high prestige than when the organizations lack prestige (Ashforth & Mael, 1989; Mael & Ashforth, 1992).
2. Organizational identification is more likely to occur in organizations that are attractive (and have attractive images) than in organizations that are unattractive (and have unattractive images) (Dutton et al., 1994).
3. Organizational identification is more likely to occur when the perceived organizational identity increases members' self-esteem (Dutton et al., 1994).

All three hypotheses suggest that organizations that are viewed favorably by members are more likely to induce identification than are organizations that are perceived unfavorably by their members. Whether couched in terms of attractiveness (Dutton et al., 1994), or more narrowly as prestige (Mael & Ashforth, 1992), each of these hypotheses emphasizes the assumption of SIT that when ingroups are seen positively, identification is more likely to occur.

Self-Categorization Theory and Organizational Identification Antecedents

As the name implies, self-categorization theory (SCT) explores how individuals classify themselves as members of social groups (i.e., the process of maximizing intracategory similarity and intercategory differences). SCT was developed by Turner and his colleagues as an extension of SIT[16] and focuses on how cognitions and group interactions affect the formation and use of social categories (Hogg, 1996; Hogg et al., 1995; Turner, 1987; Turner, Oakes, Haslam, & McGarty, 1994). In SCT, groups are represented as *prototypes*. Prototypes are "fuzzy sets that capture the context-dependent features of a group membership often in the form of exemplary group members (actual group members who best embody the group) or ideal types (an abstraction of group features)" (Hogg, 1996, p. 231). Identity formation occurs through the process of comparing ourselves to others and placing ourselves in a social field. That is, we categorize ourselves and others based on *how* similar or different we are from various group prototypes. Because it focuses on cognitive *processes,* SCT differs from SIT in that it helps answer the question of *how* members form social categories, rather than focusing on the impact of these categories on intergroup conflict.

A major tenet of SCT is that individuals can categorize themselves and others at various levels of abstraction depending on what categories are evoked by the social field. That is, they claim that whether an individual invokes a personal, social, or more abstract identity (e.g., member of the human race) depends strongly on contextual factors (Turner, 1987). As Hogg (1996) states:

> The social self-concept is context dependent insofar as specific social self-categorizations are brought into play (i.e., become the basis of perception and conduct) by the social field. The cognitive system, in seeking to maximize meaning in a specific context, engages whatever categorization best accounts for the similarities and differences among stimuli. (p. 231)

Unlike SIT, the difference between personal and social identities has little to do with attributes that define the category. Rather, personal versus social is determined by how individuals categorize themselves (i.e., what level of comparison is being made). As Turner and colleagues (1994) illustrate,

> a woman may define herself as intelligent both as an individual compared with other women and as a woman compared with men. As the only female psychologist among a

group of male psychologists, she may, depending on circumstances, make intergroup comparisons between females and males and define self as "us" (women) in contrast to "them" (men), *or* she may use her sex-category membership to differentiate herself as an individual psychologist ("me") compared with other psychologists (i.e., to enhance her individuality within the group). (p. 455)

They also note that as individuals move from a personal to a social identity, self-perceptions become *depersonalized*. That is, "individuals tend to define and see themselves less as differing individual persons and more as interchangeable representatives of some shared social category membership" (Turner et al., 1994, p. 455).

Although the process of categorization will be discussed in greater detail in the following section, there are at least two predictions of SCT that should be noted here:

1. Social identities are more likely to be salient in intergroup contexts, whereas personal identities are more likely to be evoked in intragroup contexts (Turner et al., 1994).
2. Individuals form social categories that maximize the similarities within and differences between (or among) social stimuli (Turner, 1987; Turner et al., 1994).

According to the first prediction, individuals are more likely to view themselves as members of an organization when the social context makes salient other organizations. Thus, similar to the predictions of SIT, SCT predicts that conditions that make boundaries between groups more visible—such as intergroup conflict—will increase the probability of social identification occurring for individuals. It also suggests that when the organization alone is salient, then personal identities are more likely to be evoked.

The second prediction suggests that when forming social categories, and thus social identities, individuals always seek to find that category that best accounts for the similarities and differences among stimuli (e.g., people) within the existing social context. This suggests that in organizations that are highly heterogeneous, organizational categories may not maximize ingroup similarity relative to other groups. For example, if I as a university professor found myself in an organization with an actress, a farmer, and a ship's captain, it might be difficult—especially in the absence of a strong organizational identity or mission—to find an organizational category that maximized our group's similarity in relation to other groups (cf. Ashforth & Mael, 1996). In this case, there seems little that binds us together (e.g., in terms of skills and perhaps values); therefore, a personal identity may best create meaningful distinctions (i.e., best maximize similarities and differences among social stimuli).

Moreover, when organizational members are highly similar to individuals in other organizations, then organizational identification is again difficult. In this case, an organizational categorization would not maximize differences between groups. For example, if organizational members of Hospital A do not see themselves as different from Hospital B, then members may be more likely to adopt an institutional identity rather than an organizational one. Institutional identities may do a better job of maximizing ingroup similarity and outgroup differences (e.g., an institutional identity may capture differences between hospitals and other groups, such as organizations in the computer industry). Therefore, SCT may provide insights into the conditions under which certain social identifications are more likely to occur than others.

Restated in terms of organizational identification, SCT might posit the following three hypotheses:

1. Organizational identification is more likely to occur in a social context where other organizations are made salient than in conditions where the organization alone (i.e., the ingroup) is salient. When the organization alone is salient, personal identities are more likely to be evoked.

2. Organizational identification may be difficult when members of the organization are highly heterogeneous. When organizational members are perceived as being too dissimilar, then a personal identity is likely to be evoked.

3. Organizational identification may also be difficult when members of the organization are too much like members of other organizations. When there is too much homogeneity across organizations, then more abstract identities (e.g., industry, laborers) are likely to be evoked.

When Identification?
A Summary and Commentary

Borrowing from social identity and self-categorization theory, I discussed nine major antecedents to organizational identification. These antecedents suggest that organizational identification is most likely to occur under conditions where the boundaries between one's own organization and other organizations are salient (i.e., categorizations are clear), when membership within an organization is attractive (i.e., group membership leads to self-enhancement), and when organizational categories best account for similarities and differences across individuals and groups. These nine antecedents do not represent all possible or posited antecedents (see Barker & Tompkins, 1994; Dutton et al., 1994; Mael & Ashforth, 1992). However, they do represent the major antecedents predicted by SIT and SCT, two theories that seem to currently predominate most treatments of organizational identification (Ashforth & Mael, 1989; Dutton et al., 1994; Tsui et al., 1992).

Both SIT and SCT assume that individuals compare themselves with social others as part of the categorization, and thus the identification process. Left unanswered by these theories, however, are the mechanisms whereby individuals choose their referents (Kawakami & Dion, 1995). Given that individuals are members of multiple social groups (and thus have many potential social identities), theories of organizational identification need to be more explicit about how individuals choose their "targets" of comparison (e.g., other coworkers, other organizations, other industries). According to SCT, the level of the comparison (an individual, a workgroup, or an organization) will determine whether personal, group, or organizational identifications are made. A related question concerns the mechanisms whereby particular identities become salient for individuals. In the example of the female psychologist mentioned above, Turner et al. (1994) note that to whom the female psychologist compares herself depends on "circumstances." These circumstances, however, are left largely unspecified; they do not address why certain identities are salient at times and others are not. Although some determinants of salience have been offered by SCT theorists, the motivation for why individuals choose to make particular comparisons has yet to be specified (Kawakami & Dion, 1995).

A more serious problem stemming from the predominance of SIT and SCT in guiding research on organizational identification antecedents—and organizational identification more generally—is that our views of organizational identification are based on research done primarily at the group level of analysis rather than at the individual or organizational levels. To illustrate, it is not yet clear how we might conceptualize identification at an organizational level (e.g., similar to questions about isomorphism in institutional theory, we might ask, "Under what conditions do organizations come to identify with one another?"). Likewise, although theories of rhetoric begin to address those organizational conditions that facilitate identification, our understanding of how specific organizational rites, rituals, routines, and other *processes psychologically induce or prevent* member identification is still underdeveloped (cf. Pratt, 1997a). It is also not yet clear how identifying with an organization may be fundamentally similar to or different from identifying with the kinds of social and demographic groups examined in SIT and SCT. Thus, unlike research in organizational identity that has drawn upon theories in anthropology, communications, psychology, and sociology to explain the concept (cf. Albert & Whetten, 1985; Ashforth & Mael, 1989, 1996; Cheney, 1983a, 1983b, 1991; Dutton & Dukerich, 1991; Pratt & Rafaeli, 1997), the range of theories to explain organizational identification has been restricted. One of the biggest challenges to research on organizational identification, therefore, may be to take it beyond the group level of analysis.

The first step toward meeting that challenge is to begin incorporating a wider range of theories into our thinking about organizational identification. In the following section, I will explore different theoretical processes that may lead to organizational identification. These processes should help illuminate a wider range of organizational identification antecedents (and processes) than can be provided by SIT and SCT alone.

HOW DOES IDENTIFICATION OCCUR?

Of all of the central questions of organizational identification, the one that has probably received the least attention by organizational scholars has been, "How does organizational identification occur?" Given the paucity of organizational research on this topic (Ashforth & Mael, 1989; Dutton et al., 1994), the aim of this final section is to point organizational scholars toward theoretical perspectives that may help explain how identification develops in organizational contexts. Specifically, I will review five approaches that organizational scholars may wish to pursue in explaining the formation of identification: (a) attraction-selection-attrition, (b) categorization, (c) rhetorical tactics, (d) socialization/role adoption, and (e) behavioral commitment/schema formation. I review these perspectives with two goals in mind. First, I try to identify *organizational practices* that can foster identification. Second, when possible, I try to highlight the *psychological* or *sociological mechanisms* that explain why these practices are successful.

Attraction-Selection-Attrition

The attraction-selection-attrition (ASA) framework developed by Schneider (1987) may provide insights into some forms of identification. As I mentioned earlier, one path to identification, identification through affinity, involves using one's identity to assess whether or not an organization has values and beliefs similar to one's own. Thus, identification occurs through a process that is similar to "attraction" (Schneider, 1987; Schneider et al., 1995). According to Schneider and colleagues (1995), "The attraction process concerns the fact that people's preferences for particular organizations are based upon an implicit estimate of the congruence of their own personal characteristics and the attributes of potential work organizations" (p. 749).

The ASA model also assumes that individuals who do not seem to fit with the organization will eventually leave the organization through *attrition*. Thus, organizations, over time, tend to become increasingly homogeneous. This homogeneity is also furthered as similar organizational members tend to recruit and *select* new organizational members with values and beliefs comparable to their own. Hence, selection becomes the organizational practice most closely related to organizational identification.

Although not a process model of organizational identification, the ASA model is one of the few that focuses on how individuals come to seek organizations with values and beliefs that are similar to their own. Thus, closer examination into ASA dynamics, especially as they relate to attraction, may help explain how members can come to identify with an organization before any socialization occurs. For example, attraction dynamics have been studied most extensively by scholars studying vocational choice. According to Judge and Bretz (1992), vocational choices have been found to be determined by an individual's personality and needs. However, these scholars also show that an individual's value orientation (e.g., toward fairness, concern for others, and achievement) is important in determining which organization the individual will choose to join *when an organization's values are known*. For our purposes, identification by means of affinity involves (a) individuals knowing their own values and beliefs (i.e., their own identities), and (b) organizations communicating those values to job prospects (and ultimately hiring those who fit).[17]

Categorization

Central to both SIT and SCT is the importance of the categorization process in identifying with social groups. Although most clearly addressed in SCT, scholars have recently begun to integrate SIT and SCT to more fully understand the categorization process (Kawakami & Dion, 1995). For the purpose of organizational identification, two steps must be followed if an individual is going to identify him- or herself as part of an organization: (a) the individual must perceive the organizational identity to be salient, and (b) the individual must self-categorize him- or herself in terms of his or her organizational identity.

Salience of Organizational Identities

To begin, social identities must be salient if they are to determine which social category individuals will adopt and, ultimately, how they will identify themselves.[18] Implicit in this assumption is that the salience of a social category is not equivalent with social identification. According to SCT, for example, the accessibility of a social category is only one determinant of categorization—the other being "fit." Accessibility refers to a social category being viewed as "central, relevant, useful, or likely to be confirmed by the evidence of reality" based on the past experience of the individual (Turner et al., 1994, p. 455). Similarly, Kawakami and Dion (1995) argue that salience is a precursor to categorization.

According to these authors, although the concept of group identity salience is still underdeveloped, some possible predictors of salience have been proposed:

> Examples of proposed determinants of salience of group identities are: (a) when group membership is novel, frequent, or distinctive; (b) when goals or task orientations are group-related; (c) when group affiliations and categories are emphasized and social entitativity is enhanced; (d) when groups are socioculturally and/or personally important to one's self-definition; (e) when the separation and clarity between groups are accentuated so that the perceived similarity and differences between individuals are correlated with division into group membership; (f) in intergroup competition and conflict situations; and (g) when explicit references to group identity are made. (Kawakami & Dion, 1995, pp. 558-559)

Applied to the organization, practices based on these predictors should enhance the salience of organizational identities.

Self-Categorization

Once the salience of an identity is determined, one needs to assess one's fit with that social category. Two kinds of fit are possible. The first type of fit is called *comparative* fit. Comparative fit is guided by the principle of *metacontrast,* which holds that

> a collection of stimuli is more likely to be categorized as an entity to the degree that the average differences between those stimuli are less than the average differences perceived between them and the remaining stimuli that make up the frame of reference. (Turner et al., 1994, p. 455)

From an organizational standpoint, an organization will be perceived as a social category if members within the organization are perceived as being more similar with each other than they are with nonmembers. For individuals, they will identify with Organization A if they perceive themselves to be more similar to Organization A (or the prototypical member of Organization A) than to Organization B.

A second type of fit is *normative* fit. Normative fit refers to the content of the category. Normative fit occurs when an individual's (or a group's) assessment of the similarities and differences between groups matches *shared assumptions* about those similarities and differences. For example, we may want to use the social category of "research-oriented" to distinguish between Big Ten universities and a group of midwestern liberal arts colleges. If, however, we compared the faculty of Big Ten universities with the faculty of midwestern liberal arts colleges and found out that the faculty of liberal arts colleges have more publications, on average, than faculty at the Big Ten universities, then normative fit would *not* occur. In this example, the metacontrast principle holds (the groups are more similar than different), but the direction of these comparisons did not match shared assumptions about what those differences and similarities should be. Thus, according to Turner et al. (1994), the social category of "research-oriented" would be abandoned because it fails to provide a normative fit.

In sum, categorization predicts that how an individual identifies himself or herself will depend on (a) which identities are salient, and (b) one's perceived fit with those identities. Building on my earlier discussion of SIT and SCT, identification can therefore be seen as a *very* dynamic process. Whether one invokes a personal or social identity, or whether one invokes Social Identity A or Social Identity B, will depend on the conditions of the social context (e.g., which ingroup or outgroup categories are salient), and which categories seem to best make sense of that social context (i.e., best explain similarities and differences among people). Although these perspectives do not tend to focus on specific organizational practices that foster identification, the antecedents discussed in the previous section can serve as a guide to organizational action.

Rhetorical Tactics

Unlike many perspectives that deal with how individuals change or adapt during the identification process, scholars of organizational rhetoric focus on the strategies that organizations use in order to induce identification in its members (cf. Ashforth & Mael, 1996; Cheney, 1983a, 1983b). Thus, the "process" of identification is examined at the organizational level instead of the individual or group level. Specifically, this perspective asks, "How do organizations come to persuade individual members to identify with the organization?"

Borrowing from Burke's (1937) treatment of identification, Cheney (1983b) discusses various techniques[19] that organizations use to foster identification among their members. The most important is the *common ground technique.* Here, organizations attempt to show that they share the same values as their members. There are numerous ways or tactics to induce feelings of common ground in members: organizations can (a) express concern for the individual, (b) recognize individual contributions to the organization, (c) espouse shared values, (d) advocate member benefits and activities, (e) share praise that outsiders have given the organization, and (f) communicate member testimonials (Cheney, 1983b, pp. 150-152).

A similar, but more subtle strategy is called *the assumed or transcendent we.* Here, the organization simply refers to its people as "we" in corporate publications and other communications. Organizations can also use *unifying symbols* to communicate a sense of oneness within the organization. For example, the Organization and Management Theory (OMT) artifacts (e.g., the OMT button) help show members that they belong to a single and distinct entity within the Academy of Management. Moreover, logos, stories, myths (Trice & Beyer, 1993), and even organizational dress codes may be powerful symbols of organizational unity (Pratt & Rafaeli, 1997; Rafaeli & Pratt, 1993).

All of the tactics mentioned thus far help individuals feel that they are similar to the organization; that is, they enhance identification through association. Organizations can also create identification through dissociation. This strategy, known as *identification through antithesis,* involves uniting the organization against a common enemy (Cheney, 1983b). To illustrate, a managed care organization can create unity among its physicians by talking about how the organization must fight insurance companies, because insurance companies are attempting to regulate how doctors treat patients by deciding which medications and procedures will be insured and not insured.

Although Cheney (1983b) does not provide psychological mechanisms to explain the potency of these rhetorical strategies, it appears that they can be explained by theories I have reviewed thus far. First, based on Cheney's (1983b) definition of identification (see Table 6.1), these strategies seem to appeal to members' needs for belonging to a social group. Moreover, these strategies appear to maximize ingroup similarities and outgroup differences. Organizations are viewed as unified collections of individuals sharing similar values. Those outside of the organization are seen as being both different from and as threats to the organization. As a result, intergroup boundaries are highlighted through competition. Finally, member testimonials may be integral to forming behavioral commitments among members. This mechanism for identification will be discussed later in this section.

Socialization and
Role Adoption (Identity Theory)

A fourth set of perspectives that may be useful in understanding the identification process is socialization and role adoption. Socialization is "the process by which an individual acquires the social knowledge and skills necessary to assume an organizational role" (Van Maanen & Schein, 1979, p. 211). According to some sociological theories of identity—often known simply as *identity theory*—the adoption of roles is central to the development of social identities (Hogg et al., 1995; Stryker &

Serpe, 1982). Identity theory, like social identity theory, sees the self as a product of social interaction. However, the focus and origin of the two theories are different: "Identity theory is principally a microsociological theory that sets out to explain individuals' role-related behaviors, while social identity theory is a psychological theory that sets out to explain group processes and intergroup relations" (Hogg et al., 1995, p. 255).

Socialization and identity theory offer two ways of examining the identification process. First, similar to rhetorical theories, socialization suggests a number of tactics that organizations can use to help foster identification. Second, identity theory attempts to explain how the adoption and enactment of roles lead to the formation of social identities.

To begin, socialization research has found a link between the adoption of institutionalized socialization tactics and compliance with organizational roles (Allen & Meyer, 1990; Ashforth & Mael, 1989; Jones, 1986; Van Maanen & Schein, 1979). *Institutionalized tactics* (Jones, 1986) refer to a set of socialization tactics first formulated by Van Maanen and Schein (1979). These tactics are believed to induce organizational members to passively adopt organizational roles, or assume role "custodianship." *Individualized tactics,* by contrast, are believed to promote role innovation. Recently, Ashforth and Saks (1996) have linked institutionalized socialization tactics with organizational identification.

Institutionalized socialization tactics include collective, formal, sequential, fixed, serial, and investiture tactics.[20] To begin, institutionalized socialization is *collective.* As the name implies, this tactic involves socializing organizational recruits in groups as opposed to individually. Institutionalized socialization tactics are also *formal* (as opposed to informal), *sequential* (as opposed to random), *fixed* (as opposed to variable), and *serial* (as opposed to disjunctive). This means that institutionalized socialization involves, respectively, separating new recruits from existing organizational members and clarifying the newcomers' roles, specifying a set of discernible steps that lead to the target role, providing a timetable for the completion of those steps, and using experienced organizational members to train the recruits (Van Maanen & Schein, 1979, pp. 232-247). Finally, and most surprisingly, institutionalized socialization involves *investiture* tactics, which confirm the existing identity of the recruit, rather than *divestiture* tactics, which attempt to strip away that identity.[21]

In short, one could view the socialization literature as providing a number of tactics that can foster identification. Although no strong theoretical rationale has been given for the success of these tactics, one might assume that collective socialization may trigger identification by simply assigning individuals to groups (Tajfel, 1981, 1982). Moreover, more structured tactics may also make organizational roles salient, thus leading to deindividuation (Rafaeli & Pratt, 1993) or depersonalization (Turner et al., 1994). The impact of socialization may also be explained by identity theory.

According to identity theory, the adoption and enactment of roles are a necessary and sufficient means for producing identification. Based on symbolic interactionism, identity theory sees the self as arising from social interaction via social roles: "Identity theory . . . views the self not as an autonomous psychological entity, but a multifaceted social construct that emerges from people's roles in society; variation in self-concepts is due to the different roles that people occupy" (Hogg et al., 1995, p. 256).

Specifically, identity theory sees the self as consisting of hierarchically arranged *role identities:* identities that come from the structural positions that people occupy in society (Hogg et al., 1995; Stryker & Serpe, 1982; Thoits, 1983). These hierarchically arranged role identities differ in their salience, or probability that they will be evoked across a range of situations. Salience, in turn, is determined by an individual's commitment to his or her identities. Commitments can range in quality and quantity. *Affective commitment* (not to be confused with the concept measured in the Organizational Commitment Questionnaire) is determined by the perceived importance of the social relationships associated with the identity.[22] *Interactional commitment* refers to how many roles are associated with an identity (Hogg et al., 1995).

Specific institutionalized socialization tactics may lead to role acceptance, and thus identity change, by first affecting the degree of felt commitment to organizational roles. For example, as organizations collectively socialize members into their roles with the help of experienced organizational members, organizations may enhance intraorganizational relationships, thereby increasing affective identity commitment. Moreover, as members become more senior and begin socializing others, members come to take on additional roles, thereby increasing their interactional commitment. According to role theory, increases in role commitment should lead to greater and greater levels of identity salience. Therefore, as commitment to the organizational roles increases, so too should the salience of the organizational identity. When the organizational identity is highly salient, members are more likely to view that identity as being self-referential.

Behavioral Commitment and Schema Formation

The final perspective on organizational identification that I offer is the most tentative, and it is presented briefly as a possible avenue for further research (see Pratt, 1997b). The approach borrows insights from two bodies of literature: behavioral commitment (Kiesler, 1971; Salancik, 1977; Staw & Ross, 1987) and schema formation (Markus, 1977; Markus & Wurf, 1987). The proposed link between the two is quite straightforward: Behavioral commitment leads to consistent behavior, and consistent behavior leads to changes in the self-concept.

Beginning with the self-concept, Markus (1977) argues that identity formation is linked to behaviors, in that "attempts to organize, summarize, or explain one's own behavior in a particular domain will result in the formation of cognitive structures about the self or what might be called, self schemata" (p. 64). More specifically, identity schemas are predicted to form as members try to make sense of *repeated* patterns of behavior within a particular domain or area of life. Erez and

Earley (1993) make a similar prediction in their treatment of identity. They note that a "sense of continuity and consistency helps individuals to connect events in their current social life to past experiences and to maintain a coherent view that enables them to operate effectively in the environment" (p. 29). Most recently, Weick (1995) posits that *behavioral consistency* is integral to our sense of self and how we make sense of the world around us.

Behavioral consistency in individuals is often explained by theories of behavioral commitment (Weick, 1995). Behavioral commitment is a process that "binds" individuals to behavioral events (Kiesler, 1971; Kiesler & Sakumura, 1966; Salancik, 1977). Behavioral commitment posits that all commitments begin with action. Once we act, we create justifications to explain these actions (Staw & Ross, 1987; Weick, 1995). These justifications bind us to our actions and increase the possibility that similar actions will be repeated in the future.

Although all commitments begin with action, not all actions lead to commitments. As Salancik (1977, p. 4) notes, some behaviors are more likely to lead to commitments than others. Specifically, behaviors that are volitional, irrevocable, explicit, and public tend to be the most committing, for they are the hardest to attribute to external causes (see Staw & Ross, 1987, for a more detailed explanation of the psychology of behavioral commitment). Building on these determinants of behavioral commitment, one may assume that identification with an organization will likely occur when an individual sees her or his membership as involving free choice,[23] when it cannot be reversed or denied, and/or when one confirms it in front of other people.

The link between commitment and identification may cause us to reexamine some heretofore unrelated predictors of organizational identification. For example, the behavioral commitment-schema link explains why (a) perceived choice in becoming and remaining a distributor, and (b) engaging in public displays of approval toward Amway were found to be critical mechanisms in fostering identification among Amway distributors (Pratt, 1994). It also explains why an employee giving public testimonials is a powerful tactic for inducing identification (Cheney, 1983b). Although Cheney's emphasis was on how testimonials create a common ground for many employees, it is also likely that the testimonial binds the individual employee to his or her actions when these statements are perceived to be volitional, explicit, and public. These actions, in turn, bind the individual to the organization. A behavioral commitment-schema formation perspective can also be used to reinterpret a proposition forwarded by Dutton et al. (1994). These researchers argue that the "visibility of a member's affiliation with an organization" is a key moderator in organizational identification. It is just as likely, however, that increased visibility leads to increased behavioral commitment, which leads to schema changes. Finally, the link between tenure and organizational identification (Barker & Tompkins, 1994; Mael & Ashforth, 1992) may be due to the fact that the longer an individual is with an organization, the more explicit, irrevocable, public (and possibly volitional) one's actions on behalf of the organization are likely to become. As members try to explain their organizational behaviors, they are likely to form organizational schemas.

How Does Identification Occur?
A Summary and Commentary

In this section, I have highlighted some of the organizational practices and social-psychological mechanisms that may foster organizational identification. Specifically, I reviewed five perspectives that, although not exhaustive, represent a variety of approaches to the question of how organizational identification occurs. These five perspectives were (a) attraction-selection-attrition, (b) categorization, (c) rhetorical tactics, (d) socialization/role adoption, and (e) behavioral commitment/ schema formation.

I have also argued that the question of "How does organizational identification occur?" is probably the least understood of all of the central questions of organizational identification. To close this chapter, I draw upon some of my own work and briefly suggest three major areas that need to be addressed if we are to better understand how organizational identification develops. Specifically, I believe that a more complete understanding of organizational identification involves a better understanding of (a) the role of emotions in the identification process, (b) the subtleties and complexities of identification and disidentification, and (c) the role of organizations (if any) in developing and managing multiple identifications in their employees.[24]

First, a better understanding of organizational identification must involve a better understanding of how emotions affect the process. Some clues do exist in the organizational literature. Carole Barnett and I, for example, have suggested that the creation of ambivalence among Amway distributors is critical to their eventual adoption of organizational roles (Pratt & Barnett, 1997). Borrowing on Lewin's (1958) model of organizational change (later adapted by Schein, 1987), we argued that emotional contrasts worked to "unfreeze" old behavioral routines and actions. In identity terms, ambivalence may have caused individuals to deidentify or disidentify with old role identities and may have prepared them for adopting new ones (cf. Ashforth's discussion in this book). I have also argued that ambivalence may lead to organizational identification as members attempt to resolve emotional and cognitive dissonance through the formation of behavioral commitments (Pratt, 1994; see also Brickman, 1987). These behavioral commitments, in turn, lead to identity changes. Despite insights from these and other studies, however, it is clear that more research on emotions is needed to more clearly articulate their role in the identification process.

Second, researchers need to better understand the subtleties and complexities of organizational identification and disidentification (Elsbach & Bhattacharya, 1997). To begin, few researchers have asked whether there are multiple processes of identification and disidentification. Individuals can gain or lose identities in a variety of ways. To illustrate, identifications can be added slowly over time, old identifications can become more salient, or new identifications can develop quickly under extreme conditions (e.g., the "Stockholm Syndrome"). Moreover, identifications can fade or become less salient, they can be replaced with other identifications, or they can be dramatically broken through crisis or betrayal. Each of these ways may involve its own set of psychological and sociological dynamics and outcomes. Nevertheless, at present, research does not seem to distinguish among different types of (dis)identification processes.

Our understanding of identification and disidentification is also simplistic in that we have tended to focus on how a single social identity is either adopted or lost within an organizational context. However, throughout their organizational lives, members will simultaneously be identifying and disidentifying with a whole host of social identities. The need to understand the complexities of identification and disidentification has become particularly salient to me because of a study that a colleague and I are currently conducting. In this study, we are examining how new physicians become simultaneously socialized into a profession and into an organization. Initial results suggest that as physicians are coming to identify with their organization and profession, other social identities (e.g., spouse, athlete) are becoming less salient or lost. Although we are intrigued with the findings, we have found it difficult to explain this process of identifying and disidentifying using extant theories of organizational identification.

Third, we need to better understand how and if organizations can develop and manage their members' multiple identifications. According to Cheney (1991), managing multiple identities and identifications is *the* central issue for modern organizations. However, as Barker discusses in his chapter, there is still some doubt about whether (a) organizations care to manage member identification; or (b) if they care, whether or not they can influence the process. I would add to this list of "unknowns" that (c) it is unclear whether and how organizations might manage multiple identifications (and disidentifications). In short, although the practice of organizational identification is clearly important to organizational behavior, this area of research remains relatively unexplored.

Closing Comments

Building on work in communications, psychology, social psychology, and sociology, this chapter has addressed some of the who, what, why, when, and how of organizational identification. I have described organizational identification as a fundamental human process whereby an individual's beliefs about his or her organization become self-referential or self-defining. This identification process has been posited to be related to, but distinct from, internalization, organizational commitment, and person-organization fit. Moreover, I have argued that organizational identification often occurs when individuals are experiencing strong needs, such as the need to be safe, to belong, to feel better about the self, and to fulfill holistic needs.

I have also tried to explain the antecedents, outcomes, processes, and practices of organizational identification. Although borrowing heavily from social identity theory and self-categorization theory, I have also suggested alternative theories that may prove useful in understanding how individuals come to identify with their organizations and how organizations may attempt to influence this process. Specifically, I looked at the attraction-selection-attrition model, theories of rhetoric, socialization, and identity, and behavioral commitment and schema formation.

In the process of addressing these central questions, I have raised several as well. For example, what are the roles of emotions and sensemaking in the identification process? What are the potential disadvantages of organizational identification? How is the process of identification similar to and different from disidentification? How are multiple identifications managed by individuals and organizations? Although it was the purpose of this chapter to raise these questions, it is the purpose of this book to begin to answer these (and other) questions. As I mentioned at the start of this chapter, even though the topics of identity and identification have been debated for centuries, the search for knowledge about who we are and how we become who we are remain exciting and enriching avenues for today's organizational scholars.

NOTES

1. I would like to thank Blake Ashforth, David Brandon, Peter Foreman, Paul Godfrey, Trudy Good, and David Whetten for their comments and assistance on earlier drafts of this chapter.

2. The reason I use the term "individual" is because most (if not all) treatments of identification concern individuals identifying with other individuals or groups (cf. Aronson, 1992; Ashforth & Mael, 1989) or groups trying to foster identification with individuals (cf. Cheney, 1983a, 1983b). Typically, organizational scholars have not discussed whether groups can identify with other groups. Moreover, although there has been some discussion of how organizations can facilitate individual identification, scholars typically do not talk about organizations identifying with individual members. Thus, although individuals can identify with organizations, we rarely see the converse as being true.

3. Taking this argument further, one might even argue that we ultimately identify with our *images* of others.

4. Theoretically, this path to identification may occur gradually over time, or occur more suddenly, such as what occurs during a "conversion" experience (cf. Greil & Rudy, 1983, 1984; Lofland & Stark, 1965). However, as with most treatments of identification, "emulation identification" assumes that identification with an organization is a conscious process. Whether or not identification can be said to occur without a person's knowledge remains a question for future research.

5. Incorporating internalization as a means of producing identification has been suggested elsewhere. To illustrate, Mael and Ashforth (1995) posit, "Internalization of the perceived values of a group (I believe) could also induce one to identify with the group (I am)" (pp. 310-311). Similarly, I have noted that Tajfel (1982) suggests that identification may result from the internalization of social identities.

6. The aforementioned arguments suggest that internalization is irrelevant to affinity identification. Arguing that internalization is essential to only emulation identification, however, does not *completely* distinguish the two concepts. If one takes the view that all of one's identity is socially constructed or determined, then the "affinity" path simply means that one has internalized another person's or group's values and beliefs *before* entering the organization, and that these internalized values and beliefs are now being called upon to make an assessment of individual-organizational "congruence." Similarly, Ashforth and Mael (1989) argue that one can identify with past or future organizational identities without internalizing the values and beliefs of the organization's current leaders, strategies, goals, and so on. However, this does not mean that organizational members have not internalized the values of those past or future organizational identities. It appears that as identification scholars continue to move away from Kelman's (1961) distinctions between identification and internalization, the two concepts become increasingly similar. This conceptual redundancy, however, may be the "price" to be paid if we continue to see identity as central to identification.

7. As noted in Pratt (1994, p. 3), there have been two major schools regarding the nature of organizational commitment. The first school regards commitment as a form of *value congruence* and includes affective/attitudinal (cf. Dubin, Champoux, & Porter, 1975; Mowday et al., 1982; Mowday et al., 1979; O'Reilly, 1989; O'Reilly & Caldwell, 1981; O'Reilly & Chatman, 1986; Porter & Steers, 1973; Porter et

al., 1974); normative (Varadi, Weiner, & Popper, 1989; Weiner, 1982); social exchange (Eisenberger, Fasolo, Davis-Mastro, 1990; Eisenberger, Huntington, Hutchinson, & Sowa, 1986; March & Simon, 1958); and other theories of commitment (cf. Kelman, 1961; Mayer & Schoorman, 1992; Meyer & Allen, 1991; Meyer, Allen, & Smith, 1993). These theories tend to conceptualize commitment as a state wherein an individual's values and beliefs are consonant with that of their employing organizations. The second school of theories, or *behavioral consistency theories,* include side-bet (Becker, 1960); continuance or calculative (Farrell & Rusbult, 1981; Hrebiniak & Alutto, 1972; Meyer & Allen, 1984; Rusbult & Farrell, 1983; Sheldon, 1971); and behavioral commitment (Kiesler, 1971; Salancik, 1977; Staw & Ross, 1987). These theories define commitment as a process that produces reliable patterns of actions, such as staying with an organization. Although differing radically in their orientations, both schools view consistency as being a defining feature of commitment—be it in thoughts and feelings (value-congruence) or in actions (behavioral consistency).

8. Muddying the waters further is the use of commitment by some identity scholars who talk about commitment to roles as being central to identity salience, and hence, identification (see Hogg et al., 1995). This type of commitment will be addressed briefly later in this chapter.

9. As I will discuss later in this chapter on "how people identify," behavioral commitment—although conceptually quite different from identification—may be related to organizational identification. Specifically, the behavioral commitment process may explain why some people come to identify with a particular organization.

10. Unfortunately, a more comprehensive treatment of the relationship between sensemaking and identification is beyond the scope of this chapter. My main goal is simply to suggest that the relationship deserves further examination (cf. Pratt, 1997a, 1997b).

11. It is interesting to note that self-enhancement may also drive the need to disidentify with specific groups. Recent work by Elsbach and Bhattacharya (1997) suggests that people will disassociate themselves from particular organizations, such as the National Rifle Association, because of a need to enhance positive feelings of distinctiveness and avoid negative feelings of belonging to a group that is seen as being antithetical to one's own values.

12. This relationship between identification and control is also discussed in Barker's chapter on the practice of identification.

13. Building on what I have mentioned previously about the relationship between needs and member identification, we could argue that identification may occur when people are feeling the need to be protected, to belong, to raise their self-worth, or when they would like to "be part of something greater than themselves." Many of the proposed antecedents of identification can be linked back to the deficits in safety, belonging, self-enhancement, or holistic needs (see Aronson, 1992; Ashforth & Mael, 1989; Cheney, 1983a, 1983b; Dutton et al., 1994; Kelman, 1961; Kristoff, 1996).

14. Of the two perspectives, social identity theory definitely dominates much of the current thinking on organizational identification (Ashforth & Mael, 1989; Dutton et al., 1994; Mael & Ashforth, 1992). Self-categorization theory has been mentioned in several works but has yet to be adapted to organizational identification as directly as has social identity theory.

15. Surprisingly, Mael and Ashforth (1992) did not find support for this hypothesis. In their study of college alumni, interorganizational competition did not predict identification. However, specific characteristics of their study's population may have accounted for this finding (see p. 116 of their paper for a brief discussion of this finding).

16. According to Kawakami and Dion (1995) SCT differs from SIT in that SCT "places more emphasis on the cognitions underlying the social comparison processes. Specifically, SCT attempts to provide a theoretical link between personal and group identity and to examine the interaction between intragroup and intergroup levels" (p. 554).

17. As I have mentioned, social identity theory states that individuals can feel part of a group without actually interacting with that group. Perhaps attraction may be enough to trigger perceptions of a "minimal group," and thus identification (see also Mael & Ashforth, 1995).

18. According to Kawakami and Dion (1995), salience can influence the social categorization process in at least two ways. First, the level of salient identities will influence whether individuals compare themselves to ingroup members or outgroup members. Just as intragroup contexts can evoke personal identities (Turner et al., 1994), so too can salient personal identities evoke intragroup comparisons. Similarly, just as intergroup contexts can evoke social identities, so too can salient social identities evoke intergroup comparisons. Second, the content of a salient identity can also serve to constrain social comparisons. For example, if my identity as a business school professor is salient, this will likely limit the types of social comparisons that I make. Although many social comparisons are possible, some comparisons will be

more likely (e.g., with psychology professors or with associate business school professors) than others (e.g., with female librarians in Puerto Rico).

19. In this section, I cite Cheney's (1983b) work most prominently because he provides some of the clearest and most direct explanations of specific rhetorical tactics. However, additional tactics have been alluded to by other researchers. Building from Young (1989) as well as Horvath and Glynn (1993), Ashforth and Mael (1996) note that organizations characterized by strong subgroups or by ideological divisions often use rhetorical tactics to create a sense of unity. For example, organizations that have strong normative *and* utilitarian identities (e.g., schools and health care organizations) may attempt to create unity by lauding the virtues of each identity on different occasions. Organizations may also promote *mediatory myths* (Abravanel, 1983): Sayings that attempt to make incompatible identities or beliefs more compatible (cf. Pratt, 1994).

20. There is some disagreement about which tactics should lead to role custodianship. Van Maanen and Schein (1979) believed that variable and divestiture tactics should lead to custodianship, rather than fixed and investiture tactics. The list of tactics given here is based on the empirical work of Allen and Meyer (1990), Ashforth and Saks (1996), and Jones (1986) that finds some support for including fixed and investiture tactics as institutionalized socialization tactics.

21. Within the context of institutionalized socialization, investiture may work to increase identification in the following way: Affirming a person's sense of self makes that person feel warmly toward the organization, thus increasing the probability that he or she will identify with it. However, in organizations with strong and distinctive cultures (e.g., total institutions), divestiture works best as an institutional tactic because it effectively strips away the old identity of a person and enables him or her to be remade in the organization's image (Ashforth, personal communication, June 1997).

22. Identity theory refers to members' networks of relationships associated with a role (Hogg et al., 1995). By extension, it may be interesting to link notions from network theory (e.g., network centrality, and network type) to theories of organizational identification.

23. This assertion seems to contradict an earlier prediction of mine, where I state that identification can occur under states of duress (cf. the Stockholm syndrome discussed in the beginning of this chapter). It may be, however, that identification is most likely to occur in extreme conditions: those in which there is either clearly free choice or clearly the absence of free choice.

24. In addition to my own discussion here, these (and other) topics will also be developed more fully by other authors in this book. As I have mentioned, Harquail will explore the question of emotions in identification, and Elsbach and Dukerich et al. will discuss disidentification. In addition, Ashforth will explore alternative explanations for how identification may unfold, and Barker will discuss how little we actually know about how organizations manage organizational identification.

REFERENCES

Abravanel, H. (1983). Mediatory myths in the service of organizational ideology. In L. Pondy, G. Morgan, & T. Dandridge (Eds.), *Organizational symbolism* (pp. 273-293). Greenwich, CT: JAI.

Albert, S., & Whetten, D. (1985). Organizational identity. In L. L. Cummmings & B. M. Staw (Eds.), *Research in organizational behavior* (Vol. 7, pp. 263-295). Greenwich, CT: JAI.

Allen, N., & Meyer, J. (1990). Organization socialization tactics: A longitudinal analysis of links to newcomers' commitment and role orientation. *Academy of Management Journal, 33,* 847-858.

Aronson, E. (1992). *The social animal* (6th ed.). New York: W. H. Freeman.

Ashforth, B. E., & Mael, F. (1989). Social identity theory and the organization. *Academy of Management Review, 14,* 20-39.

Ashforth, B. E., & Mael, F. A. (1996). Organizational identity and strategy as a context for the individual. In J. A. C. Baum & J. E. Dutton (Eds.), *Advances in strategic management* (Vol. 13, pp. 17-62). Greenwich, CT: JAI.

Ashforth, B., & Saks, A. (1996). Socialization tactics: Longitudinal effects on newcomer adjustment. *Academy of Management Journal, 39,* 149-178.

Barker, J. R., & Tompkins, P. K. (1994). Identification in the self-managing organization. Characteristics of target and tenure. *Human Communication Association, 21,* 223-240.

Barnett, C. K., & Pratt, M. G. (1997). *From threat-rigidity to flexibility: Towards a model of autogenic crisis in organizations.* Unpublished manuscript.

Becker, H. (1960). Notes on the concept of commitment. *American Journal of Sociology, 66,* 32-40.

Brickman, P. (1987). Commitment. In C. B. Wortman & R. Sorrentino (Eds.), *Commitment, conflict, and caring* (pp. 1-18). Englewood Cliffs, NJ: Prentice Hall.

Buchanan, B. (1974). Building organizational commitment: The socialization of managers in work organizations. *Administrative Science Quarterly, 19,* 533-546.

Bullis, C., & Wackernagel Bach, B. (1989). Are mentor relationships helping organizations? An exploration of developing mentee-mentor-organizational identifications using turning point analysis. *Communication Quarterly, 37,* 199-213.

Burke, K. (1937). *Attitudes towards history.* New York: The New Republic.

Chatman, J. (1989). Improving interactional organizational research: A model of person-organization fit. *Academy of Management Review, 14,* 333-349.

Cheney, G. (1983a). On the various and changing meanings of organizational membership: A field study of organizational identification. *Communication Monographs, 50,* 342-362.

Cheney, G. (1983b). The rhetoric of identification and the study of organizational communication. *Quarterly Journal of Speech, 69,* 143-158.

Cheney, G. (1991). *Rhetoric in an organizational society: Managing multiple identities.* Columbia: University of South Carolina Press.

Collins, J., & Porras, J. (1991). Organizational vision and visionary organizations. *California Management Review, 33,* 30-52.

Cook, J., Hepworth, S., Wall, T., & Warr, P. (1981). *The experience of work: A compendium and review of 249 measures and their use.* New York: Academic Press.

Dubin, R., Champoux, J. E., & Porter, L. W. (1975). Central life interests and organizational commitment of blue-collar and clerical workers. *Administrative Science Quarterly, 20,* 411-421.

Dutton, J. E., & Dukerich, J. M. (1991). Keeping an eye on the mirror: Image and identity in organizational adaptation. *Academy of Management Review, 34,* 517-554.

Dutton, J. E., Dukerich, J. M., & Harquail, C. V. (1994). Organizational images and member identification. *Administrative Science Quarterly, 39,* 239-263.

Eisenberger, R., Fasolo, P., & Davis-Mastro, V. (1990). Perceived organizational support and employee diligence, commitment, and innovation. *Journal of Applied Psychology, 75,* 51-59.

Eisenberger, R., Huntington, R., Hutchinson, S., & Sowa, D. (1986). Perceived organizational support. *Journal of Applied Psychology, 71,* 500-507.

Elsbach, K., & Bhattacharya, C. B. (1997). *Organizational disidentification: A study of social identity and the National Rifle Association.* Working paper, Emory University, Atlanta.

Erez, M., & Earley, C. (1993). Cultural self-representation theory. In *Culture, self-identity, and work* (pp. 18-37). New York: Oxford University Press.

Farrell, D., & Rusbult, C. E. (1981). Exchange variables as predictors of job satisfaction, job commitment, and turnover: The impact of rewards, costs, alternatives, and investments. *Organizational Behavior and Human Performance, 27,* 78-95.

Greil, A., & Rudy, D. (1983). Conversion to the world view of Alcoholics Anonymous: A refinement of conversion theory. *Qualitative Sociology, 6,* 5-28.

Greil, A., & Rudy, D. (1984). Social cocoons: Encapsulation and identity transformation in organizations. *Sociological Inquiry, 54,* 260-278.

Hogg, M. (1996). Social identity, self-categorization, and the small group. In J. Davis & E. Witte (Eds.), *Understanding group behavior, Volume 2: Small group processes and interpersonal relations* (pp. 227-254). Hillsdale, NJ: Lawrence Erlbaum.

Hogg, M. A., Terry, D. J., & White, K. M. (1995). A tale of two theories: A critical comparison of identity theory with social identity theory. *Social Psychology Quarterly, 58,* 255-269.

Horvath, L., & Glynn, M. A. (1993). *Owning a piece of the rock: Employee ownership, organizational identification, and self-management in worker cooperatives.* Unpublished manuscript.

Hrebiniak, L., & Alutto, J. (1972). Personal and role-related factors in the development of organizational commitment. *Administrative Science Quarterly, 17,* 555-572.

Ibarra, H. (1996). *Inauthentic selves: Image, identity, and social network in professional adaptation.* Working paper, Harvard University, Cambridge, MA.

Jones, G. R. (1986). Socialization tactics, self-efficacy, and newcomers' adjustments to organizations. *Academy of Management Journal, 29,* 262-279.

Judge, T. A., & Bretz, R. D. (1992). Effects of work values on job choice decisions. *Journal of Applied Psychology, 77,* 261-271.

Judge, T., & Ferris, G. (1992). The elusive criterion of fit in human resources staffing decisions. *Human Resource Planning, 15*(4), 47-67.

Kawakami, K., & Dion, K. (1995). Social identity and affect as determinants of collective action. *Theory and Psychology, 5,* 551-577.

Kelman, H. C. (1961). Processes of opinion change. *Public Opinion Quarterly, 25,* 57-78.

Kiesler, C. (1971). *The psychology of commitment.* New York: Academic Press.

Kiesler, C., & Sakumura, J. (1966). A test of a model for commitment. *Journal of Personality and Social Psychology, 3,* 349-353.

Kristoff, A. (1996). Person-organization fit: An integrative review of its conceptualizations, measurement, and implications. *Personnel Psychology, 49,* 1-49.

Lewin, K. (1958). Group decision and social change. In T. M. Newcomb & E. L. Hartley (Eds.), *Readings in social psychology* (pp. 201-216). New York: Harper & Row.

Lofland, J., & Stark, R. (1965). Becoming a world saver: A theory of conversion to a deviant perspective. *American Sociological Review, 30,* 862-874.

Lorenz, K. (1937). The companion in the bird's world. *Auk, 54,* 245-273.

Lovelace, K., & Rosen, B. (1996). Differences in achieving person-organization fit among diverse groups of managers. *Journal of Management, 22,* 703-722.

Mael, F., & Ashforth, B. (1992). Alumni and their alma mater: A partial test of the reformulated model of organizational identification. *Journal of Organizational Behavior, 13,* 103-123.

Mael, F. A., & Ashforth, B. E. (1995). Loyal from day one: Biodata, organizational identification, and turnover among newcomers. *Personnel Psychology, 48,* 309-333.

March, G., & Simon, H. (1958). *Organizations.* New York: John Wiley.

Markus, H. (1977). Self-schemata and processing information about the self. *Journal of Personality and Social Psychology, 35,* 63-78.

Markus, H., & Wurf, E. (1987). The dynamic self concept: A social psychological perspective. *American Review of Psychology, 38,* 299-337.

Mayer, R., & Schoorman, F. D. (1992). Predicting participation and production outcomes through a two-dimensional model of organizational commitment. *Academy of Management Journal, 35,* 671-684.

Meyer, J., & Allen, N. (1984). Testing the "side bet theory" of organizational commitment: Some methodological considerations. *Journal of Applied Psychology, 69,* 372-378.

Meyer, J. P., & Allen, N. J. (1991). A three-component conceptualization of organizational commitment. *Human Resource Management Review, 1,* 61-89.

Meyer, J., Allen, N., & Smith, C. (1993). Commitment to organizations and occupations: Extension and test of a three-component model. *Journal of Applied Psychology, 78,* 538-551.

Mowday, R. T., Porter, L. W., & Steers, R. M. (1982). *Employee-organizational linkages.* New York: Academic Press.

Mowday, R., Steers, R., & Porter, L. (1979). The measurement of organizational commitment. *Journal of Vocational Behavior, 14,* 224-247.

Nair, S., & Pratt, M. G. (1997, August). *Issues and identity conflicts in multiple identity environments (MIE): The case of rural physicians.* Paper presented at the annual meeting of the Academy of Management, Boston.

Neck, C., & Milliman, J. (1994). Thought self-leadership: Finding spiritual fulfillment in organizational life. *Journal of Managerial Psychology, 9,* 9-16.

Oaker, G., & Brown, R. (1986). Intergroup relations in a hospital setting: A further test of social identity theory. *Human Relations, 39,* 767-778.

O'Reilly, C. (1989). Corporations, culture, and commitment: Motivation and social control in organizations. *California Management Review, 31,* 9-25.

O'Reilly, C., & Caldwell, D. (1981). The commitment and job tenure of new employees: Some evidence of postdecisional justification. *Administrative Science Quarterly, 26,* 597-616.

O'Reilly, C., & Chatman, J. (1986). Organizational commitment and psychological attachment: The effects of compliance, identification, and internalization on prosocial behavior. *Journal of Applied Psychology, 71,* 492-499.

O'Reilly, C., Chatman, J., & Caldwell, C. (1991). People and organizational culture: A profile comparison approach to assessing person-organization fit. *Academy of Management Journal, 34,* 487-516.

Pilevsky, P. (1989). *Captive continent: The Stockholm syndrome in European-Soviet relations.* New York: Praeger.

Porter, L., & Steers, R. M. (1973). Organizational, work, and personal factors in employee turnover and absenteeism. *Psychological Bulletin, 80,* 151-176.

Porter, L., Steers, R., Mowday, R., & Boulian, P. (1974). Organizational commitment, job satisfaction, and turnover among psychiatric technicians. *Journal of Applied Psychology, 59,* 603-609.

Pratt, M. G. (1994). *The happiest, most dissatisfied people on Earth: Ambivalence and commitment among Amway distributors.* Unpublished doctoral dissertation, University of Michigan.

Pratt, M. G. (1997a). *"Sensebreaking" and encapsulation among Amway distributors: On the successes and failures of an identity transforming organization.* Working paper.

Pratt, M. G. (1997b). *Spirituality, sensemaking, and identity change: The case of Amway distributors.* Paper presented at the 15th annual International Standing Conference on Organizational Symbolism, Warsaw, Poland.

Pratt, M. G., & Barnett, C. K. (1997). Emotions and unlearning in Amway recruiting techniques: Promoting change through "safe" ambivalence. *Management Learning, 28,* 65-88.

Pratt, M. G., & Rafaeli, A. (1997). Organizational dress as a symbol of multilayered social identities. *Academy of Management Journal, 40,* 862-898.

Rafaeli, A., & Pratt, M. G. (1993). Tailored meanings: On the meaning and impact of organizational dress. *Academy of Management Review, 18,* 32-55.

Rusbult, C. E., & Farrell, D. (1983). A longitudinal test of the investment model: The impact on job satisfaction, job commitment, and turnover of variation in rewards, costs, alternatives, and investment. *Journal of Applied Psychology, 68,* 429-438.

Salancik, G. (1977). Commitment and the control of organizational behavior and belief. In B. M. Staw & G. R. Salancik (Eds.), *New directions in organizational behavior* (pp. 1-54). Chicago: St. Clair.

Schein, E. (1987). *Process consultation, Volume II: Lessons for managers.* Reading, MA: Addison-Wesley.

Schneider, B. (1987). The people make the place. *Personnel Psychology, 40,* 437-454.

Schneider, B., Goldstein, H., & Smith, D. (1995). The ASA framework: An update. *Personnel Psychology, 48,* 747-773.

Sheldon, M. (1971). Investments and involvements as mechanisms producing commitment to the organization. *Administrative Science Quarterly, 16,* 142-150.

Staw, B., & Ross, J. (1987). Behavior in escalation situations: Antecedents, prototypes, and solutions. *Research in Organizational Behavior, 9,* 39-78.

Stryker, S., & Serpe, R. (1982). Commitment, identity salience, and role behavior: Theory and research example. In W. Ickers and E. Knowles (Eds.), *Personality, roles and social behavior* (pp. 199-219). New York: Springer-Verlag.

Tajfel, H. (1981). *Human groups and social categories: Studies in social psychology.* New York: Cambridge University Press.

Tajfel, H. (1982). Social psychology of intergroup relations. *Annual Review of Psychology, 33,* 1-39.

Tajfel, H., & Turner, J. C. (1979). An integrative theory of intergroup conflict. In W. G. Austin & S. Worchel (Eds.), *The social psychology of group relations* (pp. 33-47). Monterey, CA: Brooks-Cole.

Thoits, P. (1983). Multiple identities and psychological well-being: A reformulation and test of the social isolation hypothesis. *American Sociological Review, 48,* 174-187.

Trice, H., & Beyer, J. (1993). *The culture of work organizations.* Englewood Cliffs, NJ: Prentice Hall.

Tsui, A., Egan, T., & O'Reilly, C. (1992). Being different: Relational demography and organizational attachment. *Administrative Science Quarterly, 37,* 549-579.

Turner, J. C. (1987). *Rediscovering the social group: A self-categorization theory.* New York: Basil Blackwell.

Turner, J., Oakes, P., Haslam, S., & McGarty, C. (1994). Self and collective: Cognition and social context. *Personality and Social Psychology Bulletin, 20,* 454-463.

Vandenberg, R., Self, R., & Seo, J. (1994). A critical examination of the internalization, identification, and compliance commitment measures. *Journal of Management, 20,* 123-140.

Van Maanen, J. V., & Schein, E. H. (1979). Toward a theory of organizational socialization. In L. L. Cummings & B. M. Staw (Eds.), *Research in organizational behavior* (Vol. 1, pp. 209-264). Greenwich, CT: JAI.

Varadi, Y., Weiner, Y., & Popper, M. (1989). The value content of organizational mission as a factor in the commitment of members. *Psychological Reports, 65,* 27-34.

Weick, K. (1995). *Sensemaking in organizations.* Thousand Oaks, CA: Sage.

Weiner, Y. (1982). Commitment in organizations: A normative view. *Academy of Management Review, 7,* 418-428.

Young, E. (1989). On the naming of the rose: Interests and multiple meanings as elements of organizational culture. *Organizational Studies, 10,* 187-206.

7

Identification With Organizations

Parties

Stuart Albert, Blake E. Ashforth (moderator), James R. Barker,

Janet M. Dukerich, Kimberly D. Elsbach, Mary Ann Glynn,

Celia V. Harquail, Roderick Kramer, Judi McLean Parks

For all these lifetime employees [at Imperial Oil], there develops an attachment, a loyalty, something deeper than habit, a true identification. They will work longer at Imperial than their kids live at home, than they live in one house, in one neighborhood, one city, longer than most friendships and many marriages survive. They will work at tasks more time-consuming, reward-giving and mood-determining than nearly everything else they do. "It's the best thing I ever did," they will say, as Frank says, of his decision to join the company, as his wife and children listen on and no one interrupts. Father, mother, spouse, family man, Imperial becomes part of identity itself.

—Dryden (1994, p. 182)

The concept of identification has immense potential. There are few conceptual bridges that span the interface of individual and organization (or individual and group) that truly help us understand how individuals are embedded in larger collectives. Identification, as the process through which individuals come to define themselves at least partly in terms of a collective's identity, helps explain how individuals develop ways of thinking, feeling, and acting within a social context. As suggested by

Mike Pratt's earlier review, this seminal process has implications for virtually every domain of organizational behavior, from motivation to communication, and leadership to decision making. Although we focused on *organizational* identification, the process is relevant to any collective.

Our team faced a somewhat daunting but energizing mandate: To capitalize on the potential explanatory power of identification by beginning a conversation on the key issues surrounding identification with organizations.

OUR TEAM'S APPROACH

Our team's approach to our weekend-long conversation differed markedly in both substance and style from that of the other two teams. On the substantive side, our team had the benefit of a very rich and diverse literature on individual identity, identification, and allied concepts, primarily from psychology. This literature provided a good base for our application of the concept of identification to organizational settings. Put simply, we extended scraps of existing theory into the organizational realm, whereas the other teams attempted to develop theory from scratch. Thus, in contrast to the other teams, ours began its conversation with a fairly specific set of questions, and our subsequent annotation of the conversation is more explicitly tied to the literature.

On the stylistic side, we decided at the outset to have each member (or in one case, a subteam of members) document a portion of the conversation—although we deferred matching faces to topics until the end of the weekend. We brainstormed potential topics during the first evening and derived seven that we felt mapped out the rough domain of pressing and provocative issues in organizational identification. We recognized then (and now) that these issues by no means exhaust a very fertile field of inquiry.

For the next 2 days, we talked. Our intent was to raise questions, speculate on possible answers, and surface promising leads and points of convergence and divergence—but not to rigorously pursue either closure or consensus. To do so would have forced a premature and artificial end to an open discussion. We managed to address all seven topics, although movement from one to the next was often dictated more by the clock than by any real sense that we had fully tapped an issue. As Jim Barker writes, the conversation was really going on long before we assembled and will carry on long after us.

Armed with our transcripts of the weekend (thanks again, Judi!), we each returned home to try to make sense of our designated topic. We wrestled, individually and collectively, with how best to capture our conversation in print: This proved to be the most difficult part of the process. The formal and linear style of print is a poor medium for the richness, humor, emotion, and healthy disorder of a real dialogue. At the one extreme, an edited transcript would be most faithful to the conversation, but might sound flat, be hard to follow out of its rich context, and would not allow for later reflection and embellishment. At the other extreme, a book-style essay would be hard pressed to convey the multiple voices, personalities, and excitement that characterize conversation. We selected the broad middle range, where each of us used the transcript as a springboard for a personalized narration of the conversation. We attempted to abstract the major themes, metaphors, debates, questions, and tentative conclusions and weave them into a coherent flow that was structured and yet preserved the virtues of a conversation. As you will see, each person's fingerprints are all over his or her particular write-up: There is a real diversity in style. That, too, is the essence of conversation.

THE SEVEN SISTERS

Stuart Albert's introductory chapter discussed the process of theory development and how it relates to the broad terrain of organizational identity and identification. Our team attempted to live the process of theory development, examining the more local terrain where individual and organizational identities intersect. Our survey of that terrain suggested seven intriguing theoretical questions.

The first question we examined was, "What is identification, and what does it add to the organizational literature?" We discussed the definition and meaning of identification, and how the construct is similar to and different from related constructs, such as commitment and loyalty. However, because our conversation came to encompass both identity and identification, it became evident that it would serve as a solid introduction for the book as a whole. As you may have guessed, this conversation in fact formed the basis of Stu Albert's introductory chapter.

The second question, covered by myself (Blake Ashforth), was, "How does the process of identification unfold?" We discussed the dynamics of identification—of "becoming"—in terms of several loose metaphors (imprinting, love, play, and theater) and applied the insights gained to Lewin's well-known stage model of change: unfreezing identity—changing identity—refreezing identity. Despite the term "refreezing," we speculated that identity is a perpetual work in progress.

Our third issue is captured by CV Harquail's commentary, "Organizational Identification and the 'Whole Person': Integrating Affect, Behavior, and Cognition." The basic question was, "Must one think like X, feel like X, and act like X to, in fact, 'be' X?" We recognized that most perspectives on organizational identification focus on cognition, and we considered the role of affect and behavior along with cognition in the dynamics of identification.

The fourth question, "With what do we identify?" is summarized by Kim Elsbach. We discussed how individuals have multiple organizations (and within each organization, often multiple identities) with which to identify and *dis*identify. As such, one's pattern of identification is analogous to a stellar constellation where the arrangement of stars (identification objects) is governed by various forces of attraction and repulsion.

The fifth question, "What predicts an individual's propensity to identify?" was prompted by the observation that organizations often have both true believers and heretics, as well as many other members who are ambivalent and fluctuate somewhere in between. Our thoughts on the "need for organizational identification"—

analogous to the needs for achievement, affiliation, and power—are chronicled by Mary Ann Glynn.

The sixth conversation, recounted by Janet Dukerich, Rod Kramer, and Judi McLean Parks, explored the dark side of organizational identification. Although the literature has focused on the dysfunctions of low identification, we surmised that *high* identification may also be problematic, as might both low and high *dis*identification. Thus, organizations walk a fine line in attempting to facilitate the "right" degree of identification.

Finally, with Jim Barker as our scribe, we closed by considering the question, "Can identification be managed, and if so, how?" We speculated that identification still matters, perhaps more than ever with the flattening of hierarchies and the need for involvement and flexibility, and that the management of identification is essentially the management of meaning. Thus, identity management raises ethical concerns about "Whose meaning?" and "How tightly and by what processes should meaning be controlled?"

Throughout our conversation, the implicit goal was not to provide definitive answers but to raise provocative questions that might inspire *future* conversations. After each author has recounted his or her part of our conversation, I will close with an epilogue that offers some final thoughts about where our discussion has taken us, and where it may yet lead.

REFERENCE

Dryden, K. (1994). *The moved and the shaken.* Toronto: Penguin.

Becoming:
How Does the Process
of Identification Unfold?

BLAKE E. ASHFORTH

The first of our questions pertains to how organizational members develop a connection with the organization and how they come to define themselves (at least partly) in terms of the identity of the organization and/or workgroup, department, cohort, and so on. This is a seminal issue in organizational behavior (OB) because individuals must have a more-or-less secure sense of self-in-organization, of who and where they are in the organizational setting, to respond effectively to organizational demands.

Perhaps because the issue of self-definition is so complex and the process of identification is so intensely personal (involving, as it does, a recalibration of self), our conversation was often rooted in examples from our own lives. Personal examples seemed to provide access to otherwise dense and implacable questions, acting as a touchstone for making sense of identification. At the risk of conferring more rationality on our conversation than is deserved, it's as if we were groping toward a grounded theory of identification from the data of our personal experiences. Maybe that's where a lot of OB thinking originates.

Like most conversations, ours was fluid and open-ended. Our objective was to explore the topic rather than to reach closure on specific issues. My objective here is not to faithfully chronicle the twists and turns of our conversation but to use the promising insights and examples that it generated as a springboard for a messy essay on the process of identification. A friendly warning: I will be imposing more structure on our ideas than is warranted by our actual dialogue.

BECOMING: IDENTITY AS
A WORK IN PROGRESS

Identification and other forms of attachment (or, more generally, person-organization fit) are often defined in fairly static terms as the congruence between the fixed attributes and needs of a person and those of an organization. Like a key fitting a lock, individuals are said to seek organizations that match their sense of self. It is an arrangement of convenience, where two fixed entities labor together but preserve their separateness.

What this key-and-lock metaphor denies is that identity is a perpetual work in progress. One's identity, or self-definition, is a product of social interaction grounded in specific contexts at specific times such that one's sense of self-in-organization is emergent and somewhat fluid. Thus, the *process* of identification is crucial because the nature of identity and the extent of identification are not determined by the preexisting nature of the person or organization. Individuals, groups, and the organization mutually shape one another over time and become comingled: Each level of analysis is neither static nor discrete, neither independent nor autonomous.

IDENTIFICATION METAPHORS

As our group struggled to understand the process of becoming, several recurring metaphors cropped up. Like personal examples, metaphors help one think about an issue in novel and diverse ways. Each of the four metaphors below contributes a unique perspective on identification; the trick, of course, is to determine how far to push each one.

Identification as Imprinting

Imprinting is a form of learning among some social animals whereby the young, during a specific period of their development, bond with or fixate on certain classes of objects, such as the mother, food, and the surroundings (Hess, 1973). For example, a duckling can become so highly attached to a mother-substitute, like a farmer or moving broom, that it completely ignores its actual mother. Bowlby (1969) suggested that human attachment is somewhat similar in that children learn to orient their behavior and preferences to certain people and certain ways of relating (e.g., closeness vs. aloofness).

The notion that humans have an innate preparedness to develop primary and object-specific social bonds raises some intriguing issues for identification. For one, it suggests that *people are innately predisposed to identify with social entities*—to define themselves in terms of wider social groupings—perhaps as a means of securing meaning and belonging. An entity is more likely to serve as a definitional template if it is encountered relatively early in one's life or career. For another, the imprinting metaphor suggests that *some identification objects may be mutually exclusive,* that, having bonded with a given entity, one cannot bond as strongly with others. I have lived in four major cities, but I'll always be most passionate about the sports teams from Toronto, my original hometown. Similarly, a person may develop a strong and self-defining attachment to a mentor, workgroup, or organization that continues to inform feeling, thought, and action long after the mentor has retired, the original members of the workgroup have moved on, or the organization has been disbanded. Indeed, just as imprinting may be a major source of self-definition and loyalty, it may also be a major source of inertia and resistance to change.

However, like all metaphors, the imprinting metaphor has real limits. Humans have a far more developed capacity to learn, adapt, and choose than do other species, and so they have at least the potential to radically change their attachments over time.

Identification as Love

Perhaps the process of identification is analogous to falling in love. One is initially attracted to certain kinds of occupations, organizations, and/or industries, and the more job options one has, the more likely that this attraction will play a decisive role in the eventual job choice. If the initial resonance is warranted—if one's hopes and expectations are fulfilled (and reciprocated?)—the attraction may ripen into a deep and abiding attachment. The key points of this analogy are that (a) just as one falls in love with a specific person, so too does one identify with a specific entity; (b) just as love involves affect and cognition, so too does identification; and (c) as with love, one has the capacity to identify with multiple entities, whether sequentially or simultaneously.

The metaphor of love also raises some interesting questions. To what extent can one identify "at first sight"? Is identification hedonistic? Irrational? "Blind"? Can identification persist if unrequited?

Identification as Play

The playful activities of children are typically viewed as fun and frivolous. However, in many forms of play (e.g., playing house or dress-up, playing with dolls or action figures), children tacitly adopt different roles and personae: They *experiment* with identities. As the child matures, play becomes more pointed as aptitudes and interests are pursued and refined (Salter, 1978).

Because a failed identity is a failed self, people need a protective milieu in which to develop confident self-definitions. And because play is "just for fun," it allows a person to test identities in a relatively safe and secure environment. The metaphor of identification as play, then, suggests that attractive identities are held at arm's length—are played at—until they can be publicly and privately claimed as legitimate, as truly reflecting one's self. In a sense, authenticity ("This is me") blooms from inauthenticity (Ibarra, 1996): As Kim Elsbach said, "You fake it 'til you make it." Stebbins (1990) described the self-questioning and angst that plague amateur stand-up comics when they must decide whether to quit their regular jobs and "go professional." The act of quitting signals the seriousness and irrevocability of their identity claim: Playtime is over.

However, work organizations tend to have a low tolerance for play. Notions of experimentation, role distance, and fun are often eschewed for the serious business of "work." As Reiter's (1991) account of life in a Burger King outlet suggests, individuals are usually expected to at least act as if they are fully committed to the identities implied by their occupation and organization, even if their employment is patently short-term.

Identification as Theater

Goffman (1959) characterized social life as dramaturgy in that people act out the roles they wish to claim. If their performance is judged to be convincing, they are subsequently treated as exemplars of their roles. With audience validation, they gain confidence in their portrayal and effectively *become* their roles. CV Harquail, for example, talked about "doing gender" and "doing ethnicity."

Thus, the theatrical metaphor suggests that identities are constituted through action and audience reaction. With regard to organization-based identification, one implication is that identities are selected at least somewhat *deliberately*. Indeed, an individual may consciously choose to enact not only certain identities, but certain facets of those identities. A medical intern may opt to display a warm and caring bedside manner and opt to downplay his or her technical knowledge. This raises a series of intriguing questions; for example, how much leeway do audience members (e.g., clients, supervisors, colleagues) allow the actor in interpreting, improvising, or personalizing the identity? To what extent do actors become typecast, that is, locked into limited portrayals? What identities and identity facets are prized most— and least—by actors?

A second implication of the theatrical metaphor is that identities, like theatrical roles, are *cued*. One acts "in character" when a given identity is rendered salient by the setting. In a laboratory study, Mary Ann Glynn (1994) found that individuals cued to view a task as "work" engaged it differently than did individuals cued to view it as "play": "Workers" tended to be more instrumental, efficient, and performance-oriented, whereas "players" tended to be more intrinsically motivated and to make elaborate and image-laden responses. Part of the power of organizational settings is that they tacitly tell us who to be, and thereby, what to do, think, and even feel.

A third implication is that identity performances are evaluated by critical audiences, and identification depends partly on audience applause, on *social validation*. Not only must identities be performed to exist, they must be acknowledged and affirmed by others. Affirmation indicates that the credibility gap between actor and claimed identity is narrow, instilling confidence for an even stronger performance. Ibarra (1996) describes how neophyte management consultants and investment bankers masked their initial feelings of immaturity with bravado. They adopted and refined the behaviors displayed by senior role models, winning approval from clients and colleagues. As their audience began to treat them as bona fide professionals, they began to view themselves as such. Like good actors, organizational members must offer convincing performances. One of us put it this way: "If I look the part, I convince you that I *am* the part."

HOW DO WE TALK ABOUT
THE PROCESS OF "BECOMING"?

It is somewhat difficult to talk about a fluid and continuous process because most longitudinal models in OB pertain more to stability than to change: They focus on

Unfreezing Identity	**Changing Identity**	**Refreezing Identity**
• Upending experience: crisis, opportunity, surprise, and contrast spur sensemaking • Redefinition of self (deidentification, disidentification) vs. extended or multiple definitions	• Anticipatory identification • Small wins: minor, localized, and tentative identity claims produce snowball effect • Rites and ceremonies institutionalize identity change • Identity change within social domains vs. between domains	• Social validation of identity claim; relies heavily on markers • Periodic affirmation of identity: cycles of identity salience and nonsalience

Figure 7.1. Becoming Major Themes

how one static state (e.g., job design) influences another static state (e.g., job satisfaction). The dynamism and flux that are the stuff of process are effectively hidden behind a set of hypothesized and typically linear links between blocks of frozen variables. Such models impose structure rather than truly explain change.

Unfortunately, our group did not fare much better: Our discussion almost reflexively invoked stage models to explain the process of "becoming"—and I was a major culprit. So, my approach here will be to couch the process in terms of a stage model but to take some potshots as we go.

Stage Models

Various stage models of change processes in organizations have been proposed, from Lewin's (1951) classic formulation to more specific models of work adjustment, socialization, and role transitions. The essence of these stage models is that the experience of change differs qualitatively over time as one confronts the diverse but predictable challenges commensurate with one's development. Our conversation suggested that the process of identification also has this steeplechase quality. Lewin's formulation became our default working model. The major themes of our discussion are shown in Figure 7.1.

Unfreezing Identity. Borrowing Lewin's terms, the first challenge is to "unfreeze" the individual, fostering receptiveness to identification. The very act of entering a new organization, workgroup, or role tends to be upending because the individual is confronted with novelty and ambiguity. More generally, a *crisis or opportunity,* be it personal or organizational, or a *surprise or contrast* such as disconfirmed expectations, may punctuate the mindless enactment of everyday identities and spur sensemaking (Louis, 1980). Such discontinuities may thus make salient the attributes of implicated identities, remind one of what matters most, and perhaps cause one to question taken-for-granted assumptions, values, and beliefs. In testing one's resolve, discontinuities may reaffirm an identity or cripple it. For example, a sudden layoff may cause a person to reassess his or her career choices, prompting renewed commitment or radical change (Leana & Feldman, 1992). Identification may also be constructed retrospectively: Surmounting a crisis suggests that one's bond must be strong, whereas failing suggests that one's bond is weak.

Unfreezing may require *de*identification with a social object, that is, selectively denying or forgetting those aspects of a previously valued identity that impede mobilization toward a new identity. A new supervisor may willfully forget the values and norms associated with his or her prior identity of worker that now contradict the demands of his or her new identity (cf. Lieberman, 1956). Unfreezing may also entail *dis*identification, whereby a person is galvanized not *toward* a social object (identification) but *away* from one (Elsbach & Bhattacharya, 1996). Repugnance with the platform of the Republican party may cause a person to define him- or herself as a Democrat. Disidentification may be necessary when identities are mutually exclusive or antithetical. Perhaps identities are like electrons and protons, held in orbit about a central core by competing forces of attraction and repulsion (see Elsbach's essay, this chapter).

Following the metaphors of imprinting, love, and play, "unfreezing" may be a misnomer. Rather than changing states, like ice into water, individuals may simply develop their self-definitions along existing or new paths. The issue may be less *redefinition* than *extended or multiple* definitions. Beyer and Hannah (1996) studied engineers and other professionals in the semiconductor industry who were assigned to a consortium. Beyer and Hannah concluded that individuals with longer and more diverse work experience retained more diverse latent identities, which expedited adjustment to the consortium: Their self-definitions contained more hooks on which to hang their new roles. Beyer and Hannah's research suggests that identification is strongly affected by the clarity, importance, malleability, and transferability of both *prior selves* and *possible selves* (cf. Markus & Nurius, 1986).

Finally, rather than jump-start the identification process through crisis, opportunity, surprise, or contrast, a person might simply slip gradually and unconsciously into identification. A growing appreciation of an organization's perceived virtues might ultimately lead one to internalize those virtues as an expression of self (Elsbach & Glynn, 1996). Or admiration of a leader may eventually generalize to identification with a workgroup or organization. As the imprinting metaphor suggests, people are predisposed to identify, to extend their definition of self to include valued social entities.

Changing Identity. In Lewin's (1951) model, the second major challenge is to move toward the desired state. Before assuming a new role, aspirants may engage in *anticipatory identification* (cf. Feldman, 1976), priming themselves to internalize seminal attributes implied by the role (e.g., a new MBA student may begin reading the *Wall Street Journal*). The more desired the role and the longer the lag before entry, the greater the anticipation. Occupations, organizations, and industries that project strong identities are also more likely to cue anticipation. Mael and Ashforth (1995) found that U.S. Army recruits *began* Army life with fairly high levels of organizational identification.

Consistent with the metaphors of identification as love, play, and acting is the notion of *small wins* (Weick, 1984). An individual may make a minor, localized, or tentative claim to an identity or identity facet as a low-risk means of testing the viability of a larger claim. If the claim is rebuffed, the individual can retreat more easily, preserving his or her self- and social esteem. For instance, a person can attempt to act as an informal leader of a group as a way of assessing his or her viability as a potential supervisor. Rod Kramer offered a more colorful example:

> I like to keep a lot of toys in my office, both for my kids to play with when they come to my office on the weekends, but also because they put me in a good mood. But I remember worrying what my faculty colleagues would think about this; I thought perhaps I should be more serious around work. The toys won out.

Occupational and organizational socialization processes often institutionalize small wins: Through training, work trials, and feedback, new recruits gradually colonize the domain of their targeted identity.

Organizations facilitate identity change by institutionalizing rites and ceremonies, that is, ritualistic dramas—often complete with roles, sets, props, costumes, and scripts—that are enacted before an audience (Trice & Beyer, 1993). Rites of enhancement (e.g., award ceremonies), renewal (e.g., company retreats), and integration (e.g., office parties) act out and celebrate the distinctive, core, and enduring attributes of the organization. Thus, rites and ceremonies are seductive because they render the organization's espoused identity salient and attractive, and they induce individuals to publicly behave as if they already identify with the organization. As we concluded in our later discussion of the ABCs (affect/behavior/cognition) of identification (see Harquail, this chapter), behavior is a potent datum by which actors and observers alike construct actors' identities. In rites and ceremonies, "doing" often leads to "becoming," as the heart and head follow the hands.

The notion of "changing" identity, however, is somewhat vague. Synonyms for change range from replace and transform, implying wholesale differences, to alter and modify, implying minor differences. The scope of change varies widely across episodes of identification. As Beyer and Hannah's (1996) semiconductor study illustrated, *within a given social domain* (e.g., work, family, community), the more salient and articulated a valued identity (or set of identities), the more consistent the change will be with the extant identity/identities. A person working his or her way through college as a waiter may happily abandon that work identity upon graduation, whereas another person who truly values the identity may only consider related work (restauranteur, caterer). *Across* social domains, people are far more receptive to wholesale change. Because identities are usually cued by the context (e.g., a commuter slips into her account manager persona on the drive to work and reverts to her spouse persona when her husband calls an hour later), people are quite facile at buffering or compartmentalizing identities that are primarily associated with certain contexts. Thus, people are capable of adopting identities in different domains that appear to be inconsistent, leading to what Weiner (1996) refers to as "social schizophrenia." Indeed, identities may at times be *compensatory*, as with the stern manager who doubles as a submissive spouse, and the paper-pusher who becomes a "weekend warrior" on the playing field.

Refreezing Identity. As individuals become more comfortable and confident in their enactment of a new identity, they begin to internalize and consolidate the identity as a legitimate reflection of self. However, because identities are inherently organic and fluid, Lewin's (1951) notion of "refreezing" should not be taken literally as the process of making a new identity hard, fixed, motionless, or formal.

Consistent with the metaphor of identification as theater (and love?), identity claims must be validated socially to stick. To be validated, a claim must be made salient both to one's audience and one's self. Salience is attained through the use of *markers,* that is, strong identity cues ranging from dress, jargon, and mannerisms to office decor, framed diplomas, and one's choice of social networks. Kim Elsbach mentioned that she bought an Emory sweatshirt when she accepted a position at that university: It just felt right. Haas and Shaffir (1982) discuss how medical students, from the beginning of their clinical studies, wore white lab coats and identification tags, carried medical tools, laced their talk with medical jargon, and attempted to mask their emotions. These affectations signaled to their audience of patients, supervisors, and themselves the students' claim to the role of doctor. Some Nike employees actually have the famous "swoosh" logo tattooed on their bodies (Katz, 1994). As Jim Barker put it, "As a part of acting in collectivities, we have to demonstrate what we're feeling inside. . . . We must be marked or do something to express the degree of our identification. . . . [We] display identity cues." Because one's internal psychological state is not readily accessible to others, one must adopt visible proxies that demonstrate that state.

Organizations facilitate social validation by institutionalizing temporal markers of progress known as rites of passage, and more particularly, rites of incorporation (van Gennep, 1960). Entry into a group or organization (initiation), promotions, transfers, retirements, and so on are often marked by rituals of varying formality and complexity. The process of the ritual often matters more than the content in signaling a significant change in one's identity. By witnessing and participating in the ritual, the audience is cued to regard and treat the focal person differently because he or she has become, effectively, a different person.

Following the love metaphor, just as it is difficult to imagine not loving something that one currently *does* love, so it is difficult to imagine losing a valued part of one's self-definition. Yet, as with love, identification can decay if it is not actively affirmed. Here, too, markers are essential for sustaining the salience of an identity. For example, rituals such as company retreats, religious services, anniversary celebrations, and professional conferences are held at regular intervals in part to allow individuals to periodically renew their identifications. A life devoid of regularized markers is a life devoid of identity hooks.

Similarly, periodic crises may be part of the reaffirmation cycle. Just as steel is tempered by fire, a stronger identity may be forged by ordeal, as suggested by this pastiche of quotes from our discussion: "Crises are critical incidents. . . . [They] remind you of what you most truly value . . . [and] cause you to reexamine your taken-for-granted assumptions, values, and beliefs. . . . Crises shake up mindlessness."

Finally, it was argued above that identities must be made salient to be validated and affirmed. However, because individuals are, in part, amalgams of many social identities (e.g., occupation, family, gender, religion)—where each identity is often associated with (and cued by) specific settings, and some identities may conflict—a given identity will be salient only some of the time. Seldom is continual salience required for validation; and indeed, continual salience is apt to be psychologically unhealthy. Adler and Adler (1991) discuss how college basketball players bemoaned the fact that, as local celebrities, they were seldom allowed to step out of character and simply be "themselves."

Individuals, as amalgams, are more complex and rich, and they are embedded in more diverse social contexts—are more essentially "human"—than any single identity can be (Ashforth & Mael, 1996). It is precisely because of periods of nonsalience that we come to appreciate a salient identity for what it offers the totality of who we are. When I return to my parents' home, I slip easily into the routines, patter, in-jokes, rivalries, and traditions of my family. I'm essentially a kid again. When I leave, I feel renewed and fortified, and thus capable of being an adult. The difficulty is finding and maintaining the right balance of salience and nonsalience as we juggle our identities.

CONCLUSION:
THE END OF THE BEGINNING

As attested by the variety of our identification metaphors and the number of asides in our exploration of the identification process, our conversation suggested a very dynamic and complex process where even the contours remain far from clear. Despite the structure I have imposed on the conversation, our discussion raised more issues than it answered. Promising issues for future conversations include (a) Why do people identify at all? What attracts them to certain identification objects, such as organizations? To what extent is identification intentional (conscious and purposeful)? (b) What individual and situational factors affect the trajectory and strength of identification in organizations? What are common personal and organizational markers of identification (and de- and disidentification)? (c) How are identities negotiated and transformed over time? How do individuals navigate among multiple and embedded identities, and multiple and conflicting identities? (d) How do *collective* identities emerge and change over time? What role do social processes, such as social contagion and social comparison, play in identification?

As suggested by the title, "Becoming," the issues are as open and diverse as the process itself.

REFERENCES

Adler, P. A., & Adler, P. (1991). *Backboards & blackboards: College athletes and role engulfment.* New York: Columbia University Press.

Ashforth, B. E., & Mael, F. A. (1996). Organizational identity and strategy as a context for the individual. In J. A. C. Baum & J. E. Dutton (Eds.), *Advances in strategic management* (Vol. 13, pp. 19-64). Greenwich, CT: JAI.

Beyer, J. M., & Hannah, D. R. (1996, August). *Socialization, social identity and the possible self: Who do I want to be?* Paper presented at the annual meeting of the Academy of Management, Cincinnati.

Bowlby, J. (1969). *Attachment and loss. Vol. 1: Attachment.* New York: Basic Books.

Elsbach, K. D., & Bhattacharya, C. B. (1996). *Organizational disidentification.* Unpublished manuscript, Emory University, Atlanta.

Elsbach, K. D., & Glynn, M. A. (1996). Believing your own "PR": Embedding identification in strategic reputation. In J. A. C. Baum & J. E. Dutton (Eds.), *Advances in strategic management* (Vol. 13, pp. 65-90). Greenwich, CT: JAI.

Feldman, D. C. (1976). A contingency theory of socialization. *Administrative Science Quarterly, 21,* 433-452.

Glynn, M. A. (1994). Effects of work task cues and play task cues on information processing, judgment, and motivation. *Journal of Applied Psychology, 79,* 34-45.

Goffman, E. (1959). *The presentation of self in everyday life.* Garden City, NY: Doubleday.

Haas, J., & Shaffir, W. (1982). Taking on the role of doctor: A dramaturgical analysis of professionalization. *Symbolic Interaction, 5,* 187-203.

Hess, E. H. (1973). *Imprinting: Early experience in the developmental psychobiology of attachment.* New York: Van Nostrand Reinhold.

Ibarra, H. (1996, August). *Inauthentic selves: Image, identity and social networks in professional socialization.* Paper presented at the annual meeting of the Academy of Management, Cincinnati.

Katz, D. R. (1994). *Just do it: The Nike spirit in the corporate world.* New York: Random House.

Leana, C. R., & Feldman, D. C. (1992). *Coping with job loss: How individuals, organizations, and communities respond to layoffs.* New York: Lexington.

Lewin, K. (1951). *Field theory in social science: Selected theoretical papers* (D. Cartwright, Ed.). New York: Harper & Row.

Lieberman, S. (1956). The effects of changes in roles on the attitudes of role occupants. *Human Relations, 9,* 385-402.

Louis, M. R. (1980). Surprise and sense making: What newcomers experience in entering unfamiliar organizational settings. *Administrative Science Quarterly, 25,* 226-251.

Mael, F. A., & Ashforth, B. E. (1995). Loyal from day one: Biodata, organizational identification, and turnover among newcomers. *Personnel Psychology, 48,* 309-333.

Markus, H., & Nurius, P. (1986). Possible selves. *American Psychologist, 41,* 954-969.

Reiter, E. (1991). *Making fast food: From the frying pan into the fryer.* Montreal: McGill-Queen's University Press.

Salter, M. A. (1978). *Play: Anthropological perspectives.* West Point, NY: Leisure Press.

Stebbins, R. A. (1990). *The laugh-makers: Stand-up comedy as art, business, and life-style.* Montreal: McGill-Queen's University Press.

Trice, H. M., & Beyer, J. M. (1993). *The cultures of work organizations.* Englewood Cliffs, NJ: Prentice Hall.

van Gennep, A. (1960). *The rites of passage* (M. B. Vizedom & G. L. Caffee, Trans.). Chicago: University of Chicago Press.

Weick, K. E. (1984). Small wins: Redefining the scale of social problems. *American Psychologist, 39,* 40-49.

Weiner, E. (1996, November). *Marketplace 2000: A view of the future.* Invited address at the annual symposium of the First Interstate Services Marketing Center, Arizona State University, Phoenix.

Organizational Identification and the "Whole Person": Integrating Affect, Behavior, and Cognition

CELIA V. HARQUAIL

At the very start of our weekend of conversation, we acknowledged that a significant challenge for future research on organizational identification is to address more of the "whole person" who becomes identified with the organization. Our own experience as organization members tells us that there is a lot more to being an organization member than what is captured by our current theories. Moreover, social identity theory—the very research tradition that provides a foundation for many of our current theories of organizational identification—highlights the affective as well as the cognitive nature of self-definition as a group member. Tajfel (1978) explicitly defined social identification as having both affective and cognitive components. According to Tajfel, a social identity is "the individual's knowledge that he belongs to certain social groups, together with some *emotional and value significance* [italics added] to him of that membership" (p. 31). Thus, it made sense for us to consider how organizational identification engages the feelings, the actions, the spirits, and perhaps even more of the organizationally identified person.

We acknowledged that work in organizational identification has tended to focus on the cognitive mechanisms that align an individual's identity with the identity of the organization. It has focused on how individuals "think of themselves" or define themselves cognitively as members of organizations, thus restricting theories to the rational or thought-based component of organizational identification. Although we all believed that emotions and behaviors play important roles in organizational identification—that identification has affective and behavioral components—we realized that we no longer needed to put emotions and behaviors aside while we focused on the cognitive aspects. Thus, we agreed that one pressing next step was to integrate emotions and behaviors into our definitions and models. The task we began in our conversation on the "whole person" was to expand our understanding of organizational identification to encompass the thinking, feeling, and acting person. We hoped to identify some key questions that would help explain how our emotions are engaged as we identify with organizations, and how our behaviors might induce, strengthen, and express our identification.

Quite early on in this conversation, we discovered that our ability to raise interesting, pressing questions about identification and emotion far outstripped our ability to propose plausible answers. Not only did we raise more questions than we could answer, we raised questions that, it seemed, might not even have answers.

Given the sheer number of questions raised, the amount of time devoted explicitly to the conversation about identification and the "whole person" was rather short. (It took up only 3 pages of a 45-page transcript.) One participant noted later that it appeared to her that we were trying to escape parts of the topic, perhaps because it was simply too hard to theorize good answers to these complicated questions. The harder and more complex the problems became, the less productive and energized we felt. Yet, not surprisingly, our conversations on other topics were peppered with comments and questions that related back to issues of the "whole person." Clearly, we believe that behavior, affect, and cognition are all important to identification—we are just not sure how to fit these three pieces together. The conversation related by the text to follow attempts to incorporate what we talked about directly with the sometimes isolated ideas about the whole person that came up in other conversations.

The question that we jumped to first was how tightly or loosely coupled the elements of affect, behavior, and cognition were in the overall process of identification. Although we had generally conceptualized the process as being driven by cognition, which then brought in emotion and behavior, we wondered whether the process of identification would differ if emotion "drove" identification, or if behavior did. For example, if pride in your organization's sponsorship of the Olympics drew you to identify with it more strongly, what influence would this positive emotion have on your self-definition as an organization member, or on your behavior? Similarly, if you bought and immediately began wearing a sweatshirt emblazoned with the name of the college you've just been admitted to, how would this behavior strengthen your organizational identification and influence your thoughts and feelings?

We temporarily concluded that cognition and affect were hard to untangle, whereas cognition/affect and behavior were somewhat more separable. We also concluded that it was not particularly useful to consider whether affect or cognition generally came "first" or was more important to the process of organizational identification. (The relationship between cognition and affect, we concluded, was a chronic question for the broader field of social cognition to puzzle out.) Although we believed that there were complex interrelationships between all three elements, we decided first to discuss how emotions might be important to the process of organizational identification, and later to discuss how behavior influenced the cognitions and emotions of identification.

HOW IS AFFECT IMPORTANT
TO ORGANIZATIONAL IDENTIFICATION?

The more we shared the thoughts and feelings related to our own individual experiences as identified organization members, the more confident we were in asserting that when individuals *think* of themselves as organization members, they *feel* like organization members. That is, individuals' general emotions as well as their self-specific emotions (e.g., self-esteem) are implicated by their identification with an organization. Organizational identification engages more than our cognitive self-categorizations and our brains; it engages our hearts. But exactly how are our emotions engaged as we identify with organizations? How might our emotions induce, strengthen, or weaken our organizational identification and the behaviors associated with identification?

When we discussed the place of emotion in organizational identification, we speculated that emotion might be important in several very different ways. First, emotions indicate the degree of value that individuals place on simply having their organizational identity. Emotions tell us how important an identity is to us. Because individuals become emotionally attached to their identities, when the identity or the identification relationship is threatened or affirmed, individuals are likely to experience some level of affect. In Tajfel's (1978) terms, this affect would reflect the "emotional significance" of an organizational identity to an individual. In other words, the stronger the emotions, the stronger the significance of that identity.

Second, emotions can indicate the evaluation, or judgment, that an individual has of an identity. This positive or negative evaluation is what Tajfel (1978) would call the "value significance" of a social identity. Value significance can become apparent when positive emotions alert the individual to his or her positive evaluation of an identity and when negative emotions alert him or her to a negative evaluation.

Third, emotions can also motivate organizational identification. Individuals will be drawn to identify more strongly when their organizational identities provide for positive affect, and they will be repelled from identification when their organizational identities provide for negative affect.

Affective Identification: Indicating Value

To distinguish the emotions related to being an organization member from the cognitions, researchers might call the emotional element of identification "affective identification"—the degree to which an individual values having a specific organizational identity. Use of the term "affective identification" is not to suggest that the affective and cognitive elements of organizational identification can actually be separated in either individuals' experience of identification or in researchers' measurement of identification. Rather, the term is to help researchers distinguish theoretically between the "thinking" and the "feeling" related to one's identification.

With regard to affective identification, several questions arose, including the following:

- Is affect engaged by simply "having" the identity, or is affect salient only when either the identity content or the identity relationship is threatened?
- How does the notion of affective identification influence our models of the process of organizational identification? The process must now include not only the cognitive process of "matching" characteristics that simultaneously define the self and the organization, but also the affective processes of coming to value one's organizational identification and to evaluating one's identity as positive or negative. How do individuals become affectively identified with their organization? How do they evaluate whether this organizational identity is positive or negative? (These questions are also related to

our conversation about the process of organizational identification, as recounted earlier by Blake Ashforth.)

Proposing that affect can be a signaling device that alerts individuals to where they should devote cognitive resources, we also considered what role emotions might play in getting individuals to notice and pay attention to their identification with their organization. If individuals feel emotions related to their organization's identity or to their own identification with the organization, they might be encouraged to pay attention to these emotions, try to understand them, identify their causes, and remedy the cause of any negative emotions. The idea of affect as a signal of identification triggered us to ask:

- What do different emotions tell us about our organizational identification? Is the strength of one's emotion directly related to the strength of one's identification? How do individuals use the information made available to them when they get emotional about their organization and/or identification?

Affect and the Evaluation of an Organizational Identity

Tajfel's (1978) definition of social identification ties the affective component of identification to individuals' evaluation of their group membership. Thus, organizational identification includes not only how strongly individuals feel about their organizational identity, but also how they evaluate the identity (e.g., positively or negatively). Although Tajfel refers only to individuals' evaluation of their identity, both their own private and others' public evaluations of the identity will influence individuals' emotions. As we talked about the possible roles that emotions might play in identification, we found it very difficult to separate the possible effects of the strength of identification-related emotions from the possible effects of the valence (positive or negative) of these emotions, as well as from what individuals consider as they evaluate their organizational identity.

- Is the valence of identity-related emotion the result of individuals' private evaluations of their identity or of their estimate of the public's evaluation of that identity, or both?
- How can researchers disentangle the *strength* of one's feeling about an organizational identification from the valence or *type* of affect triggered by evaluating that identification? For example, does it matter that I am strongly identified as a Caterpillar employee, even though I think that Caterpillar is an untrustworthy, bad company? Is my identification qualitatively different from that of my coworker, who is more weakly identified with Caterpillar but believes it is an honorable, good company?

Affect and the Motivation to Identify

The opportunity to experience positive affect may motivate individuals to invest more of themselves—their thoughts and feelings—into their organizational identity, thus increasing their identification. Conversely, the threat of negative affect may motivate individuals to decrease their identification. How does affect initiate, strengthen, and reflect one's organizational identification?

Affect can drive organizational identification when individuals "follow their hearts" and strive for a stronger or broader connection with an organization. Individuals may begin to define themselves as organization members (that is, to identify cognitively), where before they did not. Individuals may also increase the strength of their overall identification (both affective and cognitive) in order to experience more of the positive emotions associated with being part of the organization. These positive emotions may include the warmth of affiliation with others, enthusiasm, pride, and so on. Individuals can also follow their hearts away from the organization if they experience emotions that they interpret as negative. Negative affect can motivate individuals to temper their affective and cognitive identification, or to break off their identification entirely, to escape these emotions. For example, an individual who has been identified as a member of Texaco may reduce his or her organizational identification in an effort to reduce his or her shame over racist behavior by Texaco executives. Thus, negative and positive affect can motivate individuals to decrease or increase their organizational identification. This conversation raised again the question of alignment between feeling and thinking as an organization member. Specifically,

- Could individuals be motivated to identify or deidentify in seemingly counterlogical ways (e.g., to maintain an organizational identification that they feel negatively about, or to relinquish an identity they feel positively about)?

HOW ARE COGNITION, AFFECT, AND BEHAVIOR RELATED TO ONE ANOTHER?

As we considered the various roles that cognition, affect, and behavior might play, our discussion shifted to the process of identification; thus, the ideas here are quite related to our later conversation about identification processes. (See Elsbach's essay in this chapter. That conversation took a more longitudinal view of identification, whereas this conversation focused on a shorter cycle or span of interaction among the three elements of identification.)

We agreed that organizational identification has three intertwined elements: cognition, affect, and behavior. Under ideal conditions, these components are aligned and mutually reinforcing, so that an individual thinks, feels, and acts in a coordinated way as an organization member. At different points in the identification process, one element may lead the individual's identification while the other elements lag behind.

It would be easy to imagine that individuals' identification-related emotions and identity-relevant behaviors are outcomes of cognitive identification, and thus that our emotions and behaviors are at the mercy of cognitive identification. However, it may be that at certain times, our cognitive identification and identity-related behaviors are at the mercy of our affect. Affect may lead to cognitive identification. And, because emotions influence behaviors in general, we can expect that the emotions related to affective organizational identification will influence organizational identity-related behaviors.

- What causes cognition, affect, or behavior to take the lead in the organizational identification process? How might the overall identification process differ when affect leads identification, when cognition leads identification, and when behavior leads identification?
- Under what conditions do individuals adjust their affective identification, their cognitive identification, or their identity-related behaviors to bring their "identification system" into some balance?
- There may be situations where acting, feeling, or thinking like a member is dangerous or detrimental to the individual. A soldier who is fully identified with his or her unit may march into a hopeless battle, without thinking twice about whether this behavior is sensible. An employee might feel so positively about being an Arvin member that he or she chooses to make auto parts on Sundays rather than to fulfill his or her religious commitments. Under what conditions might individuals suppress one or more components of identification? How might individuals cope with suppressing a component of identification?

We argued about whether emotion was or was not an "equal player" in the process of identification. Perhaps, a few of us speculated, affective identification is simply an outcome of a certain, deep level of cognitive identification. Affect may indicate how deeply one's cognitive self-definition as an organization member is integrated into her or his sense of self. Ashforth (1993) and Organ (1990) have argued that the individual-organization relationship often becomes suffused with emotion over time, so that what once may have been a narrow, purely cognitive connection to the organization becomes a broader, richer, and more complex relationship with both cognitive and affective components. Following Kelman's (1958) notion of different levels of investment in a role, the lowest level of identification (what might be called "preidentification") could be simply "acting like" an organization member, without having a cognitive or affective identification with the organization. The next level might be cognitive identification, simply thinking of oneself as a member. The highest level of involvement would include emotions, so that strong organizational identification would encompass behavioral, cognitive, and emotional investment. Given either of these claims about the place of affect, there may be a hierarchy among cognitive, affective and behavioral elements of identification.

- Is it possible to have a purely intellectual (i.e., only cognitive) organizational identification? Under what conditions? Could cognitive identification without affective identification simply reflect a denial of one's emotional attachment to an identity?

BEHAVIOR AND
ORGANIZATIONAL IDENTIFICATION

Next, our conversation turned to the role of identity-congruent behavior. Recall that at the start of our conversation, we tentatively settled on the premise that cognition and affect were tightly coupled with each other, whereas behavior was only loosely coupled with cognition and affect. Although we felt comfortable proposing that behavior is an outcome of organizational identification, we realized that it was also true that behavior could be an antecedent of identification. Certainly, we can imagine a circularity in the relationships we propose between the cognitive/affective and the behavioral elements of organizational identification.

Speculating on the role of identity-congruent behavior, we proposed first that such behavior reflects a certain level of organizational identification. This argument could play two ways, with behavior reflecting either strong identification or superficial identification. Following Kelman (1958), displaying identity-congruent behavior and acting like an organization member may be the simplest and lowest level of organizational identification, existing without either cognitive or affective identification. Perhaps identity-congruent behavior reflects one's superficial experimentation with a particular identity, and that behavior "leads" identification when individuals "try on" an organizational identity. Individuals may experiment with behaviors that characterize organization members to test whether these behaviors, and thus the organizational identity, fit them. For example, the new employee who grins broadly as he says, "Welcome to McDonald's" may be experimenting with the hyper-cheery behavior common to McDonald's employees, testing whether he is ready to think of himself as or feel the emotions of a McDonald's member. This possibility raised additional questions about the role of behavior in experimenting with identities:

- What does this behavioral experimentation feel like for individuals? What do individuals have to establish through identity-congruent behaviors to encourage them to adopt or reject an organizational identification?
- Does experimentation help individuals find a balance between their organizational identification and other facets of their total identities?

It might be that identity-congruent behavior reflects not superficial identification but deep and strong identification, especially when this behavior is routine, preconscious, and/or spontaneous. For example, an individual may attend Mass regularly or make the sign of the cross automatically at the sight of an ambulance, not because he or she is experimenting with a Catholic identity but because he or she has a very strong Catholic identity.

This example raised a deeper question: What if behaving "as" a member is required before we can even say that a person "has" an identity? Doesn't going to Mass distinguish those with a Catholic identity from those without? What if identity-congruent behavior is a necessary condition for organizational identification? We disagreed whether identity-congruent behavior is simply a consequence of organizational identification or whether it is an integral and necessary part of the identification process. On one side were those who felt that behavior was a likely part of identification, but not necessary. On the other side was one who questioned whether a person really could be said to have an identity unless that person reflected that identity through identity-congruent behavior.

This participant argued that, from a variety of perspectives, identity-congruent behavior is necessary before identification can be said to exist. First, within our common cognitive paradigm that focuses on the individuals' self-definition alone, maintaining organizational identification requires identity-congruent behavior. Identity-congruent behavior is required because individuals seek continuity, congruence, and affirmation of their valued organizational identities (Dutton, Dukerich, & Harquail, 1993). Continuity requires that an identity exist over time, so an individual might need to enact his or her identity in order to keep it from decaying. Congruence requires that an individual maintain an alignment between thoughts, feelings, and behaviors. Thus, he or she will need to behave like an organization member in order to continue to feel like and to think of him- or herself as a member. Affirmation requires public recognition and validation of an identity. One critical way to be affirmed is to have others recognize and affirm your identity-congruent behavior. Even beyond these three personal motives, an individual may have to act like an organization member in order to be accepted as a member by others and maintain his or her membership.

Other participants countered that individuals can maintain their identities without identity-congruent behavior. This might be difficult, but it is not impossible. For example, individuals could define themselves as environmentalists and not recycle, if they were willing to cope with the guilt that their behaviors were not in line with their self-definition. Moreover, there are some identities that, at times, we might prefer to keep to ourselves. For example, an individual might not act like an FBI agent when he or she attends an "X Files" fan fair because his or her comfort in the situation requires hiding this organizational identity from other attendees. The process of identity negotiation, and thus the importance of identity-congruent behavior, may be more critical when individuals are new to the organization, when their self-definition as members is weak, when their affective identification is low, and when their credibility among other members and the public is low.

Our devil's advocate then suggested that we step away from the cognitive paradigm, which focuses on the individual's self-definition, and step into an interactionist perspective. In an interactionist paradigm, an identity must be negotiated (Swann, 1987) between the self and others (the social public) in order for that person to be said to "have" an identity. Identity-congruent behavior is required for identification, because an individual has to perform his or her identity and have others affirm it publicly in order for the identity to be negotiated, produced, or instantiated. In this paradigm, identity-congruent behavior is a necessary condition of organizational identification.

Although some of us found this alternative perspective unfamiliar, we were willing to entertain the idea that other theoretical perspectives would highlight the role of identity-congruent behavior. Entertaining for a moment the idea that individuals cannot be said to have identities unless they perform these identities through behaviors that define and reflect that identity (e.g., you cannot be said to be a Catholic unless you attend Mass on a regular basis), how might we adjust or expand our views about the role of behavior? What new implications are raised?

- If others do not accept or affirm that you have an identity as an organization member, how does this affect your identification? For example, what happens when no one acknowledges you as a graduate of your prestigious alma mater? Does this lack of recognition induce you to identify more strongly and to display more behaviors typical of a "Yalic," or does this lack of recognition lead you to identify less and less strongly?
- Can individuals maintain identities without enacting them, if they are comfortable with acting hypocritically?
- If behaving as an organizational member is critical to maintaining an identification, what do people do when they are not able to behave as members? When others prohibit them from expressing their organizational identification through behavior, how do individuals cope? Do some individuals get great satisfaction from maintaining a "secret identity"?
- What is the minimal amount of behavior necessary to maintain an identification? Is the act of thinking of oneself as a member enough? Are there substitutes for behavior that help maintain an identity over time?

Reflecting Back on the Conversation

Looking back over the transcripts of the weekend of conversations, I noted later how deeply faithful we were as a group to a cognitive, individually oriented paradigm of the self and of identity. Within this one perspective, there are many (too many?) rich and interesting issues to pursue. Yet we have limited our exploration into organizational identification to this one perspective—what about interactionist perspectives on identity, or relational models of the self and self-identity that depend not just on the individual but also on others? There is still much to explore.

REFERENCES

Ashforth, B. E. (1993). Political and apolitical action: Toward a reconciliation of contradictory models of organizational behavior. *International Journal of Organizational Analysis, 1,* 363-384.

Dutton, J. E., Dukerich, J. M., & Harquail, C. V. (1994). Organizational images and member identification. *Administrative Science Quarterly, 39,* 239-263.

Kelman, H. C. (1958). Compliance, identification and internalization. *Journal of Conflict Resolution, 2,* 51-60.

Organ, D. W. (1990). The motivational basis of citizenship behavior. In B. M. Staw & L. L. Cummings (Eds.), *Research in organizational behavior* (Vol. 12, pp. 43-72). Greenwich, CT: JAI.

Swann, W. B. (1987). Identity negotiation: Where two roads meet. *Journal of Personality and Social Psychology, 53,* 1038-1051.

Tajfel, H. (1978). Social categorization, social identity and social comparison. In H. Tajfel (Ed.), *Differentiation between social groups* (pp. 61-76). New York: Academic Press.

The Process of Social Identification: With What Do We Identify?

KIMBERLY D. ELSBACH

By definition, peoples' social identities (i.e., their self-concepts based on a sense of connectedness or oneness with social groups) depend on both the types of groups available with which they may choose to identify and their existing self-concepts—or "personal identities"—based on attributes that are less open to choice, such as race, gender, and age (Ashforth & Mael, 1989; Mael & Ashforth, 1992). Research on social identification suggests that people will choose to identify with groups or organizations that are congruent with their existing self-concepts and/or will enhance these self-concepts (Dutton, Dukerich, & Harquail, 1994). Yet beyond these general notions, little is known about why we define ourselves in terms of links to one set of groups or organizations versus another, seemingly similar set.

Most of the literature on antecedents of identification has focused, specifically, on what predicts employees' identification with organizations of which they are members. This research shows that things like organizational prestige, instrumentality in helping employees achieve goals, and tenure with the organization predict employees' connectedness or sense of oneness with an organization (Mael & Ashforth, 1992; Schneider, Hall, & Nygren, 1971). By contrast, few studies have examined what predicts individuals' identification with organizations of which they are not employees (e.g., clubs, churches, professional associations, or corporations that produce products and services they use; see Bhattacharya, Rao, & Glynn, 1995, for an exception), and none has examined how people make choices among organizations that would appear, at least on the surface, to provide the same types of identity enhancements to prospective identifiers (e.g., why pick the Sierra Club vs. Greenpeace to bolster an identity of environmentalism?). In these cases, it would appear that identifiers have exerted much more free choice, and even intentional effort, in connecting themselves and their self-concept to a particular organization. Furthermore, it would appear that, in cases where employees freely seek out organizations with which to identify, the characteristics of the organizations available for identification would have an important effect on their identification choice. Examining with what, in an organization, a person chooses to identify is the focus of this chapter.

In the following sections, I have reproduced parts of our discussion about the processes by which people freely and intentionally connect their identities with an organization's. Turning points and insights from this discussion centered around a set of questions about the processes of identification and how these processes were affected by individuals' identification choices. These questions thus constitute the outline of the discussion.

WITH WHAT DO WE IDENTIFY?
A DISCUSSION ABOUT IDENTITY CHOICES

Can people proactively manage the look of their social identity through their identifications?

Blake: Organizations are multifaceted, equivocal, and dynamic. This provides numerous real or imagined bases for identification. Identification is somewhat selective in that you attend to what is most compatible with your needs and values, and dismiss or rationalize away that which is not.

Kim: You might think of your identity as a stellar constellation. Depending on where you are and time of year, it looks different—so even though all the connections are the same, some are more visible at different times of year and from different vantage points. You can choose which aspects of your identity to highlight depending on the circumstances.

Rod: One might think of it in terms of *identity portfolio management.* You can switch your investment in any given identity as a type of identification management. Catastrophic losses may cause you to remove one of those identities. It's a way of demonstrating the flexibility or plasticity of the self. You can reconstitute your identity depending on changing circumstances to which you must adapt.

Blake: The same dynamics of affirmation apply in bolstering your self-esteem. When you're injured in one area (e.g., an academic gets a paper rejected by a journal), you focus on another area of your self-concept (e.g., the academic consoles herself by focusing on her successes as a parent). This type of identity management may be hard to do in isolation. If you're a misfit, you may mentally key on positive characteristics, but it's hard to maintain a positive identity unless people actively support that.

Janet: If something bad happens to your organization, you might want to play up identification with other organizations. It's a process that highlights or shadows different aspects of identifications. It also shows the advantage of multiple identities. That is, to the extent you have a rough time in one, you'll console yourself by doing something somewhere else to reaffirm your worth.

How does the distinctiveness and complexity of an individual's identity interact with the distinctiveness and complexity of an organization's identity in predicting who will identify?

Jim: A person with a complex identity may like an organization with a simple identity because it's easier to focus on only one part of their identity at a time. The more complex the organization's identity, or the more diverse the group, the more you may be likely to retreat into a simple identity. If the organization's identity is compartmentalized, then even if it has a complex identity, it may be OK. This is like Albert and Whetten's (1985) idea of an ideographic identity. By contrast, organizations with holographic identities have multiple aspects, but they all exist at all levels. It may be hard to identify with a holographic identity because so much is going on, so who can identify with all that stuff? On the other hand, because it permeates all parts of the organization, a holographic identity tends to be associated with a strong culture. So it's articulated, and one can find something to identify with.

Judi: Wilson, Keyton, Johnson, Geiger, and Clark's (1993) study of a church (comprised of overlapping self-help groups) showed that, because the church was a holographic organization, people who worked with one of its groups developed a stronger identification with the church as a whole. The local identities simply replicated the larger. If the church had been ideographic, the self-help groups would have led to a fragmented conception of the church and impeded identification with the whole.

CV: On the other hand, a person might not even see these other identities in their organization. Since identities determine (in part) what information we attend to, we may simply not attend to information about our company that isn't relevant to our identification with it. So before we ignore or suppress this information, we may not even parse it from the environment.

How are deviants important to defining the organization's identity and peoples' willingness to identify with it?

CV: If you're very different from everyone and don't find someone to affirm your identity, there may be "splitting" of the self, making it easier to deny the existence of the unsupported identity in threatening situations (e.g., a closeted gay person may behave in a very "straight" manner around those he feels oppose his gay identity). But people with marginally acceptable identities may be very functional for an organization. They may need a deviant to help define the boundaries of acceptable identities. This is what is called a radical flank effect: Radicals at fringes of legitimacy are very important to the group because they define what is acceptable and normative. We may need to keep the outliers around as a benchmark. These ideas remind us of how relational all these identities are.

Judi: Baumeister's (1986) book suggests that people who tend to rebel or actively experiment with identities that differ from those of their parents tend to be better adjusted later in life. They have a surer sense of who and why they are what they are. Those who mindlessly mimic or assimilate their parents' template don't recognize the choices they've implicitly forgone and are more vulnerable to identity threats.

What occurs during the emergent process of identification between a person and an organization?

Rod: One factor that might make it easier for individuals to identify with a group or organization initially, before they have had much concrete knowledge about or experience with the group or organization, is the various positive illusions that individuals entertain about the benefits they will derive from group membership. Recent empirical evidence indicates individuals often think they will derive more benefits from participation in one group than in others. Thus, they enter the group with relatively positive expectations, and these may help them maintain an optimistic stance regarding the benefits of group participation and keep motivation high until the real payoffs begin to roll in.

Mary Ann: But over time, perceptions may start to erode or become more complex. So when you start out, everything is simple and has a nice glow—you might overlook parts that might confuse you or upset you. Then later, you might pay more attention to them. This is one explanation for why your identifications might be changing or shifting over time.

Is it important that you have organizational disidentifications to maintain your self-concepts? Is there a usefulness to thinking about disidentifying with some organizations in order to get a grip on identifying with other organizations?

Kim: If we return to the metaphor of identifications as stellar constellations, it appears we have lots we can identify with. There may be so many options that we don't know where to place our bets. In this sense, disidentification (i.e., a sense of active disconnection from a social group) may help you to know where you are by telling you where you're not. If I have already determined what I am *not,* it may be easier to find a suitable organization with which to identify, and that identification may be stronger.

Stu: In fact, very strong cultures are likely to be defined by what they exclude, and so members may have to disidentify with some social groups in order to identify with them. This suggests that in the search for meaning, disidentification may be just as powerful a source as identification. Disidentification also underscores the salience of negative information and the diagnosticity of negative information. It's unexpected and unusual, so it tells us more about ourselves.

Mary Ann: On the other hand, it may be hard to disidentify. Just focusing on what's incongruent between you and an organization may be hard to do. Constantly thinking about what I am not and making my actions congruent with what I am not is hard to imagine (although counterculture groups tend to exist in this mode). It's much easier to make actions congruent with what I am. If we use the constellations metaphor again, it's easier to maintain orbit if you're also attracted by another, not just repulsed. If you're just being repulsed and not being attracted, you're just bouncing around because there's no place to go.

Kim: In my research on the NRA [National Rifle Association], I have found that disidentification and identification are different in significant ways. For example, with disidentification, you're in a state where you're actively maintaining negative feelings about an organization, which is something people don't like to do and is hard for them to do. So disidentification seems to require more effort than identification. It almost seems to be an "all-or-nothing" thing. Therefore, it may only be a temporary state in between identifications, or when you haven't yet found a place to identify. In this way, disidentification may be a useful tool if you're trying to get people to identify with a new company culture (i.e., first get them to disidentify with the old one). Then they're in a state they don't want to be in, and looking for something to identify with.

Jim: If we return to the notion of the complexity of organizations (i.e., Phillip Morris), can I disidentify with part of the identity and still be whole? It may be hard if you're really engaged in what you don't like.

Rod: There might be a place for "nonidentification"—a passive disconnection versus an active disconnection, like in disidentification. If identity starts to shift or decay, it creates a vacuum. And we have to fill that vacuum somehow. If your identity isn't valued in a certain culture, you have to find a value—a source of meaning for you in this culture. Organizations can make it easier or harder for us to find that meaning by making it more inclusive versus exclusive in terms of identity. It might be easier to find meaning when everything fits (weak culture) than in a strong culture, where lots does not fit.

AN INTEGRATING METAPHOR:
IDENTIFICATIONS AS
STELLAR CONSTELLATIONS

Based on this discussion, I propose that the metaphor of a "stellar constellation" (e.g., the Big Dipper or Orion) may be used to illustrate the complexity and dynamic nature of social identifications, as well as highlight questions for future research on social identifications.

In a stellar constellation, for example, the links between the stars (as a parallel to a person's identifications with social groups) are limited to the relatively small number of stars in that constellation. Stars that are far away from a given constellation may not be included in that constellation. Similarly, social groups or organizations that are cognitively "distant" from a person's social identity may be difficult to incorporate into that identity (i.e., a police officer may find it difficult to identify with an activist group, such as Earth First!, that breaks the law to promote its cause). Keeping these social groups separate from one's social identity (i.e., "disidentifying" with these groups) may also be important to defining one's self-concept (Elsbach & Bhattacharya, 1996).

In addition, depending on your location and time of year, each constellation looks different—so even though all of the connections are the same, they may vary in terms of brightness over time. In a similar manner, our social identifications may change their character over time depending on what groups or organizations are made salient to us. Playing different roles (i.e., a university professor may play the roles of teacher and scholar) may make different identifications "brighter" in one's social identity constellation (i.e., a professors' link to her university when she is teaching a class may be brighter than her link to her professional organization).

These characteristics of the "constellation" metaphor highlight two important dimensions of social identifications related to the question, "With what do we identify?" First, they suggest social identifications are complex, consisting of multiple sets of interdependent links to a variety of social groups. Second, they suggest that social identifications are dynamic. Thus, although one's social identity may be made up of an enduring set of links to the same group of organizations, that same identity may "look" different depending on one's context over time.

REFERENCES

Albert, S., & Whetten, D. A. (1985). Organizational identity. In L. L. Cummings & B. M. Staw (Eds.), *Research in organizational behavior* (Vol. 7, pp. 263-295). Greenwich, CT: JAI.

Ashforth, B. E., & Mael, F. (1989). Social identity theory and the organization. *Academy of Management Review, 14,* 20-39.

Baumeister, R. F. (1986). *Identity: Cultural change and the struggle for the self.* New York: Oxford University Press.

Bhattacharya, C. B., Rao, H., & Glynn, M. A. (1995). Understanding the bond of identification: An investigation of its correlates among art museum members. *Journal of Marketing, 59,* 46-57.

Dutton, J. E., Dukerich, J. M., & Harquail, C. V. (1994). Organizational images and member identification. *Administrative Science Quarterly, 39,* 239-263.

Elsbach, K. D., & Bhattacharya, C. B. (1996). *Organizational disidentification.* Unpublished manuscript, Emory University, Atlanta.

Mael, F., & Ashforth, B. E. (1992). Alumni and their alma mater: A partial test of the reformulated model of organizational identification. *Journal of Organizational Behavior, 13,* 103-123.

Schneider, B., Hall, D. T., & Nygren, H. T. (1971). Self image and job characteristics as correlates of changing organizational identification. *Human Relations, 24,* 397-416.

Wilson, G. L., Keyton, J., Johnson, G. D., Geiger, C., & Clark, J. C. (1993). Church growth through member identification and commitment: A congregational case study. *Review of Religious Research, 34,* 259-272.

Individuals' Need for
Organizational Identification (nOID):
Speculations on Individual
Differences in the Propensity to Identify

MARY ANN GLYNN

The notion that individuals might differ in their propensity to identify with social objects took root in our first conversation as a group. Posed as the proverbial "what if?" question, we wondered aloud: Do individuals truly have a general and universal propensity to identify? What if, like other personal attributes, individuals differ in their need to identify with social entities, and particularly with organizations? Intrigued by the creative possibilities that such an admittance would allow, our subsequent discussion turned on this single idea and its implications for organizational theory and individual behavior. Our intention was simply to think "out of the box" and to provoke further debate, theorizing, and empirical research on individuals: "identifying with" organizations.

It seemed to us that our radical notion of individual differences offered a departure from previous theories on identification. In our view, much of the existing literature on organizational identification centers on explicating the antecedents, consequences, and/or strength of individuals' identification with organizations (e.g., Bhattacharya, Rao, & Glynn, 1995; Dutton, Dukerich, & Harquail, 1994; Mael & Ashforth, 1992, 1995). Our reading of this body of work is that it focused more on a static sense of *being* identified rather than *becoming* identified (for a fuller discussion, see Ashforth's essay, this chapter). In our conversations, we purposely relaxed the assumption of universality in the need to identify. We entertained the notion that individuals might differ in their need to identify with organizations, an individual characteristic we termed *need for Organizational Identification, or nOID*. Once proposed, the concept of nOID shaped our conversation and raised a series of questions that we attempted to address. We discussed the definition, characterization, and implications of nOID; our thoughts on these issues are reported below.

WHAT IS "NEED FOR ORGANIZATIONAL IDENTIFICATION" (nOID)?
HOW IS nOID DIFFERENT FROM RELATED CONSTRUCTS,
SUCH AS COMMITMENT OR NEED FOR AFFILIATION?

As a group, we reasoned that if organizational identification involved an individual's willingness to extend the boundary of self to embrace organizational membership, then individuals might differ in their need to draw and redraw this boundary. More formally, we define the construct of nOID as an individual's need to maintain a social identity derived from membership in a larger, more impersonal general social category of a particular collective ("I am a member of X organization"). When individuals identify with an organization, they create a "socially extended self" (Brewer & Gardner, 1996, p. 84) and incorporate salient organizational attributes as part of the self (Dutton et al., 1994). This social self is distinct from an individuated personal sclf in that the former is defined in relation to significant social groups, such as organizations, and the latter is not. Although the social self can arise from interpersonal or interdependent relationships with others, it need not (Brewer & Gardner, 1996); that is, a social identity does not require personal relationship with other members of the target organization. Brewer and Gardner (1996) explain:

> Both interpersonal and collective identities are social extensions of the self but differ in whether the social connections are personalized bonds of attachment with some symbolic group or social category. . . . Collective social identities, on the other hand, do not require personal relationships among group members. (p. 83)

Thus, we conclude that organizational identification can be understood as a form of collective social identity in which individuals define themselves in terms of their membership in a particular organization and describe themselves by the same attributes they ascribe to the organization (Ashforth & Mael, 1989; Dutton et al., 1994; Mael & Ashforth, 1995). Although identifying with an organization can involve, and be sustained by, interdependent or interpersonal bonds (such as working with colleagues or reporting to a supervisor), it does not require them. For instance, an individual can perceive him- or herself to be a patron of the arts and identify with an art museum without frequenting the museum, viewing its holdings, or participating in its social or cultural programs (Bhattacharya et al., 1995).

That organizational identification can occur in the absence of direct interpersonal experiences is what distinguishes nOID from a related construct, *need for Affiliation (n-Aff)*. McClelland (1987) described n-Aff as the need to "have warm, close relationships and friendships; concerned with establishing, maintaining and restoring positive emotional relationships and avoiding conflict" (p. 347). In general, individuals with a high need for Affiliation tend to prefer to work with others, communicate interpersonally, hold meetings, and to have supervisory jobs. Although n-Aff and nOID involve both affective and cognitive categorization processes, n-Aff is expressed through specific role relationships (e.g., supervisor-subordinate, team leader-team member), whereas nOID is construed in terms of membership in more general social categories (e.g., supervisors, team leaders).

We also became convinced that nOID was different from commitment. We echo Mael and Ashforth's (1995) belief that "although identification is necessarily organization-*specific,* commitment may not be" (p. 312). Moreover, although commitment and identification can connect an individual to an organization, organizational identification involves the construction of self by incorporating the meaning of the organization and its attributes into one's self-concept, but commitment does not.

Finally, we acknowledge that individuals may differ not only in their innate need to identify with organizations, but also in their need to express, display, or "mark" their identification with organizations. Some individuals may be more (or less) eager to demonstrate publicly their identification with organizations through the markers they display, evidenced by the manner in which they dress, show corporate logos or colors (such as Nike footwear and clothing), or use language that speaks of collectivity rather than individuality (*we* versus *me*). For instance, strongly identified Coca-Cola employees might wear Coca-Cola clothes, post Coca-Cola signs in their home and office, and drink the beverage (in Coca-Cola glasses) at both work and play, thus branding themselves much like the products of the organization of which they are a member.

As a group, although we agreed that individuals could differ in the degree to which they marked their identification, we did not fully converge in our opinion of what such displays reveal about an individual's need to identify. Pointing out that identity markers are sometimes institutionally imposed (as in the case of school or police uniforms), and that the absence of markers may be as revealing as their presence, raised doubts as to the robustness of an initial hypothesis suggesting that individuals with strong needs to identify would also need to mark this identity. We concluded our discussion with the understanding that the correspondence between individuals' need to identify and their need for observable displays of organizational markers represents a fertile area for future research.

WHAT DIFFERENTIATES HIGH nOIDS FROM LOW nOIDS?

We took a coarse-grained approach and explored how individuals with a higher nOID might be different from individuals with a lower nOID. Playfully, we pictured individuals as being located along a continuum whose poles might be labeled nOID (higher need for organizational identification) versus VOID (lack of nOID).

We speculated that individuals with a higher nOID might have a stronger desire to be imprinted upon (by an organization), a higher receptivity to organizational socialization, and a marked tendency to publicly identify themselves as organizational members so as to extend the self to incorporate the organization (Belk, 1988). Conversely, we believed that individuals with a lower nOID might be characterized by a fierce sense of organizational separateness or independence, resistance to organizational socialization, and be more of a loner than a "joiner" or member of multiple organizations (Wann & Hamlet, 1994).

Although we easily described these nOID polarities, there was some discussion about the underlying processes that governed the development and expression of these individual needs. We recognized that all humans are predisposed to imprinting (because it is what makes us human), but high-nOID individuals were perceived to be "looking for something to identify with" as part of a broader search for meaning. We wondered whether a high-nOID individual lacking such a handy organizational affiliation might experience the pathology of being underidentified relative to his or her needs (see the section on pathologies of identification that follows). Moreover, we wondered whether high nOIDs might differ in the strategies they adopted to meet their needs. Could strong identification with a single organization (as in the Coca-Cola example above) be as satisfying as identification with a constellation of organizations that spanned one's work and leisure lives (as might an individual who is employed by one organization, wearing the designer clothes of another, sporting brand-name athletic wear and equipment, driving a prestigious auto, and fanatically rooting for a particular baseball team)? The group left this discussion without a firm conclusion, turning instead to uncover more fully the processes and influences that affect individuals' need to identify.

WHAT FACTORS INFLUENCE AN INDIVIDUAL'S NEED TO IDENTIFY WITH AN ORGANIZATION (nOID)?

Organizational identification is functional, helping individuals to make sense of their organizational environment and to maintain positive social identities (Kramer, 1993). In spite of its positive effects, however, individuals typically experience ambivalence in the process of identification; they become torn between dual needs for organizational inclusion and individual distinctiveness, "being the same and different at the same time." Typically, these tensions are resolved by constraining collective identities to find "optimal distinctiveness" (Brewer, 1991). Recognizing these dualities, we asked: What factors could affect an individual's need to identify strongly with an organization? Our discussion uncovered two: (a) individual differences in one's self-concept, the permeability of boundaries drawn around the self, and one's stage of personal, maturational, or career development; and (b) individual differences in the perception of organizational attractiveness or desirability.

The first set of influences seems, at least to us, to speak directly to the dilemma of balancing inclusiveness against distinctiveness: High nOIDs favor inclusiveness over distinctiveness, whereas low nOIDs lean toward the reverse. We speculated that the need for inclusiveness might relate to the boundaries one draws around one's sense of self, and by implication, how organizational membership is used to define oneself. We propose that high nOIDs, motivated perhaps by gaps in self-definition or a drive to enhance the ego, extend their self-definition to embrace organizational membership. It is organizational categories that are invoked ("I am a Coca-Cola employee") in response to the question of who I think I am; organizational membership becomes fundamental to self-description, and self-definition is impossible without it. Although some argue that the boundary of self can be extended outward via possessions (e.g., Belk, 1988), we propose the reverse—that organizations may penetrate the boundaries of self to extend inward. Thus, for high nOIDs, self-boundaries are permeable with regard to organizations, whereas for low nOIDs, self-boundaries are rigid defenses against organizational affiliations, allowing only categorizations in nonorganizational societal or work roles (e.g., I am a parent; I am an accountant; I am a tennis player).

Our discussion of the question of boundary permeability and organizational identification seemed to position us firmly within a "trait" perspective, such that nOID was viewed largely as an individual disposition that tended to generalize across various personal, situational, or organizational contexts. Several voices in the group reminded us to consider how a "state" perspective might afford alternative insights on nOID. This became the impetus for articulating some of the organizational opportunities that shaped the second set of influences on nOID that we identified.

We proposed that a heightened nOID might fill a void during periods of individual life changes, especially during transitions (e.g., geographic moves, job/organizational changes, marriage, divorce, parenthood, aging, etc.). Driven by three basic principles of self-definition (Dutton et al., 1994)—self-continuity, self-distinctiveness, and self-enhancement—individuals may experience a need to identify with organizations when there is a felt loss of meaning in their personal, social, or professional lives. Brewer and Gardner (1996) explain that "when needs for intimacy at the interpersonal level are not being met, collective identities may become more important" (p. 91). For compensatory reasons, then, prompted by a void felt within the self (whether it be temporary or more enduring), individuals may feel a stronger need to identify with an organization. Driven by crisis, opportunity, personal transition, or organizational disruption, individuals facing change in one area of their personal or professional identity might feel a compensatory push toward solidifying their identification with organizations.

Additionally, individuals may seize opportunities for self-enhancement by aligning themselves with admired or prestigious organizations (Elsbach & Glynn, 1996), thus using organizational identification as a social or professional credential to claim heightened status or legitimacy. Although attractiveness can be grounded in objective measures (such as in *Fortune*'s annual list of the Most Admired Companies), we also recognized that, like beauty, organizational attractiveness is often in the eye of the beholder; and we proposed that the beholder's eyesight might be affected by his or her nOID. As humans, we model ourselves after people whom we admire or like; so too, we mused, might high-nOID individuals be predisposed to seek and perceive attractiveness in organizations with which they sought to identify. We choose to identify with organizations that somehow resonate with our sense of self—whether idealized or actualized selves—and that, subsequently, we sometimes refashion organizations to reflect our preferences about what the firm "should" embody. Although an organization's perceived attractiveness is certainly related to a number of individual personality attributes, our ensuing discussion built on the idea that nOID and organizational attractiveness could be interrelated.

Employees who view their organizations as enjoying high performance or positive accolades might be pulled to identify themselves with these very favorable attributes. For instance, firms listed as "Most Admired," for-profit corporations that support social causes (e.g., Ben & Jerry's, The Body Shop, Tom's of Maine), or ideologically based nonprofits (e.g., Habitat for Humanity, Peace Corps) might elicit affiliations from individuals who feel a need to align with these kinds of firms. Thus, by aligning their identity with that of their firms, individuals can enhance their self-concept and bask in the reflected glory that membership provides. Consistent with a similar proposition advanced by Dutton et al. (1994), we expected that the greater the perceived organizational attraction, the greater the need to identify that individuals would experience.

Our group's discussion thus far had focused primarily on an ideal matching process, where individuals can satisfy their nOID with an available and attractive organization. Clearly, however, there can be cases of mismatch or misfit, in which individuals with high nOID do not have an available or appropriate organization with which to identify (such as the case when an elite university or country club restricts membership). Alternatively, the reverse can also occur, when low-nOID individuals are employed in firms with strong cultures that demand high individual identification (e.g., religious institutions, Mary Kay sales, Southwest Airlines). We imagined cases in which individuals' nOID and the organization's identity (with which they sought to identify) become out of sync. This could occur during periods of organizational change and reorientation, or in response to identity-threatening environmental events that precipitated a shift in organizational identity (Elsbach & Kramer, 1996), so that individuals' once-met nOID would become unsatisfied and vacuous. Additionally, when individuals' expectations of the benefits of their organizational identification outstrip their experience, needs are mismatched and go unmet. Regardless of the source of such mismatches, we hypothesized that individuals would eventually become uncomfortable and dysfunctional, and they would try to resolve these negative feelings either by exiting inappropriate organizations or modifying their needs to match organizational reality.

WHERE DO WE GO FROM HERE?

Beginning with the proposal that individuals can vary in their need for organizational identification (nOID), we defined the construct and differentiated it from the related concepts of affiliation and commitment. Clearly, for nOID to inform our understanding of the processes and outcomes that attend organizational identification, much work is needed to clarify, operationalize, and embed the construct within its nomological net and demonstrate its viability. To encourage continued conversations and research on nOID, we ended as we began, by raising questions. Some of these follow.

How can we operationalize and measure nOID? Might we construct survey scales, interview protocols, and observational techniques to uncover internal needs, external expressions of needs (markers of identification), and their interrelationship? What are the life and career circumstances that encourage higher (or lower) nOID? Is nOID fueled more by crisis and loss than by attractive organizational associations? Is nOID related to demographic characteristics; that is, do younger, less experienced employees have higher nOID than older, more seasoned executives? Are the former more compliant, easily socialized, and cooperative than the latter? Or do experience and socialization intertwine the identities of self and organization? Do organizations benefit more from hiring individuals with higher or lower nOID . . . and under what circumstances?

Finally, we would like to acknowledge that our construct of nOID may offer an unduly restrictive view of individual identification. To be consistent with the overall theme of this volume, we focused primarily on an individual's need to identify *with an organization* (i.e., nOID). Certainly, much of what has been said about nOID applies equally well to the broader construct of nID, or an individual's need to identify with any social entity or object. More generally, we can think of one's need to identify as something innately human that, as one group member stated, "brings you from your separateness to your collective." Given the multiple loci of social identities within organizations, including those delineated by institutional position (e.g., one's workgroup, department, division, job, or hierarchical level) and demographics (e.g., gender, age, or education), perhaps nOID is an oversimplification of the very complicated process of *identifying with*. That individuals may have differences in their needs to connect to, and identify with, larger social categories of which they are a part has not been fully acknowledged in the organizational literature. This idea prompted our conversations on identification; in turn, we hope that our discourse offers an impetus for others to continue the dialogue.

REFERENCES

Ashforth, B. E., & Mael, F. (1989). Social identity theory and the organization. *Academy of Management Review, 14*, 20-39.

Belk, R. W. (1988). Possessions and the extended self. *Journal of Consumer Research, 15*, 139-168.

Bhattacharya, C., Rao, H., & Glynn, M. A. (1995). Understanding the bond of identification: An investigation of its correlates among art museum members. *Journal of Marketing, 59*, 46-57.

Brewer, M. B. (1991). The social self: On being the same and different at the same time. *Personality and Social Psychology Bulletin, 17*, 475-482.

Brewer, M. B., & Gardner, W. (1996). Who is this "we"? Levels of collective identity and self representations. *Journal of Personality and Social Psychology, 71*, 83-93.

Dutton, J. E., Dukerich, J. M., & Harquail, C. V. (1994). Organizational images and member identification. *Administrative Science Quarterly, 39*, 239-263.

Elsbach, K. D., & Glynn, M. A. (1996). Believing your own "PR": Embedding identification in strategic reputation. In J. A. C. Baum & J. E. Dutton (Eds.), *Advances in strategic management* (Vol. 13, pp. 63-88). Greenwich, CT: JAI.

Elsbach, K. D., & Kramer, R. M. (1996). Members' responses to organizational identity threats: Encountering and countering the *Business Week* ratings. *Administrative Science Quarterly, 41*, 442-476.

Kramer, R. M. (1993). Cooperation and organizational identification. In J. K. Murnighan (Ed.), *Social psychology in organizations: Advances in theory and research* (pp. 244-268). Englewood Cliffs, NJ: Prentice Hall.

Mael, F. A., & Ashforth, B. E. (1992). Alumni and their alma mater: A partial test of the reformulated model of organizational identification. *Journal of Organizational Behavior, 13*, 103-123.

Mael, F. A., & Ashforth, B. E. (1995). Loyal from day one: Biodata, organizational identification, and turnover among newcomers. *Personnel Psychology, 48*, 309-333.

McClelland, D. (1987). *Human motivation*. Cambridge, UK: Cambridge University Press.

Wann, D. L., & Hamlet, M. A. (1994). The joiners' scale: Validation of a measure of social complexity. *Psychological Reports, 74*, 1027-1034.

The Dark Side of
Organizational Identification

JANET M. DUKERICH[1]

RODERICK KRAMER

JUDI McLEAN PARKS

Much of our conversation to this point has articulated the *benefits* of identification with an organization. However, there also may be pathologies associated with being under- or overidentified. At what point does identification become dysfunctional for the person and/or the organization who either cannot find an entity with which to identify, or so completely identifies with the entity (e.g., the organization) that any separate identity is lost? Or what if one cannot identify at all with the organization? To contemplate the potential pathologies associated with organizational identification, it is helpful to explain the relationship between identification and disidentification (see Figure 7.2).

As illustrated by the figure, organizational identification and disidentification can be thought of as two orthogonal dimensions. *Disidentification* is the active differentiation and distancing of oneself from the entity or organization—where one's identity is defined by *not* being identified with the organization (as Elsbach explains, this is different from *not identifying*—it is identifying *as not*). There are many things individuals are not. For example, one may not be a Republican, or an environmentalist, or a Baptist. This does not mean that the individual disidentifies with Republicans, environmentalists, or Baptists *unless* his or her identity is one in which he or she defines him- or herself specifically as *not* a Republican, *not* an environmentalist, or *not* a Baptist. In the latter case, a specific contrast or differentiation is made, disidentifying with the eschewed organization. On the other hand, *identification* is where there is a high need for inclusion and a reduced need to distinguish oneself from the organization. It is where one defines oneself in terms of one's association with the organization. Identification focuses on similarities, whereas disidentification focuses on differences. Juxtaposing these two dimensions—identification and disidentification—describes the extremes of four general states of organizational identification: apathetic identification, conflicting identification, focused disidentification,[2] and focused identification.

Apathetic identification occurs when individuals define themselves neither in terms of the organization and its identity (low identification), nor in terms of their differentiation *from* the organization (low disidentification). The organization—whether positively or negatively—simply is not central to the individual's identity. In some sense, they do not care whether they belong to the organization or not. There

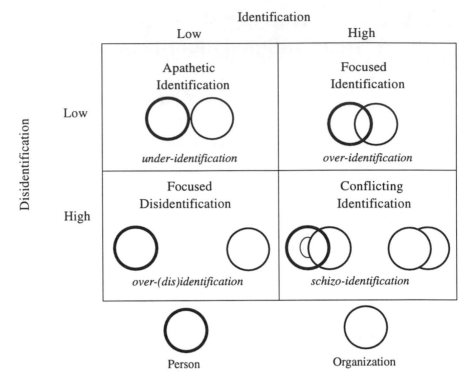

Figure 7.2. States of Identification (Within One Organization) and Their Associated *Pathologies*

is little, if any, specific overlap between the identity of the individual and the company. A pathological form of apathetic identification is underidentification.

At the other extreme are individuals who *simultaneously* identify with *and* disidentify from the same organization—what we call *conflicting identification.* Conflicting identification is a condition in which part of the individual wants to identify with the organization (merge with) and another part wants to disidentify (separate from). Key to conflicting identification is that one simultaneously identifies and disidentifies with the *same* organization. For example, members of pro-life groups may strongly identify with the organization and its antiabortion stance while simultaneously disidentifying with the sometimes violent methods some such organizations employ, finding a conflict between the protection of life on one hand and its destruction on the other. The pathology associated with conflicting identification sounds somewhat schizophrenic—like split personalities—so will be referred to as schizo-identification.

In *focused disidentification,* like apathetic identification, there is no specific overlap between the identity of the individual and that of the company. However, in the case of focused disidentification, not only is there no overlap, but the identities between the individual and the company are seen as opposing forces, repelling one another. Focused disidentification occurs when there is no overlap between the individual and the organization, *and* there is a need to define oneself by stating that one is *not* part of the organization (e.g., I am not only *not* a member of the NRA, I'm totally opposed to everything the organization stands for, so when I introduce myself to you, I am likely to tell you that I am not a member of the NRA). The pathology associated with focused disidentification is one of overdisidentification.

Focused identification occurs when the overlap between the individual and the organization's identities is great, where the individual strongly identifies with the organization, and there is no motivation for the individual to define him- or herself as *not* part of the organization (low disidentification). It is characterized by an emphasis on the collective, rather than the individual, identity. The pathology of focused identification is one of overidentification, where the self gets lost, the identity of the organization replaces self, and little of the self is left—there is little or no perceived uniqueness or differentiating factors, similar to the Borg of *Star Trek,* where there is *only* the collective.

A WAKE-UP CALL:
PATHOLOGIES OF IDENTIFICATION
AND DISIDENTIFICATION

Like many areas of organizational research, as researchers, we implicitly seem to assume that a specific behavior is uniformly "good" (e.g., organizational citizenship behavior, high motivation to perform) or uniformly "bad" (e.g., sabotage, theft, absenteeism). Yet upon closer examination, we come to realize that employees can engage in citizenship behaviors while neglecting their duties, highly motivated employees may take inappropriate risks to achieve production goals, sabotage and theft can signal dysfunctional work environments, and absenteeism can result in a refreshed and alert employee. In a similar vein, much of the research on organizational identification has focused on the *benefits* of identification, virtually ignoring the possible pathologies (with the exception of the downside of disidentification for the organization). As contrarians (perhaps a part of our identities), we think it is important to turn our attention to some of the potential pathologies for each of the four general states of organizational identification that we outlined above.

The Pathology of Apathetic
Identification/Disidentification: Underidentification

Underidentification is the pathology associated with apathetic identification, where there are dysfunctionally low levels of both identification and disidentification. To understand underidentification, we probably should emphasize the conceptual distinction between *under*identification and *dis*identification, two terms that at first blush may appear to be quite similar. Underidentification is akin to anomie, a rootlessness such that the individual or employee is not anchored to a social context. Underidentification implies indifference and lack of connection. As a trait, it may be a form of social autism: people who cannot connect to anything or anyone. In contrast, disidentification is the process of actively distancing oneself from the identification entity (see Elsbach's essay, this chapter). Disidentifiers are like an object in orbit that is repulsed by, or pushed away from, the identification entity—a concept that conjures up the notion of subversive subcultures and countercultures. Disidentification confers an identity through what one is *not*. Underidentification does not instantiate an identity, and the absence of such an identity proves dysfunctional. Disidentification *does* instantiate an identity—what one is *not*. So, underidentification is equivalent to pathologically low levels of both identification and disidentification. In many senses, underidentification is like the lack of any identity at all.

Ibarra (1996) found that there were people who were so unique that they could not find a role model to imitate, so they could not develop an authentic self in their organization. There is, perhaps, a paradox of being too unique. Those people who are so unique may also be the kind of people who find it hard to identify. They may never really take on the normative characteristics (i.e., professional role development) that are necessary for survival in a particular industry or organization. Yet the inability to identify with a social group is anxiety provoking because the individual cannot form a strong attachment (Baumeister, 1986), leaving him or her with a sense of vulnerability and rootlessness. Similarly, the simultaneous inability to *dis*identify may leave the individual not only vulnerable and rootless but also purposeless and without focus.

When one is disconnected from his or her work organization but does not want to be, there may be serious psychological consequences for both the individual and the organization. The reciprocity between the individual and the collective will not be as strong when there is underidentification. In fact, the lack of identification may lead to individuals employing different forms of reciprocity, which may engender a sense of violation in others who expected reciprocity of a certain form. For example, generalized reciprocity (where one expects to give without immediate reciprocation) may be employed and expected by members of identity groups; hence, the use of balanced reciprocity (an explicit and relatively immediate quid pro quo) may be employed and expected by those who are on the periphery of the identity group. Thus, one who does not identify may find the type of reciprocity employed by others to be incongruent and inappropriate. This may lead to lower trust and a reliance on more coercive means to control organizational members.

Individuals who want to, but are unable to identify may develop their own subculture in the organization as a substitute identification. To the extent that these subcultures have norms that are antagonistic to the organization (e.g., sabotage, unauthorized use of organizational resources), the organization may suffer. Kim Elsbach talked about a "club" she belonged to at a deli where she was employed— the "F—- the Deli" club (FTD). She and fellow employees were so disaffected by their treatment at the deli that they would intentionally damage food products so that the products would be available for employee consumption later. Had she identified with the deli, her identification might have regulated or even eliminated the subversive behavior. In this case, the subculture of the FTD was clearly opposed to the goals of the company. One can survive in an underidentified state with an organization if one has compensation in the workplace (e.g., a paycheck), an alternative identity within the organization (e.g., subversive identities, the FTD), or enough of an identity outside of the organization.

Underidentification may be a trait (related to the nOID/VOID continuum outlined by Glynn) such that there are certain people who either are incapable of establishing a connection or who just do not care to be identified with another object (a type of social hermit). There may also be situations where, out of self-protection, employees *choose* not to identify—being perhaps functional for the individual, but dysfunctional for the organization. Temporary workers are those who may be likely to underidentify with work organizations as a self-protective mechanism, just as employees who are about to be laid off may begin to soften their identification with the organization. So, at the extreme, underidentification as a trait may describe people who can*not* identify, much as they might want to.

Underidentification may also be considered as a state, such as when an organization merges or is acquired, and, for a period of time, people cannot find its identity. Individuals who strongly identified with the previous organization may find it difficult to answer "Who am I?" if they do not know what the new organization is. Perhaps they lack sufficient information for determining what the new organization is, or they are receiving inconsistent and incongruent cues and are unable to make a determination. When Borders bookstores was being acquired by K-Mart, former Borders employees were unsure of the new identity that surely would evolve ("Are we going to have blue light specials on books now?"), as well as unsure how and if they would fit in (Bridgeforth, 1992). Such uncertainty may result in employees subjectively interpreting the multiplicity of cues they are receiving, resulting in their assumption of an incongruent organizational identity that will later lead to a sense of violation and broken trust (McLean Parks, 1997).

The Pathology of Conflicting Identification:
Schizo-Identification

Schizo-identification is when one simultaneously identifies *and* disidentifies with the *same* organization, creating conflicting identities. In some senses, it is like approach-avoidance conflict in the conflict literature. Like Dr. Doolittle's Push-me Pull-you, schizo-identification creates a tension between identification and disidentification, fostering a disequilibrium in the individual's identity. This disequilibrium creates an unstable state in which the individual may experience stress akin to that of role conflict. However, this conflict will be exacerbated because one's identity is more proximate (and likely more enduring) to the self than one's role. In addition, schizo-identification—unlike role conflict, where roles may only conflict in some domains and not others—may result in complete conflict.

The dissonance created by the conflicting pulls of identification and disidentification will result in pressures for the individual to cognitively adjust, "choosing" either to identify or disidentify. This process may polarize the resulting (dis)identity, where the individual must persuade him- or herself to discard one or the other, generating reasons and arguments to support one's final position in terms of identity (e.g., Petty & Cacioppo, 1981). During this process, organizational cues may easily swing the individual to either identify or disidentify strongly with the organization, sensitizing the individual to minute cues on which they can focus in an attempt to resolve the disequilibrium. Under these circumstances, the strength of organizational cues on the individual's behavior will be enhanced, making it important for the organization to manage such cuing processes. Once the disequilibrium is resolved (if, in fact, it is), the resulting identification or disidentification will be even stronger, potentially resulting in overidentification or overdisidentification. It is also possible that the disidentification may predominate at some points in time, whereas identification may predominate at others. The strength of either could easily depend on factors such as adversity or threat, when identification might predominate as the individual's need for support and cohesiveness outweighs the disidentification. Similarly, disidentification may result during times of change or confusion, when psychological contracts may be broken (e.g., Rousseau & McLean Parks, 1993), and when the individual feels a need to distance him- or herself in the face of the unknown.

Paradoxically, although it may be a pathology in many senses, schizo-identification, perhaps, is a precursor to such frequently functional behaviors as whistle-blowing and creative change. As an aside, it is also interesting to note that the two worst forms of schizophrenia have to do with the two extremes: when one *is* the "other"— one is so like everyone else that he or she cannot see where the self starts and the "other" ends (extreme overidentification); the other extreme is narcissism, where there "is no other" (disidentifying with all others), and no commonalities or communitarian self are believed to exist.

The Pathology of Focused Disidentification: Overdisidentification

Overdisidentification may be thought of as a condition where the need for distinctiveness predominates one's need for inclusiveness. One cannot become integrated into the collective because of a need to distance oneself *from* the collective, wanting to demonstrate one's uniqueness while minimizing one's similarities. Individuals may develop such a strong disidentification with an organization that they become blinded to areas of congruence and exhibit a knee-jerk reaction, opposing any initiative or suggestion by the organization simply because the organization supports such an initiative. Overdisidentification, like hate and other strong emotions, can become all-consuming, paralyzing the individual and dominating his or her actions in the organization. The overdisidentifier will interpret his or her environments subjectively in order to be consistent with the need to disidentify; thus, a neutral event will be subjectively interpreted in a negative manner. Attributions will be personalized, such that the overdisidentifier will form internal attributions for organizational outcomes, assuming that negative outcomes were intended to be harmful to him or her personally or those things that he or she holds dear. The internal attribution will then reinforce the need for disidentification, and the process will continue.

Although it is an empirical issue, it seems intuitive that disidentifying is cognitively more effortful for employees than is identifying. From an information-processing standpoint, negative information is frequently assumed to be more diagnostic than is positive (in this case, what I am *not* vs. what I *am*). And from a perceptual standpoint (figure/ground), it is much more difficult to perceive the *absence* of something, which, in the present context, parallels what one is *not*. If, in fact, disidentification is cognitively complex, it is likely to have two implications. First, individuals who disidentify will elaborate on information that they perceive, and they will generate strong cognitive arguments to support their disidentification (Petty & Cacioppo, 1981). Second, the cognitive "sunk cost" of disidentification is greater than that of identification, potentially resulting in escalating the disidentification process. Hence, once one has disidentified, it may be quite easy to find oneself trapped in a disidentification spiral, and for the potential pathology of overdisidentification to be particularly easy to fall into and particularly difficult to reverse. At the extreme, overdisidentification may bear some similarity to paranoia.

The strong need on the part of the individual to disidentify also may negatively affect the organization. Employees who overdisidentify may come to believe that they have a "duty" to rebel or resist organizational initiatives and goals, resulting in sabotage, resistance, or aggressive behaviors aimed at the organization and its representatives. In addition, strongly disidentifying with the organization may create a presumptive distrust in other organizational members. For example, if one disidentifies with pro-life groups, one may assume that all members of such groups are untrustworthy, whether or not there is any such evidence. New information contradicting such distrust may be subjectively reinterpreted as congruent with distrust, making it difficult, if not impossible, to establish a basis for trust and future positive interactions, resulting in a lack of confidence in the collective. The knee-jerk reaction to the organization and its initiatives by the overdisidentifier means that much that is trustworthy gets discounted and much that is good gets rejected—throwing the baby out with the bathwater. In addition, the individual who highly disidentifies may be seen as a malcontent by the organization and its members, and the valid criticisms of the overdisidentifier may be given little thought or attention.

The Pathology of Focused Identification: Overidentification

Marilyn vos Savant, the holder of the highest IQ listed in the *Guinness Book of World Records*, uses the name vos Savant, assuming the French word for "knowing" as her name and thus signaling her identity. As exemplified by her name, it appears that her identity is at least partly defined by intelligence and its trappings. However, what if she was *over*identified in terms of intelligence? Overidentification seems to be the flip side of underidentification or overdisidentification. That is, overidentification may be thought of as a condition in which the need for distinctiveness or differentiation is very low compared to the need for inclusiveness. One way to evaluate overidentification is when the self becomes diminished. That is, what is special and unique about us is constrained by the connection that we have with a collective. Individuals may develop such a strong identification with an organization that they cease to think of themselves in anything other than their organizational affiliation ("I was an IBM-er for 10 years and have been an ex-IBMer now for 13 years"). It is one thing to believe in a credo and quite another to not be able to separate self from organization.

Why might we care if organizational members are overidentified? First, it is important to note that the organization can give you only a part of your sense of self. Organizational identities are somewhat flat and sterile (two-dimensional) in that they do not typically provide a fully articulated sense of self (although some normative and even utilitarian organizations, like churches or company towns, may attempt to do so). Therefore, one needs to temper the organization's autism by bringing in other aspects of self (personal identities, other social identities; Ashforth & Mael, 1996). Some organizations try to imprint on that process such that members must submerge their other identities (e.g., Army boot camp training) in order to survive. Other organizations may be more reciprocal—that is, these organizations gain some of their identity from the employees who work there. When employees must submerge their other identities and overidentify with the organization, they may lose the ability to question anything that the organization does. One needs some residual amount of identity outside of what is shared with the organization, such that one has an alternative perspective from which to evaluate organizational actions. For some organizations (e.g., the Army), there may be no desire to have employees evaluate or question the decisions that are made in the organization. In fact, such questioning may be totally counterproductive for the organization. However, such a questioning attitude may be quite healthy for another organization, fostering creativity and moving the company forward (Kunda, 1992).

There is another potentially problematic relationship between overidentification with an organization, and that concerns the possible links between strong identification with other members of the organization and its tendency to foster a kind of automatic or presumptive trust in them. There may be some deleterious organizational consequences to such presumptive trust. Specifically, in situations where identification with others is too strong and presumptive trust is too high, it is possible that individuals may become less likely to engage in necessary collective action precisely because they believe that others will do so. In other words, if individuals trust that others will come forward and take action, then the perceived need for intervention on their part may decrease. Thus, one unintended and rather ironic consequence of high levels of positive organizational identification may be that individuals underestimate the need for personal action.

These same arguments have some implications for thinking about problems of collective sensemaking and decision making in organizations. If identity-based trust fosters an overconfidence in the collective, then individuals may sometimes defer too readily to other members. They may, for example, inhibit expressions of doubt or engage in inappropriately severe self-censorship rather than press their claims as vigorously as they might, for example, with comparative strangers. In discussing the results of his famous studies on social influences, Asch (1951) pointed out that the behavior of individuals in these experiments demonstrated not only that they were influenced by conformity pressures but also that they had a basic trust in others' perceptions and judgments. In other words, not only did they trust their own senses, they also trusted others' as well, leading them to suppress their doubts. Thus, when individuals discovered that their own perceptions were discrepant with those of their fellow group members, they were perplexed and troubled. Rather than simply discount the veridicality of others' perceptions, however, they were motivated to resolve this discrepancy. They thus held back and laid low, trying to make sense of their perceptual predicament rather than drawing attention to it.

Similar lines of argument suggest that identity-based trust might, under some circumstances, impede organizational learning and adaptation. There is an important sense in which the ability of organizations to learn from experience depends at least in part on individuals' willingness to doubt and question the organization and its actions and claims. In other words, high-quality decision making requires not only the cooperative pooling of information but also the collective willingness to challenge claims about the integrity and interpretation of that information.

A second reason to be concerned with overidentification is that one's moral identity may become subsumed by the organization, and the individual may lose the ability to question the ethicality or legality of organizational actions. Brief, Buttram, and Dukerich (in press) argue that we may see collective engagement in immoral or illegal behavior when organizational leaders sanction, encourage, and reward members to perform such illegal and unethical acts. Such collective wrongdoing becomes established through the processes of sanctioning (the implicit or explicit endorsement of a corrupt practice by an authority figure), compliance (the initial obedience to the authorization to engage in a corrupt practice), and institutionalization (the process by which collective wrongdoing becomes part and parcel of everyday organizational life). Hamilton (1992) talks about "oblique intentionality," where illegal acts are performed unintentionally because of a "blindness" to accountability. This accountability is likely to be instantiated by strong identification—obliquely intending to commit an illegal act because one is intending to follow organizational directives and simply does not think about whether or not that directive is right or not. Individuals who become overidentified with the organization may be even more susceptible to these processes. Thus, they may be likely to either perform illegal or unethical acts that have been sanctioned by the organization both obliquely *and* intentionally, or they may look away when faced with evidence of such activities and try to protect the organization, perhaps even covering up (e.g., Watergate, which became one coverup after another, some innocent and some not-so-innocent).

A third and related area of concern with overidentification is that overidentifiers may not simply do wrong on behalf of the organization, but they may also suppress or cover up wrongdoing on the part of the organization. In addition, if they overidentify with an organization that is epitomized by a powerful individual, then the overidentifier, and perhaps the organization itself as an overidentifier (with the powerful individual), will be reluctant to rein in or report any wrongdoing by the powerful person. In this case, the powerful person is "too high to fall," at least in the eyes of the overidentifier. If the powerful person is punished for wrongdoing, then the identity is defiled by association with the powerful transgressor. In turn, the identity of the overidentifier will also be damaged through association. Consequently, in the eyes of the overidentifier (whether an individual or an organization), the powerful transgressor must be protected from detection and punishment. Here, overidentification includes a denial or a covert and deceitful component. In a similar vein, the overidentifier will be quite likely to punish deviants or those who would threaten the organization (or powerful transgressor), whether or not such punishment is indicated or clearly warranted. In some senses, it is as if the overidentifier begins to believe that the organization, or the powerful transgressor who epitomizes it, should be above the law, and that those who do not subscribe to the same view should be punished and their voices suppressed.

A fourth concern is in terms of threats to self-identity when one overidentifies with the organization. Individuals whose identities are defined by their organizations are particularly vulnerable to having their identities "dismantled" if, for example, they are laid off or their identities are threatened. Having one's identity threatened may damage one's perceived honor, resulting in a motivation to seek revenge (Bies & Tripp, 1996; McLean Parks, 1997). Recently, Baumeister, Smart, and Boden (1996) argued that threats to one's dignity or identity are particularly likely to result in aggressive behavior, in this case, toward the organization and its representatives. Often, aggression and other antisocial behaviors are the result of threats to identity.

In a related area of self-identity, overidentification may be a substitute for something that is missing in one's life, a more-or-less compensatory process. Mary Ann Glynn provided the example of people who identify highly with MENSA. These MENSA members tend to be very smart but may not be high achievers, so they align themselves strongly with MENSA as a compensating behavior. The underachieving MENSA identifiers also tended to dislike their work, ostensibly because their bosses were "dumber." Identification with MENSA would allow them to symbolically affirm that they were intelligent when they were not given the opportunity to demonstrate it at work. In this example, it is unclear whether the underachieving causes the overidentification (compensatory perspective) or if overidentification causes the individual to discount the importance of other available identities (e.g., with the company) because of a feeling of inherent superiority. A compensatory identity also suggests that when it is necessary to strip one of an identity (e.g., layoffs), providing an alternative identity may be one way of ameliorating the desire or need to seek revenge for the loss of the stripped identity, because another identity is filling the void.

CONCLUSION

There is a paradoxical nature to the pathologies of identification and disidentification. For example, overdisidentification is not good *or* bad but good *and* bad. Employees who disidentify are frequently disenfranchised, and their disenfranchisement may perform a valuable signaling function for the organization that some issues must be addressed. They may be an important counterpoint to an overly cohesive group or groupthink environment. However, they may also become obsessed with their disidentification, resulting in a sterile and unidimensional self-identity. Like overdisidentification, underidentification is not good *or* bad but good *and* bad. Underidentification may be appropriate during times of transition or change, or when one is sorting through the possible identities available to him or her. Underidentification may also be quite functional when in an aversive environment, but one in which disidentification is not desirable or possible. Similarly, schizo-identification is not good *or* bad but good *and* bad. Schizo-identification may be functional when it allows one to identify with particular aspects of the organization that one finds self-affirming and to disidentify with those aspects one eschews, *if* one can maintain a balance. This may also increase one's ability to capitalize on both the positives and the negatives of the identity relationship. Schizo-identification may also be a precursor to important organizational behaviors, such as whistle-blowing, encouraging necessary changes in the organization and its procedures.

Finally, overidentification is not good *or* bad but good *and* bad. Overidentification can be good and productive for both individuals and the organization. As noted above, some organizations (the armed forces, religious orders) may desire members who derive their sense of self solely from the organization. For some individuals, overidentification with an organization may satisfy a need in their lives if other identities are unavailable (e.g., one who has experienced a major life change, such as divorce, and moved to a new place to work at a new organization). However, overidentification can be dysfunctional as well. In the interests of humans growing emotionally, never going beyond identifying with the organization may create such an overdependence that the person may be one dimensional. If the organization disappears (goes bankrupt, is acquired), overidentified individuals may find themselves lost, unable to define their own identity. Overidentification that is bad includes denial, insufficient reality testing, repudiation of values previously held dear, and an inability to attend to new information and to separate one's life from the organization.

An important question for future research is whether we can identify the criteria we can use *ex ante* to determine if and when identification and disidentification will be beneficial or detrimental to the individual and the organization, and when and under what circumstances the pathologies of identification and disidentification will be beneficial or detrimental to the individual and the organization.

NOTES

1. Authors are listed alphabetically.

2. It is important to note that our discussion refers to identification *within a single organization.* Clearly, it is possible to strongly identify with one organization while strongly disidentifying with another. Conceptually, this is quite different from simultaneously identifying and disidentifying with the *same* organization, which has aspects of identity conflict and schizophrenic association, an idea we think is intriguing. Our focus is within a single organization, and we will leave the notion of the pathologies of multiple organizational identifications and disidentifications to others.

REFERENCES

Asch, S. (1951). Effects of group pressure upon the modification and distortion of judgment. In H. Guetzkow (Ed.), *Groups, leadership and men* (pp. 177-190). Pittsburgh: Carnegie Press.

Ashforth, B. E., & Mael, F. A. (1996). Organizational identity and strategy as a context for the individual. In J. A. C. Baum & J. E. Dutton (Eds.), *Advances in strategic management* (Vol. 13, pp. 19-64). Greenwich, CT: JAI.

Baumeister, R. F. (1986). *Identity: Cultural change and the struggle for self.* New York: Oxford University Press.

Baumeister, R., Smart, L., & Boden, J. (1996). Relation of threatened egotism to violence and aggression: The dark side of self esteem. *Psychological Review, 103,* 5-33.

Bies, R., & Tripp, T. (1996). Beyond distrust: "Getting even" and the need for revenge. In R. Kramer & T. Tyler (Eds.), *Trust in organizations: Frontiers of theory and research* (pp. 246-260). Thousand Oaks, CA: Sage.

Bridgeforth, A., Jr. (1992, October 25). Bordering on change: Borders bookstore chain turns a page in its history, but won't close the book on providing good reading. *Ann Arbor News,* p. C1.

Brief, A. P., Buttram, R. T., & Dukerich, J. M. (in press). Sanctioned corruption in the corporate world: A process model. In M. E. Turner (Ed.), *Groups at work: Advances in theory and research.* Hillsdale, NJ: Lawrence Erlbaum.

Hamilton, V. (1992). Responsibility and risk in organizational crimes of obedience. In B. M. Staw & L. L. Cummings (Eds.), *Research in organizational behavior* (Vol. 14, pp. 49-90). Greenwich, CT: JAI.

Ibarra, H. (1996, August). *Inauthentic selves: Image, identity and social networks in professional socialization.* Paper presented at the annual meeting of the Academy of Management, Cincinnati.

Kunda, G. (1992). *Engineering culture: Control and commitment in a high-tech corporation.* Philadelphia: Temple University Press.

McLean Parks, J. (1997). The fourth arm of justice: The art and science of revenge. In R. Lewicki, B. Sheppard, & B. Bies (Eds.), *Research on negotiation in organizations* (pp. 113-144). Greenwich, CT: JAI.

Petty, R., & Cacioppo, J. (1981). *Attitudes and persuasion: Classic and contemporary approaches.* Dubuque, IA: William C. Brown.

Rousseau, D., & McLean Parks, J. (1993). The contracts of individuals and organizations. In L. L. Cummings & B. M. Staw (Eds.), *Research in organizational behavior* (Vol. 15, pp. 1-43). Greenwich, CT: JAI.

Managing Identification

JAMES R. BARKER

We arrived at the end of our conversation wanting to spend some time examining the identification process from the organization's perspective. We wanted to examine closely how identification "works" during the course of day-to-day life as individual and organizational identities interface. That is, we wanted to talk about if and how organizations can influence, or even outright manage, the identification of their members. For our conversation, we found it helpful to view the issue of management in terms of how identification is "practiced" in day-to-day organizational life. Certainly, there is an interesting dynamic between the individual's identity and the organization's identity. Certainly, organizations create an identity through mission statements, lists of core values, public affairs newsletters, and so forth, with which they want their members to identify. Certainly, members experience a strong tension toward identifying with their organizations. But how is identification *practiced*?

BACKGROUND

To begin a conversation on the practice of organizational identification requires shifting perspective from the individual level toward the collective. That is, when we consider the issue of practice, identification becomes less a fundamentally psychological process and more a social process with two key players: the individual and the organization, each embedded in particular environmental and societal contexts. At the level of practice, we shift our thinking about identification toward how the individual and the organization work together to create what the social philosopher Kenneth Burke (1937) called a "corporate we" (p. 140).

Much of the study of identification in practice extends from the social and rhetorical theories of Burke (Cheney, 1983a, 1983b; for a recent review of related identification literature, see Cheney & Christensen, in press) and presumes an organizational, as opposed to individual, level of analysis. From this perspective, organizational identification refers primarily to the process of creating a shared sense of collective reality among an organization's members by actively enhancing the level of congruence between an organization's values and the values of its individual members. Thus, "as members identify more strongly with the organization and its values, the organization becomes as much a part of the member as the member is a part of the organization" (Bullis & Tompkins, 1989, p. 289). Such an organizational perspective on identification is readily reconciled with more socio-psychological perspectives on identity and identification, such as Ashforth and

Mael's (1989) view of identification as "the perception of oneness with or belong-ingness to a group, involving direct or vicarious experiences of its success or failures" (p. 34), around the issue of *process.* Both perspectives would see organizational identification as a process that links organization with individual and individual with organization. The issue for research and theorizing lies in the managerial ways and means of how the identification process works: How is identification practiced?

The organizational perspective presupposes that identification is an essential element in constituting the organization both as a unique entity and as a collectivity of individuals with congruent interests. Thus, the organization *needs* its members to identify with its goals, values, and objectives so that they will readily do work that helps the organization to achieve those goals, values, and objectives. When an organization's members are strongly identified with the organization's goals, values, and objectives, they are more likely to behave (e.g., make work-related decisions) that are functional for the organization (Tompkins & Cheney, 1983). Because of the organization's natural need for identification, it will actively pursue the process of constructing the identity of its members in terms of the organization's identity. Identification in practice, then, refers to how the organization actively *manages* identification.

As a point of confession, the issue of identification in practice (or managing identification) is of keen interest to me, and I actively wanted to write this section. I enjoy studying control in organizations, and issues of identification are right on the forefront of our current theorizing about organizational control. In terms of identification, we live in a curious time. On the surface, identification really should *not* be an issue. Today's world of work is an era in which people quite naturally jump from job to job. We do not appear to be as strongly committed, as unwaveringly loyal, and as identified with our employers as we were in times past. Likewise, in this era of downsizing, organizations are not as strongly committed and as unwaveringly loyal to us workers. Just looking around today's organizational scene, we would not really expect identification to matter.

Yet we know that identification still does matter, and it matters a great deal. The historical study of control clearly indicates that our methods for regulating work activity in the organization are becoming increasingly subtle and unobtrusive. Today's managers are taught to control work by getting their employees to participate more in the matters that affect the organization, such as decision making. Managers are taught to control work by getting their employees to buy in to total quality and excellent customer service as a means of increasing their productivity. And managers are taught to articulate and model core values with which their employees can identify and use to shape their own behaviors. Commitment and loyalty are not the only issues at play in identification practice. Something very subtle and very powerful is going on here, and I am interested in finding out what that something is. And now, I return to the conversation.

The issue of "managing identification" became the starting point for our discussion. As we progressed, we sought to uncover the key issues involved in managing identification, the "how" of identification practice, and to formulate these issues into coherent topics for further study. Our conversation ranged from scrutinizing the essential assumptions of identification as a management process, to the "ways and means" of this process, to the ethical requirements for managing identification. As with our other conversations, we organized our discussions around kcy questions, and our first conversation question concerned the fundamental assumption underlying the practice of identification.

CAN AN ORGANIZATION
MANAGE IDENTIFICATION?

Our first conversation question pushed us to evaluate whether or not an organization actually tries to manage identification. If we all have a need to identify with social objects, such as organizations, then perhaps the organization does not need to manage the process at all. Perhaps we naturally identify with organizations we choose to join. Are we making too complex a process that occurs naturally?

What we know about managing identification suggests that it is a very complex process and is open to being managed. When considering identity and identification issues, the organization appears to us as an entity involved in a delicate balancing act. The organization must compete with a number of other entities for the identification of its individual members (Cheney, 1983a; Tompkins & Cheney, 1983), the *constellation* of identification targets discussed in Elsbach's section. And the organization must compete well because it needs the identification of its members to ensure a unity of effort toward its goals. Although we know that individual members can actively pursue strong identification with their organizations (Tompkins & Cheney, 1983, 1985), we still find it easy to make the assumption that the organization must manage identification.

However, such an easy assumption quickly led our group to call forth two key issues. First, how can an organization know if its members have really identified? Behavioral and performance indicators of an individual's conformance to organizational values or commitment to organizational goals do not necessarily signal a high level of identification. Certainly, we can "fake" strong identification with an organization (see Jackson, 1965), which protects our investment of individual autonomy. As a group member said:

> If you simply show that you can take on the organization's perspective, and that you'll choose to act in ways that benefit the organization, then that is all that matters. If you have an appropriate level of identification, shown through behavior, you will get rewarded. If you are not identifying and it shows up in your performance, the organization will do something about it.

If, perhaps, the practice of identification only requires us to behave *as if* we identify with the organization, then we can readily choose to behave *as if* we identify, especially in times of crisis. As we discussed in an earlier section, members of an organization need some degree of freedom to negotiate their level of identification.

While discussing such indicators, we saw organizational crisis points as being particularly important and visible markers of identification as opposed to everyday behavior. When we identify with an organization, we have the ability to choose from a range of behaviors that indicate various levels of identification. In times of crisis, however, we cannot just fake our identification. Thus, if we act to defend our organization in times of crises, then we are clearly demonstrating a strong level of identification.

The opposing argument here is that although we have difficulty "seeing" the level of identification in mundane, everyday decisions and behaviors, those are the very behaviors that require an ongoing level of organizational identification. None of us denied that identification operates at a very unobtrusive level. We do not really know or perceive that we are identifying with an organization, we just behave as the organization needs us to behave (Barker, 1993; Tompkins & Cheney, 1985). As long as an organization's work life was functional, as long as it was "managed," the organization would not necessarily need to know who was highly identified and who was not.

The above point brings up the second key issue: Does the organization really care if its members have high levels of identification? One argument we debated was that the organization really does not have a reason to care about the extent to which a member identifies with it. What the organization does care about is the extent to which your identification becomes manifest in practices that are important to the organization (e.g., your making good decisions, your support for the organization, your behavior in accordance with the organization's values). And it will reward or punish you on that basis. In many organizations, there need not be a recognition of the importance of identification, or an active attempt to affect identification, such as that seen with fast-food workers below the management level or cashiers in a small hardware store. The owner of such organizations might look at you as though you were crazy if you asked him or her about the importance of employees identifying with the company.

A related view arose from considering identification in organizations that do not rely on performance-based indicators of productivity. For example, when an organization has difficulty in dictating and monitoring behavior or in measuring performance (such as a volunteer organization), the organization will experience a greater need to draw from soft, social indicators of identification. Ritualistic requirements of strong identification are often particularly appropriate for normative organizations, such as churches (e.g., ritualistic chants, symbolic candle lighting, confession) and schools (e.g., wearing school emblems, attending pep rallies), and among middle and senior managers (e.g., the old normative dress codes of IBM and EDS). Also, the greater the need for teamwork, the greater the need to demonstrate ritual allegiance to team values and identity.

The latter point calls out the counterargument to the "Does the organization really care?" question and another confessional aside on my part. Individual identification with the organization, and the organization's awareness of this identification, becomes of higher intensity in participative (e.g., team-based) organizations. In participative organizations, the ability to get the basic work of the organization done, and done well, is contingent upon identification (Barker, 1993), and such organizations are more aware of and monitor closely the indicators of identification (Barker & Tompkins, 1994). In fact, much of the effect of the corporate culture movement, inspired by such works as *In Search of Excellence* (Peters & Waterman, 1982), has been to create a heightened and intense need for organizations to manage the identification of its members (Soeters, 1986; Tompkins & Cheney, 1985). As organizations become more participative, they place more importance on the individual member identifying with the organization. Examples of this perspective include Barker and Tompkins' (1994) finding that team-based organizations *conscripted* the identification of team members; Christensen's (1995) description of how television commercials sponsored by Danish National Airlines were not aimed at customers, but rather at increasing the level of identification of its employees; and Papa, Auwal, and Singhal's (1995) account of how the members of the Grameen Bank of Bangladesh used organizational identification to control their own work behavior.

Papa et al.'s (1995) study raised a very interesting insight into the character of identification, which gave me much pause for reflection. In my study with Tompkins (Barker & Tompkins, 1994), we found that newer (and presumably less identified) members of a work team in the United States felt considerable pressure to identify with the already determined values of their longer tenured teammates. They wanted to resist this pressure but felt that they had no recourse other than to identify, or at least to signal their identification through appropriate work behavior (e.g., coming to work on time). Papa et al., however, found almost no resistance to peer pressures to identify among the members of the bank cooperative. In fact, the members welcomed the use of peer pressure to identify and saw it as essential to their cooperative's success. Papa et al. attributed this perspective, in part, to the differences between the highly individualistic culture of the United States and the more collectivist culture of Bangladesh, which strikes me as an accurate point. However, what stands out even more prominently from their study is the fact that *identification,* as we study it here, is not just a Western phenomenon; instead, it is *a characteristic of any organizing practice* and certainly a phenomenon that warrants our attention. Now, I again return to the conversation.

We left our first topic in general agreement that, yes, an organization can manage identification. The individual desires organizational identification, and although an individual can fake identification, the organization can still influence the process. What we do not clearly understand are the "hows" of this process: How does the organization assess a mental state (an individual's level of identification) through visible performance behaviors (e.g., making a decision favorable to the organization)? How can an organization know when its members are identified? How much should the organization care that its members are identified? And perhaps most importantly, How does an organization deliberately influence (manage) the identification level of its members? That point took us to our second primary discussion question.

HOW DOES AN ORGANIZATION
MANAGE IDENTIFICATION?

In the literature, the "how" of managing identification appears as an issue of organizational control. We most readily see the link between control and identification primarily in organizational decision making. Tompkins and Cheney (1985, p. 191) summarized the control-identification connection by drawing on the work of Herbert Simon:

> Simon treats identification as central to understanding the ongoing process of decision making in an organization. He explains that the act of identifying leads the decision maker to select a particular alternative, to choose one course of action over another. Simon's (1976) operational definition of identification reflects this decision-making emphasis: "A person identifies with a group when, in making a decision, he evaluates the several alternatives of choice in terms of the consequences for the specified group" (p. 205). Viewed in this sense, organizational identification reduces the range of decision: The decision maker's choice is largely confined to the alternative(s) associated with his or her personal targets of identification. From an organizational (or managerial) perspective, member identification is beneficial in that it "guarantees" that decisions will be consistent with organizational objectives, even in the absence of external stimuli (Simon, 1976).

From the standpoint of the above summary, an organization can control member behavior by enhancing, or managing, the degree of identification that a member has toward the core values of the organization. Besides articulating core values, management must also articulate decision premises that help members to reason decisions from the core values. The articulation of core values and decision premises, then, sets in motion a process of deductive reasoning from which a "beneficial" decision is made. For example, let us say that an organization has as its core value a phrase along the lines of, "Customer service is our number one priority." And let us say that a worker's manager (or the worker's team, in a participative organization) has articulated the decision premise that "we always work on our best customer's order first." If a worker is faced with two competing orders to build, and if the worker identifies with the core value, then the worker can readily deduce a functional decision: "Customer service is our number one priority. I should always work on our best customer's order first. Acme Products is our best customer, therefore, I will work on the Acme order and put the Beta Company order aside for later."

As another example, let us say that the same worker is faced with deciding between working overtime to finish the Acme order or keeping a family commitment. Then the reasoning could proceed as follows: "Customer service is our number one priority. I will have to stay overtime to finish the Acme order. I'm supposed to go to my son's ballgame right after work, but I feel I *have* to finish the Acme order (illustrating strong identification with the organizational value). Therefore, I will miss my son's game and work overtime."

The above view of "managing identification as control" quickly led us to a conceptual problem. As one of our number put it, "But I see a difference between identifying with values and identifying with the organization. Where's the organizational *entity* in this line of reasoning? What is unique to identity management that is different from managing culture?" The issue is one of whether identification occurs with the organization itself or with the constituent elements of that culture, such as its core values.

One way we engaged this issue was to consider organizational culture as being more about values and organizational identity as being more about categories. Categories are relational and invoke comparisons. Rather than just articulating values, organizations also promote a series of categorizations: "We are a research institute" instead of "We value research." Being a Top 20 research school is relational: We say we are a research school and not a teaching school. We must view our identity in relation to a set of others. The words *core* and *enduring* might reflect values, but the word *distinctive* better reflects identity because it relates to categories and comparisons. Culture is an enacted manifestation of organizational identity, so many of the same processes and principles may apply. From this perspective, an organization's mission statement would define or set up categorizations. For any given identity category, there is a set of values that corresponds to that identity. Conversely, when we speak of values and culture, the values that compose a culture are selected individually and then composed into the organization's culture. Values with an identity category come in a package; values in a culture come as individual pieces.

Naturally, such a point generated some resistance among us, as seen in these two contrasting comments from our conversation:

> I see culture as a social contract: The background or the social contract against which identities are negotiated and enacted. Culture provides a common set of assumptions, a language, a common set of experiences and metaphors, and a common sense of meaning that we can use in referencing ourselves and creating our identities and the distinct categories that define that identity. What category distinctions would be meaningful? In some cultures, it's black/white or male/female. In others, there may be other distinctive attributes that help define very different categories on which to base our identities.

And the opposing point:

> I think it's important to be careful when using the term *social contract,* especially because it invokes an exchange model, rather than a co-composition model that is part of identifying. I think in this particular case we're talking about here, the construct of social contract confuses the key issues. But I know that others are inclined to see the construct of a psychological contract as being quite so useful to organizational identification.

Another group member warned us that the values and culture argument indicated that organizations deliberately fashion their "culture" in a value-by-value piecemeal fashion. My thinking is that no particular and necessary relationship among values exists a priori in an organization. What we do is draw on the organization's culture as something of a rough draft of values and power relationships to help us construct our own identities in relation to the organization.

Another counterpoint to the above argument is that an organization's members will identify with the values that the organization puts forth as *its identity*. Shared values are at the root of what we find meaningful and coherent in any organization or other collectivity. We see this relationship metaphorically in the practice of wearing a sports team uniform (see Tompkins & Cheney, 1983, p. 139). Many organizations have espoused customer service values (there are lots of sports teams), but wearing the Dallas Cowboys uniform is special. It represents identification with a specific organization, not just with the values exemplified by that organization. Several researchers (Bullis & Tompkins, 1989; Cheney, 1991; Tompkins & Cheney, 1983) have argued that through our identification with particular values, we construct a sense of identification with an organizational entity. Papa, Auwal, and Singhal (in press), in their study of the Grameen Bank in Bangladesh, also offered a supportive argument:

> When members identify strongly with an organization, they only see decision options that are consistent with organizational values. They do not question these values because they have internalized them. Thus, members believe that their actions are entirely under their control.

As before, although we could reach general agreement on the link between managing identification and controlling work in the organization, we were less certain on the "hows" of this process: How do we construct an organizational entity out of our identification with multiple and varying organizational values? How do we proceed with managing identification in a methodical and visible manner? How do we take our analysis of managing identification to a more rigorous and fruitful level?

However, the key remaining question came from another one of our number: "For me, the drive to identify is the search for meaning more than anything else." Essentially, the management of identification is the management of meaning. The individuals who identify with an organization actually constitute that organization's identity and meaning and their own individual identities and meanings. We believed that this issue left us with an ethical problem: What are the positive and good ways of making organizations meaningful for us so that we do not end up with oppressive environments? This begged our next question for conversation.

HOW SHOULD AN ORGANIZATION
MANAGE IDENTIFICATION?

We found that our last question gave us much pause for concern and thought. For example, one of our first discussion points was embedded in the issue: "Should *we* manage identification?" Who is the "we" here, the organization or the individual member? We also found ourselves grappling with the following questions: Because organizations do manage identification, how far should we/society allow organizations to go in terms of conscripting individual identity? How will we know when an organization has gone too far or has too much influence over individuals' identities? But most of our conversation centered on the question: How can individuals manage their level (strength) and location (which value sets) of organizational identification so that their identification suits their needs (e.g., gives them enough but not too much connection and oneness)? The answer to this question appeared to us to hold the key to understanding our general discussion question of "How should we manage identification?" We never found a satisfactory answer. In the mad rush of the past 10 or so years to remake our organizations in the *In Search of Excellence* model, perhaps we have not paused long enough to consider how we "ought" to manage identification.

Current literature does not give us the answer either, but it does show us that the issue is critical. For example, Barker (1993) has argued that organizations that require high levels of identification create powerful and constraining systems of control. Barker and Tompkins (1994) found that a point existed at which an organization's members would strongly resist giving any more of their identity to the organization. Somewhat conversely, Papa et al. (in press) argued that even when an organization's members realize that their identification with an organization tightly controls their behavior, they will still support the system if they believe that the success of their organization requires that they identify at such a high level.

For us, we saw the primary ethical issue as being one of understanding exactly what the organization demands of us in terms of identification and in terms of our identity. For example, today's organizations demand that we incorporate part of the organization's identity into our own. If we do that, though, a number of ethically focused questions arise: Whose values are we asked to identify with? What right does any organization have to ask us to identify with it? What pressures can be brought to bear on the individual by the organization? To what extent is any resistance or tolerance allowed?

The issue of resistance called us back to several of the other moral and ethical questions we had raised in our earlier sections, such as our step into the "dark side" of organizational identification. Primarily, though, our discussion left us wondering, To what extent is there an opportunity for unheard or marginalized voices and/or a minority point of view? In this age of identification, is there room to be inclusive in an organization? Organizations with exceptionally strong identities in which everyone agrees may not be inclusive, and consequently may be oppressive to those who are different. One of our discussants stated the point succinctly:

> If I am not allowed to have a gay identity in my organization, and I want to resist this, what can I do? Must I deny other important parts of my identity in order to identify with the organization to the extent that I am sacrificing other parts of my life? This is the problem of the organization constraining your identity. For example, if an organization defines itself as a very Christian organization, it may prohibit a member's identity as being gay.

We did see the organization as needing to make its identity attractive to its employees. For example, a health care organization of physicians may need to have medical research as part of its identity. An organization will need to categorize its identity along lines that are attractive to the people it wants to recruit. Organizational identity must be different and distinct enough to separate it as a unique entity, but not so much so that people cannot tell what the organization is about or the organization repels those whom it wants to include. Distinctiveness implies an exclusivity and provides a legitimacy. The problem of how we *ought* to create that exclusivity and legitimacy through identification remains an open but vital question.

CONCLUSION

Our conversation revealed that most of what we know about the practice of identification is in bits and pieces, but we felt that we had identified and discussed most of those key pieces. For example, our conversation on "Can identification be managed?" became an in-depth exploration of the social process of identification practices, during which we examined a number of issues: individual/organizational exchange relationships, identification ethics, tensions between cultural values and identification categories, faking identification, resisting identification, and many others. Our conversation on identification practices was only part of the puzzle, not the solution. To borrow the words of Kenneth Burke once again, the conversation on identification was going on before we assembled, we contributed our part, and now the conversation will continue.

Out of our multiplicity (some said cacophony) of voices comes the conclusion that our three key questions—Can an organization manage identification? How does an organization manage identification? How should an organization manage identification?—are not yet answerable. Our desire now is to further this conversation toward more conceptual explorations of the intense process that occurs when organizations practice identification with and on their members.

REFERENCES

Ashforth, B. E., & Mael, F. (1989). Social identity theory and the organization. *Academy of Management Review, 14,* 20-39.

Barker, J. R. (1993). Tightening the iron cage: Concertive control in self-managing teams. *Administrative Science Quarterly, 38,* 408-437.

Barker, J. R., & Tompkins, P. K. (1994). Identification in the self-managing organization: Characteristics of target and tenure. *Human Communication Research, 21,* 223-240.

Bullis, C., & Tompkins, P. K. (1989). The forest ranger revisited: A study of control practices and identification. *Communication Monographs, 56,* 287-306.

Burke, K. (1937). *Attitudes toward history.* New York: New Republic.

Cheney, G. (1983a). On the various and changing meanings of organizational membership: A field study of organizational identification. *Communication Monographs, 50,* 342-362.

Cheney, G. (1983b). The rhetoric of identification and the study of organizational communication. *Quarterly Journal of Speech, 69,* 143-158.

Cheney, G. (1991). *Rhetoric in an organizational society: Managing multiple identities.* Columbia: University of South Carolina Press.

Cheney, G., & Christensen, L. T. (in press). Identity at issue: Linkages between "internal" and "external" organizational communication. In F. Jablin & L. Putnam (Eds.), *The new handbook of organizational communication.* Thousand Oaks, CA: Sage.

Christensen, L. T. (1995). Buffering organizational identity in the marketing culture. *Organization Studies, 16,* 651-672.

Jackson, J. (1965). Structural characteristics of norms. In I. D. Steiner & M. Fishbein (Eds.), *Current studies in social psychology* (pp. 301-309). New York: Holt, Rinehart & Winston.

Papa, M. J., Auwal, M. A., & Singhal, A. (1995). Dialectic of control and emancipation in organizing for social change: A multitheoretic study of the Grameen Bank in Bangladesh. *Communication Theory, 5,* 189-223.

Papa, M. J., Auwal, M. A., & Singhal, A. (in press). Organizing for social change in concertive control systems: Member identification, empowerment, and the masking of discipline. *Communication Monographs.*

Peters, T. J., & Waterman, R. H., Jr. (1982). *In search of excellence.* New York: Warner.

Simon, H. A. (1976). *Administrative behavior: A study of decision-making processes in administrative organizations* (3rd ed.). New York: Free Press. (Originally published in 1945)

Soeters, J. L. (1986). Excellent companies as social movements. *Journal of Management Studies, 23,* 299-312.

Tompkins, P. K., & Cheney, G. (1983). Account analysis of organizations: Decision making and identification. In L. L. Putnam & M. E. Pacanowsky (Eds.), *Communication and organizations: An interpretive approach* (pp. 123-146). Beverly Hills, CA: Sage.

Tompkins, P. K., & Cheney, G. (1985). Communication and unobtrusive control. In R. McPhee & P. K. Tompkins (Eds.), *Organizational communication: Traditional themes and new directions* (pp. 179-210). Beverly Hills, CA: Sage.

Epilogue: What Have We Learned, and Where Do We Go From Here?

BLAKE E. ASHFORTH

Our conversation on organizational identification covered a lot of ground, and yet the terrain remains only sketchily mapped. Let me close by offering some thoughts on how our conversation may help illuminate the individual-organization interface, and by offering some suggestions toward future conversations.

IDENTIFICATION AND THE ORGANIZATION

Social identities are necessarily grounded in specific social contexts at specific times. What the construct of identification adds to the organizational literature is an understanding of how individuals come to situate themselves within an organizational context. Constructs like commitment and loyalty refer to a bond between person and place, but they do not address how individuals come to fundamentally *define* themselves at least partly in terms of the organization, and thus become microcosms of the whole. Identification, then, is the fusion of self and organization, thereby helping to address one's existential needs for meaning, belonging, and even immortality.

The Process of Becoming. Our first discussion, chronicled by me, suggested that identification is a complex and dynamic process. We invoked four metaphors to help explain this process: identification as imprinting, as love, as play, and as theater. Our basic conclusion was that identification is inherently open-ended, such that identities are a perpetual work in progress.

A major implication for organizational behavior is that an individual's workplace identity (or identities) reflects an ongoing interaction between the self and the situation such that it is very difficult to predict the trajectory of identification from a static set of antecedents. Most learning occurs en route as the newcomer experiences and interprets specific and often spontaneous events. Thus, Gundry and Rousseau (1994) describe how newcomers came to understand their organization by decoding certain "critical incidents." Furthermore, as the individual learns and adapts, the meaning of such incidents may change. A newcomer may enthusiastically embrace an organization-affirming speech by the CEO, but a year later view a similar speech as cynical manipulation. Thus, to understand a given identity and its relative appeal, one must understand the process through which the identity—and attendant identification—were forged.

Identification and the whole person. Much of the organizational literature treats the individual in an atomized fashion, as a composite of demographic characteristics, personality traits, needs and wants, knowledge, skills, abilities, and so on. What's missing is a sense of the whole, of the integrity and coherence of the *person.*

Identity has the potential to provide that missing sense of the whole. CV Harquail's discussion of organizational identification and the whole person highlights the linkages between cognition, affect, and behavior—and by extension, the other qualities that typify a person. Individuals strive for a sense of self-in-situation—a social identity (e.g., loyal subordinate, go-getter, iconoclast)—to clarify how they should think, act, and even feel in a given organizational context. In the absence of a clear identity, they may socially construct one from situational cues; their own initial thoughts, actions, and feelings; and any other salient attributes. Moreover, other organizational members and constituents also strive to situate individuals within the organizational context so that they can interact effectively with them. Thus, identities serve as templates that enable both the focal actor and his or her observers to construct a coherent persona. Diffuse attributes are assembled and labeled to create a seemingly integrated whole. Identities, then, effectively *organize* and make sense of the individual.

In sum, the power of identity theory is that it may help organizational scholars and practitioners to move from atomized conceptions of the individual to a more holistic perspective.

The need for identification. Turner (1976) argued that it has become increasingly fashionable for individuals to define themselves in opposition to institutional identities: One's "true self" is revealed through impulsive acts, not institutionally approved acts (e.g., fidelity in marriage, obedience at school). According to this view, individuality and nobility lie in resistance.

In contrast, Mary Ann Glynn's discussion of nOID—the need for organizational identification—suggests that individuals have a basic (but widely varying) propensity to define themselves in terms of some larger collective(s). For high nOIDs, individuality and nobility lie in one's choice and mix of social referents. This has provocative implications for organizational behavior. Rather than view performance, commitment, cohesion, and so on as qualities that must be extracted from organizational members at potentially great cost to the members, these qualities may be viewed as healthy manifestations of a desire to identify. In this view, a loyal member is not a patsy but is simply being true to a valued self-conception. Indeed, members who forego opportunities to express an identification may be jeopardizing their psychological health.

Identifications as constellations. Kim Elsbach's discussion suggests that an individual is attracted to and repelled from certain organizational identities such that his or her pattern of identifications and disidentifications resembles a constellation of stars. This suggests that organizations that project strong identities (clear and focused) will, like bright stars, serve as salient beacons or reference points, attracting some people and repulsing others. For example, Iannaccone (1994) found that the more distinctive the practices of Christian and Jewish denominations (e.g., diet, dress, social customs), the more likely that members were to describe themselves as strong members.

In short, organizations with strong identities tend to polarize people because it is difficult to remain indifferent to highly salient entities. Conversely, organizations with weak identities will repulse few but will also attract few real adherents (leading to what Janet Dukerich, Rod Kramer, and Judi McLean Parks term "underidentification"). On balance, I suspect that it is usually better for an organization to be loved by some and hated by others than to be viewed with indifference by all. The NRA, for instance, has attained many of its legislative goals despite antagonizing much of the public (Davidson, 1993). The implication for organizations is that strong identities are preferable to weak ones, provided the former attracts a critical and resilient mass of support.

Pathologies of Identification. Dukerich et al. note that organizational scholars tend to view identification, like similar OB concepts, in uniformly positive terms: the more the better. However, Dukerich et al. describe how "overidentification" is just as much a threat to the individual and the organization as underidentification. Moreover, they note how *dis*identification represents a slippery slope that can lead the individual to rampant distrust and marginalization.

Thus, the challenge for organizational theory and practice is to determine and attain the optimal balance of inclusiveness (identification) and distinctiveness (disidentification; cf. Brewer, 1991). The optimal balance will vary widely across individuals and organizations. For example, a person with a rich set of valued social and personal identities has less need for inclusiveness within the organization, and an organization in a complex and dynamic environment has more need for member distinctiveness. At present, organizations are typically preoccupied with the inclusiveness end of the continuum, and they explicitly or implicitly support workaholism, conformity, self-censorship, and other possible indicators of overidentification. Ironically, the very success of selection, socialization, compensation, and related human resource management activities that fuse the individual and organization may consign both to failure in the long run.

Managing Identification. For decades, a shift has been underway from relatively crude external controls to more subtle and unobtrusive internal controls. Where work was once controlled through supervision, bureaucracy, and technology, it is increasingly controlled through organizational culture, empowerment, and teamwork (Tompkins & Cheney, 1985). The latter set is said to constitute "internal" controls in that the individual is induced to internalize the organization's goals, values, and norms as his or her own, and thus to become self- and peer-policing.

As Jim Barker's discussion makes clear, identification can be seen as the ultimate expression of internalized control. Indeed, Jim asserts that "identification . . . is a characteristic of any organizing practice." A major issue that arises, apart from the pragmatic aspects of under- and overidentification/disidentification discussed by Dukerich et al., is the ethical and moral implications of pushing identification. How far should organizations go? By what means? What identity content is ethically defensible? We have no ready answers, but we see a continuing dialogue as essential to the moral health of *all* organizations.

TOWARD FUTURE CONVERSATIONS

The discussion suggests at least two particularly seminal issues for future research and speculation. The first is the *process* of identification, the focus of the write-ups by Ashforth, Harquail, and Elsbach. As Mary Ann Glynn notes, existing work has "focused more on a static sense of *being* identified rather than *becoming* identified." However, if the state or outcomes of identification are indeed driven by the process, it is imperative to track the evolution of identity and identification over time. What attracts a person to some identity constellations, and what repulses them from others? How tightly coupled are the cognitive, affective, and behavioral facets of identification, and which, if any, tends to assume primacy? How do individual, social, and situational factors interact to shape identification? What are the time lines and trajectories of the process (a smooth arc? a series of stages? a chain of discontinuous events?)? What kinds of events serve as strong identity signals?

The second seminal issue is the *degree* of identification, the focus of Dukerich/ Kramer/McLean Parks, Glynn, and Barker. If the optimal degree of identification is indeed an unknown but very real blend of inclusiveness and distinctiveness, it is also imperative to investigate the boundaries of identification and disidentification. Is one's "need" for identification better characterized as a trait or state, and what individual, social, and situational factors influence that need? At what point does a given identification or disidentification become pathological for the individual and organization, and what are the indicators of pathology? To what extent are identities compensatory, such that the issue of optimization becomes one of "identity portfolio management," as Rod Kramer put it? What guidance can ethical principles offer organizations regarding identity management?

As I stated earlier, the concept of identification with and within organizations holds great promise for enriching our understanding of organizational behavior. Our team's strongest wish is that our conversation will be regarded as only an initial inquiry—one that will spark many others.

A POSTSCRIPT

Learning is largely a solitary process. One often reads, ponders, and writes alone, with only intermittent infusions of energy and ideas from colleagues and others. But it's hard to puzzle through complex and dynamic issues by oneself. And real learning—the kind that addresses questions that matter—is not always well served by the rarefied and often stuffy air of academia.

I've often thought that the most provocative and novel insights for social science are to be found not in sterile academic journals, which seem to specialize in pinning butterflies, but in the flotsam of everyday life. People try to make sense of that flotsam, to learn, by collectively comparing their experiences and budding interpretations. Toward that end, conversations are one of the major vehicles for learning.

The identity conference, organized by Dave Whetten and Paul Godfrey and sponsored by BYU, allowed 30 or so people, motivated by a common interest, to meet together in a relaxing setting. The conversations that flowed from that conference, often rooted in personal examples from everyday life, were tremendously stimulating and rewarding. I learned more from a weekend together than I could from a month alone. I don't know how successful we've been in capturing our conversations in print, but the process was an end in itself.

REFERENCES

Brewer, M. B. (1991). The social self: On being the same and different at the same time. *Personality and Social Psychology Bulletin, 17,* 475-482.

Davidson, O. G. (1993). *Under fire: The NRA and the battle for gun control.* New York: Henry Holt.

Gundry, L. K., & Rousseau, D. M. (1994). Critical incidents in communicating culture to newcomers. *Human Relations, 47,* 1063-1088.

Iannaccone, L. R. (1994). Why strict churches are strong. *American Journal of Sociology, 99,* 1180-1211.

Tompkins, P. K., & Cheney, G. (1985). Communication and unobtrusive control. In R. McPhee & P. K. Tompkins (Eds.), *Organizational communication: Traditional themes and new directions* (pp. 179-210). Beverly Hills, CA: Sage.

Turner, R. H. (1976). The real self: From institution to impulse. *American Journal of Sociology, 81,* 989-1016.

8

Epilogue
What Does the Concept of Identity Add to Organization Science?

Parties to the Conversation:

Stuart Albert, Blake E. Ashforth, Dennis A. Gioia,

Paul C. Godfrey (moderator), Rhonda K. Reger, David A. Whetten

Moderator's Note: During the Academy of Management meetings held in Boston in August 1997, some of the principal players in the identity conversation came together for a final conversation. This involved the moderators of each of the individual conversations (Blake Ashforth, Denny Gioia, and Rhonda Reger), the editors of the entire book (David Whetten and Paul Godfrey), and the author of the book's introduction (Stu Albert). The intent of this conversation was to serve as an epilogue to the book—after we had all struggled with it for a year, what were our thoughts? How did we see identity now versus how we had seen the concept a year ago?

The conversation began with a discussion of the introduction to the book, which was still a work in progress. We spent some time discussing the specifics of the book, and then the conversation turned to a more general discussion of the value of identity as a concept for organization science.

During this conversation, you will see references to a "session yesterday." This was a symposium for the Academy of Management chaired by Mary Jo Hatch and Majken Schultz (which included Denny Gioia). In this symposium, the participants attempted to recreate the conversation process that occurred at Sundance the previous September.

Paul: We see this conversation as an opportunity for us to talk about the concept of identity and the process of writing a book of conversations. What, a year later, do we still think about identity? How is the process helpful? How was what we did at Sundance helpful? What are we interested in now? We hope that this sort of thing will provide an epilogue to the book and yet give people a sense of closure without closing off. This conversation is really the end of the beginning, if you will, or the beginning of the end, and a way to close the book without a traditional academically written chapter.

⁂

Stu: Well, I have a speculation about that. The conventional view is that science was emancipated from philosophy. While nonscientific descriptions of human affairs would supply grist for scientific hypotheses, what science would do would be to purify, disambiguate, clarify those descriptions and ultimately test the explanations they contained. In the early days of the emancipation of science from philosophy, the boundary between the two was kept inviolate. I mean, there were sentry posts with machine guns to keep philosophy out of science at all costs. And what has occurred, and I may be wrong about this, is that with the second or third generation of scientists, one began to create almost a technology of science that became arid in part for lack of a connection with the larger human experience. In the early days, you had to keep certain kinds of discourse out of science for fear they would contaminate a process bent on dispelling myth and dogma. But what the current project and its format as a conversation begins to do is to reinsert or re-embed the larger human enterprise into the scientific project, legitimating a certain vocabulary as appropriate to scientific discourse, as in Rhonda's use of the word "love" yesterday. I would also include words like "agony," "wisdom"—there's a whole other set of vocabularies that conversations naturally introduce. And that reinvigorates, because it enriches and it connects to the larger phenomena. It brings these phenomena inside the tent rather than saying, "We will keep it outside and use it only as a source of ideas for scientific proofs," and if that's what this project has meant—namely, an embrace, a larger embrace of the human condition as a legitimate source of vocabulary and insights and processes—that's a significant change. Just an observation. I don't know whether it's true or not.

Blake: I'm glad that tape was running for Stu, because that really was very eloquent. To me, that kind of captures what I'm deriving from this a year later. When I started thinking about this stuff 10 years ago, it was just another construct, like socialization or commitment. It was just something that sounded intriguing. And the more we've talked about it, especially last year with that kind of in-depth reflection, the more it became clear to me that we really are talking about a very root construct that forms so much of what we do implicitly in our organization analysis. I think that, as Rhonda was saying, this core sense of who we are, what the organization is all about, and how we're embedded in these intersecting social circles really fixes us as people, as groups, in a certain place, at a certain time, in a certain cultural context. That's identity. And you can't proceed without that kind of fundamental understanding. So, to me, it really does form a strong implicit bedrock of what we do in organizational science, and it does give you access to other kinds of ways of talking about organizations that simply aren't legitimate now, like spirituality, like talking about strong emotions like love and agony. It really does open all sorts of doors for me. That's been the excitement, then, of discovering the depth and the richness of the construct.

Stu: At some point, I want to take on the whole notion of construct, and I want to argue that there's an important way in which the idea of a construct has hampered science.

Denny: At the risk of being somewhat of a devil's advocate, the statement you have made, Stu, I think is true, but I also think it reflects our blanket training in organizational study in one overriding way of seeing—and that is a positivist point of view. In fact, we should recognize that historically, the project of the interpretivists (and I consider myself one), of the critical theorists, and, more recently, of postmodernists has been to challenge the positivist mode of understanding. In essence, such scholars hold that the strong boundary with philosophy is artificially constructed or furthered by those advocating a positivist representation of the human experience. These scholars treat the conceptualization of identity as rooted in some of the same fundamental concerns as philosophers. These concerns have not been sublimated; they have been there all along. Similarly, the scholars representing this viewpoint have also been underrepresented, but they have been there continuously since the advent of positivism. Therefore, I think representatives of these domains of study would argue that they have been saying for many years that there is too great a sacrifice in trading precision, prediction, and so forth for the understanding of the essences of human experience. Positivism has made some wonderful contributions to the understanding of organizations; yet organizational study at the moment is dominated by positivists, and they have managed to construct a very strange division between the human organizational experience and the modeling of that experience—and it has cost us dearly—especially if we value the benefits of multiple perspectives on understanding.

Stu: I think that's right. One of the clear disadvantages of the construct as a bedrock part of theory construction is that it seems to suggest a spatial boundedness for which the next relevant question is always measurement, and if you listen to the way in which we just talked about the importance of identity, it's clear that the identity is an answer to a question: Identity is a *question*. It's not a construct. Or perhaps it's not either/or, but both/and. For me, the formulation of questions and the construction of means to answer them is the hallmark of science, not the definition of constructs and the search for measurement. Science is based on questions. It unites people in common purpose because people huddle together in the face of the dark, and the distinctive feature of science is the way in which you try to eliminate self-deception and search for an answer. There is for me the identity question, which is, as you put it, what is it to be human? Why are we here? Why are we doing this now? What does this mean? Identity is inexorably tied to questions of meaning. You don't measure a question, you assess its significance. You might reflect on its poignancy at a particular moment: Why does it touch you now? Why does it come about now? Is it a broad question? Is it a narrow question? You don't measure a question. So, I'll have to think through these two different worlds. There's the world of questions and the search for answers, and there's the world of constructs and how you measure them, and they haven't been completely connected.

Dave: That's really interesting, Stu. Not only is identity a useful unifying construct within organizational science, it also serves as a great bridge to other social science disciplines. It stands to reason that as disciplines mature they tend to ask more profound questions. Since organizational science is still in its infancy we would do well to tap into conversations about identity in sociology, psychology, anthropology, and even geography. Now, getting back to your distinction between identity as a construct versus a question, your comments reminded me of a conversation that I had last night with a graduate student who is interested in incorporating organizational identity into her dissertation. She said, "I went to Home Depot and asked three different employees to describe what is most core, enduring, and distinctive about their organization. I was amazed at how similar their answers were. It seems that Home Depot has a very strong identity." My response was, "Well, maybe."

Stu: In fact, their response may have nothing to do with identity.

Dave: Later in the conversation she asked how I would measure the identity of Home Depot, and I said that first of all I feel uncomfortable with any attempt to measure identity strength. Frankly, I'm wary of the tar pits of strong culture. There are a lot of dinosaurs that have died in those tar pits, and I'd just as soon not have any identity researchers follow them into the quagmire of Likert scale measures.

Stu: But if I say that identity is a question, then culture can be part of the answer. It need not be, but it can be: It can also be the total answer.

Dave: As I have thought about this recently, I've realized why the measurement of identity has never been an issue for me. My abiding interest is in studying organizations that are experiencing crises due to downsizing, or a merger, or a scandal, or something like that. By the time I show up I don't have to worry about how to engage people in a conversation about identity, that's all they want to talk about. However, since by definition the identity question is rarely raised, I'm interested in how people discuss the undiscussable, and manage the unmanageable, and resolve the unresolvable.

Denny: But, Dave, even your chapter with Stu in *Research in Organizational Behavior* in 1985 suggested ways to measure it.

Dave: Yes, it did.

Denny: That's where Jim Thomas and I took our lead for the quantitative part of the identity/image study in *ASQ* last year.

Paul: But you are not saying, Dave, that because it can't be measured it can't be observed.

Stu: No, no, no. It can be observed. If someone wants to measure how a question is answered, you can ask, how many people answer it in a particular way? Did they give a precise answer? Did they give a global answer? Did they give an "I don't know" answer? What is the purpose of measurement? Suppose we take the construct view: Why do you want to measure it? And the answer is, it seems to me, so you can relate one construct or relationship to another construct or relationship. But the same motivation applies to questions as well. What is a question related to? Well, the natural pairing is that question is related to an answer. Questions motivate the search for answers, are linked to other questions, and to a problematic situation that gives rise to them. So, looking at something as a question means asking what provoked it, what answers it, perhaps other things as well. To inquire about whether something is a construct is to ask about whether certain conditions of reliability and validity are present as necessary conditions for asking what the construct is related to. So there are probably some parallels between the question view and the construct view: Both are interested in certain kinds of external relationship between the question or construct and other questions and constructs (along with antecedents and consequences), but there is also a sense in which to ask the identity question is not to ask about measurement but to inquire about the nature of the answers that might be supplied, including the adequacy of those answers. If I find myself lost on Mont Blanc unable to answer a fundamental question about my identity that a crisis provoked, and I come down from the mountain, and because I was unable to answer the question I change my life, I don't have to measure anything—except the unanswerablity of the question.

Denny: We're going to talk about fundamental human tendencies, and one of them is to ask questions. No question about it. But once the question is asked, we go and seek answers, regardless of the form of the question.

Stu: That's right.

Denny: And so I'm not sure how revelational it is to note that identity is a question. Of course, it is a question—a question that triggers a search for an answer. It is a revelation, or at least creates the opportunity for a revelation, because the question of identity is the fundamental question. But, having posed the question, we are off chasing answers. And to me the more interesting question is, how do we choose those answers, and what answers do we get, and how do those answers depend on the perspective taken? And how do we construct identity? Do we treat it as real? Yes, we do. Is it real? No, it isn't. But, so long as we treat it as real, then it becomes real, and we act *as if* we have an identity. It gives us a medium and a means for understanding who I am at the individual level, who we are at a group level, and at an organizational level.

Dave: But, you know, I'm fundamentally less interested in finding answers to the identity question than I am in figuring out the questions for which identity is the answer. That's what got Stu and I hooked to start with, back at Illinois. We were genuinely surprised that what we considered to be a rather mild stimulus—it was something like a 1% budget cut—provoked such profound discussions about the necessary and sufficient elements of a research university.

Stu: Your use of the term "profound" is very interesting, because we have to ask whether the difficulties in measuring something that is profound is in fact a measure of its profundity. It might be. In other words, if we say, "Let's list all of the factors that contribute to the difficulty of measurement as a kind of multiple regression problem." Well, one's going to be how profound the thing to be measured in the first place. The second is going to be how good our technology of measurement is. The third might be how competent we are in applying the technology, and so on. And so, if something is difficult to measure, it might be because being difficult to measure is a property of the thing being measured, or it might simply be that we are just not very good at measuring. Now, if identity is at the core a profound question, then we should not expect measurement to be easy. And, if someone claims to be able to do so with a few phrases on a questionnaire, we should treat that effort with suspicion. The irony I suggest is precisely what makes identity so difficult to measure is precisely what is so important about it, indeed, it might be a defining propoerty. Not that there might not be simple or conventional answers, acceptable for some purposes, but that concept at its deepest level is intentionally difficult to measure.

Rhonda: What psychological construct is easy to measure?

Stu: Belief structure.

Blake: Ones that are specific, ones that have ready behavioral manifestations, ones that we talk about, ones that are emotionally loaded. But, I would argue that those aren't terribly profound ones. Look at locus of control—yeah, there are lots of things that it's relevant to, but it's not the kind of thing you can take and use to gain a deep understanding of different situations, precisely because of its superficiality.

Stu: I mean, there's something about identity that will always be a mystery. I don't who's going to claim that they know the answer to the question "Who am I?" for all time, at the deepest level.

Denny: Oh, I do! That's the core of the deeply religious view on oneself—"I am imbued by God with my essential attributes, and I don't need to ask any more questions."

[Pause]

Stu: Well, you know, what's very interesting about that—it suggests that a profound question will not admit a completely idiosyncratic answer. It's too hard a question for any individual to invent an appropriate response. Whatever answer is provided must, of necessity, draw on a cultural repository, including philosophy and religion.

Denny: Oh, I hear you. I mean, you and I might believe that. But I know a lot of people who don't believe that.

Stu: I'm providing a functional account. That is, an individual can only address a profound question by looking for answers beyond the self. Which may be another way to index or "measure" how profound a construct is. The more profound it is, the more the question demands an answer that exceeds the capability of a single individual.

Dave: Which gets back to the value of the construct. It pulls you out of the individual frame of mind and into the social, and it requires you to link a social analysis with an individual perspective. The very nature of the concept forces you to . . .

Stu: Go back and forth.

Paul: Let me follow-up on Denny's comment. My take is that religion, or philosophy, can provide a very general, template answer to the question of who I am but still may leave me waking up in the middle of the night, wondering who I am, as a physical, temporally bounded person. One reason identity is so relevant now is because of the incremental march of secularism; organizations, for many people, play the role analogous to religion in their lives, and there is a disconnect with religion. "I don't want to believe" or "I'm too skeptical to believe that who I am depends on where I end up after I die." I want who I am to be answered in a more profane (secular) dimension. I look to my work organization as a surrogate for religion in providing that template answer, so when I wake up in a cold sweat in the middle of the night, I can say, "Ah, I'm an assistant professor at Brigham Young University," and that gives me something to latch onto as I struggle with who am I and what does this really mean.

Blake: I think there's a real tension between the micro and the macro in that we do look for these sort of general belief systems—whether it's religious or cultural or whatever—to give us these answers. When it's all said and done, it always must be locally bounded, because we're tribal. People look for clusters that they can get their mind around: family, peer groups, school, work organization, church, whatever. And what we're trying to do in these kinds of situations is take this repository of values and beliefs and meaning systems, and we're trying to make sense of it at the local level with the people that we interact with. Those are the people that make these values real—they instantiate it every day. So I think identity, to really stick, has got to be something that you enact in a very local, tribal context. What makes it difficult, though, as time goes on, is that the tribes are splintering. There's less and less core agreement on what religion, or what culture, or what national values ought to prevail given all the different trends approaching the 21st century. What that does is, it makes it very hard for people to get a sense of who they are in a way that can integrate people. What you end up with is a lot of splinter groups, or you might have a core sense of self, but this often disconnects with the Zeitgeist.

Stu: The other thing that occurs to me is that, within the limited religious traditions that I know, there is always written material that deals with the difficulties of belief. Moses Mimonaides comes to mind, his guide for the perplexed. I'm sure there are many others. So, associated with the question is a path of struggle that others have gone through and presumably will always go through, which is another way of indexing the profundity of the question.

Rhonda: There are two points I want to add to the discussion. One, this discussion reminds me of the phrase "the unexamined life is not worth living." Dave and

I have had this conversation many times before. He sees identity really coming out in crisis, and that's when people think about it. I think people do think about identity in crisis, but I also think there is variance in a baseline level of individual and organizational attention to identity. In the strategy group's conversation, we use the word "heedful." How heedful are they about their identity? How much do they examine their identity at founding? Sundance was a wonderful place for this to be happening because we got this sheet of paper in our rooms about Sundance's values and heedful founding. At the founding, it talked about what they were trying to do and how they were trying to preserve their identity, which I haven't gotten in any other hotel I've ever stayed at. Marriott comes close to that, they give you a book. I think it's the Marriott story. It says to the customer, "We are conscious of our identity and proud of it. We published a book on what this is." You go to Holiday Inn, they don't have the book. And so I think there is something important about organizations that live the "examined life."

Stu: But notice the key word "story," for example, the Marriott Story or the Sundance Story. To supply an answer to the question of identity is often to reference or supply a genesis story or myth. Answers to the question of identity are rarely atemporal: They tell stories.

Rhonda: Yes, the importance of stories is a key point of the strategy conversation.

Stu: It's no accident that's the case because to connect to Blake's here and now, you have to answer the five "who, what, when, where, why," all of the things that, in this ontology, define existence. These are all the things you have to address, or your account is incomplete about a real event. And it takes the form of telling a story that touches on those elements.

Rhonda: But—and this is the other point I wanted to make—we have to be careful about saying identity is in the realm of storytelling and not in the realm of science. An awful lot of people, if they open up the book, and in the very first chapter they read, "Identity can't be measured," they will say, "Oh, well, this is like many other modern management concepts. Very nice, interesting, but I don't want to study it, because you've just told me I can't." I agree with you, it can't be measured in the sense that some of the statistically fixated want to measure things with a false of precision.

Denny: Of course you can measure it. You can invent some way of measuring almost anything. The larger question is whether the measurement has any sort of relevance or is meaningful for essential understanding, or (heaven forbid) revelation. Most extant measurement techniques don't meet that kind of standard.

Rhonda: You can be rigorous about studying identity. That's my point.

Stu: Measurement has been taken (mistaken?) for the sine qua non of science. But science is not about measurement. Science is about questions and answers. If, in seeking an answer you need to measure something, you measure it. You count it, you do whatever you need to do.

Denny: The definition of science, as accepted since Bacon, is keyed on measurement. That's what distinguishes it from other pursuits.

Stu: No, but the key word is "distinguishes." Science is about answering questions in a particular way.

Denny: With measurement as the particular way—at least in the currently dominant models of social science, which are those predicated on an assumed parallelsim between physical and social science. The presumption that there is some sort of necessary equivalance in deep structure or form between physical and social science is to me mystifying and even absurd at some level. That presumption also is one of our biggest stumbling blocks in understanding organizations. Physical and social phenomena are in many essential ways ontologically different, so why should so many scholars be so hung up on trying to force-fit physical science models to the description and understanding of social phenomena? Still, because of the predominance of this assumption, and the centrality of measurement in physical science, it is measurement that serves as the field's current guide.

Rhonda: But we have a false sense of science. Even in physics, there are many things that are theorized to exist—that cannot be measured. They're trying to build these huge, massive things, miles under the ground, so that they can measure them.

Stu: That's right, and when you get to quantum mechanics, everybody understands that the math is quite odd. We have a funny view of what makes science, and I think . . .

Rhonda: But I want to say we are in the realm of science— as much as anyone in social science is in the realm of science.

Denny: Well, even if you study relativistic mechanics, it's very intimately involved with measurement. Now it's true that when you get to the quantum level the measurements get probabilistic and precarious.

Dave: Let's make sure we finish what we were talking about regarding heedfulness. What were you thinking about along those lines?

Paul: I want to return to Stu's point that religions have a set of writings for people who struggle. And as you were talking, I thought about my identity at Brigham Young University. One of the functions that the Academy of Management serves is as a set of written and verbal traditions about how to struggle with the identity of being an academic. My mind spun ahead to sort of a Parsonian view, and an interesting question comes up: Is it possible to think about organizations playing different identity roles within a culture? For example, the Academy of Management is an identity maintenance organization, and firms and other organizastions use these identity templates and customize them—they are identity production organizations.

Stu: That's terrific.

Dave: The thing I find interesting about this whole discussion is the notion of struggle. I guess that's another measure of profundity. That helps me understand my visceral negative response to the notion of asking three employees at a store on any given day to characterize the identity of their organization. I'll take some heat for saying this, but I'll say it anyway: If there's no evidence of struggle, there's no sign of identity. For years I've used the image of peeling away the outer layers of an onion in search of its pungent core to make the point that if the people you're observing aren't crying, then whatever they're discussing, it isn't identity—yet. I think one of the reasons why many of us don't feel comfortable reducing identity to a set of scales is that they don't capture the struggle, the pain, or the profundity that are the hallmarks of identity.

Denny: An important point to make is that organizational identity tends to be tacit knowledge. For that reason, it is sometimes inaccessible; yet some knowledge of identity resides close enough to the surface that it can be accessed, if called upon. The need for access comes when identity is challenged or questioned—which is why we discover that identity surfaces or is most clearly articulated by organization members under crisis. Under normal circumstances, people articulate a kind of "party line" view of identity that is readily available by tapping the organization's publicized view of itself. That is why researchers get superficial responses in noncrisis situations because such responses are "good enough, thank you very much." I really don't need to tap myself deeply to answer organizational identity questions if everything is going OK.

Dave: And it's interesting to speculate about what organizations should do with their clarified sense of self that emerges from a crisis. How do they share this with new members who didn't experience the struggle? And, how do you prepare for future crises by having a widely shared sense of the organization's identity if it takes a crisis to, in some sense, discover your identity?

Blake: I think part of it is you don't get fully engaged until your emotions and your values are really laid bare, and I think in the normal course of organizational life, you can get by with top-of-the-head, cognitive, rational thinking, and you muddle along, not profoundly affected. But, you were saying with the crisis thing, when that happens, then your self is laid bare in the sense that you have visceral reactions to things. At that point you use that to calibrate what matters most to you. You may think you're X, and you think the organization is Y, and be quite happy with that until your emotions or values are really engaged and you think, "Hang on a second, let me think about that." So I think, it's not fraudulent, it's just that it's very hard for people to know themselves until they are fully implicated and engaged in something. That simply does not happen in the normal course of mindless life.

Rhonda: That's true, but I wonder if there's a parallel again with religion. Perhaps a prescriptive implication of our work is that we should convince organizations that they must pay attention to identity before a crisis. Having a strong sense of identity equips people to handle a crisis. This is a lot of what religion is about—they don't tell you, "Wait until you're going through a divorce and then come to church." [*Laughter.*] Come to church the whole time, maybe you can avoid the crisis, or if the crisis occurs, and then you can handle the whole situation so much better.

Dave: But you know, a key part of the oral tradition of religion and culture are the stories about hero figures responded to crises. The premise is that we can extrapolate a set of generalizable response strategies for handling our own crises. Maybe we should be having embattled hospital administrators read the Job story, or the Abraham Lincoln story, or the Buddha story.

Rhonda: Part of those stories are from the tradition of your organization, but they can also be stories from other organizations. We saw that at Intel, where they told stories about IBM, and their understanding of what had happened to IBM. They did not want to be like IBM, and they were trying to learn from IBM's experience.

Blake: I think Paul's earlier point about organizations that actually produce identity, one's that just maintain it, and other ones that are kind of oblivious to it, is really profound.

Stu: Yes, it is.

Blake: When you think about it, our tribes, these organizations, these groups that we're a part of, really vary incredibly in just how much of an answer they try to provide to fundamental questions. And a lot are very content to sort of strut through their day. I can think of a person I know very well who has zero desire to know herself beyond just working at Donut Castle and raising her kids.

Dave: Be careful about judging her.

Rhonda: She may be a whole lot more content than you are, so don't knock it. [*Laughter.*]

Blake: I think that's really profound, because what that means is there are organizations that people look to to give us these fundamental answers, and others that don't try because they're just are not in that business. And yet, being tribal, we're still looking to impute something in these places that we belong to, even if it isn't really evident. So what do we do? Well, we invent it, or we import it.

Stu: Earlier, someone asked, "What's she on?" That's really interesting because whatever destroys the questions destroys part of our humanity. Whether it's Prozac or a cult, because to be human is to reflect on these basic predicaments, including the question "Who am I?". The question is unnecessary either because it is not problematic or because something else prevents it from surfacing. If the latter, then I would say that your humanity has been degraded because being is a question.

Paul: So what would a corollary be, Stu, of an organization on Prozac? I mean, I can make sense of that on an individual level.

Dave: Speaking of humanity, what the best humanities texts do is problematize the human experience. Good literature does not simplify, it complexifies. In contrast, our scientific models simplify the human experience in hopes of better understanding it. This may be at the root of our discomfort with the push to develop "identity scales." The identity question comes from a humanities tradition, and it may not lend itself to the standard scientific methodology because it resists being simplified. It resists being categorized and analyzed and quantified because its native condition is inherently paradoxical and enigmatic. That's why we keep coming back to the concept of struggle.

Stu: I have thought about Paul's question—"Tell me what this means at the industry or firm level beyond the individual level?"—and the answer that suggests itself is as follows. The function of the business cycle—and the crisis results when many firms face life or death—is a way that capitalism, and not merely firms, renews itself. Death and the threat of death surfaces the issue: What does it mean to survive? That one was lucky, that one had a good strategy? What determines the level of competition? What is an effective strategy? What is the market? What do people really need? What do customers want? What can we provide? All of these questions become foregrounded with the business cycle. And they need to be foregrounded if society is to restructure and rethink and refresh the meaning of capitalism and the nature of competitiveness associated with any economic system. And so the identity question is posed—

Denny: I think it's important for us to make this kind of observation, and one of the things we need to do as producers of this volume is to get beyond the simple statements that there are direct parallels between every concept associated with identity at the individual and organizational level. I don't think we've concentrated enough on what's different between the levels. What aspects of identity can we point to on the organizational level and say, "It doesn't replicate that well at the individual level, but that's what makes it an interesting element. It's not necessarily a multilevel construct, but it's got some of its own distinctive features."

Stu: And the meta-twist to that is that what you're asking is the identity question with respect to the levels: What makes them different? What's special about each level that makes it different?

Denny: The one that I would go after—the one that perhaps most distinguishes identity at the individual and organizational levels—is the issue of ability to change identity itself. This is the "durability of identity" question, if you will, or the question about the "fluidity of identity" over time, and in particular, over relatively short periods of time. At the individual level, identity (or at least the perception of identity) is quite enduring. It changes, yes, but it changes slowly, such that I, as self-perceiver, hardly notice the change. "I" am constant; I see myself that way. Only if I contrast myself with my remembrance of aspects of my youthful self-image that have clearly changed do I see myself as much different (for example, I once saw myself as shy, a characteristic that is no longer a good descriptor of me). At the organizational level, however, the fluidity of identity is a much more tenable concept. The modern organization is much more quickly adaptive to competitive and environmental shifts, and if anything, the need for adaptability is increasing. The consciousness of organization members these days is one of adaptivity and adaptability, even if they don't necessarily like it. That consciousness affects and infuses identity too. So changeability arguably becomes a component of identity, which generates a kind of paradox—an enduring aspect of identity can be its very changeability. (As an organization member, I expect us to change, and I internalize that expectation as an element of my sense of my organization's identity.) Still, when we talk about the fluidity or malleability of identity, we mostly talk about incremental change processes, even if the time horizons are increasingly shorter. Yet we also need to account for those rare cases where identity is not only evolutionary but revolutionary, like the Internet services firm in Pittsburgh that transformed itself from a service provider to a hardware provider in the space of mere months. By its president's own characterization, the company "underwent a necessary identity change from a service company to a manufacturing company." No small feat, but one that was necessary to ensure survival. It does lead to some questions about how they present themselves now, and how the members see themselves, and how newcomers are socialized. But even normal organizations live in a state of changing identity to a greater or lesser degree.

Stu: But notice that turnover is a way of preserving structure—that is, turnover is an identity preserving mechanism in the sense that those who would transform the organization exit and those who are willing to accept it in its present form are allowed to enter it.

Dave: Plus the organization is forced to represent itself to the new people coming in.

Stu: Yes.

Dave: To, in a sense, reinvent themselves every time they have to explain themselves to a new bunch of recruits.

Stu: Yes.

Denny: Then you have organizations like ours at Penn State, for instance. We hire for diversity of interests in our department. We say, "Well, we're not hiring that person because that's a playmate for so-and-so. And we want somebody different."

Stu: That's your identity . . .

Denny: And I will guarantee that it changes, the collective identity.

Rhonda: But that one aspect, the identity belief that we hire for diversity . . .

Stu: That's the identity.

Rhonda: That doesn't change.

Denny: To me that's the same as saying that the only thing certain here is that we change. Well, is that a component of identity?

Stu: Sure.

Denny: But that guarantees that the identity shifts. Is that what you're saying?

Stu: No. If one year you say "We'll hire for diversity" and the next year you say "We'll hire for homogeneity," then I would say that your identity has undergone change. But if you have a consistent philosophy, "We like diversity," then that's who you are.

Rhonda: That part is enduring. But you're right. Other aspects are changing.

Denny: Well, yes, I think so. Consider that even if we are consistent in our insistence on diversity of interests as a hiring criterion, that very consistency virtually ensures a shifting collective identity. When we look at ourselves over time we don't think of ourselves as the same. I don't know how we could. Sure, some aspects of identity are stable. We have always seen ourselves as a collegial and collaborative group. But all along there have been those skeptical of the collegial portrayal, and during all my time on the faculty the metaphor of an "entrepreneurial mob" has been invoked to describe ourselves. We live comfortably with a shifting identity and a certain paradox in our self-description. Yeah, identity at the collective level is something different.

Dave: I am intrigued by your statement that identity at the social level is more vulnerable than at the individual level. I hadn't thought about that. For me, what is important to keep in mind is that, although the identity of a social group may be less enduring than the identity of a single member of the group, the identity of the group is more enduring than other group characteristics.

Denny: I think that's a good point.

Rhonda: Yes. But even at the individual level, there is a literature that claims identity looks enduring, but it's really changing. It's a life course, and as you look back you're redefining. If you think about the things that have happened, typically to individuals, over their life, their identity changes. I got married, I became a mom, and Dave knew me before all that. I mean, I'm different now.

Denny: Yes, but you're consistent with the current you. We know that from memory study.

Stu: Notice if you treat identity as a question, the question endures, although the answer changes.

Denny: Why does that help me?

Stu: Because for all levels, individual or firm, the question may be the same, but that at the firm level the answer may change over time.

Denny: Exactly. I agree with the last part of your statement.

Blake: I think at the firm level, the distribution of strong identities is incredibly skewed. You can look at organizations—the Catholic Church, that's an easy one. They've had a very strong identity that has lasted a couple thousand years now. Versus other ones, like Firestone, the entire business is not that hard to fathom. It goes back to the idea of the identity maintenance thing. To the extent that an organization is all about its values and beliefs, that is its raison d'être, versus an organization that is intent on making money and kind of post hoc on how they're going to do that. You're going to find an incredible difference in, I think, their willingness to be malleable in what they're all about. So I would say there's an incredible variation across organizations in just how enduring their identities are.

Dave: The dualism I am particularly interested in has a moral component, which means that you should expect to see a better articulation of the identity, for exactly the reason you are describing. Because, now, the value system becomes central to who we are. It's not ancillary—it's the "prime directive" for the organization. It is my sense that organizations that successfully integrate their moral and economic value systems started that way at birth, as an extension of their founders' commitment to both "do good" and "do well" or do nothing at all.

Paul: Or, Dave, if we follow the religious metaphor, they experience rebirth. Struggle and crisis initiates this rebirth, or conversion, process. Identity is formed at birth and struggles during the crisis, and then there's a rebirth. So to study this phenomenon, we wouldn't reset the clock to zero, we'd set it to a "conversion event."

Stu: Hybrids are almost by definition in a perpetual state of struggle so identity issues should be more salient and answers to the identity question more well defined because they've had a longer time to work on it. I don't know whether that's true. There's a quip that cats and dogs are alike in that they each define themselves by their difference from the other. So, within the hybrid, what makes us special is that we are composed of both oil and water, and oil and water don't mix. Our attempt to occasionally mix them is what makes us special.

Dave: Which is an interesting insight into the transformation of identity in the health care industry, which can be characterized as a shift from an ideographic to a holographic hybrid. Using your metaphor, this is the equivalent of taking separate groups of cats and dogs and trying to create one group of catlike dogs and doglike cats. The outcome is that organizational schizophrenia "morphs" into mass individual schizophrenia. In the process, members experience a double identity crisis:

Individually they are no longer a cat or a dog; organizationally they no longer define themselves as groups of cats and dogs.

Stu: What's needed, of course, is a third category, an identity that arises out of the management of these predicaments and tensions.

Rhonda: You have to read our chapter. That's one of our answers. The managing of identity. Managing the tensions. And the second answer is to talk in terms of a Hegelian dialectic that you can either manage the tension, "I'm a soccer mom and a professor forever," or I can come up with a higher level of abstraction that lets me put these together in a creative way and integrate them and have integrity in a higher way, which is the other part of the answer we have in our chapter.

Stu: That's interesting. That reminds me of Hegel's discussion of the master and the slave. Two kinds of organizations are possible. In order for the master to be a master, he needs the slave. You can either embed normative values within an economic frame, or the reverse, economic values within a normative frame or treat both values as complementary, without hierarchy, which, when they're in the same organization, produces an unstable state. That's what's happened in health care: Normative values have become embedded within the larger economic organization. And that kind of hybridization . . .

Dave: Or in some cases, it's the opposite. That's why health care is such an interesting place to study this hybridization process because you have examples of cats becoming more doglike and dogs becoming more catlike. Or, to be less oblique, some religious hospitals are privitizing and many for-profit hospital chains are striving to become more patient and community oriented.

Stu: That is, there are two routes to hybridization.

Rhonda: But there's a third route that we haven't seen in health care yet, which is for them to say economic is normative, and normative is economic. In our groups, Jay Barney presented the Koch industries case. The Hegelian synthesis is Koch's answer: These things are not in opposition, they are totally compatible.

Paul: That may work in oil and gas but be much more difficult in health care. I read at breakfast an editorial from Columbia HCA. Their new chairman essentially said, "We realize we've gone to economic excess, and we're going to now pull back and reinstill normative values." And it's interesting, because in his five-paragraph editorial, he references the founding of the company. It was about maintaining community values, using small, rural hospitals, and then they just mushroomed and grew into this huge 342 for-profit investor chain, which led to its own set of excesses, and now they want to recreate and resediment that fundamental founding imprint, which is "We're about community, we're about a health care community. We're not about taking out your spleen just because it's worth $1,200 to me, but because it is good for your health."

Stu: It connects with some work I have been doing with a professor in the law school on what we call the "rehybridization" of economic institutions, which is how you re-infuse law firms with other values other than the economic ones, which some feel have come to dominate.

Dave: We've been doing research on socially responsible businesses. We've identified about 30 *Fortune 500* companies that, according to the established rating services, have demonstrated an enduring dual commitment to "doing good" and "doing well." In examining the histories of these firms, it appears that their dualistic value system was imprinted at birth. This raises questions about the feasibility of grafting a moral value system onto a mature economic value system. It would appear that the only economically rational reasons for doing this are that the moral initiative is cost-neutral, that it is profit-enhancing (which raises questions about motive), or that the organization has sufficient slack to absorb the inefficiency typically associated with "doing good" corporate initiatives. My concern is that there is very little evidence that moral grafts can withstand the harsh evaluation of a financial downturn.

Moderator's Note: At this point the converstion continued for a few minutes. We then turned to a conversation around our reflections about the Sundance conference and the process of having conversations be the mechanism of the book.

Paul: This is the point that I made yesterday, that each of the three groups felt that they were somehow unique and outside of the other groups. Now, I remember initial reactions to Blake's topic were "Oh 'identification with' is boring." And then people said, "Well, you know, I'm kind of interested in 'identification with', and I actually like to talk about that." And then Denny's group described themselves as "antiscript," and Rhonda's group was viscerally engaged in the fact that they were on a crusade, because they felt the others had deemed them as atheoretical.

Dave: Which is interesting, and this was Rhonda's point yesterday, identity—it was there, and you know, the anthropologists said all along that identity is created in reference to the other. And that's what we were saying, that the groups that have the strongest identity, in some sense, have the strongest reaction against the other groups.

Rhonda: Going back to the initial studies that social identity theory came out of, they were trying to create groups where there would be no identification with the group. Subjects were told, "You are randomly assigned to this group, but you are in this group." They didn't see the other people in the group, they didn't exist, but they still favored members of their group over those not in the group.

Blake: And as groups are formed out of absolutely minimal criteria . . .

Rhonda: Yes! Sometimes, they were told, "You are randomly assigned."

Blake: Even that group made them think, "Oh, I guess we are a group." So a group mentality took over.

Stu: This speaks to the need for identification, the need to enlarge the boundaries of the self, and the way, once something is included within the boundaries of the self, it becomes different from what it was outside the self.

Rhonda: And imposing meaning. The world can't be random, we can't be in this group for random purposes, so there must be meaning here.

Denny: Now it comes back to me about the strategy group. As I recall, they were hands-on-hips indignant about this supposed accusation that they were atheoretical. I tried to track it down. And in fact, I did trace it to one person who made some off-handed comment, who swears he didn't say what he was accused of saying. And that it was misconstrued completely, but then it took on a life of its own, and the strategy group defined themselves in opposition to the labeling.

Rhonda: No, no! No, no! It started way before that. It's—it is embedded in the larger academic context.

Denny: Of course.

Rhonda: And I'll tell you where it started for me. Remember, I was late coming into the conference, so where the situation was between the groups was really interesting to me. For me, it started when Dave said, "You've been assigned to the 'applications of' group." I enacted, "Oh no, Dave doesn't think very highly of me." [*Laughter.*] The fear surfaces: The theory groups are the most prestigious, and I've been trying to impress him my entire career. [*More laughter.*] You know, so it was the title Dave gave to the group that enacted a whole scene that he didn't mean. And then there was another group that I think had theory or definition or something like that. We wanted to be that group. I felt like we were the outgroup, but I wanted to feel good about myself. So, then I arrived at this group and found, I think, that everyone else had the same reaction. And I think, in Dave's mind, he was thinking that we weren't really going to be coming from a theoretic perspective. But let's enact, we said, "We are Strategy and you are OT and Blake's group is OB." We were really surprised that when we made that distinction that Denny's group, you said, "We're not the OT group." We enacted the larger academy schema that gets played out, that strategy has no theory, and we're really the application of organization theory. And strategy's been saying, "No, we're not. We have our own theory, and it's separate, and it's unique." We created this worldview and got angry at other people for their roles in this worldview that they didn't create at all.

Stu: Notice that this is a discussion about the construction of identity.

Denny: And a discussion of who's constructing it.

Stu: And how it's constructed out of interaction, dialogue, labels, interpretation, the recruitment of concepts from the outside world, etc.

Paul: But identity creation is not an ex nihilo phenomenon, and a part of what we drew on to create these group identities was this identity maintenance organization, that classifies OB and OT and Strategy.

Denny: But remember that many of us concluded that we were going to humor Dave and Paul. We looked at these labels that you gave us, and said, "Okay, if they want to think of it that way, that's OK." But then Rhonda's group had an impromptu conversation at the beginning, went off, and, if I recall, came back and decided to try to negotiate with Dave about, "We don't want to do it the way you framed it. We want to do it our way. We want to tell a bunch of stories."

Rhonda: Well, this was another interesting part of the process. I missed that first night, so when Dave brought me up to speed, I shook my head and said, "Okay." Then a couple of people in my group brought me up to speed and said, "This is kind of where we are." And I'm thinking, "Okay, fine." And then Dave told me the next task he wanted the group to do, which seemed reasonable given everything I had been told. I went back to the group and said, "This is the next thing we're going to do." And they said, "No, he's nuts!" I was completely blindsided: "What, what, what have I missed?" So there really was this sort of negotiation process.

Dave: And that caught me totally by surprise. I was totally blind-sided by this, which suggests that I was so task oriented that I was insensitive to the need to form group identities and the inevitability that identities would be emerge, even under these conditions.

Denny: That's what I meant by saying, "We'll humor you," because we saw the overall vision for the conference. And in fact, the other two groups were kind of p.o.'d at the strategy group for trying to redefine the vision.

Rhonda: We wanted to redefine the vision because the vision, we thought, made us second-class citizens.

Stu: But notice the important theoretical proposition: Because identity is so profound, it necessarily is involved with questions of esteem and status.

Dave: And it's necessarily involved in the formation process—again, we're talking about birth here. It was in this birthing process that identity was being evoked. But I didn't think of this as the starting of groups, I thought of it as people coming together to perform a task and my instrumental need to produce a book out of a few brief conversations did not take into account the need for identity formation.

Paul: One thing that made it a true birthing process is this: It was not a task that people were familiar with. This was not a conference where people came and wrote a paper and presented it as a chapter in a book. I remember on the first day there was a lot of negotiation and concern about "what is this thing really going to look like." And so there was even more contextual uncertainty, and much more of a birth, because this process was something that was virgin territory for everybody.

Dave: So identity had to be created before the task could be performed, because of the uncertainty of what we were doing. This is conversation, this is a new kind of a book that nobody's ever written, so it evoked the need to establish the identity before we could get on to the task.

Blake: Well, again your identity has to be worked out over time, because it is a work in progress. And it's very hard to expect this fully formed template to just take shape. That's the nature of being. It is experiencing and learning and doing and dabbling. Well, that was kind of the nature of the process as well. It's because people were attached to the roles, the tasks that became profound for them, because they were then, in effect, labeled by that particular thing that they were attributed to.

Denny: That happened to our group at Sundance too, and I think it happened again yesterday in our symposium. I don't know what you thought of that session, but I was of two minds about it: On the one hand, I thought, "This is a small disaster." And on the other, I thought, "Hey, this is not a bad model for what went on in our creative, collaborative, conversational theory building about organizational identity." Some people got it; quite a number were clearly engaged with us. Others, perhaps justifiable, thought, "What is this about?"

Rhonda: I thought it was a great session. A thousand times better than the traditional academy session.

Denny: I hope so. At least it was a reasonable replication of the process we went through at Sundance. As far as process was concerned, we just saw ourselves as seven or eight interested people who had points of view. Initially, we were in the usual academic mode of trying to express a point of view and sell it to the others. Pretty soon, however, we discovered that we could borrow from, learn from, and develop from our other colleagues in the room, until we, and then the conversation itself, created the frame we used.

Dave: I think your take on the relationship between theory building and collaboration was very interesting. As you pointed out, most of the time when people come together to collaboratively build theory, their underlying premise is that consensus is a necessary part of the process. But consensus was not our objective at Sundance, because our goal was not to leave with a single, all-encompassing, unified theory of organizational identity. To say that we were collaborating divergently is confusing, but that is a pretty accurate characterization. Your effort to help people not only understand but appreciate this messiness was an admirable, but in retrospect, an unrealistic objective.

Blake: What we're doing is bifurcating the audience. A lot of readers are going to look at this and go, "Oh boy, this is airy fairy, make up your mind and tell us the answers, and then we'll read it." And the rest will say, "Well, this is great. You're kind of muddying up life, which is life. Let's just see how messy things can get. Let's play in the mud for awhile."

Denny: We're imposing some structure on the mud, too. We're going back post hoc and saying, "Um, we need to smooth this over a little bit."

Stu: Well, you know, this is a Merton middle-level structure. A conversation is messy, but prior to the conversation is a thought process that's even messier. A conversation is an abstracted structure of something that is even messier, namely the thought process that the conversation tries to capture. An edited written conversation is even more abstracted.

Dave: I think it's interesting to see how the different groups interpreted the charge to have a conversation and then to report the conversation in a way that invites others to join in. My initial reaction in seeing a member of Blake's group typing away furiously on her laptop during the discussion was, "Man, they're going to have the richest conversation of all because they're capturing it in real time. The rest are going to have to wade through a transcript of their tape and spend so much time trying to figure out who said what, that they'll lose track of the story line." Well, it turned out that she was only recording a very rough summary, so the richness of this communication medium was lost. Now, I personally think that how the charge was interpreted, how roles were assigned, how technology was used, and how the group identities emerged is a very interesting story. But Paul and I have been struggling with how to reconcile the expectations of publishers and readers regarding the seamless quality of well-edited books with the very messy nature of our product. Our sense has been that we can change some of the accepted formula for an edited book, but if we make too many changes we are concerned that the perceived inappropriateness of the medium will detract from the contribution of our message.

Stu: It speaks to an enduring issue which is both difficult and divides the field, namely, what is the relationship between the qualitative and the quantitative? The conversation is the sine qua non of qualitative science. A Cartesian set of propositions and proofs is the quantitative part. How do you mix them?

Paul: Stu, I beg to differ. I think the conversation is the sine qua non of human life, because qualitative research can be as vigorous and structured as a set of equations. But as I edited these conversations, my first reactions was "Oh, no," because they are conversations, and they twist and turn, and there is no sense to it. If you're not a participant in the conversation, you cannot completely understand it. And so as an editor my job became "Okay, try to tell people what happened yesterday, so when you reference yesterday, they can actually have something to understand."

Stu: This is a very profound point, namely that you had to be there, as in the expression "You had to be there," because that defines the difference between physical co-presence and virtual reality. This question is going to be revisited for generations. What is accessible only by virtue of physical presence; when must you really be there?

Dave: And that's what was inherently problematic about your session yesterday. The messiness was not simply a result of your needing to mix content and process ("This is what we did and this is how we did it"). You were also faced with a temporal messiness, in the sense that you were intent on trying to recreate a shared experience—rather than just describing the identity conference you wanted people to feel it.

Rhonda: You know what someone said to me after your session? "What is with Sundance? It must be a really spiritual place." [*Laughter.*]

Stu: But you know, the nice thing about that is that Gennette, translated into English, and other narratologists have a well-structured model of the temporal processes of unfolding narratives. Perhaps it might be possible to describe some of the messiness in a methodological piece about collaborative theory construction starting with conversations.

Rhonda: We haven't mentioned during this conversation that the book is based on Identity III. It wasn't just a scripted conversation at the end of a 2-day conversation. But it was after a 3-year bringing together of many of the same people and some different people. And part of what was so weird about the tension between our group and Denny's group was, we have been in groups with some of the same people at Identity I and II, and we didn't feel the sense of "they're the other." It also made our conversation work better because it had been this multiyear process.

Dave: And we have progressively become more structured. The first year our objective was to attract attention to the topic and to encourage people to begin talking about how they might use it. My hope was that some seeds would get planted and folks would keep thinking and talking. The next year we invited participants to make presentations about their work-in-progress.

Rhonda: And we're a product now.

Dave: That's right, we're a product now.

Moderator's Note: At this point we ran out of recording tape, and so the conversation proceeded to a rapid conclusion. Identity is a new and potentially profound way of thinking about organizations, organizational processes, and life in organizations. The identity question (Who am I?) may be the question with which both individuals and organizations must struggle in order to create a sense of meaning, and a sense of direction, for their activities. This book attempts to convey a sense that identity is a concept (or construct) in its infancy. In that spirit, we invite you, the reader, to join with us in the marvelous discovery process centered around organizational identity. *So, . . .*

9

Postscript

Observations on Conversation as a Theory-Building Methodology

PAUL C. GODFREY

In early September, 1994, Hal Gregerson knocked on my office door and asked me if I would like to attend the "Organizational Identity" conference being held that weekend. As a freshly minted PhD, I was not richly steeped in organizational identity, but I was intrigued by the construct of organizational identity because it linked well with other interests I had at the time (interests that have continued to develop). Also, the identity conference would give a young faculty member the chance to rub shoulders with some very sharp people in organization science. Identity encompasses a broad range of organizational topics (such as commitment, culture, strategy, and structure) and also includes elements of philosophy, values, ethics, and spirituality in organizations. This was the initial hook that got me interested in identity. What began as a wonderful invitation from a valued colleague reaches a major milestone in the publication of this volume.

The initial identity conference sparked my interest in organizational identity, and I saw, for perhaps the first time with clarity, the power of conversation as a method of idea generation and theory development. The first morning session of the conference, I participated in a group discussion on the topic, "What is identity?" There was much debate about whether or not there is such a thing as organizational identity, or whether it is merely an effective metaphor for organizational events (a debate that has not been resolved, as featured in the conversation edited by Denny Gioia). Dave Whetten talked for quite a while in our meeting. He began by stating that he was rather agnostic about whether identity is real or a metaphor; however, after several minutes of talking, he became adamant that identity, according to his experience, was not only something real in organizations but also something of vital importance to the moral core of organizations. I believed then, and still do now, that at the beginning of his soliloquy, Dave *actually was* agnostic about the concept, but through the process of conversation, his thoughts became clear to him and to those of us engaged in the conversation.

We chose to have this book be a series of conversations to convey to you, our reader, a concept in its intellectual infancy. There are fundamental issues about identity that are very fluid, such as how one defines the concept, and how that definition depends on the epistemological framework within which one chooses to work. We hope our conversational format has preserved this sense of infancy for you, and that it also communicates a sense of direction for the work left to do in establishing organizational identity as a viable, and useful, concept in organizational study. We hope that our book communicates a sense of beginning, rather than a definitive statement about what identity is, how it is measured, and how it is used. In the few paragraphs that follow, I hope to give you a final sense of the importance of conversation as a method for developing ideas and theories.

Conversation as a methodology for theory development is not a new, nor a radical, idea. Mary Parker Follett proposed a similar process, albeit for a different purpose, nearly 80 years ago. In *The New State,* published in 1918, she advances a concept she refers to as "interpenetration" as a mechanism for group decision making. Follett finds the traditional methods of group work, consensus building, or compromise flawed in their ability to truly maximize a group's output. Consensus fails because it looks for the solution on which everyone can agree, and most often, that agreement comes without requiring group members to think deeply about their positions or the solutions they bring forward. Although consensus builds a solution with which all feel comfortable, consensus solves disagreements by finding the first, which often turns out to be the least, common denominator between differing factions.

Compromise also results in suboptimal group work and decision making. Compromise creates what popular author Steven Covey would call a "lose-lose" situation. Both sides are forced to give up something each values in order to "split the difference" and "meet in the middle." Although compromise works, and often quite effectively, because each party has to give up something of value, it cannot be a truly maximizing framework for group work.

Follett recommends interpenetration; she also refers to it as "integration" in her later work, *Creative Experience* (1924). Integration involves group members coming together and truly listening to all positions. The purpose of this listening is to clarify understanding about others' positions as well as our own position. With a complete understanding of "where everyone is coming from," as well as the factual context surrounding the issue, the group begins a discussion that attempts to find a solution to the group challenge that meets the needs and wants of all group members. This solution is rarely present at the beginning and emerges through the process of discussion and dialogue. Integrative decisions involve a process whereby each member understands and then builds on the ideas of all others in the group. Follett argues that integration provides a superior method for group problem solving than either consensus or compromise, because only integration seeks to truly maximize the well-being of each party at hand.

The conversations recorded in this book represent, in many ways, an experiment on Follett's notion of integrative group processes; thus, I will often refer to them as integrative conversations. For example, the "identity of . . ." group (headed by Denny Gioia and found in Chapter 3) faced an early problem because each member approached the study of identity from a different paradigm: functional (positive science), interpretive, and postmodern. The conversation began with people speaking within their paradigms, and there was not much progress made. Everyone disagreed with what someone else said. The integrative process for this group lay in stepping out of their own paradigms and trying to create a language to talk about the different paradigms. You find this language recorded in Table 3.1. The group began making substantive headway once everyone understood why each paradigm held particular notions of identity, and they were thus able to lay aside the partisan debates and think seriously about the concept of identity.

The strategy group (headed by Rhonda Reger and found in Chapter 5) used integrative conversational processes to advance its understanding of the relationship between identity and strategy. Working from a large easel in the screening room at Sundance, the group began talking about how identity or strategy would change in response to environmental conditions. Over the course of several hours, they developed a very rough version of what you find as Figure 5.5 in their conversation. They continued to work on this figure to add clarity and understanding; however, no one brought even a rough draft of that figure with them to the conference. The model developed as one person tossed out an idea and someone else built on that idea. Through this iterative idea generation and critiquing process, the group clarified its collective view of how identity and strategy change together.

The "identification with . . ." group (headed by Blake Ashforth and found in Chapter 7) had its own integrative experience. I attended part of their discussion concerning the pathological elements of identification. As the group developed its thinking around this question, one member related a personal story of negative forms of identifying with an organization. Others in the group related some of their experiences with this phenomenon, and these anecdotal stories served as a launch pad for the identification of theoretical models and constructs to explain these phenomena. Again, the spontaneous process of conversation helped move theory development forward as the group mixed personal and anecdotal data into its theory development mix.

Although the experiences we had at Sundance exposed us all to the power of conversation as a tool for theory development, the process is not without its challenges and pitfalls. Let me briefly consider what I consider the chief conceptual and practical challenges in using conversation as a theory development tool.

Conceptually, the greatest challenge to making conversations work is the lack of familiarity with the form *as an organized vehicle for theory development*. We have all had great conversations with colleagues that have greatly expanded our thinking, but many of us have not had these types of sustained conversations with larger groups of people. Making the Sundance conversations work required a lot of infrastructure building. First, conversations require trust among group members if they are to work well. Most conferences provide forums to proselytize our own work or to problematize the work of others, neither of which require, or engender, trust. Integrative conversations require people to commune with one another, to give up their absolute adherence to their own position and truly be willing to learn and share with others. Integrative conversations are hard work; not only must the mind be engaged in the content of the discussion, but the heart must be engaged in respect and concern for others in the conversation. Without an atmosphere of sharing and trust, integrative conversations are not possible.

A second conceptual challenge comes from the nature of conversations. Conversations are not, metaphorically, canals that move ideas from beginning to ending with haste and dispatch; rather, they are streams that wander, overflow their banks at times, and gently meander in a general direction. The Sundance conversations took a different tack—participants knew at the outset that they came to have conversations that looked more like canals than streams. This structure forced groups to avoid wandering to some extent, and side trips had to justify themselves by adding value to the overall conversation. The impending need for a product also put some pressure on the groups, and many participants admitted that the process was different because they knew that by the end of the conference, they *had to have* something to show for all their talking. Integrative conversation, of the type we had at Sundance, worked well because there was a clear reason for the conversations and a clear output expected.

Practically, integrative conversations depend greatly on the physical circumstances. The epilogue conversation took place in a hotel convention room in Boston. The conversation was good, but after an hour and a half, everyone was ready for the conversation to end. By contrast, the Sundance conversations took place over a period of 3 days. The quiet, pastoral setting of Sundance provided a necessary backdrop for the quality of the conversations. Participants could fully engage their minds for a period of time and then find space for quiet reflection and further analysis. We could not have sustained the high level of intellectual and emotional activity needed to produce these conversations in a harried or less beautiful environment.

Another practical challenge to conversations arose as we began to put the book together. One source of inspiration for this format came from an oral history I had read about the Chicago School of Economics (Kitch, 1983). As the chapter drafts began to arrive, it became clear that oral histories are not conversations. Oral histories involve retelling, conversation entails creating something new, and something new is, by nature, more messy than the retelling of something old. Again, the streamlike nature of conversations means that they do wander, and conversations tend to reference themselves, or loop back upon themselves, in order to move forward. There were many places in the conversations where someone referenced a conversation to which, you, the reader, would have no access. This created a significant editorial challenge in preserving the essence of the conversation (because the new insight always built on the previous conversation) while helping you to have a context for understanding the unfolding conversation. Although it proved a difficult challenge to provide adequate logical structure to the conversations, it is, I believe, a small price to pay for the richness of the ideas found within the conversations.

Finally, we hope that you have not only enjoyed our conversations about identity, but that they have engaged you in some way. We hope that you will join in the study and discourse of organizational identity. As Stu Albert noted in his introduction, none of us knows for sure where the concept of identity will fit in the constellation of organizational science concepts. We hope that it occupies a prominent place. Organizational identity does not anthropomorphize organizational life, it exposes the fundamental human nature of that life. Identity facilitates the discussion of moral values and philosophical questions in the study of organizations on the same level as secular and economic questions. Identity may eventually, and hopefully, provide a strong counterpoint to the economic rationalism that so permeates our field. Whatever the outcome, we sincerely hope that you will join in the conversation.

REFERENCES

Follett, M. P. (1918). *The new state.* London: Longman's, Green.
Follett, M. P. (1924). *Creative experience.* New York: Peter Smith.
Kitch, E. W. (Ed.). (1983). The fire of truth: A remembrance of law and economics at Chicago, 1932-1970. *Journal of Law and Economics, 26,* 163-233.

About the Contributors

Stuart Albert is Associate Professor of Management in the Curtis, L. Carlson School of Management at the University of Minnesota. In addition to an interest in hybrid organizational identity, his current work focuses on the study of timing, which is the subject of a book-length monograph. An introduction to this work can be found in his article "Towards a Theory of Timing: An Archival Study of Timing Decisions in the Persian Gulf War," published in *Research in Organizational Behavior* (Vol. 17, pp. 1-170, 1995).

Blake E. Ashforth is Professor of Management at Arizona State University—Tempe. He received his PhD from the University of Toronto. His research interests include the adjustment of newcomers to work, the dysfunctions of organizational structures and processes, and the links between individual-, group-, and organization-level phenomena. His recent work has focused on socialization, identity, and labeling processes. He is currently a consulting editor for *Academy of Management Review,* and he is on the editorial boards of *Administrative Science Quarterly* and *Canadian Journal of Administrative Sciences.*

James R. Barker is Assistant Professor of Organizational Theory and Strategy in the Department of Management at the U.S. Air Force Academy. He received his PhD from the University of Colorado. Research interests focus on the development and analysis of control practices in technological and knowledge-based organizations. Recent projects include collaborative research with scientists at the Los Alamos and Sandia National Laboratories. He has also worked with a variety of public, private, and service organizations. His teaching interests focus on the application of theoretical principles to solve day-to-day organizational problems. He has taught a variety of courses that emphasize the development of critical thinking and decision-making skills. His work has appeared in a number of professional journals, including *Admin-*

istrative Science Quarterly, Communication Monographs, Human Communication Research, and *Advances in the Interdisciplinary Study of Teamwork.* He is Associate Editor of *Western Journal of Communication* and serves on the editorial board of *Administrative Science Quarterly.*

Jay B. Barney is Professor of Management and holder of the Bank One Chair for Excellence in Corporate Strategy at the Max M. Fisher College of Business, Ohio State University. He received his MA and PhD from Yale University. His research focuses on the relationship between idiosyncratic firm skills and capabilities and sustained competitive advantage. He has published over 30 articles in a variety of journals, including *Academy of Management Review, Strategic Management Journal, Management Science,* and *Journal of Management* and has served on the editorial boards of several journals. He has also delivered scholarly papers at Harvard Business School, Wharton School of Business, and a number of U.S. and international universities and has published two books: *Organizational Economics* (with William G. Ouchi) and *Managing Organizations: Strategy, Structure, and Behavior* (with Ricky Griffin). In addition, he has consulted with a wide variety of public and private organizations, focusing on implementing large-scale organizational change and strategic analysis.

Hamid Bouchikhi is Associate Professor of Management at Essec, France. He holds a PhD in management studies from Paris-Dauphine University. His main research areas are in organization theory, management, executive careers, and entrepreneurship. He has published in *Organization Science, Organization Studies,* and *Organization.* In 1997, he coedited with Martin Kilduff and Richard Whittington a special issue of *Organization Studies* on "Action, Structure, and Organizations." He is currently working with John Kimberly on organizational identity and its role in shaping strategies and managerial processes in organizations.

J. Stuart Bunderson is completing his doctoral studies at the Carlson School of Management, University of Minnesota. His current research interests include the management of pluralistic organizations (multiple identities and values) and the organization and management of professional work. His dissertation research builds on extensive fieldwork in health care organizations to develop a contingency theory of value pluralism in professional organizations.

Janet M. Dukerich is Associate Professor in the Management Department at the University of Texas at Austin. She received her PhD in organizational behavior from the University of Minnesota. Her current research interests focus on the antecedents and consequences of strong versus weak organizational identification, as well as on the processes by which individuals interpret complex, value-laden organizational issues. She recently received a grant from the Construction Industry Institute to study high-performance project teams in the construction industry. Her research has appeared in *Administrative Science Quarterly, Academy of Management Journal, Research in*

Organizational Behavior, Research in the Sociology of Organizations, Organiza-tional Behavior and Human Decision Processes, and *Journal of Business Ethics.*

Kimberly D. Elsbach is Assistant Professor of Management in the Graduate School of Management at University of California, Davis. Her research focuses on the per-ception and management of individual and organizational images, identities, and reputations. She has studied these symbolic processes in variety of contexts ranging from the California cattle industry, the National Rifle Association, and radical envi-ronmentalist groups to Hollywood screenwriters. Her work has been published in a number of scholarly outlets, including *Administrative Science Quarterly, Academy of Management Journal,* and *Organization Science,* and she serves on the editorial boards of *Administrative Science Quarterly* and *Organizational Research Methods.*

C. Marlene Fiol is Associate Professor of Strategic Management at the University of Colorado—Denver. She holds a PhD in strategic management from the University of Illinois. Her research focuses on cognitive processes in organizations, especially as they relate to strategic change, organizational learning, and innovation. Her most recent work examines the dynamic interplay between identity and reputation at the level of individuals, organizations, and communities. The purpose of this work is to determine the impact of alignments and misalignments of these internal and external beliefs on the ultimate effectiveness and health of the entity in question.

Peter Foreman is currently a doctoral candidate in organizational behavior at the University of Illinois. His dissertation is a theory-building case study of an integrated health care delivery system, investigating the strategies that organizations and indi-viduals use to manage multiple and competing identities. He has also studied how competing identity-based expectations impact rural cooperatives. His research inter-ests also include decision making, the resource-based view of the firm, institutions and deinstitutionalization, and crafting strategy. He has studied identity and cognitive processes in various settings, including agricultural cooperatives, meat packing and processing firms, ornamental horticulture (nursery) growers, biotechnology firms, and health care providers.

Charles J. Fombrun is Professor of Management in the Leonard N. Stern School of Business at New York University.

Dennis A. Gioia is Professor of Organizational Behavior in the Smeal College of Business Administration at Pennsylvania State University. His main research and writing interests continue to focus on understanding the cognitive processes of or-ganization members and how these processes affect the ways in which people make sense of their experience. His more recent work has concerned the study of organiza-tional identity and image, and especially the relationship between the two concepts (see "Identity, Image, and Issue Interpretation," with James Thomas, in *Administra-tive Science Quarterly,* 1996). In a former incarnation, prior to his ivory tower career, he worked in the real world as an engineer for Boeing Aerospace at Cape Kennedy during the Apollo lunar program. He then earned his MBA and went to work for Ford Motor Company. In the years since, he has been working in the world of academia while trying to keep one foot planted in the realm of practical reality. As evidence that he really has been working rather than simply peering from the tower, his work has appeared in many of the most visible journals in organization study. He has edited two books: *The Thinking Organization* (with Hank Sims) and *Creative Action in Organizations* (with Cam Ford). On top of that, he continues to be a member of the MBA core faculty, to do executive programs, to do his bit within the university and the community, and to try to live a balanced and rewarding life.

Mary Ann Glynn is Associate Professor of Organization and Management at Goizueta Business School, Emory University. She earned her PhD at the Graduate School of Business, Columbia University. Current research focuses on the topics of creativity, innovation, and playfulness; intelligence and learning; and organizational identity and members' identification. Her research has been published in *Academy of Management Review, Journal of Applied Psychology, Strategic Management Journal, Journal of Marketing, POETICS,* and *Journal of Empirical Research on Literature, the Media, and the Arts,* and she serves on the editorial boards of *Academy of Management Review, Organization Science,* and *Journal of Management.*

Paul C. Godfrey is Assistant Professor in the Marriott School of Management at Brigham Young University. Interests include organizational identity, strategic change, organizational change, and the philosophy of management. His work has been published in *Strategic Management Journal,* and he has written a number of articles dealing with management history and the philosophy of science and management. He and his wife, Robin, are the proud parents of three children.

Karen Golden-Biddle is Associate Professor of Organizational Analysis at the University of Alberta. She earned her PhD in 1988 at Case Western Reserve University and taught at Emory University prior to her present position. In her research, she examines the cultural and language-based aspects of organizational life. This research interest takes two particular directions. First, she analyzes how culture and identity shape organizational change. A recent article in this area is "Breaches in the Boardroom: Organizational Identity and Conflicts of Commitment in a Nonprofit Organization" (with H. V. Rao, in *Organization Science,* 1997). Second, she analyzes how scientific knowledge is constructed in organizational studies. Her most recent article in this area is "Constructing Opportunities for Contribution: Structuring Intertextual Coherence and Problematizing in Organizational Studies" (with K. Locke, in *Academy of Management Journal,* 1997). In addition, she recently completed a book, *Composing Qualitative Research* (with K. Locke, 1997), which examines writing up qualitative research for management journals. She is coeditor of the nontraditional research section of *Journal of Management Inquiry* and is on the editorial boards of *Academy of Management Journal* and *Organizational Research Methods.* She currently serves as Pre-Conference Chair and Program Chair-Elect for the Research Methods Division of the Academy of Management.

Loren T. Gustafson is Assistant Professor of Management in the School of Business and Economics at Seattle Pacific University. He earned his PhD in strategic management from Arizona State University, following 8 years of marketing and management experience in the financial services industry. His work has been published in leading journals, including *Academy of Management Review* and *Academy of Management Executive.* His paper "Using Organizational Identity to Achieve Stability and Change in High Velocity Environments" (coauthored with Rhonda Reger) won the 1995 Best Paper Award from the Managerial and Organizational Cognition Interest Group of the Academy of Management. His primary research interests include strategic change and renewal, organizational identity, managerial and organizational cognition, and strategies in turbulent environments.

Celia V. Harquail is Assistant Professor of Business Administration at Darden Graduate School of Business Administration, University of Virginia, where she teaches organizational behavior and managing creative organizations. She holds an AB in political theory from Bryn Mawr College and a PhD in organizational behavior from the Graduate School of Business at the University of Michigan. Six years were spent at Procter & Gamble, where she served as an organizational development consultant implementing team-based work systems, work system redesign, and total quality processes and as a line manager in sales and manufacturing. Her research focuses on the interaction of organizational identity and image, the symbolism of organizational and self-presentations, social identification with and within organizations, diversity, and change-oriented participation in organizations. She is currently writing about women's advocacy as a microprocess of organizational resistance and change and about how individuals can manage their organizational identification in turbulent economic environments.

Mary Jo Hatch is Professor of Organization Theory at Cranfield School of Management in England. She received her PhD from Stanford University and has taught organization theory at San Diego State University and University of California, Los Angeles and at Copenhagen Business School in Denmark. Current research interests include narrative approaches to organizational complexity theory; text and discourse analysis as applied to managerial and organizational talk; applications of postmodern thinking to organization theory and management; and aesthetics and organizing. She is also engaged in an analysis of the interactions of managerial and academic subcultures in the context of management education programs. Her articles have appeared in *Academy of Management Review, Administrative Science Quarterly, Journal of Management Inquiry, Organization Science, Organization Studies,* and *Studies in Cultures, Organizations and Societies.* She is author of *Organization Theory: Modern, Symbolic and Postmodern Perspectives,* a textbook published by Oxford University Press. She is European Editor of *Journal of Management Inquiry* and has done guest editing for *Organization Science* and *Studies in Cultures, Organizations and Societies.* She is an active members of the Academy of Management, the British Academy of Management, the European Group for Organization Studies, and the Standing Conference on Organizational Symbolism.

Anne S. Huff is Professor of Strategic Management at the University of Colorado—Boulder, with a joint appointment at Cranfield School of Management in England. She received her PhD from Northwestern University and has been on the faculty at UCLA and the University of Illinois. Her research interests focus on strategic change both as a dynamic process of interaction among firms and as a cognitive process affected by the interaction of individuals over time. She is Senior Editor for *Organization Science* and the strategy editor for *Foundations in Organization Science.* She is currently on the editorial board of *Strategic Management Journal, Journal of Management Studies,* and *The British Journal of Management.* For 1997-1998, she is President-Elect of the Academy of Management.

John R. Kimberly is Professor of Management in the Wharton School at the University of Pennsylvania.

Roderick Kramer is an Associate Professor of Organizational Behavior at Stanford University Graduate School of Business. He received his PhD in social psychology from UCLA in 1985. His research is on cooperation and conflict. He has coedited *Trust in Organizations* (with Tom Tyler), *Negotiation as a Social Process* (with David Messick), *Influence in Organizations* (with Margaret Neale), and *The Psychology of the Social Self* (with Tom Tyler and Oliver John).

Luis L. Martins is Assistant Professor of Management in the School of Business Administration at the University of Connecticut. He received his PhD in management from the Leonard N. Stern School of Business at New York University. His current research interests include reputational rankings, managerial interpretations of issues in their environment, and diversity in organizational groups.

Judi McLean Parks obtained her PhD in organizational behavior from the University of Iowa in 1990. In 1995, she joined the Organizational Behavior group at the John M. Olin Graduate School of Management, Washington University at St. Louis. She has consulted in each of these areas. Prior to coming to Washington University, she was Assistant Professor in the Industrial Relations Department at the University of Minnesota. Her research, which focuses on the "psychological contract" between employers and employees and how the nature of the employer/employee relationship is changing, has examined the impact of perceived injustice and its implications in terms of employee behaviors, organizational identification, workplace violence, and revenge. Currently, she is examining the implications of broken psychological contracts and high levels of organizational identification in predicting reactions of disaffected workers and workplace violence. Her work has been appeared in such publications as *Academy of Management Journal, Human Resources Management, International Journal of Conflict Resolution, Journal of Applied Psychology, Journal of Applied Social Psychology Journal of Organizational Behavior, Research in Organizational Behavior, Research on Negotiation in Organizations, Trends in Organizational Behavior, Organizational Behavior and Human Decision Processes,* and *Wake Forest Law Review.*

Michael G. Pratt is Assistant Professor of Business Administration at the University of Illinois at Urbana-Champaign. He received his BA from the University of Dayton and his MA and PhD from the University of Michigan. His primary research interests center on how conflicts within and between organizational and professional belief systems affect members' interpretations of and attachments to their organizations. More specifically, his interests include topics such as organizational symbolism, professional and organizational identities, socialization, organizational identification, sense making, and emotions (ambivalence) in organizations. He has examined identity conflicts within physicians and nurses. However, he has also done in-depth studies of such diverse organizations as libraries, direct-selling organizations, reinsurance companies, and group homes. His recent publications include "Organizational Dress as a Symbol of Multilayered Social Identities" (with Anat Rafaeli, *Academy of Management Journal,* 1997); "Emotions and Unlearning in Amway Recruiting Techniques: Promoting Change Through 'Safe' Ambivalence" (with C. K. Barnett, *Management Learning,* 1997); and "Merck & Co, Inc.: From Core Competence to Community Involvement" (with J. E. Dutton, 1997) in *The Public's Eye: Best Practices of Global Corporate Citizenship.*

Hayagreeva "Huggy" Rao is Associate Professor of Organization and Management and Adjunct Associate Professor in the Department of Sociology at Emory University. In his research, he studies how institutional and ecological processes lead to the creation, transformation, and extinction of organizational forms and routines. His research has been published in *American Journal of Sociology, Administrative Science Quarterly, Academy of Management Journal, Organization Science, Strategic Management Journal, Academy of Management Review, Organization Studies, Journal of Management Studies,* and *Journal of Marketing.* His recent publications include "Structuring a Theory of Moral Sentiments: Institution-Organization Co-Evolution in the Early Thrift Industry" (with Heather Haveman, in *American Journal of Sociology,* May 1997) and "Caveat Emptor: The Construction of Non-Profit Consumer Watchdogs" (also in *American Journal of Sociology,* forthcoming). He serves on the editorial boards of *Administrative Science Quarterly* and *Organization Science.*

Rhonda K. Reger is Associate Professor of Strategic Management at Maryland Business School, University of Maryland. She earned her MBA and PhD from the University of Illinois at Urbana-Champaign. Prior to joining the faculty of Maryland Business School in 1995, she served as a faculty member at Arizona State University and the University of Illinois at Chicago. She is especially interested in cognitive barriers to implementing fundamental organizational changes such as total quality and reengineering. In the international arena, she has examined international joint ventures and the international entry decisions made by smaller and medium-size firms. She is author of over a dozen articles and book chapters. These articles have appeared in journals such as *Academy of Management Review, Academy of Management Executive, Strategic Management Journal,* and *Organization Science.* She is recipient (with Loren Gustafson) of the 1995 Best Paper Award given by the Academy of Management's Managerial and Organizational Cognition Interest Group.

Violina P. Rindova is a doctoral candidate in management at the Leonard N. Stern School of Business, New York University. She has a JD from Sophia University and an MBA from Madrid Business School, University of Houston. She has published several book chapters and presented papers about corporate governance, reputation management, and corporate communications. Her current research applies text analysis to study the use of corporate communications for image and reputation management and development of competitive advantage. She serves as a reviewer for *Academy of Management Review.*

Yolanda Sarason is Assistant Professor of Strategy at the Anderson School of Management, University of New Mexico in Albuquerque. She has an MBA, as well as a PhD in strategic management, from the University of Colorado at Boulder. She has published articles on strategic management, the management of technology, and entrepeneurship in *Journal of High Technology Management, Journal of New Business Venturing,* and *Journal of Management Education.* Her dissertation focused on integrating organizational identity into a structuration theory framework and in applying this framework in an investigation of the Baby Bells since divestiture. Current research activities include a qualitative investigation of organizational identity in local hospitals and responses of these hospitals to changes in managed health care.

Majken Schultz is Professor of Intercultural Leadership at Copenhagen Business School from which she received her PhD. Her research has focused on organizational symbolism, organizational culture, organizational identity, intercultural collaboration, and change processes. She is currently in charge of a 4-year research program, "Interplay Between Organizational Culture, Identity, and Image," which includes studies of both identity consultants and companies involved in identity processes. Her work has been published in *Academy of Management Review, Journal of Management Inquiry, Organization Studies, Organization, International Studies of Management and Organization, European Journal of Marketing, Corporate Reputation Review,* and *Studies in Organization, Cultures and Societies.* In English she has published "Understanding Organizational Cultures: Diagnosis and Understanding."

J. L. "Larry" Stimpert is Associate Professor of Business and Economics at the Colorado College. He received his MBA. from Columbia University and his PhD in business administration from the University of Illinois at Urbana-Champaign. Prior to his academic career, he worked for Norfolk Southern Corporation and the Chicago and North Western Transportation Company in various research and management positions. His research and teaching interests include managerial cognition, executive leadership, diversification, corporate strategy, and organizational structure. His articles have appeared in *Academy of Management Journal, Strategic Management Journal, Journal of Management Studies,* and several other publications. He is a member of the Academy of Management and the Strategic Management Society. He and his wife, Lesley, live in Colorado Springs and enjoy hiking and backpacking.

James B. Thomas is Senior Associate Dean and Professor of Management at Pennsylvania State University.

David A. Whetten is Jack Wheatley Professor of Organizational Behavior and Director of the Center for the Study of Values in Organizations at Brigham Young University. Prior to joining the Marriott School of Management faculty in 1994, he was on the faculty at the University of Illinois at Urbana-Champaign for 20 years, where he served as Associate Dean of the College of Commerce, Harry Gray Professor of Business Administration, and Director of the Office of Organizational Research. He currently is editor of *Foundations for Organizational Science,* an academic book series, and previously was editor of *Academy of Management Review.* He has published over 50 articles and books on the subjects of interorganizational relations, organizational effectiveness, organizational decline, organizational identity, and management education. His pioneering and award-winning management text *Developing Management Skills,* coauthored with Kim Cameron, is in its third edition and was recently adapted for the European market under the title *Developing Management Skills for Europe.*